GW00733881

British History 1815–1939

W. D. HUSSEY

British History 1815-1939

CAMBRIDGE

at the University Press 1971

Published by the Syndics of the Cambridge University Press
Bentley House, 200 Euston Road, London NW1 2DB
American Branch: 32 East 57th Street, New York, N.Y.10022

© Cambridge University Press 1971

Library of Congress Catalogue Card Number: 79-149429

ISBN: 0 521 07985 3

Printed in Great Britain by Ebenezer Baylis & Son Ltd,
Leicester and London

Contents

Maps

Diagrams

NOTE: All references in the text to shillings and pence are made on the pre-decimal standard: 12 pence = 1 shilling; 20 shillings = £1

Acknowledgements

Thanks are due to the following for permission to reproduce photographs:

The Mansell Collection pp. 4, 13, 19, 34, 71, 77, 87, 89, 105, 162, 167, 199, 215, 219, 220, 224, 229, 317
National Portrait Gallery pp. 25, 40, 44, 47, 74, 86, 95
Radio Times Hulton Picture Library pp. 32, 33, 67, 70, 72, 76, 82, 83, 109, 116, 126, 128, 136, 138, 154, 155, 166, 169, 176, 177, 180, 184, 186, 187, 189, 193, 195, 198, 200, 201, 207, 208, 209, 216, 222, 227, 233, 237, 238, 245, 248, 250, 254, 255, 256, 262, 265, 268, 273, 275, 276, 277, 278, 283, 285, 290, 315, 316, 318, 319, 335, 338, 345, 346, 347, 350, 351, 352, 357, 358
Science Museum pp. 55, 56, 57, 63, 107, 109 (Bessemer converter).

The maps were drawn by Mrs M. A. Verity.

Preface

I hope this book will be of interest and use to students in schools and colleges either for examination purposes or as a general introduction to an important and formative period of British history. In the space available my aim has been to give balanced treatment to social and economic issues as well as to political, diplomatic and military matters, but in such a well documented period this has necessarily involved a good deal of compression.

British history in the nineteenth century has frequently been represented as a triumphant and uninterrupted march towards political democracy and social reform, both sponsored by a liberal-minded governing class. Modern studies have modified this optimistic view; it is now clear that political change was often opposed and that social reforms were often very limited in their effects. It is also now accepted that more weight must be given to popular forces and their impact on political and social change. In my presentation and emphasis I have tried to take both these views into account.

I wish to express my gratitude to my wife for her constant encouragement during the writing of this book, and also for her reading of the manuscript which has enabled me in many places to improve the presentation of my material. I would also like to thank the editorial staff of the Cambridge University Press for their patience and help during the long period taken to write this book.

W. D. H.

March 1971

1. The background of British history in the nineteenth century

The social framework

In 1815 the United Kingdom of Great Britain and Ireland had a population of some twenty millions: of this total England and Wales had twelve millions, Scotland two millions and Ireland six millions. These people formed a society in which class differences were clearly marked and strongly emphasized; the dividing line was between the propertied classes and those without property. Property at this time was chiefly in land, but there were increasingly important professional, merchant, and industrial classes whose wealth consisted of their stocks and shares and factories. The landed proprietors ranged from the great territorial lords with their tens of thousands of acres to the small yeoman farmer with his twenty or thirty acres. Substantial ownership of land gave an unquestioned position in the community together with political power as members of the House of Lords and House of Commons. Well housed, well fed and waited on by a host of servants these men of property whether landed or otherwise led lives which were never less than very comfortable, and sometimes elegant.

Those without property, known at the time to their social superiors as the 'common people' or the 'lower orders' were in the vast majority. As a rule they had no more than their labour which, if they were fortunate, they could sell to employers in town or country. In their ranks were the men, women and children of the cotton factories, of the mines and collieries, the farm labourers of the countryside, the craftsmen and journeymen of the skilled trades and the multitude of men and women in domestic service and, at the lowest level, the mass of unskilled and casual labour. If they had regular work they counted themselves lucky and were content with their lot, as they had to be, in a state which, except through the medium of parish poor-relief, made no provision for the destitution caused by frequent unemployment. Although from time to time there were outbreaks of mob violence in town and country, these people were as a rule law abiding, and indeed, under the adverse conditions of life and work during the period of adjustment to the changes brought by the industrial revolution in the first half of the nineteenth century, they showed remarkable restraint in their sufferings.

In this society there was no social equality. The middle classes respected and deferred to the leadership of the landed aristocracy and gentry, while the working poor saw above them the prosperous classes and their social superiors, squire, parson, gentry and middle classes: they kept their

1

distance, realizing only too well their unprotected position if they lost their work through incurring their master's displeasure. Lacking property, education, and the vote, the working masses found it an impossible task to influence a government of rich men based on an undemocratic and unrepresentative House of Commons which, in an age of great social misery, ignored the views and feelings of the common people. Politically the workers did not count, besides which the political and economic doctrines of the day said that governments could not interfere to give the poor jobs or to raise their wages; the 'iron laws of supply and demand' would decide employment and wage rates, and things must find their own level.

Although these social barriers were recognized and accepted British society was far from being an entirely stationary one; for centuries it had been possible for men to rise in the social scale by the acquisition of wealth through trade, industry or by their skill in a profession such as the law. It would also be mistaken to regard the British working classes, in spite of their numerous handicaps, as lacking in spirit or vitality; these they often showed in their leisure activities such as games or field sports, or in the formation and running of clubs and friendly societies.

The framework of government

Great Britain in 1815 was a constitutional monarchy in which the powers of the Crown were being slowly but steadily limited. Its government although undemocratic in its basis and not very efficient if judged by modern standards did however respect the rule of law and allowed its subjects more individual rights than any other government then existing except that of the United States of America. Political power belonged to the landed and propertied classes and their monopoly of this in Parliament was not shaken until measures of parliamentary reform were enacted in 1832, 1867 and 1884. The detailed work of the central government, very small in volume compared with that of today, was done by a tiny Civil Service whose members held their jobs mainly through influence and not by merit: the Home Office in 1815 had some twenty clerks. Every letter sent had to be copied by hand and ministers wrote many of their own letters to settle business which their successors of today would transact in a few minutes by telephone. Local government in town and countryside, compared with today, was little developed; it was limited to the work of the justices of the peace who maintained law and order locally and supervized the poor law and the upkeep of roads. The lack of an organized police force became increasingly felt now that the population, especially in the industrial towns, had increased so much and, because of unemployment and want, was liable to riot.

2 *Fig. 1 Population of the United Kingdom of Great Britain and Ireland. Census totals 1801–1931*

The growth of population

When the first official census was taken in 1801 it gave population figures of nine millions for England and Wales, one and a half millions for Scotland and five and a half millions for Ireland. A century later the population of the United Kingdom had risen to forty-one and a half millions. (See Fig. 1.) The chief reason for this growth of population was the steady decrease in the death rate of both infant children and adults. A factor contributing to this decrease was that the environment or general surroundings in which people lived and worked slowly improved with the provision of proper drains and sewers, better ventilation and a pure water supply. Personal hygiene also improved: greater personal cleanliness, healthier clothing, and a more varied diet made possible by increased purchasing power, all led to better health. Advances in medical science made their contribution to the declining death rate; in the nineteenth century smallpox, which hitherto had kept infant mortality rates high, was brought under control by vaccination; chloroform and antiseptics, the work of Simpson and Lister, made life-saving surgery possible. The overall result was that infant mortality was reduced and the expectation of life for adults increased: the excess of births over deaths continued to grow so giving a natural increase in the population.

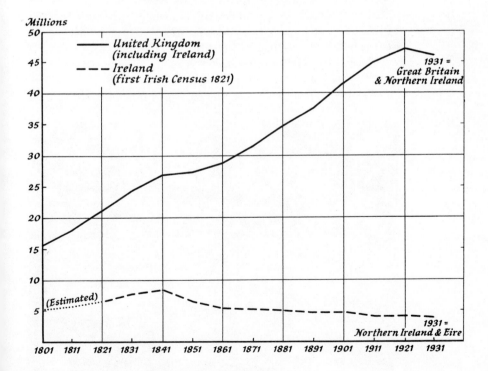

The expanding British economy

By 1815 Great Britain had passed the threshold of a revolution involving changes in her economic organization which enabled her to expand greatly the output of manufactured goods for sale at home and abroad. The origins of this change are to be found in the second half of the eighteenth century and in the thirty years before 1815 there was a sustained expansion in output and of foreign trade, both imports and exports. The process of this industrial revolution was characterized by the following features:

1. A sharp increase in population and the movement of people from the countryside to those towns which by the mid-nineteenth century had become grouped in the industrial 'conurbations' of the Midlands, Lancashire, Yorkshire, Tyneside, Clydeside, and South Wales.

2. The application of scientific knowledge for the purposes of economic activities, e.g. steam power in factories where machines and labour could be effectively concentrated for mass production, and in the development of a chemical industry essential to an expanding textile industry with its need for detergents and bleaches.

3. The exploitation of Britain's most important natural resource, coal, on which was based steam power and an iron and steel industry with its dependent heavy industries such as shipbuilding.

4. The revolution in communications brought by railways, steamships and the electric telegraph which made possible the expansion of the home market and the penetration by Great Britain of overseas markets for her ever-increasing output of manufactured goods, and the import of raw materials needed for their manufacture.

This expansion of the British economy, apart from intermittent trade

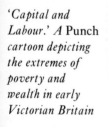

'Capital and Labour.' A Punch *cartoon depicting the extremes of poverty and wealth in early Victorian Britain*

slumps, continued strongly into the third quarter of the nineteenth century, reaching its peak in the years 1850–70. In mid-century, Britain could claim to be 'the workshop of the world', although her economic pre-eminence was soon to be challenged by rivals such as Germany and the U.S.A. As a nation Great Britain became increasingly wealthy but this wealth was very unevenly distributed and benefited a very small section of the community. While workers' wages and living standards improved slowly the contrast between the extremes of wealth and poverty in Victorian society was often glaring; Disraeli's picture of 'the two nations – the rich and the poor', given in his novel *Sybil* (1845) was an accurate one and remained so until well into the present century.

Foreign affairs

Great Britain's attitude to foreign affairs after 1815 was influenced by her experiences during the Revolutionary and Napoleonic wars. From the security of her islands Britain had continuously opposed Napoleon and had given her diplomatic, financial and military help to the European coalition which finally overthrew him between 1813 and 1815. At the peace settlement made at Vienna in 1815 Britain secured her aim of a European states system in which there was a balance of power with no one state predominating, in addition to important gains for her colonial empire. After 1815 it was the aim of British foreign policy to maintain this equilibrium in Europe as one of her 'eternal' interests since a stable Europe allowed Britain to concentrate her energies on more important matters such as economic expansion in world markets and the development of her colonial empire; to many Victorians and especially to apostles of free trade such as Cobden and Bright the pursuit of wealth through world trade was far preferable to involvement in the diplomacy and wars of continental Europe with their dangers and expense. Both the European equilibrium and Victorian complacency were shattered in the decade 1860–70 by the rise of a united Germany based on the 'blood and iron' policy of Bismarck and effected by the Prussian army. The Victorians were shocked by the ruthlessness of the new Germany and its exaltation of force; the balance of power in Europe had been radically altered by the rise of this new state which in the next forty years not only challenged the naval and economic supremacy of Great Britain but also made a bid to dominate Europe. In the face of all this a reconsideration of British foreign policy took place and this led to a cautious movement from 'splendid isolation' to *ententes* with France and Russia in the years immediately before the outbreak of World War I in 1914.

The British Empire

The nineteenth century saw the growth of a second British Empire based on what remained after the loss of the American colonies in 1783, to which were added the gains of the Napoleonic wars, mostly strategic bases such as the Cape of Good Hope, Mauritius and Ceylon, which controlled the approaches to the trading areas of India and the Far East. There was also the colonial expansion of the early nineteenth century due to emigration from the British Isles to Australia, New Zealand, Canada and South Africa. Later in the nineteenth century these white settled colonies achieved self government in accordance with the principles of the Durham Report of 1839 which emphasized that the freedom given by self government would maintain the colonial ties with Great Britain more effectively than anything else. In the twentieth century the Statute of Westminster (1931) recognized that these self-governing colonies were sovereign independent states within the British Commonwealth.

Interest in this growing empire varied a good deal during the nineteenth century. The 'Manchester School' of 'little Englanders' led by Cobden and Bright, in the 1850s and 1860s denounced colonies as useless, expensive and likely to cause wars between nations. Others saw them as an effective means of expanding British trade and of spreading both British influence and Christianity through the world. In the later nineteenth century a strong movement in favour of the British Empire took place because of the markets it provided and because of the contribution it made to Great Britain's position as a world power.

The pattern of change in the nineteenth century

British history after 1815 can best be understood by relating it to the changes brought by the interaction of political, social and economic forces within a society which because of a rapid increase in population coupled with an industrial revolution, less and less resembled the society which preceded it.

The main features of these changes are connected with:

Political reform. This involved reform of the instruments of government, e.g. Parliament, especially voting qualifications and representation in the House of Commons; of the organization and procedure of the law courts; of recruitment for the Civil Service and in the extension of its activities; the expansion of local government services. The inspiration behind this political reform was varied: some came from a liberal-minded minority of the aristocracy but a good deal more from middle-class liberal-radicals who later in the century were able to draw on the support of newly enfranchised working-class voters. The pace of reform was a gradual one because of the resistance of the politically dominant propertied classes who fought, with considerable skill, a sustained rearguard

6

action to limit reforms which would breach their monopoly of political power.

Social-economic problems. The rapidly increasing population and the steady transformation of British society from a rural society to a predominantly urban industrialized one brought large scale problems relating chiefly to conditions of life and work of the mass of the people. The exploitation of the labour of women, young persons and children in factories, workshops and mines led after 1832 to a series of Acts limiting hours and controlling conditions of work. This limitation of the employment of children pointed to another problem, that of providing primary education on a nation-wide scale. The recurrent outbreaks of cholera and typhoid due to the overcrowded and insanitary housing of the working classes in the industrial towns and to contaminated water supplies compelled parliamentary intervention by Public Health Acts which enforced minimum standards of sanitation and housing. Poverty and destitution among both able-bodied and old people was widespread in a society whose economy was subject to alternating boom and slump and where a large pool of unskilled and casual labour depressed wage rates. Victorian social conscience lagged badly over this problem and relied on the 1834 Poor Law Amendment Act and its harsh solution of the workhouse test with all the degradation that this imposed, together with the efforts of various private charitable organizations. Not till the last quarter of the century was the problem more sympathetically investigated when the revelation of widespread poverty and ill health led the state to adopt a more constructive policy towards this problem.

Working-class movements. The grinding pressure of economic forces reflected in low wages, unemployment and destitution generated working-class movements which were vehement protests against the misery of their lives and also attempts to change the situation in their favour.

(*a*) In the political field the Chartist movement was an outstanding example. At the time its aims were probably too extensive and ambitious and so drew the unswerving opposition of the upper and middle classes: Chartist leadership was also divided and not very skilful. But within eighty years of the fiasco of 1848 nearly all their programme had been enacted, and some of the Chartist leaders made a contribution to later working-class movements such as the Reform League in its efforts to influence the passing of a Reform Bill in 1867. The spread of education, the rise of a popular press and the extension of the vote by the Reform Acts of 1867 and 1884 increased the political consciousness of working men to the extent of realizing that neither the Liberal nor the Conservative Party would adequately serve their interests: these could only be

7

achieved if they had their own workers' political party. It is in the last twenty years of the nineteenth century that the origins of the Labour Party of today are to be found.

(*b*) The Cooperative movement was an attempt by the working classes to get a better deal from the economic system. Although the producers' Cooperatives of the 1820s and 1830s failed, the retail Cooperatives launched by the Rochdale Pioneers in 1844 went on to achieve a solid and lasting success with their emphasis on good quality merchandise and as much interception as possible of the middleman's profits so that their members could be paid a dividend on their purchases.

(*c*) The switch to large-scale production brought by the industrial revolution placed enormous power in the hands of the capitalist owners of the factories, machinery and working capital: they could give work or withhold it, hire and fire their workers at pleasure and drive down wage rates to the lowest possible level. The natural reply to this was for the workers in individual trades to combine in trade unions which alone could give them the strength to bargain with their employers over wage rates, hours and conditions of work, with the background threat of 'striking' by withdrawing their labour if their demands were not met. For most of the nineteenth century trade unions were faced with daunting obstacles; besides the hostility of employers, the law regarded striking and picketing as criminal offences. The success of the 'New Model' craft unions in mid-century in advancing their members' interests, followed by the removal of most legal disabilities in the 1870s firmly established trade unions in British society. In the last years of the century the movement spread with the formation of large-scale unions for semi-skilled and unskilled labour.

2. Britain after Waterloo 1815–22

The Liverpool ministry

The Tory ministry presided over by Lord Liverpool had shown a dogged and admirable persistence in the final stages of the war against Napoleon. Its treatment of the problems of the peace was much less successful because the outlook of its leading ministers had been decisively influenced by the French revolution which, they firmly believed, had shown that any change, however slight, led to the overthrow of all established institutions. Liverpool and his colleagues were therefore determined to prevent revolution in Great Britain and this explains their policy of repression of popular demonstrations and agitations for reform, which they condemned out of hand and without trying to find out what caused them.

The ministry, apart from its unanimity about the need to check revolution, was by no means united and that it kept together so long was due to the Prime Minister. Although he lacked imagination and had a horror of change, Liverpool had been carefully educated for political life by his father, an astute 'middle of the road' politician acceptable to George III. Disraeli, who rarely missed the chance of a smart remark, labelled Liverpool the 'Arch-mediocrity': this was unjust in view of the fifteen years of premiership during which Liverpool skilfully kept his ministry together. Lord Castlereagh who led for the government in the House of Commons was an able foreign secretary who had organized the European coalition against Napoleon during the three critical years after 1812 and then had shown great skill at the peace settlement. In home affairs, in which he was not much interested, he incurred popular dislike for the repressive measures of the early years of the peace. The office of home secretary, most important at this time because of its responsibility for law and order, was held by Lord Sidmouth who as Henry Addington had been prime minister from 1801 to 1804 after the resignation of the younger Pitt. Opposed to all change and inundated by letters from the justices of the peace about the revolutionary goings-on in the countryside, Sidmouth's remedy was stern repression, culminating in the Six Acts of 1819. In the House of Lords the ministry had the support of Lord Eldon and the Duke of Wellington. Eldon, the Lord Chancellor, was a Tory of Tories and a consistent opponent of reform: his last speech opposed the building of the Great Western railway. Wellington, who had no political ambitions and who despised political intrigue was useful because of his influence over George IV who was afraid of 'King Arthur'. Not all the ministers were high Tories: there was a more progressive element and

George Canning, Robert Peel, William Huskisson and Lord Palmerston were its leading members. Canning, aptly named the 'Joker', for he was an awkward card and the only one of his kind in the political pack, belonged to the Liberal Tory tradition going back to the younger Pitt; his debating skill was renowned and his devastating repartee feared. Both Peel and Huskisson were aware of the need for administrative reforms to make British government and the economy more efficient.

The Whig opposition

One piece of political good fortune for the Liverpool ministry was the weakness of the Whig opposition which in 1815 was hopelessly split by internal divisions. One aristocratic section, that of the Grenvilles, went over to the Tories in 1822 leaving Earl Grey who afterwards carried the Reform Bill in 1832, as the Whig leader. The Whigs were united in favour of Catholic Emancipation, a topic which sorely divided their Tory opponents; they opposed, sometimes rather half-heartedly, the Tory policy of repression of the Six Acts of 1819. Some of them had special interests in reform and spoke for it in and out of Parliament. Thus Lord John Russell and the Radical Whig Sir Francis Burdett both worked for parliamentary reform: other Whigs, notably Sir Samuel Romilly, Sir James Mackintosh and Henry Brougham advocated legal, humanitarian and educational reforms. But overall it would be misleading to regard the Whigs at this time as keen reformers; their belief in change and the extent to which this should go was not very different from that of the Liberal Tories.

Problems of the peace

For five years after the peace the Tories were beset with a variety of problems, most of which had economic causes. The Napoleonic wars had brought prosperity for both industry and agriculture whose products were needed for war purposes as well as for normal use by a steadily increasing population. Unemployment, during the war period, though by no means negligible, was curbed by the demand for men for the army and navy and the needs of industry and agriculture. Peace brought a rapid change for the worse. Thousands of soldiers and sailors were hastily disbanded and flung on to a labour market where unemployment was rapidly growing owing to the slump which had spread right through the economy. Almost overnight war contracts for cloth, boots, equipment, arms and ammunition were ended leading to redundant workers. The export markets were stagnant because most of our overseas customers were too financially exhausted by the war to buy our goods. The war left Britain with a greatly increased National Debt of £800 millions on which the annual interest charge was £30 millions or nearly half the national revenue.

Taxation was almost entirely indirect and unfair in its impact as far as the working classes were concerned since about two-thirds of the revenue was raised by customs and excise duties, many of which were levied on the necessities of life such as tea, sugar, beer, tobacco and on imported butter, cheese and bacon. The unfairness of the taxation system was emphasized by the speedy abolition by Parliament in 1816 of direct taxation in the shape of income tax at two shillings in the £ which had been paid by the propertied classes since 1798.

Economic distress and its consequences

In these circumstances hunger and misery were the lot of very many of the working classes. Their plight was intensified when bad harvests in 1816 and 1818 coincided with heavy unemployment due to especially bad trade. Matters were made worse by the Corn Law of 1815 which, in the interests of the rent-rolls of landlords and the incomes of their tenant farmers, prohibited the import of foreign corn until British wheat had reached the price of 80s. a quarter. In June 1817 wheat reached the famine price of 116s. 6d. a quarter, so making it impossible for the lowest paid workers to buy sufficient bread which was then the most important item in their diet and their chief energy-provider. It was in periods of intense distress such as this that trouble mounted for the government, and it took the form of rioting and popular agitation for reform. Luddism, which with its smashing and burning of machinery had first occurred in 1811–13, flared up again in the Midlands in the summer of 1816 with large-scale destruction of stocking frames at Loughborough. Political societies such as the Hampden clubs that were formed in the provinces demanded parliamentary reform: William Cobbett attacked the 'system' in his *Political Register* and mob orators like Henry Hunt harangued large meetings to the great alarm of the government. But it should be noted the more serious of the reform leaders such as Cobbett and Major Cartwright emphasized the need for peaceful agitation and warned their followers against committing illegal acts such as rioting or the senseless destruction of property.

Repression by the government

The government did not distinguish very clearly between all these agitations and disturbances. It formed its view of the situation from the magistrates' reports, often alarmist in tone, and relied too much on misleading reports from its spies, some of whom had penetrated the various popular movements. Besides this the government obstinately refused to see the connection between economic distress and political agitation; the accounts of agitation, disturbances, secret drilling, monster meetings, all pointed, so the government thought, to revolution. Consequently their

11

policy was a simple one – to take no chances, to suppress with a heavy hand all agitators, and to change nothing.

In May 1816 there were riots in East Anglia, centred in the Isle of Ely, where the magistrates were mobbed, higher wages demanded and some corn ricks burnt. In London in December 1816, meetings were held in Spa Fields, Bermondsey, by the followers of Spence who advocated nationalization of the land, and by the Radical followers of Henry Hunt. Using the excuse of the disorder that followed these meetings the government suspended the Habeas Corpus Act for a year, restricted the right of public meetings and increased the penalties for seditious speech and writings, but those it prosecuted for publishing seditious pamphlets were acquitted by sympathetic juries.

Agitation continued early in 1817 with the attempt of the unemployed handloom weavers in the Manchester area to march to London to petition the Prince Regent for reform and relief of distress. Known as the 'Blanketeers' from the blankets they carried to sleep out in at night, these demonstrators were harried and broken up by the troops before they had reached the neighbouring county of Derbyshire. Later in the same year the government received what it thought was confirmation of its fears of armed insurrection when a few hundred ill-armed workers from south-east Derbyshire set out to capture Nottingham castle under the leadership of Jeremiah Brandreth, a stocking frame knitter; Oliver, a government spy and *agent-provocateur*, had incited them to this by telling them that they must hurry up to join a national rising that had already started. They were soon rounded up by the troops; twenty-three were found guilty of high treason; Brandreth and three others were hanged, and the rest transported or imprisoned.

'Peterloo' 1819

Popular agitation revived in 1819 in the Midlands and Lancashire where unemployment and misery were widespread among the workers of certain trades especially the hand loom weavers, who faced with competition from the power loom, were struggling by frantic overwork to earn nine or ten shillings a week. Political clubs were organizing petitions, distributing propaganda and sometimes drilling secretly. At a monster reform meeting held on 16 August 1819 at St Peter's Field, Manchester, about sixty thousand people assembled peaceably enough carrying banners inscribed with demands for parliamentary reform; 'Orator' Hunt, the well-known radical speaker, was to address them. The magistrates attempted to arrest Hunt after the meeting had assembled, but as this proved beyond the powers of the special constables present, the yeomanry were sent in to take him. The huge crowd hemmed in and hustled the yeomanry who were then rescued by a charge made by the regular cavalry

12

'Britons Strike Home.' Peterloo *1819*

present and in the charge that resulted eleven people were killed and a large number injured.

The Six Acts 1819

Popular indignation over the 'Peterloo' or 'Manchester massacre' was intense: the Whig leaders condemned it and Earl Fitzwilliam, the Whig Lord Lieutenant of Yorkshire, called a meeting of protest. But the government upheld the action of the Manchester magistrates and indeed had they not done so it would have discouraged other magistrates faced with similar disorders elsewhere from doing their duty. To prevent further demonstrations and to limit popular agitation, the Six Acts or 'Gag' Acts were passed in 1819. Of these six Acts it is now generally agreed that three were not unreasonable as providing for public order and security and were essential powers for any government, viz:

1. An Act forbidding meetings for drilling and military exercises.

2. An Act empowering magistrates to issue warrants for the search of arms.

3. An Act to promote speedy trial of those accused of breaches of public order and which prevented delays on technical points by the defence, or by the Attorney-General for the prosecution.

The remaining three acts were more objectionable; they aimed at restricting the freedom of public meeting and the press:

13

4. An Act prohibiting all meetings designed to alter the law otherwise than through Parliament. No meetings of over fifty people could be held without notice to the magistrates and those attending must reside in the parish where the meeting was held. This act did not apply to meetings called by the lords-lieutenants of the counties or by mayors of corporate towns and the life of the Act was for five years only.

5. Blasphemous or seditious publications could be seized and banishment imposed for those offending a second time.

6. Pamphlets selling below sixpence were now made liable to the same stamp duty as newspapers.

The opposition of William Cobbett

In the years after Waterloo a popular spokesman and champion emerged in the person of William Cobbett (1763–1835). The son of a small Surrey farmer, Cobbett had run away to London to become a lawyer's clerk; later he enlisted in the army where he rose to the rank of sergeant-major. He carefully and intensively educated himself, paying particular attention to the writing of clear, meaningful English. In 1802 he founded his weekly *Political Register* in which for the next thirty years he attacked the evils in the state from which the people of England suffered. In Cobbett's opinion Parliament, the Church, the Law, the Services must be reformed; pensions, sinecures, paper money, war debts and the Corn Laws must be abolished. His experiences at the Honiton by-election in 1806 where the voters of that rotten borough voted for 'Mr Most' or the candidate who paid the highest price, and the fact that in one newspaper there were fifty-seven advertisements of borough seats in Parliament for sale, made Cobbett a fervent champion of parliamentary reform. With rising force and fury Cobbett thundered against the evils which oppressed the poor, fondly but quite wrongly imagining that these were unknown in England before the blight of the industrial revolution descended – a 'Merry England' in which the common man had had a sufficiency of work, good roast beef and ale. Some of his pet terms were very effective: borough-mongers, place men, pensioners and stock jobbers and 'tax eaters' (those who lived on pensions drawn from the taxes paid by the poor) were lumped together as the 'Thing'. Cobbett, who always remained a country-man at heart, despised towns as the seat of corruption and evil; his name for London was the 'Great Wen' (Wart), besides which there were all the other 'little wens'.

General distress after 1815 gave Cobbett plenty to attack. He did this in a cheap edition of his *Political Register* which because it contained no news items escaped the stamp duty and could be sold for twopence; nick-named 'Twopenny Trash' by his opponents, it had a circulation of 30,000 a week. Addressed to working-class readers it reminded them of their importance as the real producers of wealth and also of the weight of taxation their scanty wages bore: taxes on necessities such as sugar, tea, coffee, soap, paper, candles, malt and beer. For this an unrepresentative Parliament was responsible and Cobbett became the people's leader for its reform. He set out to ride all England, recounting his experiences in his famous *Rural Rides*, when he alternated between pleasure at the well cultivated countryside and fury at the sight of half-starved farm labourers. Much of the popular support for the Reform Bill was due to Cobbett who, like his supporters, mistakenly thought it would improve things for the poor. These fierce criticisms of defects in government and social wrongs embarrassed the government who retaliated by unsuccessful prosecutions of Cobbett for sedition.

The Cato Street conspiracy

The year 1820 opened with the death of the old King George III on 29 January; this was followed a few weeks later by the Cato Street conspiracy. A revolutionary desperado Thistlewood planned to murder members of the Cabinet dining at Lord Harrowby's house in Grosvenor Square; the conspirators seem to have modelled themselves on the Jacobin terrorists of the French revolution for they planned to carry the ministers' heads to the City of London where a provisional government with Thistlewood as president was to be proclaimed. The plot was betrayed by an informer: Thistlewood and his gang were arrested in Cato Street off the Edgware Road and subsequently executed.

The accession of George IV 1820

The accession of the Prince Regent as George IV brought new troubles for the Liverpool ministry. In himself George was a good deal of a liability and an expensive one at that. His past career had been discreditable: his quarrels with his father, his dissipated life and his selfish extravagances had made him despised by all classes of society. His vanity, unreliability and tendency to bluster made things difficult for his ministers who now had to deal with him not as prince regent but as king with the full powers and duties of the Sovereign. Fortunately the Duke of Wellington, of whom George was privately afraid, had sufficient influence over him to persuade him out of his worst follies although even Wellington could not dissuade him from ordering his government to start damaging divorce proceedings against Queen Caroline.

The royal divorce proceedings

In 1795 George had married Caroline, Princess of Brunswick-Bevern, chiefly to reconcile himself with his father and to get his debts paid. The marriage was unhappy and after a few years the royal couple had separ-

15

ated. In 1804 Caroline went abroad where her conduct was indiscreet, and before he became king, George had made secret inquiries about his wife's conduct in Italy with a view to divorce proceedings. Liverpool was reluctant to meet the King's wishes and hoped to persuade Caroline to reside permanently abroad in return for an increased allowance. Caroline, on the advice of Brougham, her legal adviser, refused this offer and in June 1820 arrived in England to claim her rights as queen. She was received with popular enthusiasm and as an injured woman persecuted by a worthless husband aided by unjust ministers who oppressed right and freedom wherever they saw it. A bill to dissolve the marriage and deprive the Queen of her titles was now introduced in the House of Lords by the government. In the Lords, where Caroline's conduct was ably defended by Brougham, the bill passed its third reading by a majority of only nine; Liverpool knew this meant it would never pass the Commons and therefore abandoned proceedings. Shortly after this seeming vindication of her character Caroline accepted a house and £50,000 a year voted by the House of Commons. Her popularity began to wane almost as quickly as it had arisen: in July 1821 she failed to force her way into the coronation ceremonies in Westminster Abbey and suffering under this disappointment she died in August of the same year.

3. The Liberal Tories and reform

Influence of the Liberal Tories

The disturbances after 1815 and the distraction of the attempted royal divorce had severely tested the Liverpool ministry. It now governed under less troubled conditions and in the course of the next seven years brought about some useful reforms, which were made possible by a reconstruction of the Cabinet in 1822. Of the younger and more liberal-minded Tories Robert Peel became home secretary in place of Lord Sidmouth, and William Huskisson went to the Board of Trade. George Canning, who had resigned office in disagreement with the policy of royal divorce, now became foreign secretary in place of Lord Castlereagh who on the eve of his departure for the Congress of Verona in August 1822, had committed suicide. Between 1822 and 1830 it was shown that there was a Tory reforming element ready to make British government and some of its institutions a little more rational and efficient.

The state of English criminal law

In the important office of home secretary which, apart from a break of eight months he held continuously from 1822 to 1830, Peel found many opportunities for the exercise of his practical mind and organizing ability. In 1822 the English criminal law was a barbarous jungle: the prison and convict system was inhuman and much of the legal procedure hopelessly out of date. There were nearly two hundred crimes for which the death penalty could be exacted, including such offences as impersonating pensioners of Greenwich and Chelsea Hospitals, damaging Westminster Bridge, cutting down trees, maiming cattle, being disguised on a high road, breaking down banks of rivers, stealing forty shillings or over from a dwelling-house. Although many of the death sentences passed were commuted to transportation to Australia, the English criminal code was ferocious and was inspired by the idea that the 'lower orders' could only be deterred from crimes against life and property by the threat of capital punishment. It was not surprising that juries were reluctant to convict and often perjured themselves to bring in a verdict of 'Not Guilty'; in one such case where the accused was being tried for theft from a dwelling-house, the finding of the jury was: 'as they hope for salvation, so help them God, they declare that the bills and notes for the same sum were worth only thirty-nine shillings'.

But mercifully inclined juries could only occasionally help the accused 17 as the following account of proceedings at a county Assize, and typical of the whole country, shows:

> Sentences of the Prisoners who were tried at the Wiltshire Lent Assizes 1825 before the Hon. Justice Park and the Hon. Justice Burrough:
> Elizabeth Smith for stealing a gown at Preshute – Death.
> William Maltman for stealing a watch etc. at Winsley – Death.
> Walter Hayter, 24, Robert Emery, 30, for stealing a mare and a Gelding at Standlinch – Acquitted.
> James Dursley, 14, for stealing a pair of Gaiters at Steeple Aston – 12 months.
> Robert Emmett, 16, Anthony Bateman, 16, for stealing a coat etc., at Box: Robert Emmett – Death: Anthony Bateman – Acquitted.
> Wm. Lake, 23, for stealing at Little Dunford – Death.
> John Crowther, 27, for stealing a greatcoat at Compton Chamberlain – Acquitted.
> Walter Hedges for stealing two umbrellas at Devizes – 7 years.
> William Bailey, 15, for picking a pocket and stealing two sovereigns etc. at Devizes – 14 years.

Besides the above there were fifty-one other indictments, mostly for petty thefts, resulting in fourteen more death sentences.

Peel's reform of the criminal law and prisons

Reform had been pioneered by Sir Samuel Romilly and Sir James Mackintosh. Romilly in 1808 and 1811 secured abolition of the death penalty for picking pockets and stealing linen from bleaching grounds and Mackintosh in 1820 abolition for some thirty crimes including the theft of five shillings from a shop. By 1827 Peel had abolished the death penalty for over a hundred crimes, substituting imprisonment or transportation to Australia. Some twelve offences including treason, murder, forgery, house-breaking, horse and sheep stealing, coining false money and robbery with violence remained capital crimes until Whig reforms in 1832, 1837, 1841 and 1861 eventually reduced the number to three, viz. treason, murder, and setting fire to a royal dockyard. Peel also made important changes in connection with the administration of prisons and the transportation of convicts; justices of the peace were to inspect the county prisons regularly; jailers were to be paid by salaries instead of by fees exacted from the prisoners and their relatives, and women prisoners were to be supervised by women warders.

The Metropolitan Police Act 1829

Events after 1815 had shown the urgent need for a proper police force to

A group of 'Peelers'. Early Victorian period

check mob violence, to control popular demonstrations and, with fast growing urban populations, to prevent and detect crime. The existing system of the parish constables, supplemented in some towns by night watchmen, was inadequate for the task. Peel was not without experience in this matter for when secretary for Ireland from 1812 to 1818 he had started the Royal Irish Constabulary. In 1829 his Metropolitan Police Act set up a permanent force of regularly enrolled, uniformed and paid police for the London area, directed by Commissioners of Police responsible to the Home Secretary. The appearance of the new 'Bobbies' or 'Peelers' aroused some opposition and criticism; the new police force was denounced as a threat to the liberty of Englishmen, but within a few years the value of its work in protecting life and property had been clearly shown, and in particular that the presence of an organized police force to detect and prevent crime was a greater deterrent to criminals than severity of punishment. As a result the municipal boroughs reformed by the Act of 1835 were required to establish their own police forces and by an Act of 1856 this was made compulsory for those counties in England and Wales which had not already set up their own forces.

19

Huskisson and the beginnings of free trade

The rapid development of Great Britain as a manufacturing nation with goods of all kinds to sell in the world's markets led to a free trade movement which aimed at removing restrictions to the flow of goods between countries; Adam Smith, in his *Enquiry into the Wealth of Nations* (1776), had argued that the greatest prosperity would only be attained when restrictions on trade were removed. The chief restrictions at this time were the Navigation Acts which controlled import and export trade between Great Britain and her colonies and regulated the employment of their shipping, and custom duties levied on a very wide range of raw materials and manufactured goods imported into Great Britain from abroad. Huskisson, President of the Board of Trade, made a move towards freer trade. He modified the Navigation Acts by allowing British colonies to export directly to European markets, instead of through Great Britain; his 'Reciprocity' treaties in 1824–5 with Prussia, Denmark, Sweden, Hamburg, U.S.A., and France gave their ships and cargoes equal treatment with British ships in British harbours as far as port dues were concerned. Imported manufactured goods which hitherto had paid customs duties at a very high rate were now liable to a moderate duty only, e.g. manufactured silk goods now paid 30%, cotton goods 10% and other goods were about 20%, instead of previously prohibitive rates of duty. Raw materials, which were of first importance to a manufacturing country like Great Britain, were now admitted at a much lower rate of duty: that on iron came down from £6 10s. 0d. to £1 10s. 0d. per ton; on raw silk from 4s. to 6d. and on wool from 6d. to 1d. per pound.

The problem of Catholic Emancipation

The Act of Union which in 1800 had abolished the separate Irish Parliament at Dublin and had given Ireland 100 M.P.s and 28 representative peers in the Parliament of the United Kingdom of Great Britain and Ireland at Westminster did not solve the problem of embittered Anglo-Irish relations. Apart from the resentment felt by Irishmen for the loss of their Parliament there was the grievance that the Union did not remove the political disadvantages of Catholic Irishmen. Although they could vote in elections (for Protestant candidates) no Catholic could be a member of Parliament nor could Catholics become ministers or servants of the Crown. George III's obstinacy had prevented this full emancipation of the Irish Catholics which would have given the Union a better chance of success. Twenty years after, the problem of Catholic Emancipation was the thorniest one faced by the Liverpool ministry. As it was a cause of disunity in the Cabinet they tried to stifle it as long as possible hoping thereby to maintain party unity as well as the Protestant ascendancy in Ireland.

By 1825 the problem could not be shelved any longer. This was chiefly due to the work of Daniel O'Connell who expressed the nationalist and political aims of the Catholic Irish. O'Connell's main aims were repeal of the Union and the restoration of the Parliament at Dublin, which, with full political rights for Catholics, could have led in time to self government for Ireland. To further these aims O'Connell in 1823 founded the Catholic Association which in 1824 collected a 'Catholic rent' to provide a fighting fund for a national movement to which belonged nearly all Irish Catholics. In 1825 a Catholic Relief Bill introduced by the Radical, Sir Francis Burdett, passed the Commons but was rejected by the Lords: in 1827 a similar bill was defeated in the Commons by a majority of four votes.

The ministries of Canning and Goderich 1827; Wellington 1828–30

At this critical stage the long premiership of Lord Liverpool ended in February 1827 when he suffered a paralytic stroke. The Tories were left hopelessly divided, and Canning, who favoured Catholic Emancipation could only form a ministry in April 1827 with Whig support: Wellington, Peel and some other Tories refused to serve under him. Four months later Canning died before he had been able to show his qualities as prime minister. The King tried to carry on the Canningite ministry under Lord Goderich who proved quite unequal to the task of controlling the warring party factions; in January 1828 he carried his tearful resignation to Windsor where George offered him the royal handkerchief. In the confusion that prevailed in Whig and Tory parties alike the King's choice of Wellington was the best one, since Wellington in his soldier-like way regarded this as the call of duty which he could obey without hesitation, although he thought it was 'a situation for the duties of which I am not qualified, and they are very disagreeable to me'. Change also was disagreeable to Wellington who was not in sympathy with Liberal Toryism.

Repeal of the Corporation and Test Acts 1828

In May 1828 the Whig Lord John Russell carried against the government by forty-four votes a motion for the repeal of the Corporation and Test Acts. Passed in the reign of Charles II these Acts excluded Nonconformists from all public offices, great or small, unless they had taken the sacrament of Holy Communion according to the rites of the Church of England. Conscientious Nonconformists refused to qualify but many of the less conscientious did so in a way that was sometimes scandalous; one London church catered specially for them: 'Those who want to be qualified will please to step up this way.' Although annual Indemnity Acts since 1743 had relieved Dissenters who had broken these laws, their

21

continued existence was insulting to them. The government gave way and the Bill became law after passing the Lords where the arch-Tory Lord Eldon, speaking thirty-five times and moving twenty amendments, tried in vain to stop it. The repeal of these Acts naturally encouraged the Irish Catholics to think their disabilities would likewise soon be removed.

The County Clare election 1828

Because of disagreement in the summer of 1828 over a proposal to disfranchise two corrupt boroughs, East Retford and Penryn, the Canningites Huskisson, Palmerston, and three other lesser ministers resigned from Wellington's ministry. Vesey Fitzgerald, an Irish landlord, was now made president of the Board of Trade and as was the constitutional custom at this time for newly appointed ministers, he had to seek re-election for his constituency of County Clare. An impressive demonstration of the strength of the Catholic Association now took place: O'Connell, though ineligible as a Catholic, opposed Fitzgerald. The Catholic forty shilling freeholders voted solidly for O'Connell; Fitzgerald abandoned the hopeless contest leaving O'Connell to be returned unopposed.

Catholic Emancipation granted 1829

Wellington saw that the example of County Clare would be followed throughout Ireland, and unless the Catholic M.P.'s who would inevitably be elected were allowed to take their seats, civil war in Ireland would follow. His decision to grant relief to the Catholics from their disabilities was a bold one, since he had most of his party against him. Opposition was strong from the bishops and the Church of England and above all from the King with his outburst: 'Damn it, do you mean to let them into Parliament?' Wellington's most able minister, Peel, leader of the Commons had also consistently opposed emancipation, and if he resigned the ministry could hardly survive; fortunately Peel was ready to put the interests of the country before personal and party beliefs and it was Peel who introduced the Catholic Relief Bill. It became law in April 1829 and gave Catholics the right to sit in Parliament and to hold civil and military appointments under the Crown with the exception of the offices of regent, lord chancellor of Great Britain or Ireland or lord lieutenant of Ireland. By the same Act some seventy-thousand forty shilling peasant freeholders were disfranchised and the minimum county freeholder franchise in Ireland was raised to £10 yearly worth thereby limiting Catholic Irish influence in future elections down to 1885.

Difficulties of Wellington 1829–30

Although Wellington had disposed of the thorny Catholic question, in the process he had infuriated the extreme Tories, and this, together with the earlier loss of the Canningites, made his government majorities precarious in the Commons; events generally were working against the continuation of this declining ministry. There was a revival of economic distress both in the industrial and rural areas yet the government did nothing more than declare these troubles 'beyond the reach of legislative control'. In 1829 and 1830 political activity working for parliamentary reform intensified and showed itself in various ways, e.g. the agitation carried on by Cobbett and the demands of various political unions. The London Radical Reform Association, founded in July 1829, demanded annual Parliaments, universal suffrage and vote by ballot. Early in 1830, Thomas Attwood, a banker, formed the Birmingham Political Union to press for proper representation of the middle and lower classes in the House of Commons. The example was copied elsewhere in the country and when the Whigs introduced their first Reform Bill in 1831 these political unions had an object to work and fight for.

Wellington's opposition to parliamentary reform

On 26 June 1830 George IV died, not particularly lamented, although as king he lived down some of his early unpopularity. His death, under the constitutional rule then in force, meant a dissolution of Parliament and a general election within six months. This election took place under the influence of the news from France where Charles X, who had foolishly tried to abolish the moderate constitutional liberties then existing, lost his throne in the July revolution of 1830. In addition events in France touched off a revolution in Belgium which wished to emancipate itself from Dutch rule. If foreigners could act thus for freedom so could Englishmen and this idea influenced the election contests where all grievances were channelled into the demand for reform. The Tory ministry lost ground in the election but still commanded sufficient votes to carry on. Eight days after Parliament met the Duke let fly a broadside in the House of Lords. Asked by Lord Grey what his intentions were regarding parliamentary reform, Wellington said:

'I . . . say that I have never read or heard of any measure up to the present moment which can in any degree satisfy my mind that the state of representation can be improved . . . I will go further and say that the legislature and system of representation possesses the full and entire confidence of the country . . . I am not only not prepared to bring in any measure of the description alluded to by the noble Lord but . . . I shall always feel it my duty to resist such measures when proposed by others.'

Wellington had isolated himself and his ministry. It could go on no longer against the opposition of the Whigs and many Tories, nor could

23

it beat down the demand for reform expressed almost everywhere, by moderates, by political unions, by petitions, and by Cobbett who declared: 'In short, the game is up, unless the aristocracy hasten forward and conciliate the people.' On 15 November 1830 the ministry was defeated by twenty-nine on an amendment to the Civil List proposals. The following evening Brougham was to move a Whig resolution in favour of reform; rather than face certain defeat on this the ministry resigned and the long Tory rule was over.

4. The passing of the Reform Bill 1831-2

Lord Grey and his ministry

The obstinate rejection of parliamentary reform by the Tories brought the Whigs back to power in 1830 after being in opposition for over twenty years. William IV asked Lord Grey to form a ministry; Grey undertook this on condition that a Reform Bill should be accepted by the King. Grey, now nearly seventy years old, was an aristocratic Whig whose political career went back as far as the middle of George III's reign when he had been associated with leading Whigs such as Charles James Fox and Sheridan. While believing in ordered freedom and some progress Grey had no faith in popular democracy which reminded him too much of the disorder of the French revolution: 'Grey loved the people, but he loved them at a distance' (Sir J. R. M. Butler). However, he realized the need for reform of Parliament and other institutions. His intention was that these reforms should be brought about by the ruling class to which he belonged rather than by popular agitation and pressure. His ministry, drawn from the Whigs and Liberal-Tory Canningites was decidedly aristocratic; all but four were in the House of Lords. There were some able men in his Cabinet: Lord Palmerston as foreign secretary; Lord Durham, Grey's son-in-law, capable but quarrelsome; Henry Brougham, who was made a peer and lord chancellor.

Charles, 2nd Earl Grey (by T. Lawrence)

King William IV 1830-37

During the struggle for reform the new King was called upon to make some difficult decisions. William IV, formerly Duke of Clarence, had no more than moderate abilities, but his naval career gave him a certain adaptability which helped him through the agitated political situation of 1830-2. Homely and eccentric in his personal behaviour he did not stand on royal dignity as had George IV and so gained considerable popularity. An example of this informality was his nautical turn of speech: when asked by the Royal trainer what horses were to be sent to race at Goodwood, he replied: 'Take the whole fleet; I suppose some of them will win.' To Lord Grey's apologies for asking him to go at short notice to dissolve Parliament, he said: 'Never mind that; I am always at single anchor.' Outwardly he appeared to many as an enthusiastic reformer but his sympathies were with the Tories, and he had a marked distrust of popular agitation and a strong fear of change. What he thought of the Whigs is summed up in his remark: 'Better the Devil in the house than a Whig.'

25

Grey had to use much tactful persuasion to get his acceptance of some details of the Reform Bill and a good deal more in May 1832 to wring from him the promise to create, if necessary, sufficient peers to get the Bill through the House of Lords.

Riots in the countryside

The start of Grey's ministry was not particularly fortunate. Before they could draft and present to the Commons their Reform Bill they had to deal with disturbances which swept through the southern counties of England, from Kent to Dorset. Starvation wages, the harshness of the Game Laws and the introduction of the newly invented threshing machine which deprived many farm labourers of the extra money they had earned in the winter months by hand-threshing with flails, were behind these disorders in which the hated machines were smashed and corn ricks fired. Little understanding of the causes was shown by the new government whose Home Secretary, Lord Melbourne put down the disorder with regular troops, yeomanry, a special Commission of Assize, some executions and many transportations to Australia. Such action confirmed the distrust of the Radicals for the Whigs who were now proved greater tyrants than the Tories.

The unreformed House of Commons

Parliamentary reform in 1830 had to deal with a system which had grown up during the previous four centuries, and which, because of the growth and changed distribution of population, had become unrepresentative. The greatest evils calling for reform were firstly the decayed boroughs, most of which were in the southern half of England, each returning two members, and secondly, the corrupt ways in which elections were decided in these boroughs, either according to the wishes of the individuals who controlled the pocket boroughs or by the outright purchase of votes in the rotten boroughs. The main target of the reformers was these corrupt boroughs but they had the two further aims of giving representation to the new manufacturing towns of the Midlands and North of England and of extending the vote to the middle classes. The latter, because of their property and education were thought by the Whigs to be eligible for the vote; the propertyless working classes were not.

The distribution of M.P.s

In 1830 the House of Commons of the Parliament of Great Britain and Ireland had 658 M.P.s. Of these 513 were returned for England and Wales, 45 for Scotland (Act of Union of 1707), and 100 for Ireland (Act of Union 1800). The extent to which borough representation predominated is shown by the figures for England and Wales. From the English and Welsh boroughs, the Cinque ports and the Universities of Oxford and Cambridge no less than 419 M.P.s were returned, compared with the 94 M.P.s from the English and Welsh counties. In some English counties boroughs were very thick on the ground: Cornwall had 21, Wiltshire 16, with each borough returning two members.

The 45 Scottish members were returned from 30 counties sending one each, 14 from some 60 burghs grouped together for election purposes and one member from Edinburgh. The electorate was small, being not more than five thousand and also very corrupt.

In Ireland 32 counties each returned two members, 32 boroughs one each and Dublin and Cork two members each, making a total of 100. Most of the boroughs had few voters.

Voting qualifications in the counties

Voting qualifications differed for county and borough elections and this distinction remained until it was abolished by the Reform Act carried by Gladstone in 1884. The vote in county elections was held by male freeholders who owned land of a yearly value of 40s.; this qualification had been fixed by an Act of 1430 in the reign of Henry VI when 40s. was a considerable sum. The decline in the value of money through the centuries led to many being qualified under this franchise and consequently the county elections were more representative than those of the boroughs, and also less corrupt. The reformers recognized that the county representation was one of the better features of the existing system and they sought to extend it by giving extra members to the larger and more populous counties. In 1830 each English county, regardless of size, returned two 'Knights of the Shire', except Yorkshire which sent four, having received an extra two members when the Cornish rotten borough of Grampound was disfranchised in 1821.

Borough qualifications

In the boroughs voting qualifications varied widely according to the borough. Five main types can be distinguished:

1. The 'Scot and lot' borough whose voters were those who could prove residence of not less than six months and who paid local rates and taxes. In this group there were some well populated towns, e.g. Preston and Westminster, and also some obscure villages like Gatton in Surrey.

2. The inhabitant householder and 'potwalloper' boroughs where the vote depended either on residence and not being in receipt of poor relief, or possession of a hearth for the boiling of the family pot.

3. Burgage boroughs where the vote was attached to certain houses whose occupiers could vote. Such houses were often let to outsiders with the right of voting a few days before an election.

27

4. Freemen Boroughs. Freemen were originally those who had privileged rights of trading in the town to which the right to vote was later added. Since the seventeenth century when seats in Parliament were increasingly sought after, some boroughs had restricted the number of their freemen to give closer control of elections, but many others had multiplied the number by creating honorary freemen from outside the town. This was sometimes done on the eve of an election, e.g. at Bedford in 1769 and at Northampton in 1773 when 500 and 396 honorary freemen respectively had been made. These 'outsitters' often outnumbered the resident freemen, e.g. in the election of 1831 at Coventry 235 out of 426 freemen were non-resident.

5. Corporation 'close' boroughs. In most of these the majority of the male inhabitants had been deprived of the vote which was only exercised by the very small group of the corporation, consisting of the mayor, aldermen, councillors, and a few officials.

Earlier attempts at parliamentary reform

Attempts at parliamentary reform before 1830 had been either completely unsuccessful or slight in their effect. In 1785 the younger Pitt had proposed disfranchising fifty small boroughs (with compensation to 'owners') and giving their members to the larger counties and London. The opposition was too strong and the Commons refused him leave to bring in his bill by a considerable majority. Four corrupt boroughs had been 'thrown into', or merged with the Hundred (an ancient local government area), e.g. New Shoreham (1770), Cricklade (1782), Aylesbury (1804) and East Retford (1828). The effect of this was to increase the voters since the forty shilling freeholders could vote in the borough election besides that of the county in which the Hundred was situated. The disfranchisement of Grampound in Cornwall in 1821 has already been mentioned.

Defenders of the unreformed House of Commons

Looking back from the twentieth century the need for reform of the House of Commons seems too clear to need any proof. But in 1830 there were a number of serious-minded people who defended the unreformed system, their chief argument being that this House of Commons was an essential part of the British constitution and the envy of foreigners. This constitution had worked well, and in particular it had brought us successfully through the long wars against the French revolution and Napoleon. It was therefore wrong to alter in any way the composition of the Commons lest a scheme of things which had proved itself be upset: even rotten boroughs were defended because they gave young men of talent early entry to the Commons. But these defenders were thinking in terms of eighteenth-century Britain with its much smaller and less industrialized population, and they also ignored the fact that the French revolution had spread the idea of democracy based on popular representation.

The proposals of the first Reform Bill

By the spring of 1831 a reform Bill had been drafted by a Cabinet committee of four, of which Lord Durham and Lord John Russell were the most active members. Two of its more radical proposals, vote by ballot and shortening the life of Parliament from seven years to five were dropped from the Bill before it was presented to the Commons on 1 March 1831 by Lord John Russell who had long been identified with the cause of reform. The secrets of the Bill had been closely kept and to a House, many of whose members confidently expected that no more than a handful of rotten boroughs would be disfranchised, the far-reaching changes now revealed came as a distinct shock. Incredulous or laughing derisively they heard Russell ('a little fellow not weighing above eight stone') read through Schedule A containing the names of 60 boroughs, returning 119 M.P.s, which were to be completely disfranchised. 'More yet' was Russell's comment at the end of this first slaughter, and then proceeded to Schedule B with 47 boroughs to lose one member each. The redistribution proposed was to populous towns hitherto unrepresented such as Manchester and Birmingham, and to the larger counties. In the boroughs a uniform voting qualification was proposed, viz. for male householders who occupied a house assessed for rating purposes at £10 a year or over. In the counties the forty shilling freeholders were to keep their vote, but an extension was proposed to those who occupied, as distinct from owning land, i.e. tenants who held their land on lease for varying terms of years.

Rejection of the first Bill

Once they had recovered from their shock the Tories rallied and bitterly attacked the Bill. Peel in a telling speech accused the Whigs of unfairly depriving of the vote many people in the boroughs who were qualified under the 'pot-walloper' franchise. From this opening stage an intense political agitation arose which did not die down until the Bill (the third one to be presented) became law over a year later in June 1832. Although the bill did not go as far as the radicals wanted, popular feeling rallied behind the Whigs against the Tory opposition – 'The Bill, the whole Bill and nothing but the Bill'– and so supplied a momentum which after a long struggle brought final success. Amidst great excitement in the small hours of 23 March 1831 the Bill was given a second reading by a majority of one. The Tories counter-attacked successfully when the Bill was considered in Committee, proposing that the total number of members for England and Wales should not be reduced as stated in the Bill. Defeated by eight votes Grey was granted a dissolution of Parliament by the King.

The Lords reject the second Bill

The elections returned a Commons with more reformers than before and a second Bill much like the first was introduced. By September 1831 it had passed its three readings in the Commons by comfortable majorities, although Lord Chandos carried against the ministry his amendment which would give the vote in the counties to those who occupied land on a yearly tenancy and paid a rent of not less than £50. In the Lords the Bill was defeated on its second reading by a majority of 41. The reaction of the country to this rejection was impressive and showed how strong was the popular feeling for reform. The political unions demonstrated, resolutions to pay no taxes were passed, monster meetings were staged and mobs rioted at Nottingham, Derby and Bristol. It was clear that this agitation would not subside until the Bill was passed; in Russell's words 'The whisper of a faction could not prevail over the voice of a nation' and Grey set about finding a solution. The matter was urgent as there was a risk of Parliament losing its initiative to outside political organizations such as the Birmingham Union which, with its numbers and organization, could form a National Guard and take direct action.

Political crises over the third Bill

The deadlock could be broken by the creation of sufficient peers to carry the Bill in the Lords; about sixty new peers would be necessary. Creation of peers on such a scale was disliked by the King and by many of the Lords, including Grey himself, who at this stage is reported to have said: 'Damn reform! I wish I had never touched it.' In December 1831 a third Bill was introduced and to secure its passage through the Lords Grey had to get the King's agreement to create peers, a few at first and then more later if necessary. William consented, though with many misgivings and he attempted to qualify his promise by the condition that the larger number must be 'reasonable' and not the fifty or sixty suggested. The possibility of a large creation of peers weakened the opposition of a group of more moderate peers (known as the 'Waverers'); on the second reading in the Lords in April 1832 the Bill passed by a majority of nine. Shortly afterwards when the Bill was being discussed in committee of the Lords a motion was carried against the government; Grey now asked the King to make fifty peers and on his refusal resigned with the rest of the Cabinet. Wellington was called on by the King to form a ministry which would pass a Reform Bill but one probably more moderate than that of the Whigs. It was a hopeless task for the Duke, as the refusal of the indispensable Peel to take office to pass a measure he had so strongly opposed wrecked the ministry before it was even formed.

30

The passing of the third Reform Bill

In May 1832 the agitation for the Reform Bill reached its climax. On the news of Grey's resignation and Wellington's attempt to form a ministry, the political unions of London and the provinces both of the middle and working classes braced themselves for final action. Petitions were sent to the Commons to stop supply and resolutions taken to pay no taxes until the Bill was passed. In the background there was the threat of armed insurrection, the barricades and even a republic. Francis Place, the brain of the reform agitation in London, launched his economic weapon by posting up everywhere the slogan 'To stop the Duke go for gold'. His intention was to start a run on the Bank of England by depositors, drain it of its gold reserves, and bring about financial panic and stoppage of trade. If this did not work he had a scheme ready for revolutionary rising like the July revolution of 1830 in France. The tension was reduced when the Whigs took office again after Wellington's failure to form a ministry. Before doing this Grey had received a promise, reluctantly given by King William, to create as many peers as were needed to pass the Bill through the Lords. The end was in sight: Wellington saw that the Tory position was untenable and that it was time to withdraw. Enough Tory peers abstained from voting to give the Bill a third reading by 106 votes to 22: the next day (5 June 1832) the Royal Assent was given to make it law.

Changes made by the Act of 1832

By the Act 143 seats were available for redistribution. Most of them were given to the large towns not previously represented and to the larger counties. Thus twenty-two of the larger English towns, chiefly in the industrial areas, were given two members, and twenty other towns one member each. Twenty-six of the English counties each had two members added and seven smaller counties were given an extra member. Yorkshire, which already returned four M.P.s was given two more.

The new qualifications for voting were:

1. In the boroughs male householders occupying a house assessed for rating purposes at not less than £10 a year could vote, provided they placed their name on the constituency register of parliamentary voters.

2. In the counties the vote was given to occupiers as distinct from owners of land, viz. copyholders and long leaseholders paying a rent of not less than £10 a year, and tenants at will paying not less than £50 annual rent.

It should be noted that (a) in the boroughs, resident electors qualified under the old pre-1832 franchises retained the right of voting for life, and (b) in the counties the forty shilling freeholders kept their vote.

Separate Reform Acts were passed by which Scotland added 8 and   31

Ireland 5 members to the existing totals of 45 and 100. Voting qualifications were practically the same as in England, but the Irish forty shilling freeholders disfranchised in 1829 did not recover their vote.

Moderate character of the Act: its defects

The Reform Act of 1832 was the forerunner of subsequent Acts which by gradual stages brought parliamentary democracy to Great Britain. Apart from the abolition of the rotten boroughs without compensation for their 'owners' its changes were essentially moderate ones which did not greatly affect the political ascendancy of the landed aristocracy and gentry. Borough representation was still generally excessive and in spite of the redistribution of seats southern England remained over represented. The number of electors, although increased by some 300,000 was small in relation to the population; in 1832 there were approximately 800,000 electors out of a total population for the United Kingdom of 24 millions: overall it meant that after 1832 one in seven of the adult male population had the vote. Most of the new voters were middle class, and the working classes who had provided much of the momentum to carry the Bill were left without votes; their resentment at what they regarded as a betrayal by the middle classes was one of the many factors that stimulated the Chartist movement in the later 1830s.

The Act modified but did not transform the electoral system; many of

A prospect of an election

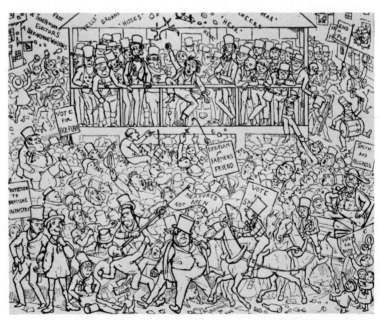

32

'The Vote Auction.' Corrupt boroughs and voters in early Victorian Britain

the bad features of the days before 1832 survived into the 1860s. There were still constituencies which could be bought as was proved by the disfranchisement of Sudbury in 1844 and St Alban's in 1852 for gross corruption; at Sudbury most of its six hundred electors had been selling their votes outright at elections held since 1832. About thirty boroughs with less than five hundred voters survived 1832 and here and in larger boroughs as well influence of various kinds was very effective. Most borough voters expected, and received, free food and drinks at election time, and sometimes money bribes as well. It was not surprising that expenses for borough elections remained high; the election for Nottingham in 1841 cost the two successful candidates a total of £12,000. Laws to prevent such bribery were obviously needed, but it was not until 1883 that a fully effective Act was passed. Under the open system of voting which was not changed until the Ballot Act of 1872, a voter's choice was known to all and he was often subject to outside influence, or even assault by the rival party's supporters. Elections remained in general disorderly and sometimes violent proceedings.

5. The Whig reforms

Nature of the Whig reforms

Towards the end of 1832 a general election on the new franchise returned a House of Commons in which the Whigs and Radicals had a comfortable majority. Lord Grey continued as prime minister until June 1834 when he resigned and Lord Melbourne took his place. During their ministries a number of important reforms were carried which made considerable changes, and which went beyond a gentle patching of existing institutions to make them work a little better. In these matters the Whigs, who believed in some reform but not too much, were driven on by their Radical wing and by reforming Tories such as the promoters of the Factory Act of 1833, Michael Sadler and Lord Ashley (afterwards Lord Shaftesbury). Public opinion in general was favourable to humanitarian measures such as the abolition of slavery and factory Acts.

The movement for the abolition of slavery

A preliminary step towards the removal of a great wrong had been taken in 1807 when the slave trade within the British Empire had been prohibited; it was now a criminal offence for British subjects to take part in the shipping and distribution of slaves from Africa to the plantations in the British Empire or elsewhere. But slavery itself remained and there were over three-quarters of a million slaves in the British Empire, most of them in the West Indian sugar islands but with lesser numbers in Cape Colony and Mauritius. While some plantation owners treated their slaves humanely there were frequent examples of cruel treatment; the condi-

'New West India Dance to the tune of 20 millions.' A cartoon by Doyle showing the liberated slaves dancing round Sir Thomas Fowell Buxton, the leader of the emancipation campaign. On the right John Bull is presented with the Bill by Lord Grey

tions of life of the field slaves who did the hard work necessary for the cultivation of the sugar cane were worst: the house slaves had an easier existence. The degradation of slavery and its utter wrongness in terms of Christian belief led British public opinion increasingly to demand its abolition. In 1823 the Anti-Slavery Society was formed for this purpose; it was organized by many noted humanitarians such as Buxton, Clarkson, Zachary Macaulay and Wilberforce. For the next ten years an intensive agitation went on with both the abolitionists and West Indian planters trying to convince the British public of the righteousness of their cause. The Jamaican planters referred to a pamphlet by Wilberforce as 'this unholy effusion from the fanaticism of second childhood, and of inveterate and reckless malice'. The planters made many telling points about the 'slavery' of the English cotton mills and the miseries of the English poor, matters in which Wilberforce showed little interest. It is notable that in the elections of 1832 for the first reformed Parliament those candidates who were in favour of abolition were generally returned.

Abolition of slavery in the British Empire 1833

In May 1833 a Bill for the abolition of slavery in the British Empire was introduced and became law on 28 August 1833. Children under six years were freed at once; slaves over this age were to be freed after serving, without payment, a period of apprenticeship, six years in the case of the field slaves and four years for the rest. Compensation of £20 millions was paid to the slave owners. The apprenticeship system was adopted to make the change from slavery to freedom a gradual one and to ensure that the planters would not be entirely deprived of labour during this period. The system worked badly and was ended in 1838. For many years the emancipated slaves were a social problem in the West Indies where little was done for their education and religious welfare except by Nonconformist missionary organizations. So great was their dislike for the scene of their former tribulation that unless absolutely obliged to, the ex-slaves were unwilling to work on the plantations for a wage. In the bigger colonies such as Jamaica and British Guiana where there was much vacant land, many of these ex-slaves became squatter-occupiers, growing food for their families rather than living as wage earners.

The need for Factory Acts

The statement of the West Indian planters that child slavery existed in British mills had a measure of truth in it. Mass production by concentrating labour and power-driven machinery under one roof had developed most in the cotton industry and here long hours were worked by thousands of men, women and children. It is clear that there were great differences in the standards of these factories: some had enlightened owners and

35

fairly good conditions but there were too many makeshift factories, often adapted from old workshops where conditions of work were very unhealthy. Many employers had risen from the ranks by their own efforts and it was usually these who troubled least about the conditions of their workers and who resented most the restrictions of the Factory Acts.

The principal aim of the first Factory Acts was to limit the hours worked by children, young persons (adolescents) and women; adult men were thought to be capable of working for unlimited hours and therefore in no need of such protection. Later Factory Acts made compulsory the fencing of flywheels and machinery, better ventilation, sanitation and cleaning facilities. Before 1833 there had been three Factory Acts (1802, 1819 and 1831) covering children and young persons in cotton and woollen mills, but the local magistrates (often mill owners themselves) had done very little to see that their provisions were enforced.

Findings of the Commission of 1833

In 1832 Michael Sadler brought forward a bill to limit factory hours to ten a day, but Parliament was dissolved before his Bill had gone beyond a second reading. A Commission was appointed by the government in 1833 to investigate conditions in factories. Its report showed the wide variety of conditions in different parts of the country regarding hours worked by children and their treatment by the overseers and adult workers under whom they worked. The commissioners found that in general children's working hours were as long as adults, i.e. between ten and twelve hours a day. They pointed out very strongly the disastrous effects of such long hours on the children's physique and health and also that their chances of any education were very small indeed. It was also clear that many children were the drudges of their parents who through sheer necessity took all or most of their wages for the family budget. The commissioners recommended that paid inspectors should be appointed to enforce any Factory Act passed and that part-time education should be compulsory for all children employed in factories.

The Factory Act 1833

Public opinion was roused by this report and in 1833 the first effective Factory Act was passed. It applied to all textile factories, except those making lace or silk goods which claimed they needed the tiny hands of small children for the fine work involved. Children under 9 were not to be employed; hours for children between 9 and 13 were not to exceed nine a day or forty-eight a week. Young persons between 13 and 18 were not to work more than twelve hours a day or sixty-nine in a week. For those under 15 there was to be not less than two hours school every weekday. Four paid inspectors, with considerable powers, were appointed to enforce the Act; they met with hostility from some, but not all, of the factory owners. There was also, owing to the lack of birth certificates, considerable difficulty in proving the age of any child; working-class parents did not want to lose the earnings of their children and often over-stated the ages of the younger children. An Act of 1836 which made registration of births compulsory eventually remedied this difficulty.

The problems of poor relief

The greatest problem tackled by the Whigs was that of the Poor Law whose working was still mainly based on the Act of 1601. This had made each parish responsible for its own poor, for providing the unpaid officials (overseers of the poor) to administer the relief given and for raising the money required by a poor rate charged on landed property. The system had been considerably affected by the Speenhamland award of 1795 which had brought wages up to subsistence level by a money allowance from the poor rates, according to the number in the family and the current price of bread. The giving of this 'outdoor relief' was very general in the southern half of England where it may have prevented mass rioting by semi-starving farm labourers during the Napoleonic wars; it also provided them with just enough food to enable them to do their very hard work. But the system led to high poor rates which hit the small farmers; employers paid low wages, and workers lost the incentive to work produc-tively as both knew that wages would be brought up to subsistence level from the poor rates.

A Royal Commission to investigate the working of the Poor Law was appointed in 1832 and reported in 1834. A dominant influence in the Commission was that of the Radical reformer Edwin Chadwick who was convinced that the problem of poverty could be solved by more efficient organization in the localities combined with close supervision by a central authority in London, and by the application of certain principles designed to deter the poor from seeking relief except in the very last resort. The Commission's report emphasized the undesirable effects of the Speen-hamland allowance system as it worked in the countryside and said these must be prevented from spreading to the industrial towns. Their chief recommendation was that 'outdoor relief' with its money allowance, except for the aged poor and sick in their own homes, should be abolished and that only 'indoor relief', i.e. within the workhouse, should be given. Those who asked for poor relief must undergo the 'workhouse test' and by acceptance of the 'house' for themselves and their families prove their destitution. The standard of living and general conditions within the workhouse were to be made unattractive to discourage all but the really destitute and to ensure that the paupers inside would not be better off than the lowest paid independent labourers outside.

The Poor Law Amendment Act 1834

These recommendations were embodied in the Poor Law Amendment Act of 1834. Poor relief was still to be provided on a local basis but there was to be a central authority, the Poor Law Commission, which with its ample powers of supervision, inspection and audit would prevent any slackness or extravagance by the local authorities.

By the Act neighbouring parishes were grouped in Unions controlled by Boards of Guardians elected by the local ratepayers. Workhouses were to be built, paid officials appointed and poor relief administered in accordance with the instructions of the Poor Law Commission, issued by its secretary Edwin Chadwick whose reforming zeal explains much of its success and also much of its unpopularity. Within a few years Unions had been formed in most parts of the country, the giving of outdoor relief to the able-bodied poor had been stopped in the South and West and the national cost of poor relief considerably reduced. The commissioners encountered most resistance to their policy of Unions and abolition of outdoor relief in the industrial Midlands and North. In these areas during trade depressions large numbers of workers might be destitute and therefore the workhouse test, because of insufficient accommodation, could not be enforced. In such cases outdoor relief, in spite of the commissioners' orders to the contrary, was often given to those in need and who were ready to work on road making or similar tasks. In some parts of Lancashire and Yorkshire determined efforts were made to prevent the formation of Unions by opposition organized by Tory factory owners such as Richard Oastler and John Fielden. Indignation ran deep against the new Poor Law; popular hatred of the Poor Law Commission, 'the three-headed monster of Somerset House' and its workhouse 'Bastilles' was one of the causes of Chartism.

The working of the Poor Law

The Victorian workhouse was a grim place made worse by the declared intention of those in authority to make it as unattractive and as uncomfortable as possible so as to deter people from seeking poor relief. In the early days of the new Poor Law many indignities were inflicted on the paupers such as the separation of husband and wife and children, the monotonous tasks of stone breaking, bone grinding and oakum picking, and the prison-like routine and elaborate code of rules, breach of which could be punished by a bread and water diet. The worst sufferers were the pauper children who started, and the aged paupers who ended, their lives in such blighted surroundings. The Poor Law Commission was ended in 1847 after an investigation into the Andover workhouse scandal when half-starved paupers had eaten the rotten gristle from the bones they were crushing. A Poor Law Board was set up under a minister

38

responsible to Parliament. This change slowly led to more humane treatment; more was done for the education of pauper children and for the medical care of the sick and aged. Unfortunately, and in spite of much private charity, the Victorian age tended to regard poverty as the result of crime or carelessness and the destitute poor often got very little sympathy. As a result a deep dread of an old age in the workhouse, ending in a pauper's grave, possessed the Victorian working classes.

The Municipal Corporations Act of 1835

The Municipal Corporations Act of 1835 reformed, for local government purposes, those boroughs in England and Wales which held charters from the Crown. A Royal Commission, although it had tended to attribute the worst scandals of a few corporations to all the others, found plenty to justify its unfavourable report. It was clear that too many of the corporations were only interested in parliamentary elections and the corruption that went with them, and that the corporate bodies represented only themselves and not the majority of the townspeople. It was also shown that some corporations misused local charitable and educational endowments, often for the private profit of their members and relatives.

The Act applied to 178 boroughs only, but other towns could apply for corporate status which would bring them under the provisions of the Act. Councillors were to be elected at local elections in which rate-paying householders could vote. The councillors were to elect a mayor and a third of their number as aldermen. Provision was made for the appointment of paid officials such as a borough clerk and treasurer, for the keeping of proper accounts and for the appointment of a Watch Committee to organize an efficient borough police force. The Act established the principle of democratic representation in local government and later in the nineteenth century this was extended to the counties and other town areas. It must be remembered that in 1835 local government activities and services, compared with those of today, were very limited.

Reform of the Church of England

Another institution needing reform was the Church of England which during the previous twenty years had not endeared itself to Whigs and Radicals by its steady opposition to reform. The evidence of a Royal Commission showed great inequalities in the incomes of the episcopal sees and Church livings. Thus the income of the bishopric of Durham, which had been increased by royalties from the development of coal mines on its lands, was £20,000 a year; that of the Bishop of Llandaff was £1,000. It also revealed that many clergy held several livings and were often non-resident, leaving the work to be done by underpaid curates. The Established Church Act of 1836 made the incomes of the bishops more equal; 39

no clergyman was to hold more than two livings. The Ecclesiastical Commission was set up to administer, for the benefit of the poorer livings, the Church property transferred by these changes. The Church was now better able to do its work among the increasing population of Victorian England; it was also helped by a spiritual revival from within, that of the Oxford movement (see chapter 13).

Legal and educational reform

Law reform which had started with Peel's changes in the criminal code was continued by the Whigs. Brougham, the Lord Chancellor, was responsible for abolishing some of the ancient procedures of the Common Law courts and for hastening the slowly grinding mills of the court of Chancery, so vividly described by Dickens in *Bleak House*. A grievance of the Dissenters was removed by the Civil Marriage Act of 1836 which allowed them to hold marriage services in their own chapels. The beginnings of state interest in education were in 1833 when the government made a modest grant of £20,000 to the National Society (Church of England) and the British and Foreign School Society (Nonconformist) to help them in their work of providing elementary (primary) schools. This grant was increased in 1839 and a Committee of the Privy Council took charge of elementary education and the inspection of these grant-aided 'voluntary' schools.

Melbourne becomes prime minister 1834

On the resignation of Lord Grey in the summer of 1834 the King sent for Lord Melbourne. The new Prime Minister was a Whig but not a very ardent one. He did not believe in sweeping reforms, and doubted if the changes since 1832 had been for the better. Personally he was for leaving things alone –'I like what is tranquil and stable.' His policy was to keep things going without stirring up too much trouble and opposition, but to appease the reforming Whigs and Radicals in his party he allowed the measures of reform described above to be enacted.

After a few months in office Melbourne resigned in November 1834. King William who more and more disliked the Whigs eagerly accepted this resignation and sent for Sir Robert Peel who returned post-haste from Italy and formed a ministry. He hoped that the impending general election would give him a majority in the Commons but the hundred or so seats gained were not sufficient. Repeatedly defeated in the Commons, Peel's premiership, sometimes known as 'Peel's Hundred Days', ended in April 1835. The Whigs came back, and apart from a short interruption in 1839 caused by the 'Bed Chamber question', continued in power until 1841. They were, however, increasingly weakened by the dissensions between the Whig and Radical groups within the party and depended a

William Lamb, 2nd Viscount Melbourne (by J. Partridge)

40

great deal on the votes of the Irish M.P.s, most of whom followed the leadership of Daniel O'Connell.

Accession of Queen Victoria 1837

On 20 June 1837 the long and eventful reign of Queen Victoria opened. Victoria was the daughter of the Duke of Kent, one of the sons of George III. She was eighteen years old but already self-possessed and aware of the great position she had come to. On the day of her accession she wrote in her diary: 'Since it has pleased Providence to place me in this situation, I shall do my utmost to fulfill my duty towards my country; I am very young and perhaps in many, though not all things, inexperienced. But I am sure that very few have more real good will and more real desire to do what is fit and right than I have.'

For the first two or three years of her reign Victoria relied entirely on Lord Melbourne who became the Queen's confidential adviser. No one was better fitted than this wise, kindly and experienced man to educate her in the political system of her realm. It was not surprising that the Queen became deeply attached to her Whig ministers and dreaded the thought of having to change them for Tories. In 1839 Melbourne's majority in the Commons became so small that he resigned and Victoria had to send for Sir Robert Peel. She found his manner stiff, and wrote: 'how different, how dreadfully different to that frank, open natural and most kind warm manner of Lord Melbourne'. Peel asked the Queen to make changes in her household which would have substituted Tory ladies for the Whig ladies of the bed chamber. Nothing could persuade her to grant this quite reasonable request and Peel consequently refused to take office. The Whig ministry was reappointed and lasted for two more years; it was kept alive by Melbourne who was reluctant to abandon the Queen to the Tories. Difficulties over finance and its inability to balance the Budget led to several defeats for the ministry. The Whigs were granted a dissolution of Parliament but the general election returned a Conservative majority and Melbourne resigned in August 1841.

6. Great Britain and foreign affairs 1815–46

Castlereagh's achievements as foreign secretary

In 1815 Great Britain's foreign relations were directed by Lord Castlereagh. Foreign Secretary since 1812, he had successfully looked after his country's interests when peace was made with France at Paris and the affairs of Europe settled at the Congress of Vienna in 1814–15. Great Britain wanted a peaceful Europe and no more Napoleons: Castlereagh had therefore worked for a settlement in which the strength of the great European powers would be equally balanced. Outside Europe he had protected British maritime and colonial interests; he prevented any discussion by the Congress of the right of search by British warships of neutral vessels carrying contraband of war and also made it clear that Great Britain would retain those colonial conquests such as the Cape of Good Hope, Mauritius, Ceylon, St Lucia, and Malta, which she considered essential for her imperial and naval power.

Due largely to Castlereagh, the Quadruple Alliance of Austria, Prussia, Russia and Great Britain which had overthrown Napoleon continued after peace had been made. Its primary aim was to ensure that France kept the terms of peace, but Castlereagh saw its possibilities as an organization for consultation from time to time between the four powers in the interests of peace. He was critical of the alternative project of Czar Alexander – the Holy Alliance – a well meaning but vague project to get all rulers to pledge themselves to rule their subjects according to the Christian principles of justice, charity and peace.

Gradual breakdown of the 'Concert' of Europe

For a few years after 1815 harmony reigned among the great powers. At the Congress of Aix-la-Chapelle (1818) it was agreed to withdraw the allied army of occupation in France and to admit France to the alliance of the four great powers. But the 'Concert' of Europe on which Castlereagh had pinned his hopes was soon to be broken. The Congress of Vienna had disregarded liberalism and nationalism in its settlement of Germany and Italy and when these forces began to attack the established order it was disagreement over their treatment that split and finally ended the Congress System. Metternich, the Austrian Chancellor, with the support of Russia and Prussia, adopted a policy of repression of liberalism in any shape or form; his Carlsbad Decrees of 1819 gagged the press in Germany and placed all politically suspect professors and students of the Universities under close supervision. Castlereagh, although the British government at this very moment were passing the 'Gag' Acts to check popular disturbance and agitation, affirmed Great Britain's belief in freedom of thought and speech lawfully expressed, and her opposition to the interference and systematic repression advocated by Metternich, in these words: 'We shall be found in our place when actual danger menaces the system of Europe but this country cannot and will not act upon abstract and speculative principles of precaution.'

The differences between Great Britain and the Holy Alliance powers, Russia, Austria, and Prussia increased in 1820 when revolutions broke out in Spain, Naples and Portugal. The Czar Alexander, under the influence of Metternich, insisted that the five great powers must intervene and suppress these revolutions. A Congress met at Troppau (Upper Silesia) in 1820; Britain and France, realizing the unpalatable decisions likely to be reached, were represented at this Congress by their ambassadors acting as observers only. The Congress issued a statement condemning all changes of government brought about by revolution and announced that intervention would take place to prevent such changes and to restore the power of lawful rulers. Castlereagh denounced this policy as being 'directly opposed to the political and constitutional system of Great Britain' which was derived from the revolution of 1688 against the misgovernment of James II. He knew how difficult it would be to justify to Parliament and British public opinion a foreign policy which involved Great Britain helping continental despots restore tyrannical rulers. The Congress of Laibach (1821), like that of Troppau, devoted its energies to suppressing revolution. Austrian troops restored the situation in Naples and Piedmont: Castlereagh while admitting Austria had a special interest in Italy made clear Great Britain's dislike of this intervention.

The problem of Spain and her American colonies

1821 saw the beginning of the Greek War of Independence which was to divide the great powers even more and also break the harmony between Austria and Russia. Meanwhile Spain and her American empire were the most urgent problem for the next Congress. Chateaubriand, the Foreign Minister of Louis XVIII of France was preparing to intervene to put down the revolution in Spain; if successful he thought this intervention would wipe out the defeat of Waterloo and plant the Bourbons more firmly on the throne of France. Great Britain, with recent memories of Napoleon's occupation of Spain, disliked this as much as the other Troppau interventions but she was more concerned about the Spanish colonies in Central and South America. They had been in revolt against Spanish rule since about 1810 and the question of their recognition as 43 independent states was bound to arise. Great Britain's interest in these Spanish dependencies was that they were potential markets for her exports. If French intervention in Spain was successful there was the possibility that in accordance with the Troppau principles it might be extended across the Atlantic to the rebellious Spanish colonies; this Great Britain could not allow.

Canning succeeds Castlereagh as foreign secretary 1822

A Congress was summoned to meet at Verona in October 1822. Because of the problems of Spain and Greece it was likely to be a critical one and Castlereagh therefore decided to go himself, but worn down by worry and overwork he killed himself on 12 August 1822. His death deprived Great Britain of an able foreign secretary who had looked after her interests well; he had consistently planned and worked on the principle that Great Britain was part of Europe and must therefore take an active interest in its affairs rather than follow a policy of isolation. Had he lived it is probable that he would have done what his successor Canning did in working for the recognition of the independence of Greece and the Spanish American colonies.

While Canning did not share Castlereagh's belief in the Congress system he heartily agreed with his policy of cutting adrift from the interfering and repressive policy of Metternich and Czar Alexander. Unlike Castlereagh who had tended to keep foreign affairs to himself, Canning was ready to give them much greater publicity and so get the backing of British opinion. He was less European and more insular in his outlook than Castlereagh ('Every nation for itself and God for us all'), and had a strong realization of essential British interests.

George Canning (by T. Lawrence)

Canning and Spanish America

In spite of British protests the Congress of Verona had given approval to French intervention in Spain. A French army marched on Madrid in April 1823, overthrew the revolution with ease, and restored the despot Ferdinand VII. While regretting this, Canning made it clear that Great Britain would not let French action go any further than Spain. What he had chiefly in mind was the situation in Central and South America where the Spanish colonies had formed themselves into independent republics. Canning was determined to prevent any reconquest of these ex-colonies by Spain from Europe with French help or the creation of kingdoms in South America for Bourbon princes. He also aimed at establishing Great Britain's influence over these infant republics and at preventing them from falling under the political and commercial control of the United States. In 1826 Canning, looking back at events, summed up his policy. 'I resolved that if France had Spain it should not be Spain with the Indies. I called the New World into existence to redress the balance of the Old.'

It was clear to Canning that more could be gained for Britain in Latin America than by associating with the Holy Alliance in Europe. The importance of the South American market to British trade carried the day; Canning saw within his grasp what had been the dream of English merchants in the eighteenth century – access to the Spanish American market. What was involved was recognition of the independence of Mexico, Colombia, Buenos Aires (Argentine). Action must be speedy as the U.S.A. had already by 1823 recognized them. The American President Monroe had also, in December 1823, issued his declaration that 'the American Continents are henceforth not to be considered as subjects for future colonization by any European powers' and that any attempt to do so would be considered as an unfriendly act. It is doubtful if the U.S.A. at this time could have enforced the Monroe doctrine, had there been intervention from Europe, without the help of the British navy. Canning was ready to fight after the decision to recognize the South American republics had been taken by the British Cabinet in December 1824. Great Britain, rather more than the U.S.A., had secured the independence of Latin America; the Holy Alliance powers might rage but they could not stop the success of Canning's policy.

British intervention in Portugal

In Portugal Canning also took action to protect British interests and prevent despotic interference. A revolution in Portugal led to the grant of a liberal constitution by King John VI who in 1821 had returned from Brazil where he had gone when Napoleon invaded Portugal in 1807. Under pressure from his brother Miguel, leader of the reactionaries, John VI revoked this constitution. Canning sent a naval squadron to Lisbon to support John VI and threatened military intervention if the French tried to repeat in Portugal what they had done in Spain. Meanwhile the colony of Brazil had revolted against Portuguese rule. With British encouragement an independent empire of Brazil was set up under Don Pedro, the eldest son of John. Pedro became King of Portugal when John VI died in 1826 but after granting a liberal constitution he resigned in favour of his daughter Maria. To preserve Portuguese independence and to help establish Queen Maria, Canning at Portuguese request sent 5,000 British troops to Lisbon. For a time the 'wicked uncle' Miguel was restrained from overthrowing the constitution.

The war of Greek Independence

In 1821 the Greeks of the Morea and Aegean islands revolted against Turkish rule. In this matter Austria and Russia could not present the

45

united front they had shown towards revolution in Western Europe. To Metternich the Greeks were rebels against lawful authority and must be suppressed, but Czar Alexander was in a painful dilemma. Rebels though the Greeks might be they were also Orthodox Christians and Russia had long claimed to be the protector of all such Christians in the Sultan's dominions; he therefore could not let them be crushed by the Sultan and his Egyptian allies. Canning was able to exploit this difference between Austria and Russia. The Greeks had driven the Turkish navy from the Aegean Sea and were taking Turkish and other merchant ships as prizes. Rather than treat the Greeks as pirates Canning recognized them as belligerents, i.e. as carrying on war in their own right as an independent power. He went no further than this because although sympathetic to the Greeks he did not want to weaken Turkey too much so as to put her at the mercy of Russia.

During 1824 the Greek cause won increasing support in Western Europe. Lord Byron's mission to Greece, ending with his death at Missolonghi on 19 April 1824, gave it further publicity. Volunteers and loans from the West began to be raised for the Greeks, now hard pressed by the Sultan who had received help from his vassal Mehemet Ali, Pasha of Egypt. The latter's son Ibrahim invaded and devastated the Morea, massacring many of its inhabitants. The Czar called a conference attended by Russia, Austria, Prussia and France. It ended in failure, with the Czar parting company with Metternich. Alexander died in December 1825 and the new Czar Nicholas I wanted agreement with Great Britain over the Greek question. By the Protocol of St Petersburg (April 1826) Russia and Britain agreed that the Greeks should have self government while remaining under the overlordship of the Sultan. Since the Sultan rejected outright this proposal Canning prepared for stronger measures. He was able to bring in France, thus leaving Austria isolated; by the Treaty of London (July 1827) Great Britain, Russia and France were to make Turkey and the Greeks accept an armistice (by force if necessary) and to secure for the Greeks the self government defined in the Protocol of 1826. The armistice was accepted by the Greeks and refused by the Sultan whereupon the three powers sent their fleets to blockade Ibrahim in the Morea and to force Turkey to make peace.

At this stage Canning died (8 August 1827) and vigour left British foreign policy until Palmerston took charge after 1830. Canning's successor, Lord Goderich, was a nonentity, while Wellington, who succeeded him in January 1828, was pro-Turkish and reluctant to carry out the Treaty of London. Meanwhile the 'untoward event' of Navarino had taken place. The allied fleets under Admiral Edward Codrington had anchored in the bay of Navarino. In a dispute over anchorage the Turks fired on some English ships and very soon a general action ensued in which the Turkish-Egyptian fleets were destroyed (20 October 1827). Greek independence was now certain but Wellington left Russia and France to put the final pressure on the Sultan. Russia declared war and defeated the Turks, while French troops occupied the Morea. As a result the London Protocol of February 1830 proclaimed the independence of Greece.

Palmerston becomes foreign secretary 1830

In 1830 Lord Palmerston became foreign secretary and for the next thirty-five years was the dominating and deciding influence in British foreign policy. Personally he was cheerful, self-confident, resourceful, and convinced of the superiority of all things British over those of foreigners. He gave the British public the comfortable feeling that foolish foreigners who tried to twist the lion's tail would very quickly be put in their place. His popularity with the British people steadily increased and in the last ten years of his life amounted to something like uncritical veneration.

Henry John Temple, 3rd Viscount Palmerston (by F. Cruikshank)

But Palmerston was much more than his countrymen's picture of a successful circus master cracking the whip to foreigners. The chief aims of his foreign policy were:

1. To maintain and extend Great Britain's influence, not only in Europe but all over the world. In particular, he worked for a balance of power much as Castlereagh had done in order to prevent domination of Europe by any one great power such as France or Russia. To this end he upheld the Vienna settlement of 1815 but accepted modifications of it such as the independence of Belgium which accorded with British interests and also checked the expansionist aims of France.

2. To protect and extend British imperial and trading interests. A major aspect of this was Palmerston's decided anti-Russian policy, involving support of Turkey and the thwarting of Russian expansion in the Near and Middle East which was seen as a threat to British power in India.

3. To champion constitutional progress against the reactionary despotisms of the Holy Alliance powers. This involved British support for constitutional regimes in France, Belgium, Portugal and Spain, and also encouragement of Liberal nationalist movements in Europe; such movements, by causing trouble, would weaken the despots' power to interfere with Palmerstonian diplomacy.

4. To enforce international agreements for the abolition of the slave trade, still active between the Portuguese colonies in S.W. Africa and Brazil. Portugal was made to sign (1842) a treaty prohibiting this trade and in 1850–1 Palmerston sent a naval squadron into Brazilian harbours to end illegal slave trading which had persisted in spite of the treaty of 1842.

In 1848 Palmerston said: 'Our interests are eternal and those interests it is our duty to follow.' Two things in particular enabled Palmerston to

47

maintain the 'eternal interests' of Great Britain; one was his own wide and expert knowledge of countries, rulers and diplomats: the other, the power of the British navy, at this time larger and more efficient than any other navy and which could if necessary be used to enforce British policy in many parts of the world.

Great Britain and Belgian independence

Belgian discontent with their status in the kingdom of the United Netherlands set up in 1815 led to a revolution in August 1830; the Dutch were expelled from many parts of Belgium. At the London Conference in the winter of 1830–1 Great Britain and France carried the plan for Belgian independence; Austria, Prussia and Russia reluctantly agreed. The hand of Palmerston was now clearly shown in the various steps leading to the final independence of Belgium. It was one of the 'eternal interests' of England that no hostile power should control the shores of the Netherlands and consequently Palmerston wanted a ruler for Belgium who would be friendly to England. Although he was acting with the French, Palmerston had to watch secret French ambitions in Belgium where they hoped to annex part of the country of Luxembourg. The French King's son, the Duke of Nemours, was offered the throne but Palmerston put pressure on King Louis Philippe to make him withdraw. Palmerston's choice was Leopold of Coburg who was Princess Victoria's uncle and friendly to Great Britain; in June 1831, the Belgians elected him king and the five great powers accepted this choice. King William of Holland rejected this settlement and invaded Belgium; a British naval force and French troops intervened to uphold the independence of Belgium. Palmerston, finding that the French troops were likely to stay in Belgium to promote French schemes for annexation threatened war if they were not withdrawn: 'Union with France we cannot permit'; Louis Philippe had to comply. In 1832, owing to the Dutch King's obstinacy, further Anglo-French intervention was necessary to take Antwerp for Belgium. Belgian independence was one of Palmerston's greatest successes: he had protected British interests, given freedom to a small nation under a constitutional monarch and had checked French ambitions.

Portugal and Spain

In Portugal and Spain civil war was raging between the supporters of constitutional monarchy and those of despotic rule. Palmerston by naval and diplomatic means, supported Queen Maria in Portugal and Queen Cristina, the regent for the infant Queen Isabella of Spain, against the two 'wicked uncles', Don Miguel and Don Carlos. His general aim was to eliminate the influence of Metternich, Czar Nicholas and the Holy Alliance powers and to attach Portugal and Spain to the two liberal

western powers, Great Britain and France. He considered that he had
done this when the Quadruple Alliance of 1834 was signed. In his own
words, 'a capital hit, and all my own doing; I reckon this to be a great
stroke'. It is doubtful, however, if this alliance really led to much. Both
Portugal and Spain were unstable and unreliable allies; neither was particularly liberal, whilst Spain was a liability, being at this time devastated
by the Carlist wars.

The Eastern Question

By 1830 the attention of the great European powers was increasingly
engaged by the 'Eastern Question' which arose from the decay of the
extensive and once powerful Turkish Empire. Turkish military power
had declined; the rule of the Sultans was ineffective and because of

Map 1   The Eastern Question to 1856

Moslem conservatism it proved very difficult to modernize the structure of government. Nationalist liberation movements were growing among the Christian subjects of the Sultan, especially in the Balkans where by 1818 the Serbs had won self government and the Greeks independence by 1830. Powerful and disobedient vassals such as Mehemet Ali in Egypt and Ali Pasha of Janina in Albania threatened the unity of the empire.

For the European powers the problem was what was to happen to the Turkish lands if and when the empire finally collapsed; all of them had their own particular interests to satisfy. Russia wanted Constantinople and control of the Straits exit from the land-locked Black Sea to the Mediterranean, and also a paramount influence over the Balkans with their predominantly Slavonic and Greek Orthodox Christian peoples. Austria's interests clashed with those of Russia in the Balkans where she feared that any Russian advance would outflank her. France regarded herself as having a 'special relationship' with Turkey going back to the treaty of alliance between Francis I and Sultan Suleiman in 1535; she wished to maintain her political influence within the Turkish Empire and in particular the religious and cultural influence of her Catholic missions in Syria and Egypt. Great Britain wanted to preserve the Turkish Empire intact and so prevent Russia approaching the eastern Mediterranean and coming too close to the strategic approaches to India and the Red Sea and Persian Gulf. It was this policy of propping up the Sultan and encouraging him to reform his government that made Britain refuse offers by Russia for an outright partition of the Turkish Empire.

The ambitions of Mehemet Ali

An early phase of the Eastern Question was the War of Greek Independence. Mehemet Ali, the Pasha of Egypt who had helped his overlord the Sultan against the rebellious Greeks, had received Crete as a reward but claimed Syria as well. The ambitions of Mehemet Ali were far-reaching; he had built up a strong army with the help of French officers and extended his rule up the Nile Valley and into Arabia. He now wanted Syria as far as the Euphrates River, and in 1832 his son Ibrahim invaded these lands. The Sultan could not stop this attack. In December 1832 a Turkish defeat at Koniah in southern Asia Minor left the way open to Constantinople. In desperation the Sultan asked for and received help from Russia. This saved Constantinople but Mehemet Ali was left in possession of Syria. Soon the Russians exacted payment for their aid: by the Treaty of Unkiar Skelessi (1833), a close alliance between Russia and Turkey was set up. The Sultan undertook to close the Dardanelles to all foreign warships but more important, made himself a political dependent of Russia; in Palmerston's words: 'The Russian Ambassador becomes chief Cabinet Minister to the Sultan.' This Russian triumph was a severe blow to the Western powers who, because of their preoccupation with Belgium and Portugal had let Russia take charge in the Near East. Palmerston bitterly regretted this inactivity, describing it in 1838 as 'a tremendous blunder'. (See Map 1.)

The powers and Mehemet Ali 1839–41

Palmerston's chance to retrieve the situation came in 1839 when the Sultan who had invaded Syria was defeated by the Egyptian army at Nessib. Turkey was now at the mercy of Mehemet Ali and worse still, in Palmerston's eyes, of Russia as well. In his view, Turkey must be protected, kept intact, and reformed; Mehemet Ali must be crushed. Palmerston regarded him with intense dislike because his empire in Egypt, Syria and Arabia cut right across the new routes to the East, although it is clear that Mehemet Ali was not basically hostile to British commercial interests in this area. At this stage a rift appeared in the Anglo-French understanding; France, because of her interests in Egypt and Syria, supported Mehemet Ali's claims. At this unwelcome news, Palmerston turned to the other powers, including Russia, whose ruler saw the chance to exploit the breach in Anglo-French relations. The result was the agreement in July 1840 between Great Britain, Russia, Austria and Prussia to impose their terms on Mehemet Ali: if he accepted he would get Egypt as a hereditary possession, and Syria for life: if he refused he might lose everything. Relations between France and Great Britain became very strained because of Palmerston's inadequate consideration of the French viewpoint; war between the two nations was a possibility. Meanwhile, a joint British and Austrian naval force arrived off the Syrian coast and with the Turks, defeated the Egyptians. Mehemet Ali had to yield and gave up Syria, recovering Egypt as an hereditary possession. His submission was followed by the Straits Convention (1841) between the powers and the Sultan; this closed the Straits to foreign warships in time of peace, and made the five great Powers the protectors of the Turkish Empire instead of Russia. Thus the treaty of Unkiar Skelessi had been set aside and this was a success for Palmerston, but in getting it he had unnecessarily humiliated France and committed Britain to propping up Turkey.

War with the Chinese Empire 1839–42

In 1839 a dispute arose with the Chinese Empire over the export of opium from British India in return for the purchase of China tea and silks. The Chinese government forbade the opium trade but found it difficult to stop the large scale smuggling that took place; they also demanded that the British merchants in Canton should surrender their stocks of opium. In keeping with their aim of saving China from penetration by European

51

traders and influences they tried to prevent all trade with Great Britain, and rashly fired on a British warship. This brought the wrath of Palmerston on their heads; a short war followed in which Canton and its forts were bombarded by a British squadron. By the Treaty of Nanking (1842), the Chinese ceded Hong Kong and opened five places for trade – the so-called 'Treaty ports' of Shanghai, Canton, Foochow, Amoy and Swatow. They also paid compensation for the confiscated opium. The 'Opium War' was concerned with more than the opium trade; it was part of the policy of Great Britain and other powers of breaking the self-imposed isolation of the Chinese Empire and so opening a great trading area and a large mission field. Palmerston can be criticized for forcing a pernicious drug like opium on the Chinese but he believed that modern European civilization must be brought to China, even by gunboats. Later in Palmerston's career a second war with China followed, between 1856 and 1860. (See chapter 11.)

Anglo-French relations 1841–6

Soon after the Straits Convention was signed in July 1841, the Whigs went out of office; in Peel's ministry which followed, Lord Aberdeen was foreign secretary. His methods were more conciliatory than those of the headstrong and dictatorial Palmerston. In particular, Aberdeen tried to improve Anglo-French relations which had been harmed by Palmerston's attitude over Mehemet Ali; some progress was made in this direction and visits between the British and French royal families took place in 1843 and 1845. But incidents continued which caused friction between the two nations; the searching of French vessels by the ships of the British anti-slavery patrols off the West African coast were resented and relations were strained by the Pritchard affair. Pritchard was a Protestant missionary and British consul in Tahiti in the South Pacific who had become involved in a protest movement when a French protectorate over this island was proclaimed, and for which he was unceremoniously deported by the French. British indignation was soothed by an official apology and compensation for Pritchard. In 1846 the relative harmony between the two nations was shattered by the affair of the Spanish marriages, by which Louis Philippe unscrupulously attempted to advance the fortunes of his dynasty, only to lose the friendship of Britain in the process.

Relations with the U.S.A. 1818–46

Since the conclusion of the unnecessary war with the United States in 1814, Anglo-U.S. relations had improved, though they were still far from cordial. During the years between 1815 and 1850, considerable progress was made in marking out the frontier between British North America and the United States. In 1817 the two countries agreed that no warships

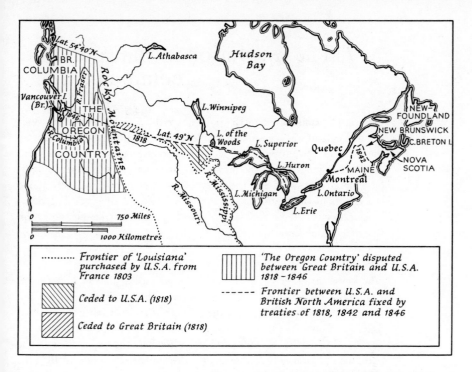

Map 2   The frontier in North America 1818–46

should be kept on the Great Lakes. In 1818 it was decided that the boundary between the U.S.A. and British North America should run along the 49th parallel of latitude westwards from the Lake of the Woods, as far as the Rocky Mountains. In the east, the frontier between the British colony of New Brunswick and the State of Maine was in dispute until fixed by the Webster-Ashburton Treaty of 1842. It proved more difficult to decide the frontier from the Rockies westwards to the Pacific. Flushed with their success against Mexico in 1845 which added Texas to the Union the Americans demanded a frontier of 54° 40″ North. Had this been conceded it would have meant the loss of Vancouver Island and most of British Columbia but the diplomacy of Lord Ashburton led the Americans to abate their demands and by the Oregon Treaty of 1846 the frontier continued along the 49th parallel of latitude to the Pacific. (See Map 2.)

C

7. The revolution in transport and communications

The rapid population growth and industrial development of early Victorian England was accompanied by a revolution in transport brought by the railways: the movement of people and goods was no longer dependent on the restricted pace of the horse-drawn vehicle or canal barge. To this leap forward in speed and the conquest of distance on land were added the effects of the steamship on the trade routes of the world, and the acceleration of news and information by the electric telegraph and speedier postal services.

Rise and decline of the coaching system

The better roads made by the turnpike engineers such as Telford and Macadam had brought a great extension in the number of coaches and had raised the average speed in the case of the crack coaches to about ten miles per hour. At the time of the first introduction of railways in the 1820s and 1830s the coaching services were expanding, especially over the main trunk routes between the great towns of the Kingdom. In 1833 the 'Telegraph' did the London to Manchester run in eighteen hours; in 1837 the average number of mail coaches leaving London nightly was thirty, and there were twenty-two coaches working daily on the London to Birmingham run. Railways led to a decline in the coaching industry with its vast establishment of horses, drivers, postillions and ostlers, but this decline was gradual until the long-distance railways were opened in the late 1830s and early 1840s; the opening of the London to Birmingham railway in 1838 reduced the number of coaches from twenty-two to four daily. Only on cross-country routes not served by a railway could the coach survive for the time being until the railway network pushed into these remoter areas.

Early experiments in locomotives and railways

The birthplace of the railways was the colliery areas of Durham, Northumberland and South Wales, where primitive tramways, some with wooden rails, had been built in the eighteenth century to haul coal from the pits to loading points on the river estuaries. The Surrey Iron Railway, authorized by an Act of Parliament in 1801 showed that the method could be applied outside colliery areas; using horse-drawn wagons on iron rails there was an attempt to link the Thames at Wandsworth with the Surrey countryside around Croydon. In the early years of the nineteenth century

SURREY
Iron Railway.

The COMMITTEE of the SURREY IRON RAILWAY COMPANY,

HEREBY, GIVE NOTICE,. That the BASON at *Wandsworth*, and the Railway therefrom up to *Croydon* and *Carfhalton*, is now open for the Ufe of the Public, on Payment of the following Tolls, *viz.*

'or all Coals entering into or going out of their Bason at Wandsworth,	*per Chaldron,*	3d.
'or all other Goods entering into or going out of their Bason at Wandsworth - -	*per Ton,*	3d.

'or all GOODS carried on the said RAILWAY, as follows, viz.

or Dung, - -	*per Ton, per Mile,*	1d.
or Lime, and all Manures, (except Dung,) Lime-ftone, Chalk, Clay, Breeze, Afhes, Sand, Bricks, Stone, Flints, and Fuller's Earth,	*per Ton, per Mile,*	2d.
or Coals, - -	*per Chald. per Mile,*	3d.
nd, For all other Goods, -	*per Ton, per Mile,*	3d.

By ORDER of the COMMITTEE,

W. B. LUTTLY,
Clerk of the Company.

andfworth, June 1, 1804.

important pioneer work was done on the application of steam power to rail transport by Trevithick, Blackett, Blenkinsop and Stephenson. All four built locomotives which, although crude and cumbrous, were capable of hauling heavy loads along rails.

The Liverpool and Manchester railway

It was the Stockton and Darlington railway which showed that railways had other possibilities besides the carriage of bulky goods such as coal. Opened in 1825 and originally designed to haul coal from the Durham

Opening of the Stockton and Darlington railway 1825

coalfield to Stockton-on-Tees for shipment to London, this railway, using Stephenson's 'Locomotion No. 1', tried passenger traffic as an experiment. Its success was encouraging to the promoters of the Liverpool and Manchester railway which had been first projected in 1824 to provide cheaper and speedier transport of goods between the two towns than that of the water carriers of the Bridgewater Canal and the Mersey

Museum drawing of Stephenson's 'Locomotion' 1825

Navigation. The promoters confidently promised speedier and cheaper carriage of goods by rail but they were more cautious about passengers, e.g. 'as a cheap and expeditious means of conveyance for travellers, the railway holds out the fair prospect of a public accommodation, the magnitude and importance of which cannot be immediately ascertained'.

The Liverpool and Manchester railway, opened in September 1830, can be regarded as marking the start of the Railway age in Great Britain. The line was constructed by George Stephenson (1781–1848), a self-educated engineering genius, who mastered both the problems of laying the track and of building the locomotives to run on them. He persuaded the directors to use steam instead of horse-power, and it was appropriate that his engine the 'Rocket' should have won the Rainhill trials (1829) which decided the matter. The 'Rocket' was the father of modern locomotives: it incorporated several novel features, among them sloping cylinders with pistons directly connected to the driving wheels (in contrast to the curious 'cats-cradle' overhead gear of Stephenson's early locomotives). It also incorporated two of Trevithick's ideas of a tubed boiler 57 and forced draught from the exhaust steam, both of which gave faster steam raising; a reversing valve gear and safety valve device were also other novelties. From the very start the railway was a great success. People flocked to experience the novelty of travelling by steam power; in the year 1831 over 400,000 passengers were carried, and the directors were apologizing because so few engines could be spared for goods traffic.

Creation of a trunk line system

Within a few years of 1830 companies were formed to build trunk railways linking the principal towns, and connecting branch lines. The Great Western Railway Company was formed in 1833 to join London and Bristol and the same year saw the promotion of the London and Birmingham railway: in 1834 and 1836 respectively there were formed the London and Southampton and the Eastern Counties, the latter linking London, Norwich and Yarmouth. The anticipation of large profits led to unwise promotion of new companies and heavy speculation in railway shares. This 'railway mania' reached its peak in the years 1844–8 when over 600 separate lines involving more than 9,000 miles were authorized by Parliament. In the 1840s the amalgamation of smaller lines to form trunk lines started; the movement was headed by George Hudson, the 'Railway King'. Hudson, originally a linen draper of York, had first turned to banking and then to promoting and directing railways. By 1844 he controlled over 1,000 miles of line and for a time was able to deceive the shareholders in his companies and the investing public at large by paying high dividends which came not from earned profits, but from capital. The fear that the projected Great Northern railway from London to York would spoil the revenues of his 'Kingdom' led to his creation of the Midland railway by the amalgamation of the Midland Counties railway, the North Midland and the Birmingham and Derby line. The London and North Western was formed in 1846 by the union of the London and Birmingham with the Grand Junction railway from Birmingham to Liverpool. These unions eventually brought about a national trunk system, improved 'through' running, and by establishing strong 'spheres of influence' made it difficult for rivals to build competing lines.

Obstacles to railway construction

Before construction could be started the companies had to raise money from their shareholders, survey the line, and, most important, get Private Acts of Parliament giving them powers to build and run their lines. Such Acts were necessary because the building of any railway would affect property rights, e.g. land might have to be acquired compulsorily and rights of way passing across the line of the railway modified.

58   Much company money was spent at this stage in getting these Private

Acts against the strong opposition which was organized to prevent the Bills passing. Canal companies, coach proprietors, turnpike trusts naturally opposed railways, and were sometimes joined in their opposition by rival railways running, or planning to run, over neighbouring territories. Other aggrieved parties were landowners and corporations who saw their amenities threatened by that belching monster, the early locomotive. The Headmaster of Eton College opposed the Great Western line to Windsor on the grounds that it 'would interfere with the discipline of the school, the studies and amusements of the boys'; similarly the Universities of Oxford and Cambridge entered their protests and used their influence to keep the railways well away from the University precincts. In many cases the opposition of noble landowners was polite blackmail to make the railway companies pay high prices for the land they needed and sometimes to build what were virtually private stations for the benefit of the landlords and their estates.

I. K. Brunel and the Great Western railway

Construction of these early railways was a major engineering feat involving many deep cuttings and high embankments which were built by the muscle power of thousands of 'navvies', equipped with no more than picks, shovels and wheelbarrows. These 'navvies' were almost a race apart with their own distinctive dress and habits; they terrorized many a neighbourhood with the drinking bouts and brawling which inevitably followed pay-day. From the survey of the line to its opening, much depended on the engineer in charge. Isambard Kingdom Brunel was the most inventive and imaginative of these engineers. Appointed engineer of the Great Western railway at the age of 27, his survey for the line drew the generous tribute from George Stephenson: 'I can imagine a better line, but I do not know of one.' Constructed between 1836 and 1841 the Great Western was distinguished by its easy gradients (in the first eighty-five miles from London it did not exceed 1 in 660) giving high speeds, by its finely designed bridges (as at Maidenhead), its cuttings and viaducts and by Box Tunnel which was nearly two miles long. Brunel regarded his construction of a London–Bristol rail link as the first stage of a new era of trans-Atlantic communication which would use steamships operating from the port of Bristol.

The 'Battle of the Gauges'

To get high speed and smoothness of travel Brunel rejected the 4 ft 8½ ins gauge used by Stephenson, contemptuously referring to it as 'the coal wagon gauge'. Instead, he used one of 7 ft which achieved his aims but led to considerable difficulties since nearly all other companies used the 4 ft 8½ ins gauge. It meant great inconvenience to passengers and freights 59 whenever the gauge changed. A 'Battle of the Gauges' now raged between the rival camps. To show what the broad gauge could do, Brunel built the first 'Great Western' locomotive with 8 ft driving wheels and a boiler working at 100 lbs to the square inch pressure. Although this hauled the London to Exeter express over the 194 miles at an average speed of 55 miles per hour, the Parliamentary Commission reported in favour of the narrow gauge. In 1846 the Gauge Act ordered that no future British Railways were to be built on any other gauge than 4 ft 8½ ins unless special parliamentary permission was given. The Great Western railway did not finally give up the broad gauge until 1892.

State intervention

By 1840 railways had become a matter of considerable concern to Parliament; it was felt that this new invention with its unchallengeable superiority in the transport of passengers and goods must be brought under some degree of control. There was the danger that the railways would be able to establish and exploit a monopoly of inland transport, and there was also the question of safety of passengers. It was significant that even in the 1840s when *laissez-faire* doctrines emphasized that economic activities were best left to private individuals there should have been a minority in Parliament which favoured state ownership of railways.

By an Act of 1840, amended in 1842, the Board of Trade was given general supervisory powers over railways. Its consent was needed before new passenger lines could be opened, and the Board's inspectors could withhold this if they considered the new line of unsatisfactory construction. In 1844 a Parliamentary Select Committee under the chairmanship of Gladstone, President of the Board of Trade, made a detailed investigation of railway organization, operational methods, and rates charged; its findings led to the Railway Act (1844). This Act (which did not apply to the 2,000 miles of railways authorized by Parliament before 1844) had two main provisions:

(*a*) companies were obliged to run at least one train a day in each direction, stopping at every station, with covered third class coaches and with fares not exceeding a penny per mile; previously third class passengers had received poor treatment, being herded like cattle in open trucks and sometimes charged as much as 2½*d*. a mile;

(*b*) the Board of Trade, if authorized specifically by Parliament, could buy out any new railway after it had been operating for 21 years.

Economic and social results

By the end of 1850 just over 6,000 miles of railway had been laid in Great Britain and in the same year 67 million passengers were carried. The economic and social results of railways were far-reaching. They provided faster and cheaper transport for mails, newspapers, and other goods, whether raw material from the ports of entry to the factories or the manufactured goods going to the ports for shipment overseas. Agricultural produce of a perishable nature could now be carried quickly to the markets of the big towns. Both the coal and iron industries expanded to meet the railways' need for fuel and material for the construction of the permanent way, locomotives and rolling stock. Railway building and the operation of the system provided employment for the ever-growing labour force. Rival forms of transport such as coaches and canals were hard hit; the former were driven out of business by mid-century, and of the latter many were bought out by the railways, with only a few surviving precariously. Socially, the middle and working classes were most affected; they became more mobile whether for work or pleasure. For the middle classes, railways made possible the annual seaside holiday, or for the poor the cheap day excursion to the sea. Many of our seaside resorts date from the railway age, while the dormitory suburbs of the great towns, especially in London, were the direct result of the establishment of railways.

The early steamships

In the early years of the nineteenth century there had been successful attempts on both sides of the Atlantic to apply steam power to ships. In 1802 Symington had demonstrated his *Charlotte Dundas* on the Forth and Clyde canal, and in the U.S.A. Fulton had built *Clermont* in 1807 to work on the River Hudson between New York and Albany. The first steam-propelled ship in regular use in Great Britain was the *Comet* built in 1812 for service on the Clyde estuary. A pioneer crossing of the Atlantic from west to east was made in 1819 by the American ship *Savannah*, but owing to the limited bunker capacity its engine was only used for a small part of the voyage. By the 1830s steam power had shown its possibilities for use in ships; in 1840 the Cunard trans-Atlantic service started, to be followed by other lines such as the Royal Mail and Peninsular and Oriental.

The propulsion of these early ships using steam power was by means of paddle wheels. The method had certain disadvantages, especially in bad weather, when a listing ship meant that either the port or starboard paddles would be more or less out of the water. The advantages of screw propulsion were shown in 1838 by the *Archimedes*, and gradually this method superseded paddle propulsion, especially for ocean-going ships. Brunel applied it in 1843 to his *Great Britain* which was novel in a further respect, that its hull was made of iron. Until well after mid-century steam was regarded as auxiliary power for vessels and almost all 'steam ships' carried and used sails. This was due to the relative unreliability of marine

61

engines, their extravagant consumption of coal (which took up valuable cargo space) and the absence of bunkering stations on the main sea routes of the world. In the period 1860–80 the development of the double and triple expansion marine engine gave a much more economical and efficient engine and although the brilliant performance of the sailing clippers such as the *Cutty Sark* sometimes surpassed those of the steamships of the day, ocean-going sailing ships were rapidly declining after 1880. It was these improved steamships which made possible the transport of cargoes of prairie grain from North America to Great Britain at such cheap rates that even after cargo and freight had been paid for, the importer could undersell the British wheat producer in his own market.

The electric line telegraph

In 1820 the Danish physicist Oersted had discovered that currents passing through a magnetic field had the power of deflecting a needle placed in that field. Cooke, a former officer in the English East India Company's army, and Wheatstone, a professor of science at King's College, London, followed up this by producing an electric needle telegraph for which they were granted a patent in 1837. In their instrument the needle was pivoted within a magnetic field and by alternating the current passed through the field the needle would move either left or right and point to the required letter of the alphabet printed on a frame placed behind the needle mounting. The new railways were the first to show a practical interest in this invention which made possible the transmission of information over a distance between two places connected by line or cable. In 1838 the Great Western railway started with a thirteen-mile link on its system between Paddington and West Drayton, and extended this to Slough in 1842. London was linked with Dover in 1846 and in the same year the Electric Telegraph Company was formed. By 1852 there were over 4,000 miles of telegraph line in Britain, most of them belonging to the railways.

Overseas links by means of submarine cables soon followed. In 1851, due to the work of the Brett Brothers, a cable link was laid between Dover and Calais; cables across the North Sea and Mediterranean soon followed. A trans-Atlantic cable proved more difficult; a link was established in 1858 but, owing to a defective cable, lasted for a few months only. It was not until 1866 that the *Great Eastern*, Brunel's ship which had been a failure as a passenger liner, and now employed as a cable layer, established a permanent line between Valentia in S.W. Ireland and Newfoundland. The importance of the trans-Atlantic cable was chiefly a commercial one; it made possible a world market in which buying and selling orders could be made within a few minutes by telegraph. Before 1866 a business house in London dealing with the U.S.A. by sea mail could not expect a reply to its offers before nearly three weeks had elapsed.

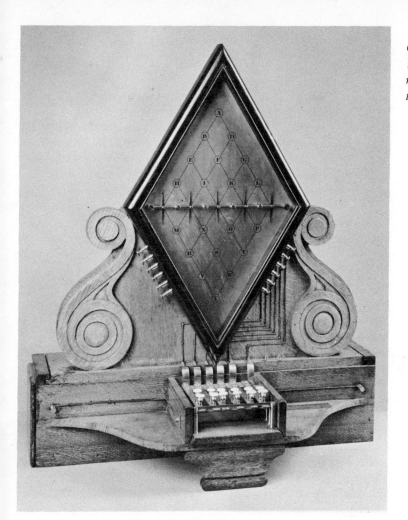

Cooke and Wheatstone's five needle electric line telegraph

8. 'Self-help' movements

Causes of 'self-help'

In the thirty or forty years after 1815 the condition of the British working classes was deplorable. This was due to a combination of adverse circumstances in which the workers were almost completely unprotected against the hazards and adversities of life and work. Wages were low, unemployment frequent, housing and working conditions bad, food poor, with the fear of the workhouse in old age: all these combined to make it an age of insecurity for the mass of the people.

The reforms made by both Whig and Tory governments, while checking some of the worst abuses such as the exploitation by industry of the labour of women and children, did not reach down to the hard core of the working-class situation, and the governing classes and the Parliament they controlled made it abundantly clear that they were opposed to any radical transformation of the society in which they held so comfortable and assured a position. The reaction of the British working classes was a mixture of protest movements such as Chartism combined with 'self-help' organizations, a number of which emerged in the first half of the nineteenth century. Bearing in mind the many handicaps which beset the working classes at this time these movements were a remarkable achievement; more important they were the starting point of the British Labour movement which in the twentieth century by the mobilization of its political and economic power has substantially changed the structure of our society. These pioneer movements reflect the inescapable need of the workers of early Victorian Britain for the expression of their political grievances and aspirations, and for 'self-help' organizations which would give some security and meaning to their lives.

Friendly Societies

In 1815 workers could not combine in trade unions to bargain for better wages because such action was a criminal offence by the Combination Acts of 1799. Besides these laws forbidding collective action the individual workman was subject to the law governing relations between master and servant under which disobedience such as leaving his job without notice was a criminal offence. The Combination Acts applied to employers but they openly disregarded this and used the Acts to keep wages down by intimidating workmen who refused their terms of employment or who asked for more pay. In spite of these restrictions some unions did exist but they had to keep their activities well concealed, often under the dis-

64

guise of a Friendly Society which was not illegal. Working class solidarity was developed by these Friendly Societies with their provident schemes whereby members could make some provision for illness, unemployment and funeral expenses by voluntary insurance contributions. Most societies had their social side; in their lodge meetings the individual had to express himself in conformity with an accepted code of manners: 'no eating, swearing or indecent songs in the lodge room, and all must address their remarks to the chair'. These societies were especially strong in the industrial areas and were an inseparable part of a working man's life well into the twentieth century when many of their insurance functions were supplemented by state schemes.

The repeal of the Combination Acts

The repeal of the Combination Acts was brought about by the efforts of Francis Place, a self-educated Radical and skilled in political propaganda and lobbying. As a young journeyman breeches-maker Place had led an unsuccessful strike in 1793 for which he was blacklisted by the employers, unemployed for a year, and with his wife reduced to near starvation. Later he had become a prosperous master craftsman but his earlier experiences influenced him to work for the repeal of the Combination Acts from 1810 onwards when the ruthless prosecution of the compositors of *The Times* for combining and striking aroused his indignation. By patient canvassing of M.P.s who were sympathetic and with the help of the Radical M.P. Joseph Hume, Place succeeded in getting a Parliamentary Committee appointed in 1824 to consider the matter. The evidence brought before this committee, both written and that of the working men witnesses, was chiefly inspired by Place. Subsequently an Act to repeal the Combination Laws was passed, almost without the majority of M.P.s realizing what was happening. It was now lawful for workers to form trade unions, to strike and to persuade others to do so. The immediate result was the formation of trade unions, many strikes, and the reconsideration of the matter by Parliament. In 1825 another Act repealed the one of 1824; it gave a bare right of combination by allowing workers to discuss and bargain collectively with their employers about wage rates and hours of labour; strikes and persuading others to strike by means of peaceful picketing remained illegal and criminal acts, and with this very limited freedom the British trade union movement started its career.

Robert Owen and trade unionism

Place thought that once trade unions were legalized, agitation would die down and that 'all will be as orderly as even a Quaker could desire'. He was mistaken and during the next ten years under the influence of Robert Owen the movement had an interesting if unsuccessful phase. Robert 65

Owen (1771–1858) was already well known for his New Lanark mills where since 1799 he had given his employees good working conditions and encouragement in their work, decent housing and schools for adults and children. Owen believed that the industrial revolution had brought the possibility of abolishing poverty and substituting plenty in its stead, and although he had been a successful capitalist, by 1820 he had become a fervent believer in socialist-cooperative principles by which the new methods of production could be used for the benefit of the community rather than for private profit. Industry must produce on a cooperative basis and distribute its products in the same way and in 1832 he set up a number of 'Labour Exchanges' where the goods made by producer cooperative societies could be exchanged, their price being fixed by reference to the cost of the raw material and the 'labour value' involved. For a year or so these 'Exchanges' had some success but by 1834 they had run into difficulties because the range of their goods and prices were uncompetitive with those of ordinary shops. In 1833 Owen's ideas were accepted by the Operative Builders Union which now planned to take over the building industry and encouraged by this Owen at the end of 1833 launched the Grand National Consolidated Union to include all workers, skilled or unskilled. This Union aimed at ending capitalism and replacing it by workers' control of industry on a cooperative basis, followed by a political take-over by a workers' 'Parliament'. Its membership was probably not less than half a million but only a small fraction of these could pay the membership dues and consequently the Union was quite unable to meet the demands for strike pay for those who had been locked out by their employers. Both government and employers had united to meet the threat presented by the G.N.C.T.U.; the prosecution, conviction and transportation to Australia in 1834 of six farm labourers of Tolpuddle in Dorset for taking an oath of secrecy, illegal under an Act of 1797, when forming a branch of the G.N.C.T.U., struck fear into the movement; employers coerced their workmen by refusing to employ them unless they signed the 'document' by which they renounced their union membership. By the end of 1834 the Grand National had collapsed, but some unions of the building trades, engineers, cotton operatives and miners survived on a local and precarious basis.

The 'new model' craft unions

A recovery for trade unionism came in the 1850s with the success of the Amalgamated Society of Engineers. This was formed in 1851 by the amalgamation of the various craft unions of skilled mechanics and fitters in the engineering trades. It gave its members protection against their employers in the matters of hours and conditions of work and also an extended range of benefits such as pay during strikes, unemployment and

Membership certificate of the Amalgamated Society of Engineers. Mid-nineteenth century

sickness. The high rates of contributions for these benefits made the 'new model' unions rather exclusive bodies; only the better-paid skilled craftsmen could afford to belong to them.

The A.S.E. was efficiently organised on a national basis with a general secretary and central executive which alone took decisions and gave instructions to the local branches over strike action and strike pay. It very soon came into conflict with the employers over its demands for the abolition of piece work and overtime enforced by the employers at 67 ordinary rates of pay. In 1852 the engineering employers locked out their workers and after three months forced them back to work on their terms. In spite of this defeat the A.S.E. survived and went on to increase its membership and funds.

The example of the A.S.E. with its emphasis on a central organization spread to the building trades in the later 1850s; after a struggle with the employers who were trying to force their workmen to sign the 'document' renouncing trade union membership, the Amalgamated Society of Carpenters and Joiners was founded in 1860. In the same year the London Trades Council was formed; this became the framework through which the leaders of the important craft unions, known as the 'Junta', could organize political pressure for reform of the laws restricting trade union activities; it foreshadowed the later Trades Union Congress, founded in 1868 to coordinate trade union interests and activities.

The background of Chartism

Chartism was a movement of the British working classes to achieve the ambitious programme of political rights contained in the six points of the Charter. Recent studies have increasingly shown the complexity of the movement both as regards its causes and the attitudes of its leaders, and also that it had two aspects – national and regional, the latter often being strongly marked. While political aims influenced the better-paid craftsmen of Lovett's London Working Men's Association, social-economic factors were more important in promoting Chartism in the provincial areas of the North, North-East and East Midlands where the movement was a protest against the bad conditions of life and work of the 1830s and 1840s. The low wages, frequent unemployment, lack of security, the harsh Poor Law, and the low housing standards made men ask if life had any meaning at all; it is significant that Chartism was strong in areas where hand industries such as broad cloth and stocking weaving, nail making, wool combing and calico printing had been adversely affected by the mechanization of the industrial revolution. The Charter pointed a way out of all this misery and this explains the intense fervour with which it was supported. If the six points were accepted and became law Parliament would be substantially changed in character and laws to improve working-class conditions could be confidently expected.

The 'six points' of the Charter

The movement started in 1836 when William Lovett founded the London Working Men's Association which aimed at uniting the better-paid workers in a demand for the vote. It also tried to give the public information about the bad conditions of the working classes. In May 1838 the People's Charter was published; it was drawn up by Lovett with the help of Francis Place and contained what they thought to be the essentials of a working-class democracy. In its final form the Charter contained six demands:

1. Universal suffrage, i.e. votes for all men over 21.
2. Vote by ballot, i.e. secretly, as opposed to the existing system where the voter openly declared his choice.
3. Annual parliaments, i.e. a general election would be held every year. This, based on the advanced democratic idea that frequent ascertainment of the will of the electors was necessary, was unpractical.
4. No property qualification for M.P.s, thus enabling working class men to sit in Parliament. By an Act of 1710 there was an income qualification of £600 a year for a County member and £300 a year for a Borough member.
5. Payment of M.P.s. This was necessary to enable working men M.P.s to take their seats if elected.
6. Equal electoral districts, i.e. each M.P. should be returned by approximately the same number of electors.

Chartist action in 1838–9

The London Association sent speakers to the provinces to popularize the Charter which was enthusiastically received in the Midlands and North. Thomas Attwood, a Birmingham banker and M.P. interested in curing industrial depression by putting paper money into circulation rallied the Birmingham Political Union behind the Charter. But neither Lovett nor Attwood could compete with the more militant section of the Chartists in Lancashire and Yorkshire, where Feargus O'Connor held sway. O'Connor was both a powerful speaker and effective journalist with his own newspaper the *Northern Star* to publicize the Chartist cause. The first active phase of Chartism was in 1838–9. Torchlight meetings were held; a People's Convention or 'Parliament' met at Birmingham and declared the right of the people to arm; a 'Sacred Month' or general strike was to follow if Parliament rejected the Charter. A petition to Parliament with over 1,000,000 signatures asking for laws to make the 'six points' effective was presented by Attwood; in July 1839 the Commons rejected it by 235 votes to 46. Riots took place in Birmingham but the threatened general strike did not occur. In November there was an isolated rising of Chartists in Monmouthshire where some Chartists under John Frost attacked the troops in Newport. Lovett and O'Connor were imprisoned and Frost transported to Australia.

The divisions in the movement

The events of 1839 revealed a split in the Chartist ranks. Lovett essentially believed in 'moral force', i.e. that Chartism must work by peaceful

persuasion, particularly of the middle classes. Opposed to this policy were the 'physical force' Chartists who favoured strikes and risings; O'Connor himself was careful not to advocate physical force openly but many of his speeches gave it encouragement. The second attempt of Chartism in 1842 and its final effort in 1848 were both directed by O'Connor. A second petition to Parliament to accept the Charter was presented in May 1842 with over three and a quarter million signatures; besides the demand for the 'six points', the petition contained protests against poverty, the new Poor Law, the new police forces and the inequality of incomes. Its rejection by the Commons by 287 votes to 49 was followed by rioting, strikes, and industrial sabotage which aimed at stopping factory production by removing the safety plugs from the boilers. Peel's government took strong action; troops were deployed in the Midlands and North where many strikers and rioters were put on trial and imprisoned or transported for their part in these disturbances. After this suppression Chartist activities died down because the free trade policy of Peel stimulated economic activity so bringing increased employment and better wages.

The Chartist petition of 1848

In 1848 the revolutions in Europe encouraged the Chartists to renew their efforts; a People's Convention met and drew up a third petition. On 10 April 1848 the Chartist deputations assembled on Kennington Common from where they intended to cross the Thames and present the petition to the House of Commons. A large force of troops, police and special constables had been assembled to protect London from any lawlessness; the

A Chartist procession at Blackfriars in support of the Charter in 1848

Chartists were not allowed to cross the river and the petition was finally taken by O'Connor in three cabs to the House. When examined it was found to have just under 2 million signatures instead of the 5,700,000 claimed, besides which many bogus signatures such as 'Queen Victoria', 'Duke of Wellington', 'Pugnose', 'No Cheese' were recorded. The ridicule created by this exposure enabled the government to ignore the petition and it also hurried on the decline of Chartism, which during the next ten years maintained a shadowy existence under divided leadership; some followed O'Connor until he was certified insane in 1852, with another group under G. J. Harney and Ernest Jones moving towards a workers' Socialist Party. Other ex-Chartists linked up with the Radical Liberal movement of the 1860s which played a part in the agitation for the extension of the parliamentary vote eventually granted by the Reform Act of 1867, while trade unionism and the cooperative movement attracted other former Chartists.

As a mass movement with some revolutionary undertones Chartism was heartily disliked by the governing classes of Victorian Britain who did all they could to stifle it and to minimize its importance. Yet it is significant that within the next eighty years all six points of the Charter, except the unpractical demand for annual elections, had become law. Chartism also influenced mid-Victorian governments, albeit reluctantly, towards a more enlightened policy of social legislation which was reflected in a considerable extension of the Factory and Mines Acts and the beginnings of minimum standards of public health. Finally there remains the contribution made by Chartism to working-class solidarity with its own leadership.

The Cooperative movement and its aims
The retail Cooperative movement of 1844 was one of the most successful examples of 'self-help'. Before this date there had been a few isolated retail cooperative stores in both England and Scotland, and the plans of Robert Owen in the 1820s and 1830s for 'Villages of Cooperation', self-

71

governing communities producing and distributing their products on a cooperative basis. There had also been 'Exchange Bazaars' and 'Equitable Labour Exchanges' which valued producers' goods in 'labour hours' and issued their own currency labour notes for buying and selling of these goods. It was the Rochdale Pioneers of 1844 who put the movement on a firm and workable basis. One evil they fought was that of the 'tommy shop' run by the factory owner which sold inferior quality goods to employees; the aim of the Pioneers was to provide retail stores where members could buy the necessaries of life of good quality at a fair price, and at the same time to eliminate the middleman's profit for the benefit of members. Every member no matter what amount of capital he subscribed would only have one vote, thus ensuring democratic control and would only get a fixed rate of interest on his capital. Members would get a dividend depending on the amount of their purchases; this was a popular feature and an incentive to membership. Trading was strictly cash, with no credit given, thus encouraging thrift rather than debts. Pure and unadulterated goods only were sold, a novelty at the time when the poor consumer was unprotected against unscrupulous shopkeepers. There were also provisions for education of members.

Success of the Rochdale Pioneers

On 21 December 1844 the Pioneers, most of whom were flannel weavers, opened their shop in the ground floor of a warehouse in Toad Lane, Rochdale. Their capital, painfully scraped together, was £28; the shop at first opened only in the evenings and sold essential groceries, to which were added, a few years later, meat, drapery, clothing, boots and clogs. At the end of the first year their sales totalled £710: ten years later they had risen to nearly £45,000. This success led to the rapid spread of cooperative retail stores, especially in the Midland and Northern industrial areas.

The surviving members of the Rochdale Pioneers. From a photograph taken in 1860

A natural extension of the movement was the founding of Cooperative Wholesale Societies in the 1860s. These at first bought goods wholesale for resale to the various consumer Cooperative Societies; later they manufactured their own products, starting with boots, biscuits and soap. By 1900 the Cooperative Wholesale Society had factories making a large range of products and also owned dairy farms at home and tea plantations overseas.

Emigration

One important expression of 'self-help' was emigration which provided a solution to the harsh economic pressures which affected thousands of industrial and agricultural workers in nineteenth-century Britain. (See Fig. 2.) For these people a move to the new lands of Canada, the U.S.A. and Australia held out hope of a better life; it could hardly be for the worse. Since 1815 there had been a steady flow of emigrants which greatly increased after 1840; the famine of 1845–6 led to a mass Irish emigration chiefly to the U.S.A. The sufferings of the emigrants on the long sea passages in overcrowded ships with insufficient food supplies led to a series of Acts of Parliament after 1828 regulating conditions on such ships.

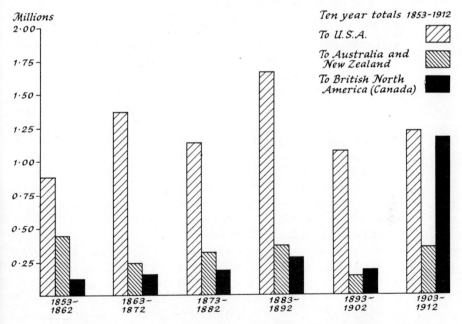

Fig. 2   Emigration from the United Kingdom 1853–1912

9. The ministry of Peel 1841–6

Peel's political career before 1841

Sir Robert Peel who became prime minister in 1841 had a long political career behind him going back to 1809 when, at the age of 21, he had become M.P. for the Irish pocket borough of Cashel. After holding junior office he was promoted in 1812 to the chief secretaryship for Ireland, where he learned much about that troubled land's political and religious problems. His work as Home secretary for reform of the criminal code and police between 1822 and 1830 has already been described. His 'Hundred Days' as prime minister in 1834–5 achieved little of importance apart from showing him as a leader of a revived Tory-Conservative party. Owing to the Queen's action over the 'Bed Chamber Question' he had been prevented from taking office in 1839; in opposition from 1839–41 Peel dominated the House of Commons and was a merciless critic of some measures of the Whig ministry, while supporting them on measures of change he thought justified.

Sir Robert Peel
(by J. Linnell)

The attitudes of Peel

In many respects Peel was a portent of nineteenth-century Britain as it moved into the new industrial age based on steam-power, iron and steel, and railways. He was the son of a wealthy cotton spinner and as such, the representative of a new social class that had risen to wealth, social position and political power on the back of the industrial revolution. His great advantage was that he understood the trends of his age and its most urgent needs. He was far more at home in the world of finance, trade and industry than were the landed aristocracy of both his party and the Whigs. His outlook was essentially practical and flexible; he repeatedly stated his determination not to be bound by strict party doctrines if the needs of the country required otherwise. He looked forward rather than backwards as his 'Manifesto' in 1835 to the electors of his constituency of Tamworth showed: 'I consider the Reform Bill as the final and irrevocable settlement of a great constitutional question.' He made it clear that he would not oppose reforms if they led to 'the firm maintenance of established rights, the correction of proved abuses and the redress of real grievances.'

Peel took office at a time of widespread social and economic distress which the Whig ministry had done little or nothing to alleviate. There was large-scale unemployment, due to the trade depression of 1838–42; in 1841, one person in eleven was receiving poor relief: dear bread and taxes on necessities like tea, sugar and soap made the lot of the poor a hard one.

'Curious Ins and Outs, or the Disputed Thunder.' A cartoon showing the Whigs accusing the new Tory ministry of Peel of unfairly taking credit for Whig successes in foreign policy, and of being hostile to the repeal of the Corn Laws

The Chartist movement which reached its height during Peel's ministry, reflected both the determination of the working classes to improve their condition and also their utter disillusionment with the Whigs and their promises. At the same time, the Anti-Corn Law League which was a middle-class movement, put forward its demands for the abolition of the Corn Laws. But Peel had his own ideas of how best to deal with the needs of his country: he suppressed Chartism, and held off the Anti-Corn Law League until the events of 1845–6 forced his hand. His Cabinet was a strong one and included some able young men, three of whom, Aberdeen, Stanley, and Gladstone, subsequently became prime minister.

The budgets of 1842 and 1845

In March 1842 Peel introduced the first of his celebrated budgets. He was faced with a situation in which the budget was £2⅓ millions on the wrong side. His solution was to change the Whig method of relying on indirect taxation from customs duties on imports and from excise duties on goods consumed inside the country. Instead he proposed direct taxation of income, thus reintroducing for a period of three years that income tax which had been levied first by Pitt in 1798 and which had been abandoned in 1816. At a rate of 7d. in the £ levied on all incomes over £150 a year Peel estimated that this income tax would produce sufficient revenue to enable him to reduce the customs and excise duties. Such reduction would benefit Britain's industries which would get their raw material

75

more cheaply, and also the ordinary man who would pay less for many of the goods he consumed; lower duties would eventually lead to increased consumption. At this time, Great Britain had a complicated tariff or list of duties levied on about 1,200 different commodities; many of these duties were quite unproductive, e.g. there were 349 different commodities where the duty on each one brought in less than £100 a year in revenue. Peel now reduced the duty on 750 of these, fixing it at 5% on raw material, 12% on semi-manufactured articles and 20% on fully manufactured imports.

The budget of 1842 was the first step towards Peel's own declared aim: 'We must make this country a cheap country for living.' It brought freer trade, soon to be followed by free trade in the 1850s and 1860s. The re-introduction of income tax made it possible to shift some of the burden of taxation from the poorer classes who had hitherto paid a disproportionate amount on necessities on to the shoulders of the middle and upper classes. The budget also showed Peel's realization that Britain was changing fast from an agricultural to an industrial country and that the needs of the industrial workers for cheap food must come first. This was equivalent to an admission that the Corn Laws must go, but Peel made it clear in 1842 that he was not prepared to go as far as that.

By 1844 the results had exceeded expectation. Income tax yielded more than was forecast and gave a surplus of £1½ million; helped by the lower costs of raw material and by the growing demand for labour and material for railway building, trade and industry revived. Two excellent harvests in 1842 and 1843 made bread cheaper. In 1845 Peel followed up with another effective budget; many of the duties on goods and raw materials which had been reduced in 1842 were now completely abolished and the rates on semi-manufactured and manufactured goods were cut to 5% and 10% respectively. Income tax, whose buoyant revenue made possible these remissions of indirect taxation, was still regarded as a temporary measure but it was now renewed for another three years.

The Bank Charter Act 1844

To this restoration to health of public finances, Peel added his Bank Charter Act of 1844 which mainly concerned the Bank of England, and which had as its aim the prevention of financial crises. At this time, notes issued by all banks, great or small, were convertible, i.e. the holder of a £5 note (or upwards) could demand that the bank of issue should exchange it for five gold sovereigns. Many of the smaller country banks issued more notes than the value of gold in their vaults and in times of crisis they were often faced with a run on the bank by note holders wanting payment in gold. Often they could not meet these liabilities; they closed their doors and went 'bust'. Peel's aim was to limit the issue of paper money, over-issue of which he considered the chief cause of financial crashes. The Act of 1844 divided the Bank of England into two departments, one for normal banking activities and the other for issue of notes. The Issue Department could issue up to £14,000,000 worth of notes without gold cover but all notes beyond this sum must be backed by an equivalent amount of gold; other banks could not increase their existing issue of notes. On the whole the Act had good results: it prevented inflation by over-issue of paper money and established confidence in a pound based on gold down to the outbreak of World War I in 1914.

The Royal Commission on mines and collieries

Social reform also had a place in Peel's plans. The driving force within his party was Lord Ashley (Shaftesbury), who in 1840 secured the appointment of a Royal Commission to investigate the conditions of work of women and children in mines and in trades and manufactures other than the textile industry. The Commission's report on mines and collieries shocked public opinion. It showed that in most coal mines the employment underground of women, young persons and children was the rule; there were many cases of children as young as five or six years old going down the pits, with eight or nine as the usual age. The youngest children were employed as 'trappers', i.e. opening and closing the ventilating doors in the shafts, a task which meant sitting in darkness for eleven or twelve hours a day. The older children were employed as 'hurriers'; half-naked and in total darkness they moved along the narrow tunnels, some not more than two feet high, from the coal face to the main shaft, dragging coal sleds with a load from anything from one and a half to five hundredweights. An eleven-year-old boy 'hurrier' in Scotland told the commissioners: 'The work is as said (sad) as ever laddie put his hand to.' Women and girls were employed in carrying heavy loads, either along the galleries or up the ladders of the pit shaft. The report emphasized the frequency of fatal accidents which were often due to a lack of safety precautions or to explosions from 'fire damp'; ventilation often failed and there were fatal accidents to miners going up or down the main shaft because of

A child 'hurrier' drawing coal 1842

defective ropes hauling the cage or because control of the pit head engine was entrusted to inexperienced or careless boys. The effects of these conditions and the hard labour involved meant stunted bodies and an expectation of life not exceeding fifty years.

The Collieries and Mines Act 1842

As a result of these revelations a Collieries and Mines Act was passed in August 1842 which forbade the employment underground of women, girls, and boys under ten. Some attempts were made to inspect conditions underground and to introduce safety regulations, e.g. boys under fifteen were not to be in charge of engines where human lives depended on them. This pioneer Act was followed by two others: the Coal Mines Act of 1850 which provided paid inspectors and for the compulsory reporting of accidents, and the Mines Regulation Act of 1860. This last Act introduced further safety regulations and check-weighers to check the amount of coal hewn by the miners. The aim was to stop the miners being cheated by their overseers and employers, but further legislation was needed to enforce their rights in this respect.

Factory Acts 1844 and 1845

The Royal Commission also dealt with the employment of children in calico printing, potteries, bleaching and dye works. Their report showed conclusively that conditions were worse than in textile factories but the Factory Act Peel passed in 1844 dealt only with textile factories. A first bill introduced in 1842 was withdrawn because of the violent opposition of the Nonconformists to the proposal to place factory schools under Church of England control. The second bill introduced and passed in 1844 dropped the proposals for compulsory factory schools but introduced some new and important principles connected with safety, e.g. machinery was to be fenced: it was not to be cleaned by young persons or children while it was in motion. The hours of women were not to exceed those of young persons, i.e. twelve a day, or sixty-nine a week with no night work. Children's hours were reduced to a 'half-time' basis with a maximum of six and a half a day. In 1845, due to the untiring efforts of Ashley, a Print Works Act was passed which prohibited the employment of children under eight in calico printing works and also night work for women and children. It also placed print works under the supervision of the Factory Inspectors and made provision for part-time education of children under thirteen.

Peel and Ireland

Peel made attempts to pacify Ireland but any success he had was overshadowed by the tragedy of the potato famine in 1845–6. Catholic

Emancipation in 1829 had removed a grievance but the bigger one of the Union of 1800 remained: Daniel O'Connell was the leader of the Irish at Westminster. When Peel took office O'Connell became hostile and agitated for the repeal of the Union of 1800, which, if granted, would have restored to Ireland her Parliament at Dublin. Mass meetings were held at which O'Connell urged the Irish people to stand firm for their rights; of his voice on these occasions an enthusiastic Irish peasant said: 'You'd hear it a mile off and it sounded as if it was coming through honey.' But O'Connell miscalculated, thinking that Peel would give way as had happened over Catholic Emancipation in 1829. Peel announced that repeal of the Union would not be granted and troops were poured into Ireland to suppress any armed rising. O'Connell called a monster meeting for 8 October 1843 at Clontarf. The day before, the government forbade the meeting, and surprisingly, O'Connell gave way. Later he was tried for conspiracy and convicted but on appeal the House of Lords reversed the verdict. After this O'Connell's influence declined and he died while on a pilgrimage to Rome in 1847.

Peel had successfully asserted the authority of the law but he recognized the limits of force when he said in 1843: 'It is clear that mere force will do nothing as a permanent remedy for the social evils of Ireland.' He now made a definite attempt to conciliate the Irish. Catholics were given a share of government appointments; an increased money grant was made to the Catholic training college for priests at Maynooth. Three Queen's Colleges for higher education were founded; two for Catholics at Cork and Galway and one at Belfast for Protestant Dissenters. Unfortunately, these well meant proposals met with a hostile reception. The intolerant Protestant sections of Peel's party opposed the Maynooth grants; the Catholic bishops and clergy condemned the 'godless' colleges; only the College for Protestants at Belfast flourished.

In 1844 Peel secured the appointment of a Royal Commission presided over by Lord Devon to investigate the land problem in Ireland and in particular to report on the relations between landlords and tenants. As a result of its work a Bill was introduced in 1845 to give Irish tenants the right to compensation for improvements they had made to their holdings, such as erecting farm buildings, draining and fencing the land. Owing to strong opposition the Bill was withdrawn for amendment but the Irish famine and the fall of Peel's ministry prevented anything further being done. Nearly thirty years later, Gladstone took up the work of Irish land reform and it was to the Devon report that he turned for the general picture of the Irish land problem.

Irish over-population and dependence on the potato
The Irish famine of 1845–6 showed with appalling clearness the dreadful

social and economic state of Ireland and also how little Acts of Parliament could do. Since 1800 the population had been growing at a rapid rate. The estimated figure for 1800 was 5,000,000: the first census returns of 1821 gave 6,802,000; that of 1841, 8,200,000. This startling increase had been brought about by early marriages and by the cultivation of the potato. The potato was an easily grown, easily cooked vegetable which thrived even on the poor peaty soil and high rainfall of Ireland. Together with milk and vegetables the potato was the only readily available food for a country with at least two millions too many people. Unlike Britain, Ireland had not experienced an industrial development which had absorbed the growing population. Her economy, except in Ulster, was almost entirely agrarian, a fact which led to relentless pressure on all available land. The result was intense competition for land which forced rents up to absurd levels. The landlord let his land to middlemen who in turn sub-let in minute plots at high rents to the peasant labourers. Several millions of these peasants were utterly dependent on this land system, the potato and poorly paid casual labour. They bore their sufferings with amazing fortitude and patient acceptance: 'If I had a blanket to cover her, I would marry the woman I liked; if I could get potatoes enough to put into my children's mouths I would be as happy and content as any man and think myself as well off as my Lord Dunloe.' But failure to pay the high rent meant ruthless eviction from the holding and mud cabin; there was no legal protection for the tenant and starvation followed. It was little wonder that crime flourished in Ireland and that prison, where a daily ration of seven pounds of potatoes was prescribed, had few terrors.

The Irish famine 1845–6

The famine of 1845–6 brought matters to a head. It showed the fatal results of dependence on a single crop whose failure meant that several millions of Irish must either starve or emigrate. In 1845 there were nearly 2,000,000 acres of potatoes mainly grown in spade-cultivated plots of less than one acre. There had previously been local failures of the potato crop but the loss of the 1845 crop was a general one. In western Europe the potato crop was attacked by a fungus which first destroyed the foliage and then rotted the potatoes in the ground. Ireland suffered more than any other country: by the end of October the bewildered peasants saw their food for the winter gone. This calamity together with the poor corn harvest in Great Britain led to Peel's decision to repeal the Corn Laws. The long political struggle over this repeal meant that Ireland suffered meanwhile, but the government made an attempt to relieve distress by importing maize, known to the Irish as 'yellow dust' or 'Peel's brimstone'.

Public relief works, building roads and drainage projects were also started but the real tragedy came with the failure of the potato crop for the second time in the autumn of 1846. In the winter and spring of 1846–7 the full effects of this were seen with hundreds of thousands of deaths from the starvation, typhus, scurvy, dysentery, and cholera which followed in the wake of the famine. The situation was one which would have taxed the resources of any well-organized state of today; the poor internal communications of Ireland in 1846 made distribution of relief stores very difficult. The British government with its firm belief that economic forces must work themselves out with as little interference as possible from the state, did far less than it should have done. Somewhat callously it repented of its earlier decision to make relief grants in 1845–6; in the second year of famine it threw the burden of relief on to the local Irish Poor Law authorities. The results were disastrous; the Irish workhouses were besieged by starving people whom the bankrupt Poor Law authorities, unable to collect their poor rates, could do little to relieve. Eventually the government was forced to make further grants and the government relief measures and those of the voluntary bodies, notably the Quakers, were intensified. Work was found for some 700,000 labourers, mostly on roads, some of which led nowhere in particular. Soup kitchens dispensing soup, bread, or maize porridge were set up in the summer of 1847. By the autumn of that year the good corn harvest and the blight free potato crop brought these relief measures to an end.

Mass emigration followed. Between 1846 and 1851 over a million Irish emigrated, most of them to the United States. They took with them not only their long historical remembrance of the wrongs done to Ireland by England through the centuries but also the bitter memories of the famine. It is not surprising that they provided money and encouragement for the Fenians and other Irish Nationalist bodies seeking the independence of Ireland. But after the famine Ireland remained a vexing problem for Great Britain: the problem was that stated by Disraeli in 1844: 'A starving population, an absentee aristocracy, an alien Church, and the weakest executive in the world.'

The Anti-Corn Law League

The last two years of Peel's ministry were dominated by events leading to the repeal of the Corn Laws in 1846. While it was the Irish famine in 1845–6 which finally forced his hand in this matter the ground had been prepared beforehand by the work of the Anti-Corn Law League. Founded in Manchester in 1838, its programme was simple: the abolition of the Corn Laws, or as it put it, the abolition of the bread tax. The League was organized and financed by middle-class manufacturers whose business ability and wealth enabled them to organize and finance propaganda for this cause on a large scale: using the new penny post and railways,

81

9,000,000 pamphlets were distributed and speakers sent to all parts of the country. The leaders of the movement in and outside Parliament were Richard Cobden and John Bright.

The League attacked the Corn Laws and the landlords who benefited by them. The Corn Law of 1815 had prohibited the import of foreign wheat when the price of English wheat was below 80s. a quarter. In 1828 it had been modified by a sliding scale which varied the duty on foreign wheat according to the price of English wheat. Peel in 1843 had reduced the duties under this scale so that when English wheat was 50s. a quarter the duty on foreign wheat was 20s., decreasing to 12s. at 60s. and 1s. at 73s. This did not satisfy the League who constantly explained to the middle and lower classes that they were being taxed to fill the landlords' pockets. They also argued that if foreign wheat was imported duty free the countries sending it would buy British manufactured goods in return. The working classes in their distress accepted the aims of the League for cheap bread, although they distrusted the middle-class organizers of the League whom they knew as the employers who gave them long hours and low wages, and who, like Bright, opposed factory Acts. It was not difficult for the landowners to make the point that the Anti-Corn Law League wanted cheap bread so that they might cut wages.

Repeal of the Corn Laws 1846

The majority of the landlords who comprised Peel's party were fanatical believers in the Corn Laws but there was also a substantial minority who realized that by using the new methods of 'high farming' British agriculture could compete with duty free imports of foreign corn. As in the case of other major political problems, Peel's attitude was one of flexibility and prudent calculation; his own economic beliefs had become increasingly those of a free trader and this made it very difficult for him to reject

the arguments of the Anti-Corn Law League for repeal. Besides this his political shrewdness told him that if this movement for repeal which commanded popular and nationwide support was resisted, another and more dangerous one might take its place in the shape of a renewed and irresistible demand for a further round of parliamentary reform to the detriment of the landed classes whose control of the House of Commons, in spite of the Reform Act of 1832, remained largely intact. With his parliamentary majority Peel could have rejected repeal as long as he remained in office, but he deliberately chose otherwise and his decision was made after the wet summer of 1845 leading to a poor grain harvest in Britain and the failure of the Irish potato crop; in November 1845 he proposed the suspension of the Corn Laws to permit importation of relief supplies of grain. This led to a split in his Cabinet and on 5 December he resigned; Lord John Russell, who had recently announced his conversion to repeal, tried to form a Whig ministry but failed and Peel returned to office a fortnight later. He announced his intention first to reduce the duty on imported corn and then to abolish the Corn Laws by 1849. Stormy debates followed, in which two-thirds of Peel's party were organized by Lord

83

George Bentinck and Disraeli against what they regarded as a great betrayal. Bentinck, a sporting landowner, did so because, in his own words, 'I don't like to be done.' Disraeli, whose injured vanity could not forgive Peel for denying him ministerial office in 1841, mounted a brilliant and venomous attack in which he accused Peel of treachery and of having no political principles. With Whig support, the repeal of the Corn Laws was carried in the Commons on 25 June 1846 by a majority of 98; three days later it passed the Lords, but the same day Peel was in a minority of 73 over a Coercion Bill to check disorder in Ireland. He at once resigned and his great ministry was at an end. In his resignation speech Peel took full personal responsibility for the reversal he had made in Tory policy; he paid tribute to the reasoned eloquence of Cobden which had caused this change. He referred with pride to the achievements of his ministry in securing peace abroad and growing prosperity at home; he expressed the hope that his efforts to remove taxes from food would be remembered by the working classes.

Results of repeal

Repeal split the Tory-Conservative Party into two groups: the free trade Peelites, who eventually joined the Whig Party, and a right-wing protectionist group; the latter, under Derby and Disraeli, formed the basis of a revived Conservative Party in the 1860s and 1870s. On the economic front repeal meant that foreign corn could now enter duty free apart from a nominal registration duty of 1s. a quarter and also that the principle of cheap imported food, so vital to the growing population of Victorian Britain and its industrial economy geared to export markets, had been firmly established. Yet events after 1846 hardly fulfilled either the hopes of the repealers or the gloomy prophecies of the protectionists. Although imports of foreign grain trebled, in the years 1850–70 the average prices of wheat and bread in Britain were only very slightly below those of the pre-1846 years. This was due to growing demand from an increasing population and to the interruption in foreign supplies caused by the Crimean War, the American Civil War and Bismarck's wars against Austria and France. In these circumstances British farmers found they could still grow corn profitably and the years from 1850 to 1875 have been called 'the golden age of British farming'. It was not until the 1880s that the free trade policy brought ruin; railways and steamships poured in a flood of cheaply produced prairie grain from the U.S.A. and Canada at a price with which the British farmer could not compete.

10. Whigs and Peelites 1846–55

Opposition to political reform

With the repeal of the Corn Laws in 1846 Victorian political life entered a clearly marked phase which lasted till the death of Palmerston in 1865. During these twenty years the ministries in power displayed a distinct coolness towards the extension of the parliamentary vote; they generally gave the impression of a wish to postpone popular democracy in Great Britain for as long as possible and so to maintain intact the existing aristocratic political structure as modified by the Reform Act of 1832. In matters of administrative reform this period produced a good deal of socially important legislation, affecting public health, factory acts, and criminal law. Finally during these years the British economy became fully committed to a free trade policy.

This defensive attitude in mid-century towards political reform was inspired and shaped by a number of factors. The decisive rejection of Chartism and its radical political demands was a clear indication of a widely based parliamentary opposition to popular democracy and that the extension of the vote was likely to be a very gradual matter indeed. The upper and middle classes had benefited most from the profits of a successful industrial revolution linked to a free trade policy and accordingly wanted no fundamental changes in the society they dominated. Even the working classes were affected by their small share of the new prosperity insofar as it promoted their acceptance of a society in which by hard work, thrift and 'self-help', working men might advance themselves socially and economically. The Radical movement of the time, although it had notable personalities such as Cobden, Bright and J. S. Mill, was thinly represented in the House of Commons and was distrusted by Victorian opinion. Again, once the issue of free trade had been settled, the basic differences in the political beliefs of Whigs, Peelites and Tories were slight as far as the maintenance of the existing political system was concerned. Finally there were the political effects of the repeal of the Corn Laws which split the Tory-Conservative Party into free trade Peelites and protectionist Tories. The Peelites, who included the ablest of the Conservatives, remained a distinct political group until they merged with the Whig-Liberal Party in 1859; the protectionist Tories under the leadership of Derby and Disraeli emerged in the late 1850s as a revived Conservative Party. This division into Whigs, Peelites and Tories promoted instability and floating votes, sometimes making an assured majority for the government of the day doubtful, and inducing

85

an atmosphere of coalitions and shifting political alliances in which sharp personal rivalries between party leaders were often present.

The Russell ministry 1846–52

On the resignation of Peel in June 1846, Lord John Russell formed a Whig ministry. Apart from Palmerston who became foreign secretary again, it had few men of ability and was only able to survive because of the divisions in the Conservative Party. The aftermath of the Irish famine occupied the ministry's attention for the next two years involving provision of relief and the repression of disorder and crime. The year of revolutions in Europe, 1848, caused little disturbance in Great Britain, apart from the third and last petition for the Charter by Feargus O'Connor (see Chapter 8). In the same year there was a major outbreak of cholera with a high death rate which emphasized the importance of the Public Health Act recently enacted.

Lord John (1st Earl) Russell (by Sir F. Grant)

The problem of public health

The government was obliged to face the serious problem of public health arising from the growth of population and of unplanned urban areas with generally insanitary environments. Many of the new towns had grown so rapidly that little or no attention had been paid to the layout and building of houses for the working population. The poorly paid workers could afford no more than low rents and they must be as near their work as possible. The aim of the speculative builder was therefore to build as cheaply as possible and in as little space as possible. An account of the houses of the poorest classes of Manchester in the 1840s describes them thus:

> The walls are half a brick thick, or what bricklayers call 'brick noggin' and the whole of the materials are slight and unfit for the purpose. They are built back to back without ventilation and drainage, and like a honeycomb, every particle of space is occupied. Double rows of these houses form courts with, perhaps, a pump at one end and a privy at the other, common to the occupants of about twenty houses.

Chadwick's 'Report on Sanitary Conditions' 1842

Such appalling conditions were common; all the large towns had their rabbit-warrens and rookeries where the poor lived in overcrowded conditions which actively promoted the killing diseases such as typhoid, smallpox, cholera and tuberculosis. It was the large-scale epidemics of the 1830s which led to official investigation. The industrious social reformer, Edwin Chadwick, besides his concern for Poor Law reform, was also keenly interested in public health. In 1842, under instructions from

86

Parliament, he drew up his *Report on the Sanitary Condition of the*
Labouring Population, which revealed many disturbing facts. The population of the poorest part of Leeds was described as living in houses:

> with broken panes in every windowframe, and filth and vermin in every
> nook. With the walls unwhite-washed for years, black with the smoke
> of foul chimneys, without water, with corded bed-stocks for beds, and
> sacking for bed-clothing, with floors unwashed from year to year . . .
> uncared for by any authority but the landlord who collects his miser-
> able rents from his miserable tenants. Can we wonder that such places
> are the hotbeds of disease?

The unhealthy state of the towns was shown by Chadwick's investigation of the average ages at which the working classes died; he gave seventeen years for Manchester, compared with thirty-eight for the rural
county of Rutland. At the same time, it was observed that the number of
births was more than sufficient to replace the high percentage of deaths;
the insanitary environment of the workers did not affect their powers of
reproduction. In the countryside the farm labourer's cottage was usually
small, badly built and damp, but the occupants had more fresh air and
sunlight than in the congested industrial towns; this, in spite of their life   87

of unremitting toil, low wages and restricted diet, gave them a slightly greater expectation of life.

Chadwick's recommendations

Chadwick's main conclusion was that disease among the working classes was due to dirt caused by inefficient disposal of human excreta, together with overcrowding in damp and ill-ventilated houses. He urged the need for a system of proper sanitation based on water-borne sewage, adequate street cleaning and removal of refuse, and above all, an abundant water supply. This last was essential if standards of cleanliness were to be established and proper drainage effected. Before 1850 few towns had piped water supplies; water was usually sold by the gallon or bucket; at Bradford one penny was charged for three gallons; at Carlisle it was one penny for eight gallons. Chadwick was confident that if these improvements were made, disease would be checked with a consequent reduction in the expenditure of the Poor Law authorities on the relief of the sick and consequently destitute poor.

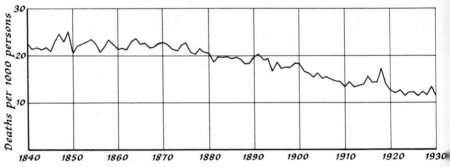

Fig. 3   Death rates: England and Wales 1840–1930

The Public Health Act 1848

The report of Chadwick was followed in 1843 by a Royal Commission which confirmed his findings and recommended the creation of a Board of Health in all large towns. A Public Health Act was enacted in 1848 which created a Central Board of Health; in areas where the death rate was over 23 per 1,000 it could compulsorily set up local Health Boards; elsewhere it could do so if 10% of the inhabitants petitioned for this to be done. In spite of the lack of full compulsory powers, this health Act marked the beginnings of an improvement in public health; the local boards which were set up under the Act often did good work in their areas by drainage schemes, abatement of sanitary nuisances and the provision of a pure water supply. The aims of the Act of 1848 were also supplemented by some typically piecemeal mid-Victorian legislation. Common

88

lodging houses, or 'doss houses', which were used by large numbers of
semi-vagrant and poorly paid workers, were regulated by Acts of 1851
and 1853; the keepers of these houses were to maintain minimum sanitary standards on pain of losing their licenses. In 1855 an Act gave local
authorities power to inspect insanitary houses and to enforce abatement
of any nuisances they caused.

Palmerston and the Don Pacifico Affair 1850

Russell was not helped by the exuberant, and, at times, high-handed
action of his Foreign Secretary Palmerston who had offended the Queen
by his anti-Austrian attitude during the revolutions of 1848, when he
condemned Austrian treatment of their Italian and Hungarian political
prisoners, and later when he welcomed the Hungarian patriot Kossuth
on a visit to this country. But public opinion supported him over these
matters, and even in the rather extreme action he took in the case of Don
Pacifico. Pacifico, a Jewish money-lender living in Athens, claimed British
citizenship because of his birth at Gibraltar. During a riot a Greek mob
had burnt and pillaged his house for which he claimed extravagant and
unjustified compensation. Palmerston zealously supported this claim and
forced its payment by the pressure of a naval blockade of Greece early in
1850. Subsequently he successfully defended his action in a lengthy
speech in the Commons: every British subject, in the same way as the
Roman citizen was protected against personal wrongs within the Roman
Empire by reason of his citizenship, had the same right to full protection,
no matter in what country he might be.

89

Dismissal of Palmerston and resignation of Russell 1852

The Queen, disappointed by Palmerston's triumph in the Pacifico affair, now demanded that he should not, under pain of dismissal, alter the foreign dispatches once they had been seen and approved by her. Palmerston did not comply with this instruction, and even sent some dispatches without showing them to the Queen at all. Somewhat rashly, and without informing the Queen or consulting his Cabinet colleagues, Palmerston openly expressed his approval of the *coup d'état* of 2 December 1851, by which Louis Napoleon Bonaparte had overthrown the Second French Republic. Russell was now obliged to dismiss him, but a few weeks later (February 1852) Palmerston took his revenge, his 'tit for tat with Johnny Russell', by moving and carrying against the government an amendment to a Militia Bill. Russell thereupon took the opportunity to resign and was succeeded by a Tory ministry formed by Lord Derby, leader of the protectionist wing of the party; Disraeli at last achieved his aim of ministerial office as chancellor of the Exchequer.

The Derby-Disraeli ministry, February–December 1852

The new ministry was a minority government and relied on the tolerance of the Peelites to keep it in office; its protectionist character was suspect, although it now discreetly abandoned this losing card. A general election in July gave it a few more seats but its lack of an assured majority in the Commons brought its downfall when the budget proposals were debated in December. Disraeli's proposals were ingenious: a reduction in the malt tax to please the landed interest; a lower duty on tea; a novel distinction between earned and unearned income in the levying of income tax, with a lower rate on the former; the partial extension of income tax to Ireland, and an increase in the rate of house tax to make good the loss of revenue arising from the tax reductions. In the final debate Disraeli made a fighting speech defending his budget, but a powerful counter-speech by Gladstone sealed its fate: defeated by 305 to 286 the ministry resigned.

The Aberdeen ministry 1852–5

On paper, this ministry looked a strong one. Lord Aberdeen was a Peelite and he brought in other able men whom Peel had encouraged, notably Gladstone, Graham, and Sidney Herbert. Lord John Russell held office for a year as foreign secretary while Palmerston, quietly biding his time, was home secretary. Yet the ministry did not live up to its apparent promise and cracked under the strain of the Crimean War.

In domestic matters, the most notable achievement was that of Gladstone as chancellor of the Exchequer. In his first budget of 1853 and all subsequent ones he showed an impressive grasp of state finance, and also a determination to complete the free trade policy of Peel. (See chapter 12.)

Compared with the attenuated efforts of today Gladstone's budget speeches were marathon affairs lasting for several hours, during which he made few references to his papers and carried with obvious ease in his head all the facts and figures he needed. He planned a reduction of income tax (then standing at 7*d*. in the £) by gradual stages over a period of seven years leading to its abolition by 1860. On income tax, 'this colossal engine of finance', as he called it, Gladstone was eloquent. He said it was immoral; it tempted politicians to be extravagant and tax-payers to practise fraudulent evasions. Public money was private money, taken from individuals for public use and must therefore be used with economy and not squandered. He saw this as a reserve power for the emergencies of war, and ironically enough this was not far away when Gladstone spoke thus in 1853.

The causes of the Crimean War

The intervention of the powers in 1840–1 had saved Turkey from both Russia and Mehemet Ali, but the 'Eastern Question' intensified as the Turkish Empire continued its decline; the Sultan could not defend his empire unaided against Russia, nor could he modernize his government. The European powers watched, Great Britain anxiously, and Russia eagerly, for the collapse of this empire. In 1845 Czar Nicholas visited England and urged the need for Anglo-Russian cooperation, should this collapse happen. In a conversation of 1853 with the British Ambassador at St Petersburgh he went further and suggested that the Turkish Empire should be divided, with Great Britain taking Egypt and Crete, leaving Russia with control of the Balkans and Constantinople. Great Britain received these suggestions with reserve because she feared Russian designs and in particular that Russia would gain control of the Straits and become a Mediterranean naval power at the same time as she expanded in the Middle East towards the Persian Gulf and the approaches to India.

Tension increased when Napoleon III, to secure the support of the French Catholics, championed the claim of the Catholic Church to the custody of the 'Holy Places' in Palestine, notably the church of the Holy Sepulchre at Jerusalem. The Greek Orthodox Church controlled this church and were supported by Russia on the grounds that the Sultan, by treaty, had recognized Russian claims to be the protector of Christians in the Turkish Empire. The Czar sent Prince Menschikoff to Constantinople to force a treaty from the Sultan confirming these claims, including those to the 'Holy Places'. Aberdeen's Cabinet was divided over this matter, but their Ambassador at Constantinople, Lord Stratford de Redcliffe, took the line of stiffening Turkish resistance to the Russian demands. By July 1853, the Russians had invaded the Danubian Principalities of Moldavia and Wallachia and the British and French fleets moved up to

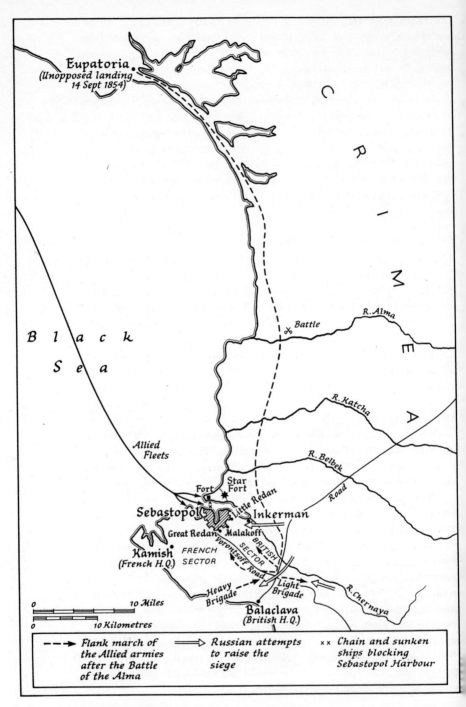

Map 3   The war in the Crimea 1854–5

the entrance to the Dardanelles. A Note drawn up by the ambassadors of the powers at Vienna and which reaffirmed the treaty rights of Russia to protect the Christian subjects of Turkey was presented to the Sultan, who eventually rejected it as he was reasonably certain that Britain and France would intervene if Russia invaded Turkey. By October 1853, Russia and Turkey were at war. Early in January 1854 the French and British fleets entered the Black Sea, concentrating off the Russian naval base of Sebastopol; by the end of March Britain and France were officially at war with Russia.

Defects of British military organization

The army Great Britain sent to the Crimea suffered from certain defects. Although many of its men had been on active service in India and other parts of the British Empire, as a whole it had not engaged in large-scale warfare since 1815. Its organization had been too much dominated by the Duke of Wellington who had opposed major changes largely on the grounds that none were required for an army which had beaten Napoleon. In the interests of economy, Parliament, since 1815, had cut down establishments, kept pay low, and left unchanged the bad conditions of service for the private soldier. Of its officers, the command and staff were often elderly; Lord Raglan, the Commander-in-Chief was aged 66, and a veteran of the Peninsular and Waterloo campaigns. The regimental officers were brave gentlemen, but averse to professional zeal and proud of their amateur status. The worst feature was the organization in Whitehall, behind the army; responsibility for control and supplies were divided between a medley of authorities each of which could shuffle off its responsibilities to another department. There had been no planning for an extended campaign in the field with its need for extra field and medical stores, tents, warm clothing, supply and transport, as the Crimean winter of 1854-5 tragically showed.

The invasion of the Crimea 1854

The original plan of the Anglo-French command was to drive the Russians out of Moldavia and Wallachia. Consequently their armies landed (July 1854) at Varna on the western coast of the Black Sea, but the Russians, chiefly to conciliate Austria, evacuated this area in August. The decision was then made to land the allied armies in the Crimea with the aim of capturing Sebastopol before winter set in. Between 14 and 18 September the allies made an unopposed landing at Eupatoria, about fifty miles north of Sebastopol. The British army was about 25,000 strong and the French 30,000; because of the shortage of transport they started their campaign without field stores and hospital equipment. Their advance south to Sebastopol was opposed by the Russians on the line of the River

Alma, but the passage was forced and the Russians driven off. Raglan wished to follow up this victory but the French commander, St Arnaud, refused. It is possible that an immediate advance would have led to a further defeat of the Russian field army and the quick capture of the fortifications on the northern shore of the harbour of Sebastopol. Instead, the decision was taken to march the allied armies round the eastern flank to the plateau south of Sebastopol chiefly because this area had a few small harbours through which supplies could be drawn. Raglan chose the harbour of Balaclava thereby giving the British army the eastern sector of the siege operations and the flank most exposed to attack from Russian forces attempting to relieve Sebastopol. The French had the better protected sector to the west.

Before the winter set in the Russian field army made two attempts to raise the siege. On 25 October they made a thrust at the British base area around Balaclava, but this attack was held by a Highland regiment and by a charge of the Heavy Cavalry Brigade. Then followed the charge of the Light Brigade under Lord Cardigan who, misinterpreting a not very clearly worded order from Lord Raglan, charged the Russian guns at the head of a valley a mile distant, suffering heavy casualties in the process. The second Russian attempt was on 5 November when part of the Russian field army crossed the Chernaya river from the east to combine with a sortie by the Sebastopol garrison in an attack on the British right at Inkerman. After fierce hand to hand fighting in the fog the Russians were repulsed.

The Crimean winter of 1854–5

The allied armies now spent a terrible winter on the plateau before Sebastopol. In mid-November, a hurricane swept through the Crimea, destroying buildings, tents, shelters and sinking supply ships in Balaclava harbour. This disaster forced the British army to winter in cruel conditions in the open, short of food, clothing and fuel. Disease caused by starvation and exposure, rather than the enemies' bullets took the heaviest toll. A flood of sick and wounded poured down to the base hospital at Scutari, suffering agonies during the journey over the Black Sea in the overcrowded transports; cholera, dysentery, typhus and scurvy raged. The British army began to melt away; during January and February 1855 nearly 14,000 men were in hospital.

Failure of the British medical services

The Army medical department proved incapable of dealing with these casualties. It had no ambulances in the field, its base hospitals were insanitary and short of stores and nurses. Worse still was the division of responsibility between the Commisariat, which controlled ordinary

94

rations, and the Purveyor who controlled invalid foods and hospital stores. Red tape prevailed among the officials of these two departments with the result that, although there was invalid food and clothing in store they could not be issued to the half-naked sick in the hospital wards because the regulations did not permit, or the stores had not been officially surveyed. William Howard Russell, war correspondent of *The Times*, had sent back disturbing despatches after the Battle of the Alma. 'Not only are there not sufficient surgeons . . . not only are there no dressers and nurses . . . there is not even linen to make bandages . . . the French are greatly our superiors . . . their medical arrangements are extremely good, their surgeons more numerous and they have also the help of the Sisters of Charity . . . these devoted women make excellent nurses.' The British public was both stupefied and enraged by these revelations. The government then asked Miss Florence Nightingale to go out to Scutari with a party of nurses.

The work of Florence Nightingale

Florence Nightingale, much against her family's wishes, had trained in nursing and had acquired a detailed knowledge of hospital administration. She accepted the invitation and arrived at Scutari on 4 November with thirty-eight nurses. Scutari hospital was a converted Turkish barracks, large, verminous and insanitary; one of the chaplains recorded that as he wrote down the messages of the dying men the paper became covered with lice. Her reception was cool; some of the medical officers were jealous and resentful of what they thought was female interference. Her relations with the Purveyor who could not issue urgently needed stores until a Board of Survey had 'sat on' them were even worse. The hospital was soon filled to overflowing and the medical authorities were overwhelmed by the sick and wounded from the Crimea. Amid the terrible scenes of the sick and dying the iron will of Florence Nightingale never wavered. From private funds at her disposal she provided clothing and invalid foods; more important, she achieved her main object of proving the value of women as nurses whose work did much to raise the morale of the sick and wounded. Florence Nightingale, moving through the wards by day and night, won the hearts of the soldiers, establishing an extraordinary influence over them, for never before in their sickness and suffering had they been treated so humanely. But the death rate in the hospital during the winter of 1854–5 remained high, since many of the patients died from the fevers they caught in the noxious atmosphere of the Scutari wards; it was found that the hospital's foundations were over a great cess-pit and that the water supply passed through the rotting carcase of a horse. When these defects were remedied and spring arrived, the death rate fell rapidly, helped by the nursing and better food.

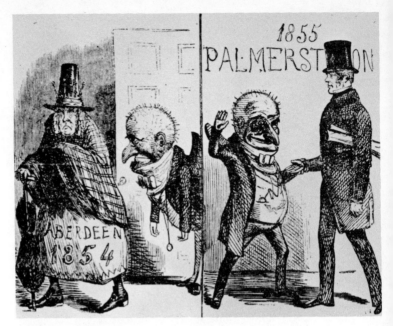

'Seeing the Old Year out and the New Year in.' Mr Punch welcomes the resignation of Lord Aberdeen and his replacement by Lord Palmerston in 1855

Parliamentary enquiry into the conduct of the war

The sorry tale of mistakes, incompetence and defects that the war had revealed, led to a public demand for a searching inquiry. In January 1855 Roebuck, a Radical M.P., moved and carried by 305 votes to 147, a motion to appoint a Parliamentary Committee 'to enquire into the conditions of the army before Sebastopol and the conduct of those departments of the government whose duty it has been to minister to the wants of that army'. Because of this vote of censure, Aberdeen resigned and Palmerston became prime minister. The Roebuck Report (June 1855) placed general blame for the war disasters on the Cabinet. It showed the inefficiency of the War Office where responsibility was divided between the secretary of State for War and the secretary at War, which made firm decisions difficult to get. The senior civil servants were shown to be irresolute, sheltering behind the rules and passing the responsibility to other branches. The report made it clear that the decision to invade the Crimea was a hurried one and one which ignored the difficulties of a winter campaign and its requirements.

Allied occupation of Sebastopol, September 1855

In the summer of 1855 the allies mounted their final assault on Sebastopol. The first attack in June failed chiefly due to a last-minute change in plans by the French commander. After an intensive artillery bombardment lasting twenty-three days a second attempt was made on 8 September: the

British were repulsed in their attack on the Redan but the French captured the Malakoff position which dominated the defences. On 10 September 1855 the Russians withdrew to the north side of the harbour, leaving the ruins of Sebastopol to the allies. In spite of this defeat the Russian position was still strong and her enemies hardly dared embark on a winter campaign in south Russia. Austria now became a mediator between the two sides but made it clear to Russia that if she did not agree to peace, Austria would join the allies against her. An armistice was agreed in January 1856 and was followed by a peace conference at Paris.

The Peace of Paris 1856

The Peace of Paris, signed on 30 March 1856, embodied the following terms:

1. The Black Sea was neutralized and the 1841 Convention closing the Dardanelles to foreign warships in time of peace was confirmed.

2. Russia's claim to be the protector of the Christian subjects of the Sultan was set aside.

3. The powers guaranteed the independence and integrity of the Turkish Empire; the Sultan promised reforms, but these were not carried out.

4. The Principalities of Moldavia and Wallachia were given self government. In 1859 they were united and later became the kingdom of Rumania.

5. Various matters of international maritime law such as the abolition of privateering, the regulation of blockade, and the searching of neutral ships for contraband in time of war, were settled.

Great Britain could look back with little satisfaction on the course and conduct of this war. The revelations of inefficiency, in spite of sustained attempts in high quarters to minimize them, could not be entirely disregarded and led to some administrative reform of the War Office, the army, and Civil Service over the next twenty years.

11. The ascendancy of Palmerston
1855–65

Palmerston becomes prime minister 1855

In his seventieth year the veteran Palmerston became prime minister. His political reputation had grown with the passage of years, and British public opinion placed him head and shoulders above his rivals: Lord John Russell was distrusted, Gladstone was thought too erratic and Derby had refused to take office. The mismanagement of the Crimean War had offended British opinion which felt that only Palmerston could lead the country to victory, largely on the ground that in the past he had shown that he would stand no nonsense from troublesome foreigners. But in some quarters Palmerston was deeply distrusted; Queen Victoria and her husband could hardly conceal their dislike for Lord 'Pilgerstein': the Queen could not forgive him for his cavalier alteration of the foreign despatches after she had read and approved them. Disraeli, bitterly disappointed because his leader Derby had refused to form a ministry, spoke wildly of Palmerston as 'an impostor, utterly exhausted and at the best only ginger beer and not champagne, and now an old painted pantaloon'. Nevertheless the blithe self-confidence of Palmerston was what was needed at this juncture and he positively warmed to the task of chastising the Russian bear. Neither was he perturbed by the early resignation from his ministry of the Peelites, Gladstone, Graham and Sidney Herbert, who resented the Roebuck motion for an enquiry which was bound to reveal mismanagement by the Peelite ministers of Aberdeen's government. Palmerston replaced them and with his reconstructed ministry did a good deal to improve Britain's effort in the later stages of the war.

War with China 1857–60

In 1857 the Indian Mutiny (see chapter 14) and China occupied his attention. The Chinese had arrested on a charge of piracy the lorcha (schooner) *Arrow* from Hong Kong which rather doubtfully claimed to sail under the British flag. Because of this insult Canton was bombarded and war with China followed. A vote of censure against his policy was passed by 16 votes whereupon Palmerston got a dissolution of Parliament and fought a general election on the China issue. The electors were carried away by the splendid picture of Palmerston chastising the insolent Chinese and gave him an increased majority; Cobden and Bright, two of his bitterest critics, lost their seats. With the cooperation of France, Palmerston could now increase the pressure on China and force open the door a little wider.

'*Pam – winner of the Great National Steeple-chase.' Palmerston was an easy winner of the general election in 1857.* (Punch cartoon)

An Anglo-French force captured the Taku forts at the mouth of the Peiho river leading to Tientsin and Peking; extensive concessions were then made by the Chinese, including eleven more 'treaty ports', the right of travel in the interior, the granting of diplomatic representation in Peking, and permission for Christian missionaries to work in China. Later the Chinese refused to ratify the draft treaty and only did so after another Anglo-French expedition had forced its way inland and occupied Tientsin and Peking (1860).

Administrative reforms 1855–7

Ambitious programmes of radical reform were disliked by Palmerston who thought that the business of government was to govern and 'not to go on legislating for ever'. Notwithstanding, some useful administrative reforms were made during this ministry.

(*a*) The Northcote-Trevelyan report of 1854 had made sweeping criticisms of the recruitment, organization and efficiency of the Civil Service. To improve matters the Civil Service Commission was set up in 1855; its first examinations were not competitive but more in the nature of qualifying tests to ensure that candidates satisfied the requirements of the department recruiting them. The open competitive principle was finally established by Gladstone in 1870.

(*b*) The Cambridge University Act of 1856, following a similar one for

99

Oxford in 1854, brought about many of the reforms recommended in 1852 by the Royal Commission on the Universities. Dissenters were no longer obliged to submit to religious tests as a condition of admission, or on taking the Bachelor's Degree; university government became more representative and the admission to Fellowships and Scholarships less restricted.

(c) By the Police in Counties and Boroughs Act (1856) it became compulsory for those counties and boroughs which had not yet done so, to set up a regular police force in their areas.

(d) Down to 1857 the only way a divorce might be obtained in England was by lengthy proceedings in the ecclesiastical courts followed by a private Act of Parliament, both difficult and expensive processes for the average person. In 1857 the Matrimonial Causes Act set up a new court for divorce and matrimonial causes with power to grant a decree of divorce or an order for judicial separation.

Fall of Palmerston 1858

In January 1858 the Italian revolutionary Orsini attempted to assassinate Napoleon III; the bombs he used were made in Birmingham and the conspiracy planned in England. Palmerston, unlike his usual defiant self, went out of his way to appease the violent French protests by introducing a Conspiracy to Murder Bill which would have made any attempt to commit murder abroad from England a serious crime. His popularity with his countrymen temporarily slumped; the mob hooted at him in Hyde Park and a combination of Tories, Radicals and Peelites turned him out of office by 234 votes to 215.

The Derby–Disraeli ministry, February 1858–June 1859

Lord Derby now formed a government with Disraeli as chancellor of the Exchequer; it was a minority government but survived for over a year because of differences between Whigs, Peelites and Radicals. Among its measures were the Government of India Act (see chapter 14); an Act permitting Jews to sit in the House of Commons without taking the usual oath 'on the true faith of a Christian', and one abolishing the property qualification for members of Parliament.

On the initiative of Disraeli the ministry made a modest attempt at parliamentary reform, but their Bill was defeated (see chapter 15). The health of the very rapidly growing Greater London area was improved by an Act of 1858 which gave the Metropolitan Board of Works, then the only central municipal authority, legal and financial powers to carry out a comprehensive drainage scheme. By building 82 miles of giant sewers, sewage which previously had run straight into the Thames in its course through London, was carried eastwards to discharge far out into the

Thames estuary. In June 1859 the ministry was defeated on a motion of no confidence and their resignation brought back the evergreen Palmerston.

Palmerston's last ministry 1859–65

The prestige and political skill of Palmerston enabled him to form a Cabinet that included aristocratic Whigs like Lord John Russell, Peelites such as Gladstone, and a few Radicals. Gladstone, by accepting office, turned his back for ever on his first party, the Tory, and led the Peelites finally into the Whig–Liberal camp. He proved a difficult chancellor of the Exchequer for he disliked the expenditure on armaments and fortifications undertaken by Palmerston because of growing suspicion of French hostility. The chimneys of No. 10 Downing Street, said Palmerston, were constantly smoking from the letters of resignation sent him by Gladstone.

There was one matter on which Palmerston, Gladstone and Russell were united, and this was the cause of Italian unity. Palmerston had long sympathized with the Italian struggle for freedom from the rule of Austria and the petty despots; Gladstone in 1851 had visited Naples where he had seen the savagery with which King Ferdinand II treated his political prisoners. When Piedmont–Sardinia with French help attacked Austria in Lombardy in 1859 Palmerston's government did not conceal its sympathies, though this led to difficulties with Queen Victoria who supported Austria. In 1860 Garibaldi's invasion of Sicily and the Neapolitan mainland was indirectly assisted by the benevolent presence of British warships; Foreign Secretary Russell justified the invasion by reference to English history when William of Orange, in 1688, had delivered the country from the tyranny of James II.

Great Britain and the American Civil War 1861–5

The American Civil War which started in April 1861 raised some awkward problems for Great Britain where majority opinion was against the slavery that existed in the Southern Confederate States which had broken away from the Union, but where there was also sympathy for the Confederate States on the grounds that having joined the U.S.A. voluntarily they should have the right to leave the Union in the same way. British upper-class opinion regarded the Southern planters as gentlemen in contrast to the rough-and-ready Yankee Northerners, while Great Britain's economic interests were closely linked with the South because the mighty British cotton industry, whose exports in 1861 were worth £50 million, was heavily dependent on Southern cotton. Again, the Southern States favoured free trade, taking British manufactured goods in payment for their cotton whereas the North was an up and coming industrial rival who favoured high protective tariffs. As the war proceeded the effect on the

101

Lancashire cotton industry was disastrous. In anticipation of the war two and a half million bales of cotton had been imported in 1860 but by 1862 imports had dropped to 70,000 bales and this led to unemployment and privation for nearly half a million textile workers. Only the import of small supplies of cotton from Egypt and India prevented a complete collapse of the industry.

Soon after the war started the British government declared its neutrality in the struggle but its relations with the Federal government were heavily strained by the *Trent* incident. In October 1861 an American warship stopped the British steamer *Trent* in the Atlantic and took off two Southern envoys, Mason and Slidell, who were on their way to London to canvass support for the Confederate cause. Palmerston demanded the return of the two men within seven days, and an apology for this violation of British neutrality. A stiff note, fortunately moderated by the good sense of Prince Albert, was sent to Washington, followed by reinforcements to Canada; President Lincoln released the two prisoners.

The Federal government complained of British merchant ships which attempted to evade its blockade of the Confederate ports. A bigger grievance was the damage caused to Federal shipping by Confederate commerce raiders which the British government had allowed to be built in British shipyards. The most notorious of these raiders was the *Alabama*, built on Merseyside; due to a suspicious mixture of mischance and delay on the part of the British government, the *Alabama* was launched in July 1862 and allowed to get away to sea. She took on her guns at the Azores and sank many Federal ships in the Atlantic before she herself was destroyed (June 1864) off Cherbourg by the U.S. cruiser *Kearsage*. The U.S. government demanded compensation which Palmerston refused and it was not until 1870-1 that Great Britain paid the £3¼ million compensation awarded by an international arbitration court.

The Polish rising 1863; the Schleswig-Holstein question 1863–4

The last three years of Palmerston's career were clouded by failure over the Polish rising and the Schleswig-Holstein question. It was not so much that Palmerston had lost grip or that in Russell he had a changeable and tactless foreign secretary, as the fact that times had changed; there were new forces in Europe, notably Bismarck and the Prussian army against which Palmerstonian pressure was ineffective, and gunboat diplomacy useless.

The Polish rising of 1863 was caused by Russian oppression of Polish nationality and by the introduction of conscription. Great Britain was sympathetic to Polish nationality and Napoleon III even more so. Russell encouraged the French to think Britain would join them against Russia over Poland but later backed out when he realized that war might result.

Russia, with Prussian support, ignored the French and British diplomatic protests and suggestions for a congress on the Polish question. The Poles were crushed by Russia and Bismarck was rewarded by the end of any Anglo-French friendship, a fact which helped him in his aggressive policy during the next seven years.

The Schleswig-Holstein question was even more revealing. This complicated matter was due to the peculiar relationship of the Duchies of Schleswig and Holstein with Denmark whose king was also duke of Schleswig and duke of Holstein. Schleswig was predominantly Danish but Holstein was German-speaking and a member of the Germanic Confederation of 1815. In March 1863 the Danish king announced that Schleswig would be incorporated with Denmark while Holstein would remain separate. German nationalist opinion resented this step and agitated for the Germanic Confederation to prevent the plan being carried out. In July 1863 Palmerston made an injudicious speech in which, referring to possible interference with the rights and independence of Denmark, he said: 'those who made the attempt would find in the event that it would not be Denmark alone with whom they would have to contend'. Naturally enough this was taken by the Danes to mean that Great Britain would fight on their behalf if they were attacked and on invasion by Prussia and Austria in February 1864 they appealed to Great Britain for aid. While British opinion condemned the wanton aggression of Prussia and Austria, there was a strong peace party in the Cabinet and Palmerston realized that without an ally and with only a small army Great Britain could not go to war. Queen Victoria (although her eldest son Edward, Prince of Wales, had married the Danish king's daughter Alexandra in 1863) declared her 'heart and sympathies are all German' and referred to the anxiety caused her by 'those two dreadful old men', Palmerston and Russell, who might, in spite of everything, intervene on behalf of the Danes. Bismarck had called the bluff of Palmerstonian diplomacy; Denmark was invaded, defeated and deprived of the two Duchies. The blame for this diplomatic defeat was not all Palmerston's. Great Britain in her great prosperity had become complacent and short-sighted about foreign affairs: year in and year out the pundits of the 'Manchester School' such as John Bright and Richard Cobden had preached the need for Great Britain's absolute abstention from continental politics.

Death of Palmerston 1865

A general election was held in 1865. Its outcome was considerably influenced by the material prosperity achieved by Britain's rapid economic growth and by the skilful policy of Gladstone as chancellor of the Exchequer; the humiliation and discredit over the abandonment of Denmark were forgotten and a majority supporting Palmerston was returned.

Before the new Parliament met, Palmerston died in October 1865; with his death ended an era not only on foreign affairs, but in domestic politics as well. Reform at home had long been held back by Palmerston's easy-going conservatism and dislike of 'legislation for ever', but in 1865 Great Britain was fully ready for another round of political and social reform.

12. The 'workshop of the world'

Great Britain's economic advance

From 1800 to 1850 there was a rapid development of the British economy and its resources, leading to a peak of prosperity in 1850–75. This economic growth, which was greater and more consistent than anything achieved in the twentieth century, was due to a combination of factors. It reflected the readiness of enterprising men to risk their capital and to apply their organizing abilities to profitable production of goods for expanding markets at home and abroad. Increased and cheaper production was made possible by labour-saving machinery powered by coal-fired steam engines, helped by the bulk transport facilities provided by railways and steamships. The emphasis was on factory manufacture of consumer goods and on heavy industries such as iron and steel, shipbuilding and coalmining. Agriculture, although its efficiency and output increased in this period, became increasingly a junior partner in the British economy. It was this industrial revolution which made Britain in the mid-nineteenth century 'the workshop of the world', a position she was to hold until industrial rivals such as Germany and the U.S.A. appeared at the end of the century.

The Great Exhibition of 1851

The Great Exhibition of 1851 provided evidence for the world of all this progress. In the Crystal Palace, the great glasshouse designed by Joseph Paxton, were displayed the products of British and foreign industry – locomotives, machinery, textiles, hardware, furniture, china and glass. Many of the articles for domestic use were made in the over-elaborate,

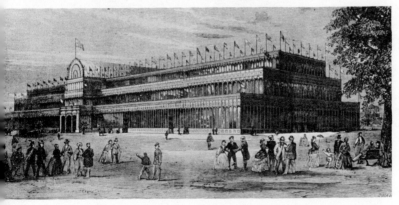

The Crystal Palace 1851

105

A child's cot. An example from the Great Exhibition which shows the Victorian fondness for excessive ornamentation

over-ornamented and ugly designs so beloved by the Victorian age. Novelties abounded: sportsmen's knives with eighty blades; unsinkable deck-chairs; pockets that could not be picked; corsets that opened instantly if their lady wearers should faint or have other mishaps. Six million people, including many foreigners, visited this Exhibition made accessible by the Railway age. Besides being a spectacle for the general public it was an impressive proof of the industrial progress of Great Britain; its promoters, including Prince Albert, Queen Victoria's husband, congratulated themselves that they had struck a blow for freer trade and peaceful progress.

106

Look yonder where the engines toil;
These England's arms of conquest are.
The trophies of her bloodless war:
    Brave weapons these.
Victorious over wave and soil,
With these she sails, she weaves, she tills,
Pierces the everlasting hills
    And spans the seas.
        (W. M. Thackeray, *May Day Ode*, 1851.)

*Maudslay's
original screw
cutting lathe*

Growth of a machine-tool industry

The basis of Britain's expanding industrial system was the increasing application of steam power to more and more machinery. This new machinery was a great improvement on the somewhat clumsy wooden contraptions used by the pioneers of mechanization such as Hargreaves, Arkwright and Crompton. The products of local millwrights were now inadequate for the general mechanization of industry; machines made of metal, durable and accurate in their working, were essential. The need for these led to the growth of a machine-tool industry, on which the development of all industrial revolutions depends. This industry produced firstly, machines which could turn, plane, cut and drill metal, and secondly, precision gauges for measuring accurately. The lathe invented by Henry Maudslay in 1800 with its traversing slide-rest gave speed and accuracy in the turning of metal and made possible the cutting of screw threads. Joseph Whitworth, a pupil of Maudslay, invented a metal planing machine of great accuracy and also micrometer gauges which were essential for the precision measurements needed by engineers. In 1839 James Nasmyth designed his steam hammer to meet the need of the builders 107 of the *Great Britain* steamship who were experiencing difficulty with forging the large paddle-wheel shaft for this vessel. On these inventions was founded a modern engineering industry which by 1850 was making locomotives, rolling stock, rails, iron ships, marine engines, textile and other industrial machinery. While Britain's industrial future clearly lay with machine production, in 1850 there were still many industries of considerable output which relied on hand processes with few mechanical aids, e.g. nail making, chain making, shoemaking, cutlery, agricultural implements and clothing, while even in the mechanized textile industries a few hand loom weavers lingered on into the 1860s.

The importance of coal

A dominant factor in the industrial revolution was coal which was essential for steam engines (stationary and locomotive), for smelting iron ore, for gas manufacture, for a chemical industry, and for domestic use. Output and the size of the labour force both increased sharply after 1850; from 57 million tons in 1851 the output had nearly doubled by 1871 with a total of 117 million tons. Reliable figures for the labour force do not exist until 1873 when the official return gave a total of 514,000 employed above ground and underground; probably the figure for the early 1850s is about 250,000. The increased output reflected the soaring industrial demand, and also the technical advances in the industry such as steam-powered winding gear, and fan ventilation which made possible the working of deeper pits. Coal became an important British export, especially after 1870 when the demand for coal for steamships on the ocean sea routes sharply increased. In 1851 exports totalled $3\frac{1}{4}$ million tons; by 1871 they were $12\frac{1}{4}$ million, and by 1900 had nearly quadrupled at 44 million tons.

The British iron industry

In 1850 the most important industrial metal in Britain's economy was pig-iron. This could either be used as cast iron, hard and rather brittle, or wrought iron after the 'puddling' process which made it stronger and more malleable. Wrought iron held the field because steel, a superior rival, was available only in small quantities and at high cost from the crucible process developed by Huntsman in 1750. It was wrought iron which made the early Railway age possible, providing the metal for locomotives, track and bridges. In the size of her output, Great Britain led the world at this time: in 1871 she produced about $6\frac{1}{2}$ million tons of pig-iron out of an estimated world total of 12 million tons. After 1850 new iron fields were opened up in North-east England (Cleveland), Furness (Cumberland), in Lincolnshire and Nottinghamshire. The older centres of iron manufacture in Staffordshire, Shropshire and South Wales now declined in output.

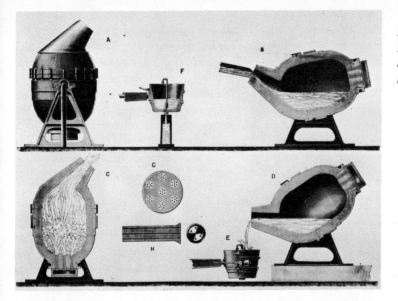

The Bessemer steelmaking process

The age of steel was brought by Henry Bessemer's process, the details of which he had worked out in 1856; by 1859 it was in commercial production. The Bessemer process involved placing the pig-iron in a cylindrical converter and passing a powerful air blast through the molten mass which burnt out the silicon and carbon impurities. Steel is iron in which the carbon content is exactly controlled and therefore Bessemer, after his carefully timed process had eliminated the carbon originally present,

added the required amount of carbon by means of a mixture of carbon and manganese, known as ferro-manganese. A major drawback to the Bessemer process was that it would not work with iron ores which had any phosphorus content; only pig-iron smelted from the non-phosphoric haematite ores could be used, and it was not until 1879 that the use of phosphoric ores became possible after the Gilchrist-Thomas cousins had discovered that a limestone lining to the converter would absorb the phosphorus in the iron ore. The Bessemer process cut the price of steel by over a half, but the adoption of steel as a constructional material was relatively slow until the 1880s, since wrought iron remained much cheaper, if less efficient, than steel.

The 'open hearth' process

Bessemer's invention was followed by the Siemens-Martin 'open hearth' process of steel making, developed between 1866 and 1869. Siemens had already invented a regenerative furnace which was designed to prevent loss of heat from hot gases escaping up the chimney. Using gas fuel in this furnace, Siemens obtained temperatures high enough to smelt pig-iron and pure iron ore together, driving off the carbon and silicon, and adding manganese as required. This process was more economical in fuel and easier to control than the Bessemer process and it had the added advantage that the steel product could be sampled while being made. It also produced a 'mild' steel which was better suited to boiler-making and for plates of ships' hulls than the Bessemer steel.

The chemical industry

Chemical products were essential to the industrial revolution and their manufacture had been given a powerful impulse by the needs of the textile industry whose various processes called for large quantities of chemicals: chlorine, sulphuric acid and lime chloride for bleaching; caustic soda for scouring the raw materials such as greasy wool. Potash and soda were needed by glass and soap makers; alum for fixing the vegetable dyes then used. Between 1856 and 1870 the discoveries of William Perkin founded the coal-tar dye industry. He showed that a number of valuable by-products could be obtained from coal, and produced from coal-tar an artificial purple aniline dye; later in 1869 he produced an artificial red dye to take the place of the 'Turkey red' vegetable dye which had been made for centuries from the madder root. In spite of Perkin's pioneer efforts a British synthetic dye industry was slow in developing, and the lead was lost to Germany.

Importance of the textile industry

110 In 1850 the textile industries held a predominant position in Great

Britain's industrial organization. At this time the cotton, wool, silk and linen industries employed just over 950,000; of these industries cotton was by far the largest, with just over 500,000 workers. In many ways the cotton industry by its early adoption of power and machinery symbolized the growth of industrial Britain. Directed by enterprising men who had been reared in the hard school of competition, the industry sought and obtained a world market for its cloth and yarns. In 1851 cotton exports were worth £30 million; in 1861 £46¾ million, and in 1871, £72 million; the only check to this expansion had been a temporary one in 1861–5 during the American Civil War when supplies of raw cotton from the Southern States dwindled to a mere trickle, causing a sharp contraction of output and hardship for the Lancashire cotton workers.

Banking, currency and credit

The intensive economic activities of Victorian Britain would not have been possible without a developed banking system, a sound currency, and ample credit facilities.

In banking the private banks which had provided much of the capital for the financing of the early industrial revolution were becoming less important; their note issues had been brought under strict control by the Bank Charter Act of 1844, and after 1850 they had to meet increasing competition from the joint stock banks with their greater capital resources and branches operating on a regional or national basis. The wider facilities offered by the joint stock banks made possible the extended use of the cheque for the settlement of debts. At the summit of the banking system was the Bank of England which besides being the government's banker increasingly became a central bank and 'bankers' bank' to the joint stock and private banks.

Victorian economic society had the advantage of a stable currency, linked to gold, and which was not subject to a steady decrease in its value through creeping inflation such as our century has experienced. The currency in circulation was the gold sovereign and half sovereign, supplemented by convertible banknotes, mostly those issued by the Bank of England. The total monetary supply of the country was basically determined by the amount of its gold holdings and also by the control over note issues imposed by the Bank Charter Act of 1844.

The money credits needed by British traders and manufacturers to pay for their imports and to realize the proceeds of their exports was provided by the discount and finance houses. Using their own resources supplemented by extensive short term borrowings from the Lombard Street money market, these houses made credits available on terms profitable to themselves against the bills of exchange drawn by importers and exporters. This credit system worked well, but from time to time crashes occurred notably in 1866 when the finance house of Overend, Gurney Ltd failed for over £5 million due to its overtrading in bills which were not honoured by the drawers at maturity and by advancing too much money for speculative enterprises.

Limited liability companies

At the beginning of the nineteenth century the normal form of association for trading, as distinct from the 'one man business', was the partnership consisting of two or more partners who put up the capital required. The partnership organization had disadvantages notably that all the capital subscribed by the partners, and also their purely private assets as well, were liable for the satisfaction of debts contracted by the partnership. Some other form of organization which would limit the liability of those participating in the enterprise was needed. The joint stock limited liability company was the answer, and the formation of these was made possible by the Companies Acts of 1856 and 1862. The important principle established by these Acts was that of limited liability, i.e. that the liability of the company for debts was limited to the amount of its capital and consequently the liability of shareholders was limited to the amount of money they had subscribed for their shares in the company. It now became possible to tap the savings of the thrifty Victorian public for new and productive enterprises.

Great Britain and free trade

The adoption by Great Britain in the mid-nineteenth century of a free trade policy was the direct result of the growth of her manufacturing industry, her merchant shipping and her increasing population. Adam Smith, the prophet of free trade, had said that wealth would be most effectively achieved when the flow of goods between countries could move freely and without interference by customs duties or other restrictions. Great Britain, with an ever increasing flow of manufactured goods, looked to the world market in which to sell them, and any doctrine which would make this market easier of access had her enthusiastic support. Likewise, the two imports she needed most, raw material for her factories, and food for her workers, would be cheapest if they entered Great Britain duty free and such cheapness would lower her production costs and prevent the cost of living, on which wages were based, from rising. It was free trade and the advantages she held in the techniques of production that made Great Britain an efficient, low cost producer who could under-sell all her other rivals in the markets of the world.

A decisive step towards free trade was taken by Peel in his ministry of 1841–6 with an extensive reduction of duties in his budgets of 1842 and 1845 and by repeal of the Corn Laws in 1846. Another impediment to trade was removed when the most important survival of the Navigation Acts, viz., that British colonies must ship their exports in British or colonial ships, was repealed in 1849, thus giving exporters or importers a free choice of ship at the most advantageous freight rate. British free trade policy also cast a critical eye on the preferential rates of duty that had long been enjoyed by colonial exports in the British market, on the grounds that free trade meant equal opportunities for all in a competitive world market. As a result colonial preferences began to be reduced; the outstanding example was in the case of sugar; by the Sugar Duties Equalization Act of 1846 the duties paid on colonial sugar were to be equalized by 1852 with those paid by imports from foreign countries. The British West Indies were hard hit by this as they found themselves unable to compete with the large-scale sugar producers of Cuba and Louisiana who still had slave labour.

The details of British free trade policy were filled in by Gladstone in his budgets as chancellor of the Exchequer between 1853 and 1861. Starting in 1853 with extensive reductions or abolition of duties on a wide range of goods, by 1861 the only import duties levied by Great Britain were on beer, wines, spirits, tea, coffee, sugar, timber, tobacco, gold and silver plate, playing cards and dice; some of these were abolished before 1900. Gladstone's 'crown and summit' budget of 1861 had been influenced by Cobden's success in negotiating a free trade treaty with France in 1860. The terms of this provided that France undertook not to levy duties of more than 30% on British imports, and removed her former ban on the import of fine quality British textiles; in return Great Britain reduced the duties on imports of French wines and brandies and abolished duties on French manufactured goods.

The Victorian champions of free trade such as Cobden and Bright regarded free trade not only as economically right but also as having the wider purpose of promoting international peace in which all nations would be linked together by the ties of peaceful trade. It was not until the later 1880s when Great Britain first felt industrial competition from other nations such as Germany and the U.S.A. that the merits of free trade were questioned.

Carried by a merchant navy which grew from $3\frac{1}{2}$ million tons in 1850 to $5\frac{3}{4}$ million in 1868, British exports went all over the world. The chief markets were in India, Australasia, U.S.A. and Western Europe; the development of railways, steamships, and telegraph cables all helped to make these markets more accessible to British trade. In return, Britain imported great quantities of foodstuffs and raw materials, e.g. grain, meat, iron ore, wool, cotton, flax, sugar, tea and coffee for her steadily growing industries and population.

113

British overseas investment

Besides goods, Britain had by the mid-nineteenth century become an exporter of capital. The profits of the industrial revolution were not squandered; Victorian society believed in thrift and for the wealthy the very low rate of taxation (income tax fluctuated between 2*d*. and 6*d*. in the £) made it possible to save a large proportion of their income: prosperous Victorians lived soberly if comfortably and were not generally addicted to extravagant spending on luxury goods. British capital financed the building of railways in the U.S.A., Canada, India and the Argentine. These investments yielded annual interest payments and brought large orders for the British iron, steel and engineering industries. Between 1850 and 1870 about £25 million was lent annually and by 1870 British overseas investments totalled about £900 million.

The trade cycle

The economic activity of Victorian England tended to fluctuate between boom and slump. The characteristics of this trade cycle, which were more pronounced than the present-day recessions and full employment, were a period of rising demand leading to full production and employment followed by a decline in demand leading to stagnation in production and a high unemployment rate. Thus for some years after 1850 Britain was very prosperous until a decline set in about 1856–7; revival followed in a few years and the early 1860s were buoyant apart from the distress caused to Lancashire by the cotton famine due to the American Civil War of 1861–5. In 1867–8 trade was depressed, but a revival soon set in and lasted until about 1874–5, at which point, a sharp decline started and continued well into the 1880s. This last slump was one of the indications that Britain's leadership as the workshop of the world was now being challenged by competition from the newer industrial organizations of other countries, such as Germany and the U.S.A.

13. Victorian society

General considerations

There is a vast amount of historical evidence on which a general account of the structure, ideas and attitudes of Victorian society can be based. In attempting this a balanced approach is necessary because the Victorian age has aroused strong feelings in commentators of the twentieth century. Generally they have been very critical of the Victorian age and have condemned it outright as superficial in its beliefs and hypocritical in its moral outlook, particularly in the realm of sexual morality. Recently, and perhaps under nostalgic, 'good old days' influences, the trend has moved away from this sweeping criticism to discover values and stability in Victorian society which are lacking in the 'permissive' and turbulent society of the 1970s. A further point is that the term 'Victorian age' is a general one, and misleading to the extent that it comprised three distinct eras: early Victorian from about 1830 to 1850; mid-Victorian 1850 to about 1870, and late Victorian from 1875 to 1900. The mid-Victorian era is the one which is most representative of the characteristics and attitudes of Victorian society.

The Victorian social structure

In contrast to our own society in which class distinctions and differences have become somewhat blurred, Victorian society had a definite and clear-cut structure which was recognized, understood and accepted by Victorians. At the summit of society was the monarchy; Queen Victoria by her long reign and personal conduct did much to exalt the reputation of monarchy and give it a nationwide respect which hitherto had been lacking. While a few Victorian intellectuals advocated a republic, the monarchy was widely accepted and believed to be the corner-stone of the whole framework of British society. Rivalling the importance of the monarchy as a social force were the landed aristocracy and gentry whose ownership of great estates gave them a monopoly of social and political influence. These landowners were 'kings' in those parts of the countryside where their estates were located; their influence radiated from their castle, hall or mansion over the countryside; the tenant farmers almost always voted for the candidate supported by their landlord, while the rest of the neighbourhood accorded its respectful admiration and usually followed his lordship's lead in local as well as national politics. This class provided many Cabinet ministers and dominated the membership of the House of Commons well into the second half of the nineteenth century.

Working-class group 1855

A mid-Victorian family group 1863

116

Underpinning this upper level of English society were the middle classes. Here distinction existed between an upper layer consisting of professional men such as doctors, lawyers, clergy of the Church of England, rich bankers and prosperous merchants, and a lower one of those who were engaged in general trade and business; those of the upper section, many of whom had close relationships with the landed gentry, were considered 'gentlemen', but not those of the lower section. Below the small business-man there was a gradation downwards into the lower middle classes which eventually merged with the skilled workmen who made up the bulk of the 'respectable' working classes. Some of these hoped by their own efforts to move up the social ladder but all dreaded a movement downwards through some stroke of economic calamity. At the bottom of the social pyramid were the humble poor; the majority were the unskilled workmen, the farm labourers, domestic servants, all of whom thought themselves lucky if they were in reasonably secure and permanent work. Finally at the very lowest level there was a mass of very poor, permanently destitute people, e.g. those in low-paid casual employment, tramps and beggars.

A pronounced characteristic of this society was that it was a deferential society; all its members were much aware of their particular place in society and they respected the status of their superiors and sometimes despised those below them. This system had its advantages; people knew where they stood and it made for an ordered and stable society. It was also modified by the fact that British society was not lacking in fluidity: it was always possible for people to move up the social scale by their own efforts especially if these led to the acquisition of wealth. Two particular factors assisted in the maintenance of this deferential society: one was the exceed-ingly unequal distribution of wealth and the other was the very narrow basis of education. This last factor gave an extraordinary advantage to the upper layers of Victorian society to dominate the minds of the classes beneath them. This could be done in various ways: by the social example and behaviour of the upper classes; by the influence of the clergy over their parishioners and by the confident and dogmatic assertions of the Victorian intellectual establishment: all of these were accepted without very much questioning by their social inferiors.

In Victorian society the family was a most important social unit and more so than today. The Victorian family was distinguished by the strength of the ties between its members. Family solidarity was main-tained to a great extent by the concentration of authority in the father of the family whose views, wishes and beliefs were unquestionably accepted by his wife and daughters and often by his sons. Victorian social thinking favoured this situation and English law upheld paternal authority in various ways. Both politically and legally the position of women was inferior and their true function was thought of as being that of wives and 117

E

mothers if they were married, and if single, as ornaments of the family circle, provided the financial means of the family permitted this; only the lower middle classes and below sent their women out to work.

The importance of the individual

One of the strongest beliefs of Victorian society concerned the individual as such. There was a widespread belief in the individual and his capacity to do two things: firstly to achieve moral progress, i.e. to make himself a better man in the eyes of God and secondly, by the cultivation of virtues such as hard work and thrift to improve the position of himself and his family materially in society. Moral progress had a close connection with the Victorian attitude to religion, and in particular with Evangelical Christianity which in itself was a continuation of the Puritan tradition of the seventeenth century, with its emphasis on earnest conduct, God-fearing ways, full employment of time and avoidance of frivolity and luxury. It was firmly believed that the individual could make a success or failure of his or her life and that the decision involved was a rational and objective one; it ignored those irrational and subconscious forces of which the twentieth century became so painfully aware. At the popular level Samuel Smiles proclaimed the doctrine in his widely read works on *Self Help* and *Thrift*; Anthony Trollope made it a central feature of his delineation of character in his novels and the poet, W. E. Henley, proclaimed it with his 'I am the master of my fate: I am the captain of my soul'. This assertive individualism had certain results in the realm of politics and economics: people wanted to be left alone in the direction of their lives and economic activities. State legislation, however well intentioned and necessary, was often resented by the Victorians as an unjustified interference with the individual's right to manage his own life as he thought best.

The belief in progress

Among the major beliefs which coloured the outlook of a wide section of Victorian society was their confident belief in progress of a sustained and cumulative kind. Looking at their external situation they saw a rapid advance in scientific knowledge and control of the natural environment; the industrial revolution had brought a revolution in communications and the ability to produce manufactured goods on a vastly increased scale: medical science gave the possibility of control of disease which would give an increase in the expectation of life. This material progress was welcomed by the Victorians who thought its benefits would spread through the world if free trade became the rule and the 1851 Exhibition gave visual proof of such progress in action. The belief in progress was supported by the intellectuals of the early and mid-Victorian age. Macaulay, writing at the beginning of the age in 1835, stated: 'The history of England is emphatically the history of progress': the evidence for this lay close at hand; it was the manifest increase of wealth, population, knowledge and liberty. Charles Darwin's *Origin of Species* (1859), although it had disquieting results for many Victorians in the field of religious belief, nevertheless was seen as supporting the idea of progress because the theory of evolution contained the idea of an upward movement by man towards perfection.

While belief in progress was widespread, there were also doubts and anxieties which increased after 1850. The stability of society appeared to be threatened by popular agitation; universal suffrage was opposed because it would surrender political power to the ignorant mob. There was also anxiety about Christian faith and its certainty; the old dogmatic beliefs established by religious revelation and a literal interpretation of the Bible had been rudely shattered by the ideas of the geologists and biologists, such as Lyell and Darwin. The reaction of intellectual Victorians to this erosion of faith varied: some became total disbelievers; others, while they could not believe in Christianity, nevertheless defended it on the ground of social utility, while some took refuge in the authority of Roman Catholicism.

Distrust of intellectual values

One trait of Victorian society was its distrust and fear of intellectual learning and disciplines; other 'values', such as those of business methods, utility, and practical action were preferred. The question was often asked: What was the use of art and philosophy?; compared with practical action they appeared to be useless. This attitude had been fostered by the industrial revolution and its emphasis on practical results derived from deliberate manipulation of the material environment. Thus Samuel Smiles, 'the mentor of the aspiring working classes', played down intellect and emphasized instead the achievements of persevering men such as George Stephenson whose education had been in the hard school of practical experience. The economic events which had made Britain the 'workshop of the world' and brought such an increase of wealth, also strengthened the Victorian belief that practical and utilitarian considerations must govern the pursuit of knowledge, because this could then be used to make more money. Macaulay, whom Matthew Arnold labelled 'The great apostle of the Philistines' glorified the idea of utility leading to progress and denounced philosophy as sterile and poetry as a deceptive fantasy.

Matthew Arnold's criticisms of Victorian values

In his *Culture and Anarchy* (1869), Matthew Arnold brought under stringent criticism these attitudes of Victorian society. His main theme was 119 the absolute need for cultivation of the mind and a feeling for beauty as opposed to 'the anarchical tendencies of thoughtless action'. As an inspector of schools Arnold had been brought into close contact with middle-class Nonconformist Victorian society whose attitudes and values he found uniformly repellent. His main classification of Victorian society was that of Barbarians and Philistines. The Barbarians constituted the Victorian upper classes whom Arnold admitted had many good qualities but also singular failings in the realm of culture. He saw them as possessing such good qualities as the belief in the individual's right to manage his own life, and a passion for field sports and manly exercise. But:

'the chivalry of the Barbarians, with its characteristics of high spirits, choice manners and distinguished bearing, what is this but the attractive commencement of the politeness of our aristocratic class? . . . In general its culture is exterior chiefly; all the exterior graces and accomplishments, and the more external of the inward virtues, seem to be principally its portion. It now, of course, cannot but be often in contact with those studies by which, from the world of thought and feeling, true culture teaches us to fetch sweetness and light; but its hold upon these very studies appears remarkably external, and unable to exert any deep power upon its spirit.'

Victorian middle-class society was described by Arnold as the class of Philistines. To Arnold their life seemed dismal and illiberal; it was obsessed by merely material things, such as the production of wealth, the creation of material objects; its failing was that it had no awareness of the things of the mind or the love of beautiful things. To Arnold the term Philistine gave 'the notion of something particularly stiff-necked and perverse in the resistance to light and its children'. Worse still, Arnold saw that the ideas of the Philistines were being communicated to the aspiring working classes of the better sort. Finally, at the very bottom of the English social scale, Arnold saw a mass of ignorant people which he termed the Populace.

Tendency to dogmatism

A characteristic of our own day is uncertainty of belief. This would have seemed strange to the Victorians who in many respects were prone to a rigid dogmatism. To them truth was easily and conclusively ascertainable by quite ordinary people provided the rules of logic and reason were followed. To some extent this dogmatism was a product of Victorian individualism, i.e. the individual as part of his belief in himself was entitled to like or dislike what he chose; in fact much of this Victorian dogmatism was no more than shallow prejudice based on inadequate knowledge.

It was also the product of ready acceptance of pronouncements on politics, religion, morals and art made by social superiors, persons in authority, and recognized critics. This dogmatic attitude was also shown, as most Victorian novels testify, in the judgement of personal character which stood or fell under the stern and rigidly applied test of right or wrong, regardless of extenuating circumstances.

Religious worship

An account of Victorian society requires some account of the part played by organized religion. For the majority of Victorians religion meant allegiance either to the established Church of England or to the Non-conformist groups, such as Wesleyan, Baptist, and Congregationalists; after 1850 the Roman Catholic Church increased its numbers because of the influx of Irish immigrants.

It is sometimes believed that every Victorian, almost without exception, regularly attended church or chapel on Sundays. This is incorrect as the evidence collected in the Census Report of 1851 shows. Its findings were that about 50% of those able to attend a place of worship on Sunday did not do so; most of the congregations were drawn predominantly from the middle classes and to a slightly lesser extent from the upper classes. The bulk of those who did not attend were adult working people, although they had been brought under religious influences as children in the primary and Sunday schools. 'The myriads of our labouring population are as ignorant of Christianity as were the heathen Saxons at Augustine's landing.' Among the reasons given for this indifference of the working classes to organized religion was the fact that, especially in the Church of England, attendance emphasized the inferiority of the working classes who could not afford to pay for a pew or seat in the church and conse-quently were pushed into the back of the church away from their social superiors; the Church of England was far too much identified, especially in the countryside, with the maintenance of the established social order. Joseph Arch, the radical Warwickshire countryman who organized trade unions for farm labourers in the 1870s, gives a biting account of this in his *Autobiography*:

'In the parish Church the poor were apportioned their lowly places and taught that they must sit in them Sunday after Sunday all their lives long. They must sit meekly and never dare to mingle with their betters in the social scale. It was an object lesson repeated week after week, one which no one could mistake, and it sank deep into my mind. I can remember when the Squire and other local magnates used to sit in state in the centre of the aisle; they did not, if you please, like the look of the agricultural labourers. Hodge sat too near them, and even

121

in his Sunday best he was an offence to their eyes. They also objected to Hodge looking at them, so they had curtains put up to hide them from the vulgar gaze. And yet, while all this was going on, while the poor had to bear with such high-handed dealings, people wondered why the Church had lost its hold, and continued to lose its hold, on the labourers in the country districts.'

The Evangelicals and Broad Churchmen

A leading force in the Church of England at the beginning of the Victorian age was the Evangelical movement which carried into the nineteenth century some of the fervour that had been generated by the Wesleyan religious revival of the eighteenth century. The Evangelicals emphasized a personal religion centred on individual salvation and this accorded well with middle-class Victorian individualism, although there were some upper-class supporters, notably Lord Shaftesbury. They were often fundamentalists believing in a literal interpretation of the Bible and although shaken by the evolutionary theories of Darwin they generally remained impervious to new ideas. Another group was that of the Broad Churchmen, among them Thomas Arnold, headmaster of Rugby. These men had liberal reforming tendencies and realized that the Church of England must modernize its organization and redistribute its revenues if it was to make any impact on a society that was rapidly becoming industrialized; hence their support of the Whig reforms in the 1830s.

The Oxford movement

A more controversial movement within the Victorian Church of England was the Tractarian or Oxford movement which arose from the activities of a distinguished group of Oxford clergymen fellows, mostly at Oriel College. The leading figures were John Keble, John Henry Newman and Edward Pusey. Initially they were motivated by an exaggerated fear of Liberalism and reform which they thought might destroy the Church of England. In July 1833 Keble preached the Oxford Assize Sermon on the theme of 'National Apostasy' in which he protested against the government's intention to reform the Protestant Church of Ireland by suppressing some bishoprics and devoting part of their revenues to secular purposes. More important was the publication and circulation by the movement of a series of *Tracts for the Times*, ninety in all. These were directed mainly at the clergy, explaining the nature and doctrines of the Church and emphasizing its spiritual mission and authority. The historic traditions of the Catholic Church were fully discussed and explained with the aim of proving that the Anglican Church was not only the true Church but also a Catholic Church. Great emphasis was laid on the Apostolic Succession as the basis of ecclesiastical authority exercised by those

122

ordained. The Tractarian movement, or the Oxford movement, as it soon came to be called, raised widespread opposition from the Evangelical section of the Church of England, both clergy and laymen, many of whose beliefs in the Protestant Church of the Reformation were grievously offended by the emphasis laid by the Tractarians on the Catholic character of the Church and by the acceptance of what they regarded as Romish errors: they said that the Tractarians should be logical and join the Roman Catholic Church. A crisis for the movement arrived in 1841 when Newman published Tract 90 in which he said that the thirty-nine Articles, the statement of belief to which all Anglican clergy were bound to subscribe, were capable of bearing a Catholic interpretation. For this the University of Oxford condemned Newman who in 1845 was received into the Roman Catholic Church. Although the secession of Newman and a number of his associates was a heavy blow for the Oxford movement, it survived to make an important contribution to the vitality of the Church of England in the second half of the nineteenth century. One of its most important results was to give the Church of England a sense of being a Church rather than a department of state. It emphasized that the Church was both a divine society and a sacred mystery. It gave the Church a far clearer idea of its doctrines, beliefs, order of worship and the importance of its sacraments. It reaffirmed the importance of the priestly office and for the layman it emphasized the importance of life as a continued pilgrimage to God, in which he was sustained by prayer and sacraments rather than being buoyed up by a sudden conversion experienced once for all. Important also was the emphasis that Christianity was for all ranks of society, not merely the well-to-do. The movement built and served churches in the poor areas where newly founded Anglican religious orders of monks, friars and nuns worked side by side with the secular clergy.

While the Oxford movement had its enthusiastic followers it aroused a good deal of suspicion in the mind of the average Victorian which was generally attuned to a Protestant outlook. It brought a division in the Church of England which crystallized into three main sections: the High Church Anglo-Catholic section opposed strongly by the Low Church Protestant group with a middle-of-the-road Anglicanism as a third group. Public controversy arose in the third quarter of the century over ritualism, or the practices of a Catholic nature that many advanced followers of the Oxford movement introduced into their churches, e.g. reservation of the Sacrament, confession, the use of incense, and the sprinkling of the church with holy water. The legality of these practices was often challenged by indignant Protestant members of the congregation; unfortunately it could only be determined by resort to secular courts culminating in the Judicial Committee of the Privy Council. An attempt to remedy this situation was made by the enactment of the Public Worship Regula-

123

tion Act of 1874; this strengthened the disciplinary powers of the bishops over the clergy and made it possible for clergy or parishioners who were offended at irregular practices to bring their complaints before the provincial courts of the archbishops of Canterbury and York.

The Protestant Nonconformists

Victorian Nonconformity, organized in four main groups of the Wesleyan Methodists, Baptists, Congregationalists, and Unitarians, was particularly strong in the industrial towns of the Midlands and North; it also was well established in many country districts where the tradition went back to the persecutions of the seventeenth century. The message of these religions was directed to the individual to encourage him to lead a better and more moral life and this coincided with the aspirations to self improvement so marked in the Victorian age. Whilst most Nonconformist chapels had their regular ministers they provided many opportunities for the part-time lay preacher. The distinction between church and chapel was a very real one in Victorian society, especially in the smaller towns and country districts. It showed itself in various ways, e.g. social prejudice on the part of churchgoers who thought themselves superior to Nonconformists; quarrels over the expenditure of money from the rates on Church schools which the Nonconformists thought unjust, and a tendency for church-goers to support the Tory Party while the Nonconformists were ardent supporters of Mr Gladstone and the Liberal Party, which in consequence had to be careful not to offend the 'Nonconformist conscience'. In the nineteenth century the Nonconformists secured the removal of various legal disabilities, e.g. the abolition of the Test Act in 1828, which was followed by the legalization of marriages in their own chapels. Later they were admitted to university degrees and fellowships at Oxford and Cambridge; finally, in 1868, they were freed from compulsory payment of Church rates, which had been a long-standing grievance.

The Roman Catholic Church

The growing number of Roman Catholics in England led the Pope in 1850 to appoint bishops for England with appropriate territorial titles. There was nothing unreasonable in this but the announcement of it was made in a somewhat tactless and arrogant fashion; at once a howl of wrath went up from Victorian England about 'Papal aggression'. It stirred up something that was very strong in popular Victorian imagination, the bogey of 'Popery'. In a rather naive fashion many otherwise sober-minded Victorians regarded the Pope and his priests as a threat to the liberty of the individual and the nation. This was nothing new; it stemmed from the sixteenth century and its recollection of the persecutions in Queen Mary's reign; it had been sustained by the Gunpowder plot and the 'Popish plot' in the reign of Charles II. Bigoted Victorian Protestantism fastened on certain features of the Roman Catholic Church which it disliked intensely and irrationally. Among these were the celibacy of the priest and the special role assigned to him. The unmarried priest would surely seduce innocent girls in the confessional and there were swarms of tendentious pamphlets and trashy novels which told lurid and improbable tales of innocent girls who were abducted into convents where they were tortured to death. The practice of auricular confession was seen as a powerful threat to the unity of the family; the cunning priest through the confessional would influence the wives and daughters so as to undermine the paternal supremacy of the husband. The outcry was so great that the Prime Minister, Lord John Russell, was forced to take action. He wrote an open letter to the Bishop of Durham describing 'the late aggression of the Pope upon our Protestantism' as 'insolent and insidious'. He also contrived to throw some of the blame for the situation upon the Romish practices advocated by the Oxford movement. He followed this up by securing the enactment of the Ecclesiastical Titles Act of 1851; this prohibited under penalties the assumption of any ecclesiastical titles already taken by the clergy of the Church of England. In the event the Act remained a dead letter, was never enforced, and was repealed in 1871.

The Victorian achievement in the arts

An account of Victorian society requires some consideration of its achievement in the arts; this often reflected those values and attitudes which have already been described. On a broad view this achievement was an uneven one with an impressive contribution to literature, both prose and poetry, counterbalanced by a much less creative one in painting, architecture and music.

The major Victorian novelists give us an extended picture of all levels of Victorian society in town and country. Dickens depicted the vigorous, sprawling life of popular society in early and mid-Victorian England with its joys, sorrows and social evils; George Eliot described life in the small towns and villages of provincial England as it came under the influence of the political and economic changes of the age; Trollope portrayed with astonishing fidelity the patterned lives of the Victorian 'leisured' upper classes; Hardy, a late Victorian, in contrast to the optimism of earlier writers, struck a more realistic if pessimistic note about the harshness of life, and especially for the toiling men and women of rural England.

The Victorian achievement in painting and architecture, although present day opinion sees more merit in it than previously, compares unfavourably with that of Victorian literature. One reason for this was that to a great extent it had lost the values and principles that had inspired the

work of its predecessors without acquiring any new values of comparable worth. The values of classical art which lasted until the Regency period immediately preceding the Victorian age, and which reflected the taste of the aristocratic society of the eighteenth century had been emphatic ones. They insisted on form, proportion, symmetry, and suitability for its purpose of the object created; ornamentation and decoration were kept subordinate to the main theme. In their abandonment of these values the Victorians turned to painting of a reproductive and descriptive kind which lacked creative content, and in architecture to a revival of medieval Gothic styles, often with much trivial detail and excessive ornamentation.

Influences affecting Victorian art values

What were the reasons for this change in values? Perhaps the explanation is that it was a product of middle-class Victorian society, that Philistine society which Arnold had criticized. It reflected their obsession with material things, the narrowness of their culture and their lack of ideas and critical faculties. All they asked of painting was that it should be faithful to nature, a mere reproductive copy giving the illusion of reality. For them art had no unique creativity or meaning; they regarded art forms as adjuncts of their newly acquired prosperity which would reflect their social status. Their anti-intellectual attitudes and cult of the practical gave them a basic contempt for the artist whom they regarded as wasting valuable time which might be more profitably spent in making money. Taine, a Frenchman and an acute observer of English society in the 1860s and early 1870s commented that according to *Punch*, the faithful mirror of Victorian middle-class opinion: 'Musicians are represented as salaried monkeys, who come to make a noise in the drawing room. Painters are bearded artisans, unkempt, shabbily dressed, badly educated, conceited, hardly one degree raised above photographers'. The invention of photography in the late 1840s and its widespread practice by the 1860s seemed to many to make the artist superfluous. The camera could give that faithful, natural reproduction which was what the Victorians wanted far more quickly and cheaply than the craftsman painter. Another adverse influence was that of the industrial revolution which had ensured the triumph of mass production over individual craftsmanship working to a sound design; this was especially seen in the realm of domestic equipment such as furniture, fabrics and china. Many of the exhibits at the Great Exhibition in 1851 were hideous examples of the tasteless standards of Victorian industrial design; vulgar, excessive, and whimsical ornamentation was the rule, producing such oddities as tables resting on the heads of swans and door knockers of elephant's heads.

The accepted qualities of Victorian art

What did the Victorians especially look for in their art forms? One quality was respectability: they strongly disapproved of visual art with a disturbing content, such as nudes in painting and sculpture, and of literature which dealt realistically with relations between the sexes. They justified this attitude by the belief that art which appealed to sensual feelings was wrong; instead it must be directed at man's higher and better nature.

The Victorians expected art forms to be faithful copies of nature, reproductions which could be recognized and so understood. They also thought it desirable for paintings to tell a story with a moral or to depict a panorama of action from everyday life, such as Frith's *Derby Day*, and *A Railway Station*, which all could recognize and understand.

Lastly there was a marked element of escapism in Victorian art which took the form of a regression into the past. The growth of historical studies, and at the popular level, reading of romantic historical novels such as those of Sir Walter Scott, awakened the interest of the Victorians in the Middle Ages which appeared to them as an idealized Christian age, and worthy of imitation. The paintings of the 'Pre-Raphaelite' group, especially those of D. G. Rossetti, E. Burne-Jones, and J. E. Millais, often contained reconstructions of these medieval values and attitudes. Victorian 127

The Law Courts,
Carey Street front
1882

architecture was similarly influenced to adopt a 'neo-Gothic' medieval style which with its spires and pointed arches stretching up to heaven, was believed to have a morally elevating effect upon its beholders. Of the many surviving examples of Victorian neo-Gothic the best examples are its churches and colleges; less acceptable are its private houses and municipal buildings. Thus many Victorian houses had crenellated parapets, castle turrets and pointed church windows; the functional purposes of public buildings were not helped by their neo-Gothic facades with a clutter of ornamentation and ethical illustration and which are displayed by so many Victorian town halls, railway stations and public offices.

St Pancras
Station: built
1868–71. An
example of neo-
Gothic influences
in Victorian
public buildings

The reaction against Victorian values

In the late Victorian age after 1880 there was a reaction against these art values. William Morris protested against the Victorians' obsession with irrelevant ornamentation, especially in their homes; he saw no reason why they should not have domestic furnishings that were both beautiful and useful. Believing that the industrial revolution and its mechanical methods had corrupted art forms, Morris attempted a revival of hand craftsmanship to correct this. Victorian painting came under attack from the 'Art for art's sake' movement, which believed that the artist was quite independent of society, had no duty necessarily to society, and was not bound to attempt to communicate with it. It did not matter at all if conventional society was shocked, or was unable to understand what artists were doing. It was a quest for a more creative approach to art, which the movement found conspicuously absent in the paintings of the Victorian academic 'establishment'.

14. The development of the British Empire

Colonial expansion after 1815

British colonial expansion went steadily ahead in the early nineteenth century. To those colonies (mostly in the West Indies) which remained after the loss of the thirteen American colonies in 1783 were added the conquests of the Napoleonic wars, together with new white-settled colonies in North America, Australia and after 1840 in New Zealand. The value of this empire was that it provided the strategic bases and trading posts needed by the expanding overseas trade of Great Britain; later its importance as an outlet for emigrants from the growing population of the British Isles became evident. The decisive factor of trading interests is shown by the conquests of the Napoleonic wars. Thus in the Caribbean the French island of St Lucia was taken because of its excellent harbour; Trinidad was conquered from Spain as a trading base with South America; the conquests from the Dutch of the Cape of Good Hope and Ceylon (with its fine harbour of Trincomalee) and from the French of the islands of Mauritius and the Seychelles gave control of the sea routes of the Indian Ocean. This control was extended further east by the acquisition of Singapore in 1819 and the cession by the Dutch of Malacca in 1824; in 1842 the capture of Hong Kong gave a foothold for Britain's trade with China. The second half of the nineteenth century saw a rapid expansion of the white settled colonies in British North America, Australia and New Zealand, followed in the last years of the century by the creation of numerous British colonies and protectorates in tropical Africa.

Crown colony government

The humanitarian movement which achieved firstly the suppression of the slave trade (1807) and later the abolition of slavery (1833) within the British Empire also publicized the idea of trusteeship, i.e. Great Britain had a responsibility for the peoples of her empire: government must be just and must prevent inhumanity or exploitation. This doctrine of trusteeship influenced the development of Crown colony government which differed sharply from the old representative system of government set up in the white-settled colonies of the seventeenth century. Crown colony government was a concentration of power in the hands of a governor who represented the Crown, and who ruled in accordance with the colonial policy of the British government. He was not hampered by obstruction from a representative assembly of the local white planters or settlers, as had been the governors of the white settlements in America and the West Indies in the seventeenth and eighteenth centuries. It therefore became possible to enforce official policy which in particular aimed at limiting the abuses of slavery before emancipation took place in 1833, and afterwards in preventing oppression of native peoples under British rule.

Crown colony government was applied to the conquests from France, Spain and the Dutch and for which the wholesale introduction of British representative institutions was unsuitable. In the second half of the nineteenth century it was also applied to those colonies and protectorates Britain acquired in tropical Africa such as the Gold Coast, the Nigerias, Kenya and Nyasaland. In their early stages some of the new white-settled colonies, e.g. New South Wales and New Zealand had Crown colony government, but the system became increasingly unpopular with them because it was very different from the representative form of government which people of British origin thought to be their birthright. By the 1840s there was an increasing demand from the Australian colonies for representative government based on the British pattern. But shortly before this, events in British North America led to the Durham Report of 1839; this established principles which determined the subsequent development of self government in the British Empire.

British North America

The British North American colonies 1815–37. In 1815 the British North American colonies consisted of Lower Canada (Quebec), Upper Canada (Ontario), Nova Scotia, New Brunswick, and Prince Edward Island. Upper Canada and New Brunswick had been mainly settled by the United Empire Loyalists, who were Americans who wished to remain under British rule after the thirteen American colonies had gained their independence in 1783. After 1815 there was a wave of emigration from the British Isles chiefly to Upper Canada and the maritime colonies of Nova Scotia and New Brunswick; these emigrants brought with them a demand for political change and a more representative form of government. In Lower Canada, where the French Canadians predominated, growing tension arose from their dislike of the English official element who ruled them. In Upper Canada the new settlers resented what was known as the 'Family Compact' of the older settlers who monopolized political power and who were held to be responsible for an unsatisfactory land settlement programme. The leader of these malcontents was William Lyon Mackenzie, a Scottish emigrant. In Quebec the French Canadian elements in the Assembly of Lower Canada were under the leadership of Louis Joseph Papineau; their demand for a greater share in their government was rejected by the British government. In 1837 in both provinces there were small and unsuccessful rebellions against British government.

The Durham Report 1839. In 1838 the British government sent out the Earl of Durham as governor-general of British North America to investigate the causes of all this unrest. From this mission resulted the celebrated Durham Report of 1839. The Report condemned the monopoly of power of the 'Family Compact' in Upper Canada, the abuses in the making of land grants, and the excessive privileges of the Anglican clergy over the 'clergy reserve' lands. It also reviewed emigration, the use of public lands, and communications; it declared that the root cause of the troubles in Lower Canada was the racial conflict between the French and English. Its main recommendations were that the Canadas should be granted responsible government for their own internal affairs, while the imperial government reserved control over constitutional changes, defence, foreign relations and the regulation of trade. Lastly, it recommended that there should be a union of the two Canadas to end racial conflict and produce a common nationality. Durham was mistaken here because he optimistically thought that in time the French Canadians would be assimilated to English ideas and culture. The British government accepted the recommendation for union and in 1840 passed an Act of Union which set up a united province of Canada with a governor, an Executive Council, a Legislative Council and an elected Assembly. In this assembly there were English and French Canadians who were ready to work together for responsible government made possible by the declaration of the British government in 1846 that where conditions were favourable, the inhabitants of settled colonies should be allowed internal self government. A new governor of Canada, Lord Elgin, was appointed in 1847 to carry out this policy; in 1848 he called upon the majority party in the Assembly to form a government, thus introducing responsible government. Soon afterwards New Brunswick and Newfoundland achieved responsible government, while Nova Scotia had anticipated Canada in 1846.

The federation of 1867. A federation of British North American Colonies was enacted in 1867 because of the need for the greater strength that such closer union would give. There were grounds for thinking that the United States of America having defeated the Southern Confederates in the Civil War of 1861–5 might follow this with a conquest of the British North American colonies. Other reasons were economic, e.g. trade would be increased if a federal union was made, and only a federal government could command the resources necessary for the building of a transcontinental railway across the Rocky mountains to the Pacific Coast. Great Britain supported the idea of federation because she knew

132

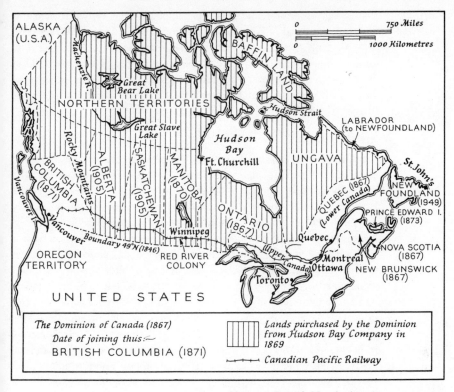

Map 4   *British North America 1791–1914*

the difficulties of defending her North American colonies against invasion
by the U.S.A. In 1866 a London Conference accepted the plan of union
with four provinces as founder members of the federation, viz., Nova
Scotia, New Brunswick, Ontario and Quebec. The Federation was set up
in 1867 by the British North America Act and within six years it was
extended by the addition of other North American territories, viz. Mani-
toba (1870), British Columbia (1871) and Prince Edward Island (1873);
Newfoundland held aloof and did not join the federated Dominion of
Canada until 1949.

Growth of the Dominion of Canada. A condition on which British
Columbia had agreed to join the federation was that the Dominion government should build a transcontinental railway within ten years. This was
done by the Canadian-Pacific railway, a private company, which started
work in 1880; by 1885 there was a link across the Rocky Mountains to
the Pacific. The railway played a great part in the development of the
prairie provinces as it could bring in settlers and take out the grain crops   133

that the virgin prairie land grew in such abundance. Between 1896 and 1914, over two and a half million emigrants entered Canada, attracted by the free land that the government was offering in the prairies. The Dominion of Canada's population which was three and a quarter million in 1867 increased to nearly six million by 1914, and two new prairie provinces, Alberta and Saskatchewan were added to the Dominion federation in 1905.

Australia

The foundation of New South Wales. It was the first voyage of Captain Cook in 1769–71 that had drawn attention to the possibilities of Australia and New Zealand. The loss of the thirteen American colonies obliged the British government to find somewhere else for convicts who previously had been sent to America. From this need resulted the colony of New South Wales, which started in January 1788 when Governor Arthur Philip landed 700 convicts and their military escort at Sydney Cove on the fine harbour of Port Jackson. For the first thirty years New South Wales was predominantly a convict colony, although some free settlers had arrived, attracted by trading and farming possibilities. By 1815 two important developments had taken place: one was the introduction of the merino sheep which laid the foundations of the great Australian wool industry, and the other was that some exploration of the interior had been made, notably the crossing of the Blue Mountain range which in 1812 revealed vast plains in the interior suitable for sheep farming.

The convict system. After 1815 about three or four thousand convicts were sent out from Great Britain every year. Their background varied a great deal; some had committed petty thefts; others had more serious criminal records. The convicts were employed in various ways in the colony, e.g. in the government labour force to make roads, build barracks and ports, while others were assigned to free settlers who could use their labour. Liberty was regained by serving the full term of their sentence to transportation or by the grant of a conditional or absolute pardon or by release on 'ticket of leave'. Those with a conditional pardon were free in every respect except they could not return to Great Britain; an absolute pardon meant that they were completely free: a ticket of leave carried liability to recall to government service. The convict system made possible the foundation of a colony but by 1830 its degrading effects on social and public life were only too obvious.

The era of settlement 1820–60. The formative years in Australian history were between 1820 and 1850 when new colonies were founded, free settlers began to arrive in numbers, the interior was explored and an

134

economy based on sheep farming was built up. The new colonies that were founded during these years were:

(*a*) The island of Van Diemen's Land, later known as Tasmania, had originally been part of the colony of New South Wales, but in 1825 it was made a separate colony. It began to flourish after the measures of Governor Arthur who rounded up the desperate bushranger convicts who raided the sheep runs and farms of the free settlers. In 1856 it became a self-governing colony.

(*b*) In 1829 a settlement known as the Swan River colony was made on the west coast of Australia. Its growth was very slow; emigrants from Great Britain were more attracted to New South Wales or South Australia: twenty years after its foundation its population did not exceed 5,000.

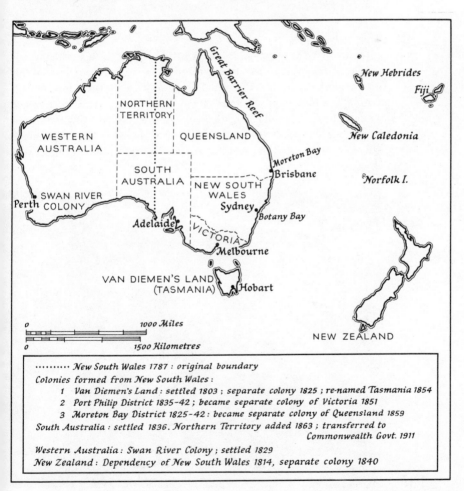

Map 5   *The colonization of Australia and New Zealand*

Settler's hut in Australia 1849

(c) In 1836 the colony of South Australia started with a settlement at Adelaide; the colony was a free one and did not admit convicts and this may explain why it attracted a good type of settler. After a few difficult years the colony began to flourish and by 1850 there were over 50,000 settlers. Its foundation and settlement had been considerably influenced by the ideas of the 'systematic' colonizer, Edward Gibbon Wakefield, who had emphasized the need for organization and proper utilization of land resources.

'On the Road' 1872. A scene in the interior of New South Wales.

(*d*) Although Victoria had an unofficial existence as a separate colony for some years, it was not recognized as such until 1851. It was carved out of New South Wales and was made by the movement of settlers from that colony into the wide plains around Port Philip. When it was given a separate existence in 1851 there were 80,000 settlers, but in this year the discovery of gold at Ballarat and Bendigo revolutionized the situation. A frenzied gold rush took place and a flood of emigrants from Europe and elsewhere raised the population of Victoria to over half a million by 1860.

(*e*) The last colony to be set up was Queensland, which was created out of New South Wales in 1859. The first settlements here had been in the early days when a penal camp for refractory convicts had been established at Moreton Bay and where later the capital city of Brisbane was founded.

The advance to self-government 1850–60. Between 1830 and 1850 many free settlers had entered Australia; their radical political views led to a demand for self government such as had been granted to Canada. Before this could be given it was necessary to end the convict system which a Parliamentary Committee in Great Britain in 1837 condemned as thoroughly bad. A gradual abolition of transportation to Australia followed: after 1840 New South Wales, and after 1853 Tasmania, took no more convicts, but Western Australia which was very short of labour admitted convicts from 1849 to 1868. An advance to self government from the modified Crown colony government under which the Australian colonies were then governed now became possible; in 1850 the Australian Colonies Government Act gave the four Australian colonies power to draw up new constitutions for themselves which would be submitted to the British Parliament for enactment. By 1856 all four colonies had been granted constitutions which gave them the responsible self government of Canada and the other British North American colonies. Queensland received this in 1859 when it was created a separate colony; Western Australia, because of its slower development, not until 1890.

New Zealand

The Treaty of Waitangi 1840. In 1769 Captain Cook on his first voyage had shown that New Zealand, discovered by the Dutch in the seventeenth century, consisted of two islands; he had named it as a British possession but no official action was taken at the time to uphold this claim. By 1800 there had been an unofficial penetration of the islands by traders, whalers, convicts and missionaries and this forced the Governor of New South Wales to proclaim in 1813 that the two islands were dependencies of New South Wales and under British protection, thereby enabling some control to be exercised over British ships and their crews which visited the islands. 137

By 1830 the British government was under pressure from missionary societies to protect the Maoris from the traders who were selling them gin and muskets; there was also a demand for action by several British companies hoping to colonize these islands before rival French companies did so. In 1840 the British government sent Captain William Hobson to negotiate with the Maori chiefs for the cession of sovereignty to the British Crown. This was done in February 1840 when Hobson made the Treaty of Waitangi with the Maori chiefs of the North Island; by this treaty the Maoris ceded all sovereignty over their lands to the British Crown. In return the Crown guaranteed to the chiefs and tribes their lands and estates, stipulating that if they wished to sell their land, the Crown should have the first right to purchase it. The Maoris of New Zealand were placed under the protection of the Crown and received the rights and privileges of British subjects.

The Maoris and the land problem. In May and June 1840 Hobson proclaimed British sovereignty over North and South Islands respectively and in August of the same year New Zealand was created a separate colony by an Act of the British Parliament. Early settlement in the North Island was hampered by the official policy laid down in the Treaty of Waitangi. The settlers found that the government had the first right of purchase of any land the Maoris wished to sell, but as the government had no funds it bought no land and so prevented the settlers getting the land they wanted; eventually the Crown relaxed its rights of first purchase and allowed the settlers to buy direct from the Maoris. A further difficulty of the treaty was one of interpretation: did it apply to the waste or 'wild' lands not occupied by the Maoris, or should these unoccupied lands have

The beginnings of Canterbury colony in South Island, New Zealand 1853

138

been excluded from the operation of the treaty? In defence of their lands the Maoris destroyed a number of the early settlements in North Island and it was only through the governorship of George Grey that the colony began to progress. He showed a sympathetic attitude towards the Maoris and brought the land question under partial control by making it unlawful for settlers to buy land from Maoris without first obtaining a licence from the government. It was also under his direction that the settlement of South Island was carried out; there were few Maoris in this island, and consequently fewer disputes and difficulties arose over the purchase of their land rights. The settlement of South Island was carried out between 1848 and 1852 by two groups inspired by the ideas of Edward Gibbon Wakefield; Scottish Presbyterians settled the Dunedin area in 1848, and Christchurch, a little further to the north, was settled in 1850 by the Canterbury Association organized by the Church of England.

Governor Sir George Grey. Much was done for the colony by Sir George Grey; during his first term of office from 1845 to 1853, he worked to promote the welfare of the Maoris. The essentials were to maintain law and order among them and to protect them in cases of dispute or exploitation by Europeans; special provisions were made in the law courts to protect them in this respect. More difficult conditions faced Grey during his second period of office as governor from 1861 to 1867. Pressure on the vacant lands was growing because of the increasing white settlement and the Maoris had banded together in a nationalist movement to defend their lands, their separate culture and customs. A prolonged military 'police' operation followed against the Maoris for nearly twelve years (1860 to 1872) but entrenched in their stockaded strongholds the Maoris proved difficult to defeat and even if defeated proved an elusive enemy. The solution of the problem came after these wars: it was to treat the Maoris more generously, to give them fair prices for their land and the full rights of citizenship. This policy was eventually adopted and the Maori population which had been declining in the nineteenth century made a recovery in the early years of the twentieth.

South Africa
The Cape Boers and British rule 1815-36. When the Dutch ceded the Cape of Good Hope in 1815 Great Britain obtained the 'half-way house' she had long desired on the sea route to India and the East. She also became the ruler of the 25,000 Dutch 'Boer' inhabitants of the Cape and relations with this singular and stubborn people were strained from the very start. It was the Boers living in the interior and on the frontiers who proved most troublesome; they were pastoral farmers with large farms out on the wide veldt grazed by their horses and herds of cattle.

Self sufficient and self reliant and with a sincere if narrow religious faith they saw themselves as a chosen people, like the Israelites of the Old Testament, and the heathen Bantu (Kaffir) peoples around them as their natural slaves.

The humanitarian movement had influenced British colonial rule towards treating native peoples with more consideration and greater understanding. The Boers found such an attitude incredible and resented the criticisms made of their treatment of the natives by the English missionaries; they were offended by the decision of the British government that the evidence of a Hottentot against his master should be accepted by a law court. The abolition of slavery was also unpopular but it is doubtful if this was the major cause of the Great Trek as some years before 1833 the frontier Boers had become restless and wanted to move away from the hated British rule. There was also an increase in their population which made it necessary to find new farms elsewhere, and they knew there was sufficient land for this beyond the colony; reconnaissance expeditions had brought back glowing accounts of good land with plenty of water and game.

The Great Trek 1836–48. The Great Trek started in 1836 and continued for about twelve years. The frontier Boers sold their farms and with their wives, children, servants and cattle, moved into the interior. The women and children travelled in the trek waggons drawn by teams of oxen. At night a defended laager or camp was formed by outspanning the oxen, and forming the waggons into a circle within which were the women and children. The trekking parties varied in size: some were several hundred strong, others much smaller. The trekkers crossed the Orange River; one party went northwards across the Vaal River, while another group turned eastwards towards the Drakensberg Mountains which they crossed and then came down into the fertile land of Natal. Their leader, Piet Retief, went to negotiate with the Zulu king Dingaan. On their second meeting Dingaan treacherously murdered Retief and his sixty-nine companions. Later the Zulus were defeated by Andries Pretorius at the battle of Blood River in 1838.

The trekkers then set up the Natal Republic, but this was short lived because of British intervention. The British government did not wish to let Natal pass under Boer control because with a sea coast on the Indian Ocean it had some importance on the route to India. In 1842 the British government sent troops to Natal to protect the Bantu peoples from Boer interference, followed by a Royal Proclamation in 1843 which made Natal a British colony under the supervision of Cape Colony. The answer of the Natal Boers was a drastic one; they abandoned their new homes and trekked back over the Drakensberg Mountains. Some settled in the

Orange Free State, but most of them went northwards across the River
Vaal where they founded several farmer republics, eventually united into
one, the South African Republic, but more generally known as the
Transvaal Republic.

British policy towards the Boer Republics 1848–77. The British
government wanted to control the movement of these trek Boers but
found that South Africa was a vast country and the expense involved was
too great; it alternated between a policy of control and one of leaving the
trekkers alone. In 1848 the Governor of Cape Colony, Sir Harry Smith,
proclaimed British sovereignty over the district between the Orange and

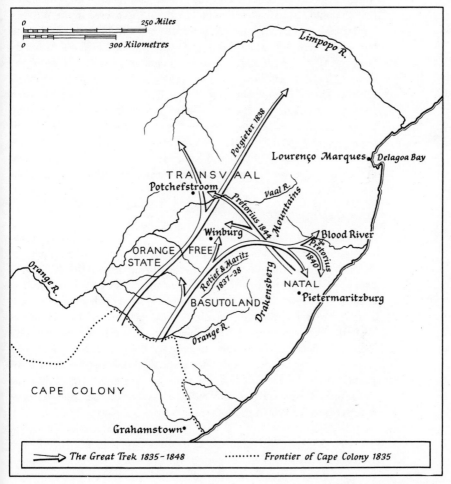

Map 6   The Great Trek

Vaal Rivers; the Orange Free State Boers rose in revolt but were defeated in 1848 at Boomplatz. This conflict with the trekkers, together with frontier wars with the Bantu peoples of Kaffraria decided the British government to limit its commitments in South Africa. In January 1852 the Sand River Convention gave independence to the Boers beyond the River Vaal, with the stipulations that the Boers should prohibit slavery and allow British subjects free access for trade; by the Convention of Bloemfontein, February 1854, Great Britain gave up her sovereignty over the Orange River territories, and gave independence to the Boers here on the same terms as for the Transvaal Boers.

For the next twenty years the Boer Republics were left more or less alone but there were incidents which confirmed them in their dislike of British policy. In 1867–9 a diamond field was discovered in the Western borderlands of the Orange Free State; the exact frontier was in dispute but the Orange Free State claimed that the diamond field lay within its territory. The British disregarded this claim and in 1871 annexed the district (Griqualand West) to Cape Colony and in 1873 made it into a separate Crown colony; the Orange Free State Boers felt they had been cheated. The Transvaal Boers resented an arbitration award which gave a disputed piece of territory on their western frontier to independent tribes, thereby keeping the Boers off the 'missionaries' road' to the north. But far greater troubles followed from the annexation of the Transvaal to the British Crown in 1877; this brought a stormy period of Anglo-Boer relations (see chapter 17).

British India

The company and the Maratha princes. In the first half of the nine-teeth century there was steady expansion by the East India Company of its political power in India. The intrigues of Napoleon with the Maratha princes of central and western India were regarded by the company as a prelude to renewed French intervention in India and which must be prevented by war against these rulers. The victories of the Marquess Wellesley between 1802 and 1804 obliged the Maratha princes to receive British residents at their courts to cede territory, and to conduct their foreign relations by permission of the company, while the successful campaigns of the Marquess Hastings between 1817 and 1819 against the marauding Pindaris broke the military powers of the Maratha confederacy and confirmed the supremacy of the company.

The first Afghan War 1839–42. In their policy of expansion north-west India became increasingly important to the company. The extension of Russian power in the Near and Middle East during the 1820s and 1830s alarmed the company who feared Russian control of the land approaches

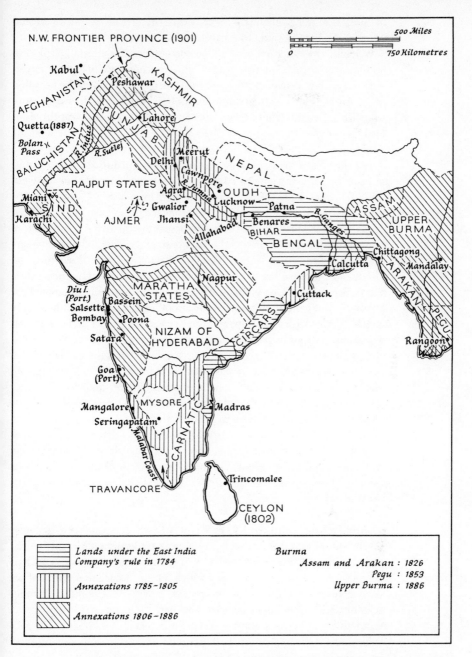

Map 7   The growth of British India 1784–1886

to India through Afghanistan. This led to the first of two unsuccessful attempts by British India to control Afghanistan.

When in 1839 an army of about 20,000 entered Afghanistan to place a pretender on the Afghan throne in the interests of the British government the intervention proved disastrous; the difficult country and the hostility of the Afghans led to a treaty of evacuation in 1842 but in the withdrawal from Kabul virtually all 16,000 men involved were killed, captured or died from exposure.

The Sikh Wars and the annexation of the Punjab. In spite of this setback the company continued the extension of its control of north-west India. In 1843 it provoked a war with the Amirs of Sind who were defeated at Miani and their territories annexed; this gave the company control of the approaches of the Bolan pass into southern Afghanistan. A more difficult proposition was the Sikh state in the Punjab lying between the Rivers Indus and Sutlej. The Sikhs practised a purified form of Hinduism and were warrior groups who had been formed by their ruler, Ranjit Singh, into a powerful state with an efficient army organized on European lines and with some European officers. Ranjit Singh had been on good terms with the company but after his death in 1839 relations got worse and led to war in 1845–6. The fighting qualities of the Sikhs were clearly shown in this war, but they were defeated and the Punjab was at the disposal of the British. It was not annexed but a British Resident, Sir Henry Lawrence was installed at the capital, Lahore; his reforming zeal offended the Sikhs, who thought their religion was being attacked and in 1848 they made an attempt to recover their independence. The new Governor-General of India, Lord Dalhousie, was determined to break the Sikh military power and after several costly battles this was achieved by General Gough in 1849. On his own responsibility Dalhousie annexed the Punjab regarding it as a vital area for the defence of British India on the north-west.

Control of the company by the Crown. Simultaneously with the move to paramount power in India the company's trade and political organization came under increasing control by the British government. This had started with the India Act of 1784 which set up a Board of Control of six privy councillors to supervise the general policy of the company and its relations with the Indian princes. Further, the company's charter was renewable every twenty years by Act of Parliament, thus giving the opportunity for a searching review of its activities and limitation of its powers; on renewal of its charter in 1813 and 1833 respectively, the company lost its monopoly of the Indian and Chinese trades. The 1833 renewal also defined the company as a political agent for the Crown, holding its

144

lands in India 'in trust for His Majesty, His heirs and successors, for the service of the government of India'. The last renewal in 1853 took away the right of the company to make appointments to its service and introduced the system of open competition by examination for this purpose. In view of this dwindling of the company's independent political power it seems likely that even if the mutiny of 1857 had not intervened the company would have come to an end sooner rather than later.

The policy of 'westernization'. The increasing emphasis on rule rather than trade brought with it the application of western ideas to British India. Although these could usually be justified on humanitarian grounds and in the interest of more efficient government they often conflicted with Indian social and religious customs. Lord William Bentinck, governor-general from 1828 to 1835 prohibited the practice of 'suttee' whereby Hindu widows were burnt alive on the funeral pyres of their husbands. He also suppressed the 'Thagi' or 'Thugs' who were robbers and ritual murderers who infested the highways and inns of India, and who were dedicated to the murder of travellers and merchants as a sacrifice to the death goddess Kali. On the advice of his secretary, T. B. Macaulay, the celebrated historian, Bentinck made English the medium of instruction in the government controlled schools thus placing an emphasis on western knowledge rather than Indian culture and civilization.

The policy of 'westernization' was the keynote of the governor-generalship of Lord Dalhousie (1848–56). He proceeded from the assumption that many of the princely states suffered from bad and oppressive government and would benefit by coming under British rule. His doctrine of 'lapse' whereby childless rulers could not adopt a son to succeed them without consent of the company led to the annexation of three Hindu states, Satara (1848), Jhansi (1853) and Nagpur (1854); in 1852 on the grounds of misgovernment the Moslem Kingdom of Oudh was taken over. In his wish to give India the benefit of western progress Dalhousie pioneered the building of trunk roads and railways and the extension of primary, secondary and university education along western lines.

The Indian mutiny 1857–8. Various explanations have been given of the causes of the Indian mutiny even to the extent of representing it as a nationalist revolt against British rule. In its narrowest aspect it was a mutiny of the Bengal native army but in its wider aspect it reflected the discontent of influential forces in Indian society against the westernization policy of the previous thirty years. The princes feared the policy of 'lapse' and annexation; Hindu society saw itself threatened by the disregard shown for the rigidities of its caste system when castes were

145

mingled in railway travel and the low caste prisoners cooked the food for those of higher caste in the prisons; western education had been proclaimed superior to Hindu and Christian missionaries were assiduously seeking converts.

Of the three native armies of Bengal, Bombay, and Madras that of Bengal was by far the largest and the most disaffected. The high caste Hindus of this army resented the changes that had been made in British India; they disliked the General Service Enlistment Act of 1856 with its obligation of service overseas instead of only in India, because travel on the high seas made them polluted persons. There had already been a small mutiny in 1852 when a regiment of the Bengal army refused to sail overseas to fight in the Burma campaign. Another cause of the mutiny was that many of the British officers were out of touch with their men and hardly realized the extent of their grievances. The immediate cause of the outbreak was the greased cartridge for use with a new Enfield rifle; before loading the cartridge had to be bitten by the soldier to expose the powder. A rumour circulated that these cartridges were smeared with the fat of cows and pigs; to the Hindu, the cow was sacred and to the Moslem the pig was unclean, and defilement would result for both if they used these cartridges. Orders were issued for the cartridges to be withdrawn but it was too late, for early in 1857 regiments were refusing to use them and in May 1857 the sepoys at Meerut mutinied and shot their officers.

The mutiny spread to the remainder of the Bengal army in the Upper Ganges Valley and the existence of British India was now threatened by nearly 100,000 well-trained mutineers, with infantry, cavalry, and artillery. The few British troops in India were hastily reinforced and as the native armies of Bombay and Madras remained loyal the British could concentrate on the recapture of Delhi from the mutineers who may have intended it as a capital of a revived Mughul Empire. The struggle fluctuated in the summer of 1857 with British successes and reverses; in the United Provinces, Lucknow was relieved for the first time, but Cawnpore was lost to be followed by the massacre of 125 British women and children by Nana Sahib. In September 1857 Delhi was recaptured and in November of the same year Lucknow was finally relieved by Sir Colin Campbell. The mutineers fought well but they had no concerted plan of campaign and by the end of 1857 the greater number of them had been rounded up and disarmed. In 1858, the rebel strongholds in north central India including the key fortress of Gwalior were captured and by June 1858 the mutiny was over.

The Government of India Act 1858. A settlement of affairs was now made by the Government of India Act of 1858 by which the East India Company was abolished and the Crown became the sovereign ruler of

British India; as its direct representative the governor-general was given the additional title of viceroy. A secretary of state responsible to Parliament for India was appointed, with an India Office in Whitehall taking the place of the old Board of Control; he was to be advised on Indian affairs by a Council of India of fifteen members. An attempt to allay the fears caused by 'westernization' before the mutiny was made in the Queen's Proclamation of 1858 which assured the Indian peoples that their religion and customs would not be interfered with; it held out the hope that they might in the future participate in the government of their country, and also recognized the titles of the Indian princes, subject to their allegiance to the British Crown.

British tropical Africa

Down to 1800 Great Britain like other European powers had been chiefly interested in Africa as a source of slaves and because its coast provided staging posts on the long sea voyage to India and the East. The abolition of the slave trade in 1808 and the geographical discoveries in Africa after 1800 in which British explorers such as Park, Clapperton, Lander, Burton, Speke, Livingstone and Baker played a prominent part, changed this situation. The vast interior of Africa and its native peoples became an area of colonization for the European powers; it held out the possibilities of trade, of supplies of tropical produce such as palm oil and rubber, and of mineral wealth, e.g. diamonds, gold and other metals. It was also seen as a great Christian mission field; in Great Britain especially this was linked with the aim of the anti-slavery movement to stop the slave trade at its source in the interior of Africa. In the last quarter of the nineteenth century a 'scramble for Africa' by the European powers took place; Great Britain took the lead in this when in 1882 she occupied Egypt to protect her imperial 'lifeline' of the Suez Canal.

West Africa

The Gold Coast. The abolition of the slave trade by Great Britain in 1808 left her presence in West Africa much in doubt but eventually this was maintained for the purpose of naval anti-slavery patrols (based largely on Freetown in Sierra Leone), and because of trading interests which wanted to keep the footholds given by the Gold Coast forts. This position in the Gold Coast was consolidated by the work of Captain George Maclean who between 1830 and 1845 made treaties with the tribal chieftains of the coastal area thereby giving the peace in which trade could flourish. In 1874 the coastal states were annexed to form the colony of the Gold Coast to which was added in 1900 the Ashanti territory of the interior.

The Nigerias. British influence in the Niger delta lands started with the annexation of Lagos in 1861, largely to stop slave trading. Twenty years later this was increased by the trading activities in the delta of the National African Company which in 1886 became the Royal Niger Company with a charter which gave it powers of government in the area. To stop French encroachment from the north the company extended its influence inland over the middle Niger lands; this was done by the campaigns of Captain Lugard who made a great name for himself in the history of British tropical Africa, first as a soldier and later as an administrator. In 1899 the charter of the Royal Niger Company was revoked and its administrative responsibilities were taken over by the British government. By 1900 British Nigeria was in being with the colony and protectorate of Lagos and the protectorates of Southern and Northern Nigeria.

East Africa

British interest in East Africa arose from her wish to secure control of the Indian Ocean of which the East African coast was a part, and from the aim of suppressing an extensive slave trade controlled by the Arabs of Zanzibar and supplied by raids they conducted in the interior of East Africa. From 1822 onwards British pressure was steadily exerted on the Sultan of Zanzibar to stop this trade both at sea and in the interior; by 1876 this had been achieved at sea but the trade was far more difficult to suppress on the mainland.

Uganda and Kenya. British action was also stimulated by the establishment of the colony of German East Africa (Tanganyika) in 1884; a partition treaty divided the mainland between Germany and Britain, giving the latter what later became Kenya. As in West Africa the extension of British influence inland was the work of a chartered British company, in this case the Imperial British East Africa Company. Its base was at Mombasa on the coast from where it had penetrated inland to Lake Victoria, thus making contact with the Bantu kingdoms of Uganda. The presence of this company prevented the establishment of a German colony in Uganda; the Anglo-German Treaty of 1890 recognized that Uganda was within the British sphere of interest, and also fixed the boundaries between German and British interest from the coast inland as far as the Belgian Congo. Because the B.E.A. Company lacked the resources to administer Uganda, a British protectorate was proclaimed there in 1894, while the other areas between the coast and Lake Victoria under the company's control were taken over and in 1895 the British East Africa Protectorate (later Kenya) was set up. Between 1897 and 1902 a railway was built from Mombasa to Kisumu on Lake Victoria, followed by white settlement and economic development of the Kenya Highlands by mixed farming and the establishment of coffee and sisal plantations.

Central Africa

The Rhodesias and Nyasaland. In pursuit of his aim of establishing British supremacy in Africa Cecil Rhodes had obtained in 1888 a mining concession from the Matabele ruler Lobengula which covered the vast lands between the Limpopo and Zambesi rivers. To exploit this concession Rhodes secured a royal charter in 1890 for the British South Africa Company which occupied the area later known as Rhodesia and brought in British and Boer settlers. Later the company's influence was extended north of the Zambesi over lands known as Northern Rhodesia. East of the Rhodesias lay Nyasaland along the lake of that name where in 1892 a British protectorate had been proclaimed in order to protect the mission stations and traders and to stop the Arab slave raiding in this area.

F

15. Parliamentary reform in the mid-nineteenth century

Distrust of democratic reform

After the 1832 Act no further major reform of Parliamentary voting and representation was achieved until 1867 because neither Whigs nor Tories believed in the principle of full democratic representation. They thought that Parliament should represent distinct 'communities' and 'interests' such as those of the counties, boroughs, landowners and businessmen, and regarded the democratic idea of 'counting heads' on a 'one man, one vote' basis as incapable of giving adequate recognition of these interests. The middle classes who had been enfranchised in 1832 followed the lead of their social superiors in this matter and were generally unwilling to share their newly-gained privilege with the working masses below them. The wholesale rejection in the 1840s of Chartism and its democratic demands reflected these upper- and middle-class attitudes. Nevertheless, neither Whig nor Tory ministers after 1850 could disregard entirely the demands for parliamentary reform made on behalf of the increasing number of 'respectable' working men. Their reaction, characteristically, was to introduce measures of parliamentary reform which were designed to hold off the threat of popular democracy by cautious extensions of the franchise to householders, counterbalanced by giving the vote to minority 'interests', and by a redistribution of seats which would keep a voting balance between the boroughs and the counties.

Russell's Reform Bills of 1852 and 1854

In 1849 the Prime Minister, Lord John Russell, although he had previously described the 1832 Reform Act as 'final', decided to introduce a new Reform Bill. This was strenuously opposed by a majority of his Cabinet; the Bill was outlined in 1850 but it was not finally brought forward until 1852. It proposed to reduce the qualification for the vote in both the boroughs and the counties, e.g. in the boroughs from a £10 rateable value to £5 and in the counties by a reduction of the long-lease qualification from £10 to £5 and in the case of the tenants-at-will from £50 a year to £20 a year. The resignation of Russell in February 1852 brought an end to this Bill.

In 1854 Russell brought forward another Reform Bill which proposed to reduce the household qualification in the boroughs to a £6 rateable value and place the lowest occupation franchise in the counties on a £10 a year basis. More significant was the attempt to cater for minority interests by what were known as the 'fancy franchises'. Thus it was proposed to give the vote to those who had a salary of not less than £100 a year, to university graduates, to those paying not less than 40s. income tax, and to those who had small investment incomes from government stock. These 'fancy franchises' were thought to be justifiable because they were 'the rewards of both enterprise, industry and thrift' and as such appealed to the spirit of the age and were acceptable to those who wished to reform Parliament but who did not wish to follow the path of democratic household suffrage; they were unacceptable to radical opinion because they would increase the number of plural voters and were an obstacle to the achievement of truly democratic voting. The Bill proposed a redistribution of fifty-two seats taken from the small boroughs which had survived the Act of 1832; these were mostly safe aristocratic Whig seats which explains the unpopularity of the measure with Russell's own party. The onset of the Crimean War in 1854 provided a convenient excuse for abandoning this Bill.

The Conservative attempt in 1859

The Whig efforts at reform were imitated in 1859 by a Conservative ministry under Lord Derby and Disraeli. Disraeli believed that the vote could safely be given to the better paid working men and that many of them would vote Conservative; a Reform Bill would give an opportunity to remodel the constituencies in the interest of his party by a judicious redistribution of seats. The underlying intention of the Bill of 1859 was to increase votes and representation in the counties where Conservative strength chiefly lay. In the counties £10 householders would become qualified and there was to be a redistribution of about 50 seats to the counties. The 'fancy franchises' of Russell's Bill of 1854 were repeated in the Bill of 1859 with some additions, e.g. members of learned professions were to have the vote as well as graduates, and for the first time the principle of giving votes to male lodgers who paid a minimum rental of £20 a year was introduced. Disraeli defended his novelties by calling them 'lateral extensions of the franchise', but in May 1859 a motion was carried against the government by Lord Russell which condemned the Bill because it did not provide any extension of the vote in the boroughs.

Whig proposals in 1860

In 1860 when the Whigs returned to power under Palmerston, Russell introduced another Reform Bill. This proposed to reduce the qualification for voting to £6 annual value for householders in the boroughs, and in the counties tenants paying not less than £10 a year would be given the vote. There was also to be a redistribution of seats, mostly to be taken from about twenty-two of the smaller boroughs and these seats were to be divided between the bigger counties and some of the bigger towns. Little enthusiasm was shown for the Bill and it did not get further than the Committee stage on the second reading.

The growing demand for reform after 1865

With the death of Palmerston in 1865 the great question of parliamentary reform entered a new and decisive phase. Palmerston had firmly and successfully applied the brake to parliamentary and other reform, which he disliked on principle and his political influence and reputation were not adversely affected by this. After his death the Whig and Tory party leaders, Russell and Derby, both realized that parliamentary reform must come and were therefore willing to accept it if only for party advantage. At the popular level the forces of reform were mobilizing; the extension of primary education and the growth of a popular press both contributed to the demands of the better off working men for the vote. Events abroad contributed to the idea that democracy was in the ascendancy; the victory of the North in the American Civil War and the unification of Italy were seen as victories for the popular cause: the demand was that the aristocratic British constitution must be modified to give the people a share of their just political rights. In 1861 and 1864 Sir Edward Baines, M.P. for Leeds, had introduced a Private Member's Bill for reform. In the debate on the 1864 Bill Gladstone made an eloquent pronouncement in favour of extending the vote to the more responsible of the working classes: 'And I venture to say that every man who is not presumably incapacitated by some consideration of personal unfitness or of political danger is morally entitled to come within the pale of the constitution'.

Failure of the Whig Reform Bill of 1866

Palmerston's successor as prime minister, Earl Russell, had a majority of 70 and wished to pass a Reform Bill before he retired from politics. Accordingly Gladstone was entrusted with the introduction of a Bill; this dealt only with voting qualifications and had no provisions for the redistribution of seats. It proposed to reduce the qualification in the boroughs to £7 annual rateable value and in the counties to £14 annual value. A great parliamentary debate ensued in which the supporters and opponents of parliamentary reform joined battle. The strongest opposition to the Bill came from a discontented section of the Whig Party led by Robert Lowe, and which was nicknamed by John Bright the 'Adullamites' (a Biblical reference to the discontented young men who joined David in the wilderness in the cave of Adullam). There were forty to fifty of them and with the help of the opposition they were able to carry an amendment against the government forcing it to add redistribution clauses to the original Bill.

152

In a series of trenchant speeches Lowe made attacks upon the very idea of democracy. His major argument was that the test was good government, not political justice; he showed complete disbelief in the idea of natural political rights for all men. In a democracy, said Lowe, the intelligent, educated minority would be swamped by ignorant rabble-rousers, and a working class with the vote would infallibly bring wasteful use of public money and an excessive amount of interfering government legislation. It would be far better to keep the government in the hands of an elite of intellect and ability and if necessary make judicious and periodical readjustments to the constitution from time to time. In his own words:

'A consideration of the speeches delivered on both sides will show the arguments in favour of democracy are mostly metaphysical, resting on considerations prior to, and therefore independent of, experience, appealing to abstract maxims and terms, and treating this peculiarly practical subject as if it were a problem of pure geometry. The arguments against a democratic change, on the other hand, are all drawn, or professed to be drawn, from considerations purely practical. The one side deals in such terms as right, equality, justice; the other, with the working of constitutions, with their faults, with their remedies, with the probable influence which such changes will exert. Are both these methods right, and if not both, which of the two?'

The government's proposals for redistribution were not liked. They involved the grouping of boroughs with less than 8,000 people in order to provide 49 seats for redistribution. The opposition and the Adullamite Whigs attacked it and in June 1866 an amendment to substitute rateable value for rental value in the boroughs was carried against the government, by 315 to 304; 48 Liberals voted with the opposition. A week later Russell and his Whig ministry resigned and a minority government headed by Lord Derby and Disraeli took office.

The Reform Act of 1867

The malcontent Whigs declined to join the Derby government which was in a minority of 70. The decision of the Conservative ministry to embark on a Reform Bill reflected two forces: firstly the need for the party to gain political initiative and secondly the strength of the reform agitation in the country at large. The situation attracted Disraeli, now chancellor of the Exchequer and leader of the Commons, because of the opportunity it gave of winning working-class votes for the Conservative Party. It took some time before proposals for a Bill could be made final; there was considerable dissension within the Cabinet and some ministers were opposed

'The Derby 1867.'
Dizzy wins with
'Reform Bill'.
(Punch cartoon)

to household suffrage under any conditions whatsoever. The Bill as finally presented proposed to give the vote in the boroughs to all householders regardless of the rateable value of the house they occupied, provided that they paid their rates directly and personally and not through the practice of 'compounding', i.e. paying the rates as part of their rent to the landlord who then made a consolidated payment to the local authority. In the counties the minimum qualification was to be the occupation of a house rated at not less than £15 a year. It also proposed a number of 'fancy franchises' whereby those who paid 20s. income tax yearly or who had £50 in the Savings Bank should have the vote.

Gladstone made strenuous attempts to amend the Bill so as to fix the qualification for a vote in the boroughs at a £5 rateable value. His attempt failed, largely because of the skill shown by Disraeli in the debates and also because Disraeli could rely on the support of some of the Radicals in the Liberal party who approved of his Bill. The price of this support was concessions such as the reduction of residence from two years to one in the boroughs to qualify a voter, and the grant of votes to male lodgers who occupied unfurnished rooms worth not less than £10 a year. A more startling amendment which Disraeli accepted was one which abolished the 'compound' householder; this meant that all householders must pay their rates personally and so automatically qualify for the vote in the boroughs regardless of the rateable value of the house they occupied. Disraeli's acceptance of this amendment was due to a lightning decision he made amidst the pressure of debate in the Commons; it brought about household suffrage in a way that he had not originally intended and as a result about an extra half-million voters were created. For the counties a minimum qualification of £12 a year rateable value was fixed instead of the original £15. A redistribution of seats was also effected; by taking one member from small boroughs with less than 10,000 inhabitants and dis-franchising four others completely, forty-five seats were available. Of these, twenty-five were given to the counties, nineteen to the boroughs,

'A Leap in the Dark.' Britannia's horse, *'Disraeli'*, dashes headlong at the hedge of *Reform.* (Punch cartoon)

155

and one member to London University. By adding nearly one million new voters the Act brought the total of the electorate in England and Wales up to two million and because of its acceptance of the principle of universal male household suffrage was a much more radical Act than its predecessor of 1832. Its implications, because of the political power it now gave to the lower classes were disturbing for men of both parties. Three of Derby's Cabinet resigned before the Bill was carried: Derby himself described it as 'A leap in the dark': even Gladstone and Bright were distrustful of it because they disliked the idea of extending the vote down to the 'dregs of the population'.

16. Gladstone and Disraeli 1868–80

The Gladstone–Disraeli duel

Although there may be a tendency to exaggerate the part played by individual politicians in the political history of any age, the personalities and political rivalry of Gladstone and Disraeli certainly dominated the period from 1865 to 1880. Both men had active political careers before 1865 but it was in the following fifteen years that the battle between them was joined in earnest. They had an attentive audience since Victorian people showed a relatively greater interest in politics than the British public today; they had also the time and stamina to digest the lengthy reports of parliamentary debates that most newspapers carried. The political rivalry of the two men remained sharp because of their wide differences of outlook, temperament, education, political beliefs and conduct. Basically they appealed to two quite different tendencies in their countrymen: Gladstone to the earnest, self-improving, God-fearing elements of Victorian society; Disraeli (like Palmerston) to a somewhat aggressive and rising tide of popular imperialism.

Their early careers

William Ewart Gladstone (1809–98) was the son of a Liverpool merchant with interests in West Indian sugar and coffee plantations and who could afford to educate his children well: the young Gladstone was sent first to Eton, and then to Christ Church, Oxford. In 1832 he had the offer of an easy seat in Parliament; he stood as a Tory candidate for the pocket borough of Newark and was elected. In the House of Commons he soon attracted favourable attention, and Sir Robert Peel, in his short ministry at the end of 1834 to the beginning of 1835, gave him minor office as under-secretary for the colonies. In Peel's ministry of 1841–6 Gladstone became vice-president of the Board of Trade; two years later promotion came when he entered the cabinet as president of the Board of Trade. In 1845, on a matter of conscience, he resigned because he disagreed with Peel's proposal to give financial grants to the Roman Catholic seminary at Maynooth in Ireland. But he soon returned, and in December 1845 he became colonial secretary; a year later he went into temporary political exile when Peel was overthrown after the repeal of the Corn Laws. In 1852 he became chancellor of the Exchequer in Lord Aberdeen's ministry, a mixed ministry of Peelites and Whigs. He quickly showed his financial ability by introducing a brilliant budget in 1853, and after the interruption of the Crimean War of 1854–6 he resumed with a series of   157 budgets which completed the free trade policy of Peel.

Gladstone's comfortable and assured start in political life contrasts sharply with that of his rival. Benjamin Disraeli (1804–81) was the eldest son of Isaac Disraeli, a man of letters whose family was Jewish, having settled in this country from Italy in the middle of the eighteenth century. Young Benjamin Disraeli had a very indifferent sort of education; baptized a Christian, he was sent to a Nonconformist academy at Walthamstow, but he left at the age of fifteen and for the next few years educated himself by studying the classics. At seventeen he was articled to a solicitor, but he soon lost interest in the law and speculated unsuccessfully on the stock exchange. As a young man Disraeli cut a somewhat startling figure, chiefly because of his flamboyant clothes, often appearing in purple or green velvet trousers, a fancy waistcoat and with his hair in ringlets; conventional people were suspicious of this brilliant and disreputable young man who at the age of twenty-two had already published a successful novel entitled *Vivian Gray*. He continued his education abroad, and visited the Mediterranean and the lands of the Near East. Compared with Gladstone his early attempts at political life were disappointing and humiliating. He stood three times unsuccessfully as an independent Radical for High Wycombe, but was not daunted by failure because in 1834 he said to Lord Melbourne, then prime minister, 'I want to be Prime Minister.' After his third failure he realized that he must join a party, and he became a Tory, standing as their candidate at Taunton in 1835, but again he was defeated. Finally in 1837 at Maidstone he was elected to Parliament. His first speech in the House of Commons was a complete failure, partly because of his strange appearance and his stilted language. It was received with cat-calls and laughter, but before he sat down he told his audience that the time would come when they would hear him. By contrast, Gladstone's maiden speech in the Commons, which lasted fifty minutes, showed considerable knowledge, was effectively delivered, and was respectfully received. Disraeli persevered, and his third speech in the House received some cheers: likewise he battled on in society, where he made his mark by his brilliant eloquence, his sarcasm, his wit and his knowledge of worldly affairs.

Gladstone's political beliefs

It is often observed in politics how men, in their younger days, express advanced opinions while in their old age they adopt conservative ones. With Gladstone it was the very reverse. He started as a Tory, in fact the hope of the 'stern, unbending Tories', but his whole political life showed a movement from right to left, and as he grew older he became more liberal and more radical in his outlook. Increasingly, he believed in democracy and that on broad, major issues, the people would decide correctly:

'I will back the masses against the classes.' He thought all men except the 'dregs of the populace' had a natural right to the vote. He became a democratic champion, the hero of millions to whom he appeared as a man of integrity and righteousness. To Gladstone, democracy could be best promoted by legislation to remove social discrimination and political inequalities, so that individuals would have a more equal chance of improving their status in society by their own efforts. Unlike Disraeli, Gladstone showed little enthusiasm for intervention by Acts of Parliament which affected the lives and environment of the people at large.

Gladstone constantly asserted that the state should conduct itself economically; the expenditure of the welfare state of today would have horrified him. He thought that taxation should be kept as low as possible, thereby encouraging people to save and preventing the squandering of money on less worthy objects. As chancellor of the Exchequer, Gladstone would have thought himself wrong if he had not made savings wherever possible, even 'candle ends'. Although this attitude became increasingly unfashionable, in his later career after 1880 Gladstone clung to it and a factor influencing his final retirement from politics in 1894 was that he thought the naval estimates were far too extravagant. His love of economy also influenced his attitude to imperial and foreign affairs, in which Great Britain should be careful not to become too involved, since this would lead to higher taxation.

Gladstone believed that politics had a moral basis and therefore all political questions should be determined on the basis of right or wrong; this was in accordance with his earnest and religious approach to politics. Once he had convinced himself of the righteousness of any cause he was incapable of compromise and his torrential energy and oratory poured forth in support of it. By contrast Disraeli lacked these fixed principles; his attitude was largely governed by expediency which meant that the right policy to be followed would be the most advantageous one, irrespective of moral right or wrong. Although the outstanding Liberal of the later Victorian period and with a great public reputation, Gladstone was somewhat inept as a party politician; his Cabinets and party were often baffled by his unpredictable moves and by the adoption of unpopular and politically unprofitable policies such as Irish Home Rule which split the Liberal Party in 1886.

Disraeli's political ideas

Throughout his career, Disraeli showed a more flexible attitude to politics than Gladstone and for this two factors were responsible. Firstly, Disraeli was consumed by political ambition and because of his birth and upbringing, he had much prejudice to overcome; he must therefore dazzle the British public by seizing and exploiting every opportunity. Secondly, he belonged to and finally led a party which had to be educated out of old-fashioned ideas and made to adopt vote-catching new policies.

From his speeches, novels and political tracts, certain political ideas can be traced. Disraeli proclaimed a somewhat sentimental belief in the 'Throne, the Church and the Aristocracy', regarding them as the cement that held society together and whose acceptance and maintenance were the guarantee of good government. Like all Conservatives Disraeli expressed a belief in leadership from above; he had no belief as had Gladstone in popular democracy, or that men had a natural right to the vote, which he thought was a privilege to be earned by deserving working men. His 'Tory democracy' was no more than rallying the masses, especially those of the growing industrial towns, under the party banner, with leadership from above and with a programme which was a mixture of social reform and imperialistic flag-waving. In sharp contrast with Gladstone, Disraeli believed in social reform of a collective and positive character; his novel, *Sybil, or the Two Nations* published in 1846 showed that he was aware of the appalling conditions of life and work of the working classes, and that intervention by Parliament was essential to improve matters. Lastly, Disraeli in his later years became the prophet of British imperialism. In a celebrated speech at the Crystal Palace in 1872 he drew a picture of a self-governing empire linked by a common tariff and with a central organization on which all the self-governing colonies should be represented – a forecast of the later idea of Imperial Conferences, and in our own day of the British Commonwealth; the perceptive Disraeli had seen that imperialism would be acceptable to the British people because it flattered their self-esteem.

In his personal relations with Queen Victoria, Disraeli showed great skill. He knew that she responded to flattery which he did not hesitate to use whenever possible. He wanted to exalt the Crown in national life and the addition of 'Empress of India' to the royal titles in 1876 was his idea. To the Queen, Disraeli appeared as a sympathetic, understanding man, whom she was glad to have as prime minister. Very different was the case of Gladstone, who after 1870 became intolerable to her because of his attempts to make her give up the seclusion of her widowhood and take a more active part in public life. Later in the 1880s Gladstone appeared to the Queen as a dangerous radical who was turning things upside down. Always she found the lectures of Gladstone unbearable, and complained that he treated her, not as a woman, but as a department of state.

The emergence of the Liberal Party

Disraeli became prime minister in March 1868 when Lord Derby resigned; 'Yes; I have climbed to the top of the greasy pole.' He was confident that the working men he had enfranchised by the Act of 1867 would return him with a majority but at the general election in the autumn of 1868 the Whigs and Liberals had a majority of 112, and Gladstone, not Disraeli, became prime minister. The Conservative defeat was due to the superior political appeal to the new electors of the Liberal Party led by Gladstone. A Liberal Party had emerged during the 1860s from a grouping of the more progressively minded Whig aristocrats and gentry, the middle classes and the newly enfranchised working men. Gladstone provided the link between all these diverse elements: the aristocracy and gentry accepted him as a landowner and because of his connections with them by marriage; to the middle classes he represented Liberal politics as a means of moral progress and emancipation from inequalities, while to the working classes, and especially to their large Nonconformist element, he identified Liberalism with Christian conscience. Here was a new political party which could finally make the transition from the old constitution dominated by the landed aristocracy to one more fitted to the needs of a mainly industrialized society in which the political rights and demands of the middle and lower classes were being increasingly recognized. In 1868 the Liberal Party had a dynamic which was lacking in the Conservative Party; it was not until Disraeli played down his earlier theme of 'The Throne, the Church and the Aristocracy' and made collective social reform and imperialism the main planks in his programme that Conservatism made an effective appeal to the electorate.

Gladstone's first ministry 1868–74

When called upon to form a government Gladstone was preoccupied with the Irish problem, as his celebrated remark 'My mission is to pacify Ireland' revealed, and in 1869–70 he made his first attempt to achieve this (see chapter 18). In other directions his ministry embarked on a programme of reforms for which the country, after the stationary policy of Palmerston, was more than ready. These reforms were concerned with the abolition of privileges and the removal of disabilities with the aim of giving greater equality of opportunity for the individual, or with administrative reform of organizations such as the army and the law courts.

The Education Act 1870

An important landmark in the provision of a state system of primary education was the Education Act of 1870, largely due to W. E. Forster, vice-president of the Privy Council, then entrusted with the administration of the money grants made since 1833 to the 'voluntary' schools organized by the various religious denominations. Gladstone was not himself very enthusiastic about the measure, but there was a strong demand for it from the radical wing of the party who, under Joseph Chamberlain, had organized a National Education League to press for

161

William Ewart Gladstone. A photograph taken at his country house at Hawarden, where his hobby was tree felling

universal free and compulsory education outside the control of the religious denominations.

By the Act local and elected School Boards were set up with power to levy an education rate, to build and staff schools where the existing provision by the voluntary denominational and charity schools was inadequate. The government grants to the voluntary denominational schools were increased. In the new Board Schools there was no denominational religious teaching and parents could, if they wished, withdraw their children from the weekly Scripture lesson. The Act did not establish free and compulsory primary education, although the School Boards had limited powers to compel attendance in certain cases and to pay the fees of the children of very poor parents.

Civil Service and University reform: the Ballot Act

In 1870 appointments to most branches of the Civil Service, with the exception of the Foreign Office, were made dependent on fully competitive examinations. At the Universities of Oxford and Cambridge religious tests were abolished in 1871; these had prevented men who were not members of the Church of England from holding scholarships and fellowships or from being admitted to higher degrees. By the Ballot Act of 1872 voting at parliamentary elections was made secret; hitherto the voter had openly declared his choice. This Act reduced intimidation of electors and made elections less disorderly, but it did not prevent various kinds of direct or indirect bribing of voters which continued until 1883 when the Corrupt Practices Act was enacted.

Trade union legislation 1869–71

Gladstone moved cautiously towards improving the status of trade unions. The movement had been alarmed by the judgment of the court of the Queen's Bench in the case of *Hornby* v. *Close* (1867) in which the Boilermakers' Society failed in the action they brought against one of their secretaries who had embezzled union funds. The court held that because a trade union at common law was an unlawful society, and in spite of the fact that it had registered itself as a Friendly Society, it was not entitled to any protection of its funds from the Friendly Societies Act. The Trade Union (Protection of Funds) Act of 1869 partially remedied this, allowing unions to sue defaulting officials. A Trade Union Act of 1871 went further giving trade unions legal status but a Criminal Law Amendment Act of the same year, by imposing heavy penalties for molestation, watching, besetting and intimidation during a strike, made it virtually impossible for unions to support their demands by strike action. Picketing even of the most orderly and peaceful kind was likely to incur penalties under this Act.

Local government and public health

The rapid growth of population, particularly in the urban areas, made necessary the provision of local health and sanitary services. Gladstone, a firm believer in strictly limiting the scope of the state's activities, was not over-enthusiastic about the extension of powers that would be involved if this was done. In 1871 the Local Government Board (forerunner of the Ministry of Health and Local Government) was formed out of the existing departments which dealt with local affairs. Of these the Poor Law Board was the most prominent and its unprogressive and stingy attitude was for many years far too influential in the new Board. By a Public Health Act of 1872 Urban and Sanitary Rural Districts, whose areas of authority coincided with those of the Poor Law Unions, were set up. It was not until the Public Health Act of 1875, carried by Disraeli's ministry, that these Boards were given fully effective powers and duties in the matters of health and sanitation.

Cardwell's army reforms

An urgent need was reform of two historic institutions, the army and the law courts. The Franco-Prussian War of 1870–1 in which the machine-like efficiency of the German armies had triumphed over the reputedly mighty French army, disquieted British opinion. It was asked whether our army was large enough or efficient enough in command and organization. In 1870–1 Gladstone's able secretary of state for War, Edward Cardwell now carried through, against widespread opposition from vested interests, an extensive reform of recruitment, organization, and command.

To build up a reserve of trained soldiers the short service principle was introduced by enlisting men for six years with the colours followed by a reserve service liability of a further six years. The infantry regiments of the line, hitherto known by numbers were now assigned to county districts and took for the most part county names. On this reorganization, Cardwell based his 'linked battalion' system whereby one battalion was at the home depot with the other one serving abroad. The home battalion was concerned with training recruits which were drafted at intervals to the overseas battalion.

Other measures included the combining of the various branches of the War department into a unified War Office under the secretary of state for War to whom was now subordinated the commander-in-chief. The change which provoked the greatest opposition was the abolition of purchase of commissions in the infantry and cavalry regiments. Under this system, officers on entry to the service purchased their commissions; promotion to higher ranks was achieved by buying the commissions of senior officers who were retiring. While there were able and efficient officers in the army there were too many unsuitable ones and too little promotion by merit. Yet the officer caste and aristocratic opinion fervently supported the system largely on the grounds that an officer corps of gentlemen amateurs was far preferable to one of a more professional kind. The House of Lords obstructed the reform, but Gladstone persuaded the Queen to abolish purchase by Royal Warrant. The Cardwell reforms increased the size of the army and its reserves and also its general efficiency, though the South African War of 1899–1902 was to reveal other defects, notably the lack of a general staff.

The Supreme Court of Judicature Act 1873

The creaking edifice of the English legal system was made more rational by a reorganization in 1873. The Act of this year dealt firstly with the two distinct systems of common law and equity then existing; it combined the two systems and henceforth common law and equity were to be administered concurrently in all courts, and where any conflict arose between them, the rules of equity would prevail. Secondly, the courts were reorganized into (*a*) the high court of justice, with its sub-divisions of chancery; Queen's bench; probate, divorce and admiralty; and (*b*) the court of appeal which heard appeals from the decisions of the judges of these sub-divisions.

Gladstone and foreign affairs

In foreign affairs Gladstone's attitude was peaceful and conciliatory. Soon after the outbreak of the Franco-Prussian War he secured international confirmation of the 1839 guarantee of Belgian neutrality, but he failed to dissuade the victorious Bismarck from annexing Alsace–Lorraine. When Russia in October 1870 denounced the clauses of the Treaty of Paris 1856 which neutralized the Black Sea and prohibited Russian naval bases in this area, Gladstone and his Foreign Minister Granville, lacking any support from other European powers, could only protest; a conference of the powers held in London (January 1871) affirmed the sanctity of treaties, but also cancelled the Black Sea clauses. Gladstone's belief that the rule of law rather than force should govern international relations was put into practice by his reference to an arbitration tribunal of the claims of the U.S.A. for the damage done to her shipping in 1862–4 by the commerce raider *Alabama* (see chapter 11). When the arbitrators awarded the U.S.A. £3¼ million against Great Britain, Gladstone paid this, although his action was unpopular and regarded as damaging to British prestige.

Resignation of Gladstone 1874

The numerous reforms carried since 1868 had offended many different interests and after 1871 Gladstone's ministry began to lose ground as the by-elections showed. The upper classes disliked the army reforms; the Nonconformists thought the Education Act favoured the Church of England schools; working men resented the restrictions on peaceful picketing; the Licensing Act of 1872 had antagonized the brewers and distillers. In March 1873 the ministry was defeated in the Commons on a Bill which proposed to set up a new Irish University for Roman Catholics. Gladstone resigned, but resumed office a week later because Disraeli refused to form another minority administration. Disraeli knew that the political tide was running strongly in favour of the Conservatives and accordingly pressed home his attack on what he called 'the incessant and harassing legislation' of the Gladstone ministry. In January 1874 Gladstone made a sudden decision to seek the verdict of a general election; this followed in February and amply confirmed Disraeli's expectations, giving the Conservatives a clear working majority of about fifty over Liberals and Irish Home Rulers combined. Gladstone's resignation quickly followed and the Queen summoned Disraeli to form a ministry. 165

'Paradise and the Peri.' Disraeli wins the general election in 1874. (Punch *cartoon*)

The Disraeli ministry 1874–80

Disraeli was now aged seventy; his health was failing, but he retained much of his political skill and resourcefulness. He formed a cabinet of able men; among them was R. A. Cross who as home secretary was responsible for the factory, housing, and trade union legislation enacted between 1874 and 1878. Disraeli himself was preoccupied with imperial and foreign affairs but gave his blessing to social reforms which were in keeping with the 'Tory democracy' he had preached in his earlier years and which he realized, were essential for contemporary British society. Whereas Gladstone's reforms had been somewhat narrowly concerned

166

with the improvement of the condition of the individual by the removal of discrimination, inequalities and the pressure of patronage, those of Disraeli had a considerably wider social purpose and sought to improve the general conditions of life and work for the mass of the population. This legislation was not new as the Factory Acts of the 1830s and '40s showed, and some of it was permissive and so not compulsory for local authorities, but overall it was important and foreshadowed the social legislation of the twentieth century. Although little or no public money was involved in implementing this legislation it was attacked on principle by the supporters of *laissez-faire* who objected to interference with property and other rights, but a testimonial came from a trade union M.P., Alexander Macdonald in 1879: 'the Conservative party has done more for the working classes in five years than the Liberals have in fifty'.

Benjamin Disraeli

Factory, housing and labour legislation 1874–8

In 1874 a Factory Act restricted the working week to fifty-six and a half hours and raised the minimum age for employment of children from nine to ten years. This was followed in 1878 by a Factory and Workshops' Act which consolidated existing factory laws and in particular forbade the employment of children over ten years for more than 'half-time', with 'half-time' education, which was not finally abolished until the Education Act of 1918.

By the Artisans Dwellings Act of 1875 a number of towns in England and Wales were given permissive, but not compulsory, powers to demolish insanitary houses and rebuild them. Relatively little use was made of these powers although there were a few notable exceptions, e.g. in Birmingham considerable improvements were made under the direction of its energetic mayor, Joseph Chamberlain.

Gladstone's trade union legislation of 1871, while conceding legal recognition of trade unions, had also created a number of criminal offences which made strike action almost impossible. Trade unionists' grievances over this were met by the Conspiracy and Protection of Property Act of 1875 by which a combination of workers acting in contemplation or furtherance of a trade dispute with their employers might lawfully do any act which if committed by one person would not be punishable as a crime; peaceful picketing, with emphasis on the 'peaceful' aspect, was made possible by the Act – but 'lightning strikes' by employees of gas and water supply undertakings were made illegal. In the same year the Employers and Workmen Act brought equality to the contractual relationship between employers and employees; henceforth any breach of contract was a matter for civil damages whereas previously by the Master and Servant Act of 1867 breach of contract by a workman (but not by an employer) could lead to criminal proceedings.

167

Public health legislation 1875

The existing piecemeal legislation governing public health was amended and consolidated by the Public Health Act of 1875 which was the work of Sclater Booth, president of the Local Government Board. This Act remained the framework of the system down to 1936 and was notable for the compulsory duties it laid on local authorities in connection with the enforcement of public health; hitherto many of these authorities had evaded their responsibilities in a careless or obstructive way. By the Act the local Sanitary Boards were compelled to appoint medical officers for health; to supervize the installation of water-borne sewerage and drainage in urban areas; to carry out the removal of household and industrial refuse. Supervisory powers were given over the building of houses, and the building of cellar dwellings was prohibited. Powers were also given for the control of infectious diseases such as smallpox by making these compulsorily notifiable, by the official disinfection of infected premises and by the maintenance of fever hospitals. Unsound food could be condemned and destroyed; those responsible for insanitary 'nuisances' could be compelled to abate them. A parallel measure was the Sale of Food and Drugs Act (1875) which was directed chiefly against the adulteration of foodstuffs; it had long been a common practice of unscrupulous manufacturers and retailers to use the stomachs of the working classes as receptacles for sugar adulterated with sand, bread whitened by alum, and beer spiced with thirst-producing salt. Public analysts were authorized by the Act to detect such adulteration and prosecutions could be brought against the offending manufacturers and retailers.

Merchant shipping; open spaces; education

In 1876 and afterwards the tide of reform slackened due partly to Cabinet preoccupation with imperial and foreign affairs and partly because of the disorderly behaviour of the Irish Home Rulers who began a systematic obstruction of debates and government business in the Commons. Disraeli himself became a peer and went to the Lords in August 1876 with the title of Lord Beaconsfield.

Of the reforms of 1876 three deserve mention. Since 1871 Samuel Plimsoll, Radical M.P. for Derby, had been agitating against the hazards to merchant seamen's lives from undermanned, overloaded, unseaworthy 'coffin' ships and his protests had led to an Act in 1873 which gave power to prevent unseaworthy ships from putting to sea. Further protests by Plimsoll (including a scene in the Commons where he denounced opponents of the Bill as murderers) and his trade union supporters, resulted in the Merchant Shipping Act of 1876; this established the principle of the 'Plimsoll' or load line for ships, but not much more, and further legislation was needed in 1894 and 1906 to make Merchant Shipping Acts more comprehensive and effective. The Enclosure of Commons Act made private enclosure of the few remaining open commons and woodland such as Epping forest difficult, thus preserving them as open spaces for public benefit. In education, because sufficient primary schools had been built as a result of the Education Act of 1870, it was now possible to enforce a measure of compulsory attendance. By Lord Sandon's Education Act of 1876 children up to ten were to attend whole time; between ten and thirteen they could not leave to become 'half-timers' unless they had obtained a proficiency certificate in the 'Three R's'; School Boards were ordered to appoint attendance committees and officers to enforce this regulation.

'Empress and Earl.' Queen Victoria, now Empress of India, confers a peerage on Disraeli

169

A 'forward' imperial policy

Before he took office, Disraeli had proclaimed the Conservative Party champions of the British Empire and its advancement. The risks of a 'forward' imperial policy were clearly shown during his ministry for besides some successes there were also expensive failures; the latter were chiefly due to the ill-judged policies and actions of the representatives of the British government in South Africa and India. It was a tribute to the skill of Disraeli that success was attained in matters he controlled personally, notably the purchase of the Suez Canal shares.

By 1875 the huge debts of the Khedive Ismail of Egypt forced him to sell his last remaining asset, his holding of seven-sixteenths of the share capital of the Suez Canal Company. To forestall purchase by French interests, Disraeli, on his own initiative and against strong opposition from his Cabinet, bought the shares for £4 millions which was advanced by the banking house of Rothschild. Parliament subsequently ratified the purchase and voted the money to repay the advance; Gladstone not only denounced the transaction as unconstitutional but mistakenly called it a bad bargain, and suggested that Disraeli should be impeached. The purchase did not give the British government majority control of the Suez Canal Company, but it meant that British representatives were appointed to the Board of Directors where they could use their influence to secure a reduction of tolls levied on shipping, important because British shipping was the greatest user of the canal. Besides its importance to Great Britain's maritime interest, Disraeli saw the Canal as a vital link in the route to British India and the East.

In 1876 Disraeli followed with another imaginative stroke. Parliament conferred the title of 'Empress of India' on the Queen. Critics attacked the title as unnecessarily ostentatious, but Disraeli realized its significance in India where the principle of monarchical rule was well established; it would also emphasize British supremacy and that the British Crown was the successor of the Mughul emperors.

The forward policy ran into difficulties in South Africa, and Afghanistan. Disraeli's Colonial Secretary Lord Carnarvon, aimed at the federation of Cape Colony, Natal, the Orange Free State and the Transvaal Republic. The annexation of the Transvaal (1877) and the Zulu War (1879) followed, and when the Conservative ministry resigned in April 1880, the Transvaal Boers were about to rise in arms to recover their independence. The attempt to secure the north-west approaches to British India by establishing British influence in Afghanistan, whose ruler was suspected of being too friendly with Russia, also proved disastrous. A British Resident and his staff, installed after a first successful invasion, were massacred and the Gladstone ministry was forced to send in another expedition to retrieve the situation (see chapter 17).

170

Revival of the 'Eastern Question' 1875

A major problem for European diplomacy arose with the revolt in 1875 of the Christian subjects of Turkey in the Balkans. In Disraeli's view British interests would be adversely affected by these risings which with Russian support would certainly weaken the Turkish Empire, the maintenance of which was a declared aim of British policy. Furthermore, Disraeli feared the aggressive aims of Russia in the Eastern Mediterranean and Middle East which he saw as a threat to the Suez Canal route to India and the East. His pro-Turkish policy was made difficult by the atrocities of May 1876 when some 12,000 Bulgarian Christians were cruelly massacred by Turkish irregulars. Unfortunately Disraeli, misled by the pro-Turkish British ambassador at Constantinople, questioned the accuracy of reports of the massacres, referring to them as 'bazaar gossip'. Gladstone saw his rival had slipped; in his pamphlet *The Bulgarian Horrors and the Question of the East* he fiercely attacked Disraeli for his support of the Turks, 'the one great anti-human species of humanity'.

'Let the Turks now carry away their abuses in the only possible manner, namely by carrying off themselves . . . one and all, bag and baggage they shall, I hope, clear out from the province they have desolated and profaned . . .'

Disraeli's anti-Russian policy

At the end of 1876 a conference of the European powers, at which Lord Salisbury represented Great Britain, met at Constantinople with the aim of persuading the Sultan to reform his government and make concessions to his Christian subjects. The Turkish refusal led the Russians to declare war in April 1877 and their armies entered the Balkans. Although held up by the Turkish defence of Plevna conducted by Osman Pasha the Russian successes alarmed British opinion to the extent that Disraeli's (now Lord Beaconsfield) hand was strengthened and the fiery denunciations of Gladstone correspondingly weakened. With the Russians approaching Constantinople and the Turks asking for an armistice the question for the British Cabinet was how Russia could be stopped and Turkey preserved without a war. There were divisions in the British Cabinet over the action to be taken shown by the fact that the order to the British Mediterranean fleet to move up the Straits to Constantinople was given and then countermanded no less than three times.

The San Stefano Treaty; the Congress of Berlin 1878

Following an armistice the Turks were forced to sign the Treaty of San Stefano in March 1878. This virtually eliminated Turkish power in Europe, setting up a large Bulgarian state with an outlet to the Aegean Sea. Its terms were unacceptable to Great Britain and also Austria– 171

Map 8   Frontiers proposed by the Treaty of San Stefano 1878

Hungary, who saw its Balkan aspirations blocked by Russian influence over the Slav states there. Beaconsfield insisted that a conference of the powers should be called to discuss the revision and added force to this demand by calling up the army reserves and bringing 7,000 Indian troops

172

Map 9   *The Settlement made by the Berlin Congress 1878*

to Malta. Lord Salisbury who played a leading part in the modification
of San Stefano treaty, now replaced Lord Derby as foreign secretary. In
June 1878 the Berlin Congress of the powers assembled, Bismarck acting
as the 'honest broker'; Beaconsfield and Salisbury represented Great
Britain.

The Congress witnessed the usual diplomatic bargaining and bluff,
including one by Beaconsfield, who threatened to leave the Congress if
certain British demands were not conceded, but most vital points had
been settled before the conference assembled by secret conventions
between the powers. Thus, Great Britain and Russia had agreed to reduce
the big Bulgaria of San Stefano and so restore Turkish control of southern
Bulgaria. It was agreed beforehand that Austria–Hungary should take
over the administration of Bosnia–Herzgovina, that Russia should have

173

south Bessarabia, and Rumania the Dobrudja. By another secret agreement Turkey, in return for a promise to defend the Sultan's dominions in Asia, granted Great Britain the right to occupy Cyprus. While Russia gave way over Turkey in Europe, the Congress sanctioned her annexation of considerable Turkish territory in Asia Minor bordering on the southeast Black Sea, including the port of Batum.

The Treaty of San Stefano had been destroyed; Turkey had been preserved, and the Russian advance checked. Beaconsfield was elated by his success. At a reception at the Austrian Embassy in Berlin, he was asked: 'What are you thinking of?' Characteristically, he replied: 'I am not thinking, I am enjoying myself.' Returning to London with Salisbury, he announced that they had brought back 'peace, and a peace, I hope, not without honour'. The preservation of peace in circumstances very similar to those which had led to the Crimean War twenty-five years earlier was certainly an achievement.

Difficulties of the Conservative ministry 1878–80

By contrast the last phase of Beaconsfield's ministry was beset by a rising tide of troubles at home. A pronounced depression in trade developed leading to unemployment (in 1879 11% of trade union members were out of work) and wage reductions. British exports were finding it more difficult to enter foreign markets protected by rising customs duties, while free trade left the British market unprotected. A flood of cheap grain from the U.S.A. and Canada began to pour in, which with the bad harvests of 1878 and 1879 and widespread disease in cattle and sheep, shook British agriculture to its foundations. Ireland, almost an entirely agricultural economy and with few industries, was worst hit. Irish grievances found expression in the agitation for Home Rule, started by Isaac Butt in 1873, but directed after 1878 by the far more forceful Charles Stewart Parnell; by organizing systematic obstruction in the House of Commons Parnell brought government business to a halt. The formation of the Irish National Land League, directed against landlords and the payment of rent to them, and of which Parnell became president, was an equally alarming development for the government (see chapter 18). Reviving Liberalism saw its chance in all these difficulties and Gladstone, in a marathon of political oratory known as the Midlothian campaign, attacked the record of the government, particularly its imperial policy which he denounced as having 'weakened the empire by needless wars, unprofitable extensions and unwise engagements.' At a general election in March 1880 the Liberals gained a majority of 137 without taking into account the 65 Irish Home Rulers who were returned. Lord Beaconsfield resigned, to die a year later, and Gladstone's second ministry took office.

17. Gladstone's second ministry 1880–5

'The ministry of all the troubles'

In the general election of March 1880 the Liberals were helped by an efficient party organization, especially in big provincial towns like Birmingham; they won 347 seats against the Conservatives 240. While Gladstone had used radical appeal to get his majority, his Cabinet did not reflect this: no less than six ministers were in the House of Lords and represented the aristocratic Whig section of the Liberal Party, although radical Liberalism had some forceful spokesmen in the Commons, e.g. Chamberlain, Dilke, and Labouchere. In spite of its assured majority the life of this ministry was far from easy and it was known as 'the ministry of all the troubles'. For this the thorny problem of Ireland, with which Gladstone was preoccupied, was largely responsible (see chapter 18); Gladstone's leadership of his Cabinet was also erratic, with much conflict between the Radical and Whig sections of the party. The growing economic depression in industry and agriculture for which the Liberals had no positive remedies, also added to their difficulties.

Withdrawal from Afghanistan 1880

One of the first tasks of the new ministry was to clear up the situation in Afghanistan. After the murder of Sir Louis Cavagnari, the Resident at Kabul, the British forces returned to Afghanistan. Abdul Rahman, a nephew of the former ruler Sher Ali, was recognized in July 1880 as ruler of Afghanistan. He entered into treaty relations whereby Great Britain controlled his foreign relations and guaranteed his position against external aggression; in return the British gave up their claim to maintain a resident at Kabul. After dealing with rival claimants to the throne which involved extensive military operations including the celebrated march of General Roberts from Kabul to Kandahar, a distance of over 300 miles through trackless and difficult country which was accomplished with a force of about 18,000 men in three weeks, the British forces withdrew.

The Transvaal recovers independence 1881

In the Transvaal the Boers were demanding the restoration of the independence they had lost when their republic had been annexed to the British Crown in 1877. Gladstone had attacked this annexation before he was returned to power and naturally enough the Boers expected that he would restore their independence. He was slow in doing this and towards

175

the end of 1880 the Transvaal Boers took up arms to recover their independence, after first rejecting a proposal in June 1880 for the federation of the four territories of Cape Colony, Natal, the Transvaal and the Orange Free State. In February 1881 the Boers decisively defeated a small British force under the High Commissioner, General Sir George Colley, who had occupied Majuba Hill, commanding a pass through the Drakensburg Mountains into Natal. This defeat was resented by British opinion, but Gladstone gave way and by the Convention of Pretoria, August 1881, restored independence to the Transvaal, 'subject to the suzerainty of Her Majesty', a vague claim of sovereignty which irritated the Boers; other restrictions were also imposed, notably that the republic must conduct its foreign relations through Great Britain.

'Gladstone invading Egypt 1882'

The British occupation of Egypt 1882

When faced with events in Egypt which threatened British interests, Gladstone, in the rather unpredictable way that was often characteristic of him, followed a policy as ambitious as Disraeli would have advocated in similar circumstances. In 1880 British interests in Egypt were twofold; the first was the responsibility we shared with France since 1878 for the administration of the 'Dual control' of the Egyptian finances, and secondly, our interest in the vital link in imperial communications, especially with India and the East, provided by the Suez Canal.

In 1881 a nationalist revolt broke out in Egypt, headed by Arabi Pasha, an officer in the Egyptian army, in protest against Turkish influence over the Khedive Tewfik, and also against the influence and privileged position of foreigners in Egypt, especially those who controlled, under the debt payment arrangements, various parts of the Egyptian administration. By the beginning of 1882 the Khedive's authority was seriously threatened by Arabi Pasha and his followers. France and Great Britain, the powers most interested, made it clear that they would prevent any further attempts to overthrow the Khedive. In May the French and British fleets were sent to Alexandria; in the following month there were anti-foreign riots in Alexandria leading to the deaths of over fifty Europeans. At this stage France withdrew from the operations in support of the Khedive. The fortifications of Alexandria were bombarded by the British fleet in July 1882 and a few months later a British force was landed to secure the Suez Canal which was achieved by the defeat of Arabi Pasha's army at Tel-el Kebir, September 1882. The British government now decided to occupy Egypt for an indefinite period; this would assure control of the Suez Canal

177

route and also make possible the provision of better government for Egypt. The British Agent and Consul-General, Sir Evelyn Baring, afterwards Lord Cromer, dominated the government of Egypt from 1884–1907. He improved the condition of the peasants by reducing taxation and promoted the economic prosperity of Egypt by an ambitious programme of public works, especially for irrigation. The waters of the Nile were brought under control for this purpose by the building of various barrages and dams, notably the Aswan Dam in Upper Egypt. Great Britain did not annex Egypt which remained nominally a province of Turkey, with its own ruler the Khedive and his Egyptian ministers. It was not until 1914 that Great Britain declared a protectorate over Egypt.

Great Britain and the Sudan

The control now established over Egypt involved Britain in another matter in which she was far less successful. To the south, stretching to the Equator and beyond, was the Egyptian province of the Sudan. Egyptian authority over this had never been very firmly established and in 1881 their rule was overthrown by Mohammed Ahmed, who was better known as the Mahdi, or the 'guided one.' He and his warrior followers, the Dervishes, opposed Egyptian rule because they considered it corrupt and oppressive and because they considered the Egyptians as bad Moslems. With the consent of the British government who lent them General Charles Gordon for the purpose, the Khedive's advisers decided to evacuate the Sudan.

Gordon had previous experience of the Sudan as governor-general in the employment of the Khedive Ishmail from 1874–9. It was this that probably led him to disregard his orders to evacuate the garrisons and to decide to stay at Khartoum, thinking that he could retrieve the situation. As the Dervish armies controlled nearly all the Sudan this was a serious miscalculation and by the middle of 1884 Gordon and his Egyptian army were surrounded in Khartoum. It was now urgent that the British government should send a rescue expedition, but the Cabinet delayed making a decision in favour of this until rather too late. The commander appointed, Wolseley, did not reach Egypt until September nor enter the Sudan until November. The advance guard of this relieving force reached Khartoum two days after it had been stormed and Gordon killed on the night of 25/26 January 1885. The Anglo-Egyptian forces withdrew; the Sudan, except the Red Sea port of Suakin, was lost and not reconquered until 1898. Gladstone incurred great unpopularity for this defeat which was resented by British opinion from Queen Victoria downwards.

Parliamentary reform 1883–5

Gladstone was under considerable pressure from the Radicals in his

Cabinet to enact measures of parliamentary reform which would continue the work of 1832 and 1867 in the direction of popular democracy. The result was three Acts dealing with the prevention of corrupt practices at parliamentary elections, the extension of the vote to householders in the counties, and the redistribution of seats to give more equal representation of the constituencies.

The Corrupt Practices Act 1883. The problem was that bribery and corruption, in spite of an increased electorate and reforms such as the Ballot Act of 1872 were still prevalent and particularly so in the small boroughs. Large sums were spent by candidates in bribing electors, sometimes directly but more often indirectly, e.g. 'treating' with food and drink or by the employment of unnecessarily large numbers of paid stewards, clerks and 'helpers'. Control of election expenses was the heart of the problem, and this was achieved by the Act. It fixed the total amount that could be spent in any constituency in proportion to the number of its electors; this meant in practice a few hundred pounds in contrast to the thousands that had frequently been spent in the past. The candidate could only have one agent who was responsible for expenses and whose accounts were to be audited within a month of the election. Corrupt practices were strictly defined and included bribery, 'treating', undue influence and persecution; for committing such offences candidates, agents and electors were liable to penalties including disqualification, fines and even imprisonment.

The County Franchise Act 1884. This made the qualification for voting in the counties basically the same as that in the boroughs as provided by the Reform Act of 1867, e.g. all male householders and £10 lodgers. As a result nearly two million householders, mainly agricultural labourers and miners now became voters providing that their names were on the register of voters and that they were not disqualified by the receipt of poor relief.

The Redistribution Act 1885. Conservative criticism was expressed through the House of Lords which refused to pass the Franchise Bill unless the government agreed to a redistribution of seats and an adjustment of the constituency boundaries. Hence the Redistribution Act of 1885; by it all boroughs with less than 15,000 inhabitants lost their separate representation and were merged in the counties in which they were situated, and boroughs with less than 50,000 inhabitants lost one member. The remainder of the country was divided into single member constituencies apart from twenty-two medium sized boroughs with between 50,000 and 100,000 inhabitants which retained two members each. The total number of the House of Commons was raised by 12 to 670.

'Come Hup! I say – You Ugly Beast.' A cartoon depicting Gladstone as Mr Jorrocks and Lord Salisbury as the horse 'Artaxerxes'. Lord Salisbury had led the Tory majority in the House of Lords against the passage of Gladstone's Reform Bill of 1884

The combined effect of these three Acts was to advance democracy in Great Britain and Ireland, although some men and all women had not yet got the vote. Other results were that the great increase in rural voters made it increasingly difficult for the landed aristocracy to keep their former unquestioned control of elections in the countryside; the creation of a mass electorate greatly increased the importance of the party organizations and their propaganda, for it was this which could decisively influence the way the votes were cast at an election; in Ireland the enfranchisement of the peasant householder increased the already considerable control over Irish elections held by Parnell and the Home Rulers.

Domestic reform

Gladstone's programme of domestic reform was hampered not only by the organized obstruction of the Irish Home Rulers but also by the inroads on parliamentary time made by the case of Charles Bradlaugh, atheist M.P. for Northampton. A somewhat undignified debate continued intermittently for several years as to whether or not Bradlaugh could be allowed, before taking his seat in the Commons, to make an affirmation instead of the usual Christian oath of allegiance taken by all M.P.s. Nevertheless some socially important reforms were enacted. The Employers' Liability Act of 1880 provided that if a workman was injured at work through the negligence of his employer or the employer's agent, he might get compensation. The Act remained ineffective because many employers employed their workers only on condition that they 'contracted out' which meant that the workers agreed that the provisions of the Act regarding compensation should not apply to them. The Nonconformists secured the removal of a long-standing grievance in 1880 when a Burials Act was enacted which allowed them to bury their dead with their own services in the parish churchyards. School attendance up to the age of 13 was made compulsory in all primary schools. In 1882 the Married Women's Property Act improved the status of women in respect of control of their own property; it gave women for the first time control of their own separate property, which hitherto on marriage had passed under the control and disposition of their husbands. The Settled Land Act of 1883 made possible the sale of landed estates which had been 'tied up' in strict settlement in the hands of trustees for the benefit of successive generations of the families concerned. This removal of restrictions on the sale of settled land led gradually to the break-up of many of the great landed estates; the process reflected the declining social and economic importance of land in an industrialized society.

Events leading to Gladstone's third ministry

The unpopularity brought by the disaster of Gordon at Khartoum, together with dissensions within the ministry over a proposal to give local government to Ireland, led Gladstone to resign in June 1885 after a defeat in the Commons over the budget. The Queen sent for Lord Salisbury who somewhat unwillingly formed a government. No elections could be held until November because a new parliamentary register of electors in conformity with the Franchise Act of 1884 was being prepared. Salisbury's government therefore was a minority government and it lasted only seven months (see chapter 18).

To win over the new voters enfranchised by the Act of 1884 the radical wing of the Liberal Party under the leadership of Joseph Chamberlain prepared what was known as the 'unauthorized programme' which advocated free primary education, provision of smallholdings, disestablishment of the state Churches in England, Scotland, and Wales, and increased taxation to provide money for social reforms. At the general election in December 1885 this programme won many seats for the Liberals in the countryside, but on the whole the towns turned against Gladstone. The Irish vote by order of Parnell was given to the Conservatives. The final result was 335 Liberals, 249 Conservatives, and 86 Irish Nationalists whose votes made Parnell the arbiter between the other two parties. He soon demonstrated this when in January 1886 upon the assembly of the new Parliament, he abandoned his flirtation with the Conservatives and joined the Liberals to pass an amendment to the address in reply to the Queen's Speech. Defeated by a majority of 79, Salisbury resigned, and Gladstone, now committed to Home Rule for Ireland, formed his third and short-lived ministry at the beginning of February 1886 (see chapter 18).

181

G

18. The Irish problem 1865–1914

The elements of the problem

In the second half of the nineteenth century the problem of Ireland intensified for the British government. Politically the legislative Union of 1800 with Great Britain was unacceptable to Irish nationalist feeling which regarded it as a device to strengthen English domination over Ireland. With this rule was associated an Established Church, the Protestant Church of Ireland, wealthy and privileged, but a stranger in a land where seven-eighths of the population were Roman Catholics. Economically there was an urgent land problem, aggravated by the bad relations that existed between landlords and tenants. Although the famine of 1845–6 and the emigration that followed it had reduced the population of Ireland by two millions, there was still insufficient land. The reason for this pressure on the land was that the population had few other means of subsistence; the industrial revolution, except in Ulster, had largely by-passed Ireland and consequently alternative occupations for the surplus population were lacking.

The land problem

The evils in land tenure described by the Devon Commission in 1845 still existed twenty years later. There was the same pressure on the land leading to sub-division into smaller and smaller holdings let at high rack rents. There was the grievance (except in Ulster) that landlords refused to recognize the tenant's right to compensation for any improvements he had made to his holding. There was the same ruthless eviction in case of non-payment of rent and the only protection for the poverty-stricken peasant farmers lay in violence organized by secret or semi-secret societies, whose methods were murder, assault or intimidation of landlords, their agents, or those who became tenants of the lands of evicted peasants. The situation was thus hopeless and government after government was forced to rule through Coercion Acts which suspended the right of public meeting and habeas corpus and increased the powers of magistrates and police. For the landlord, the only way of improving his position was the anti-social one of wholesale eviction; if this was done there was some chance of consolidating the holdings and letting the land in a larger unit to a substantial tenant who could farm the land properly. Failing this, the land had to be let in small units at high rents which the tenants could not pay, so leading to eviction. While some of the great Protestant Anglo-Irish landlords were absentees with land agents administering their estates locally and enforcing evictions, not all Irish landlords came into this category; a number were resident and made attempts to improve their estates and help their tenants. But the agrarian situation in Ireland, as in Great Britain, worsened in the 1870s and 1880s because of the sharp fall in prices for farm produce which made it even more difficult for the peasants to pay their rents.

The Fenians

A new force entered Irish politics in the 1860s. This was the Irish Revolutionary Brotherhood, or as they were usually known, the Fenians. Founded in the U.S.A. in 1858, the organization sought to end the connection with Great Britain and to set up an independent republic, thus differing sharply from the more constitutional movement led in the 1840s by Daniel O'Connell, which wanted no more than the repeal of the Union and the re-establishment of an Irish Parliament and government at Dublin. The strength behind the Fenian movement lay in the fact that it was inspired by Irish-Americans, many of whom had been forced out of Ireland by the famine and who hated the memory of British policy. In the United States many of them had prospered and were so able to give considerable financial support to the Fenian movement. The British government could neither stop these Fenian activities in the U.S.A. nor the flow of money which was skilfully used to promote agitation in Ireland and to relieve the victims of eviction. The revolutionary violence of the Fenians was shown in 1866 in an attempted invasion of Canada from the United States, followed, in 1867, by an attempt to seize Chester Castle. Later in the same year a bomb explosion organized by Fenians killed twelve people in or near Clerkenwell Gaol, London.

Disestablishment of the Protestant Church of Ireland 1869

These outrages were a sharp reminder for British politicians of the problem that lay on their doorstep. On becoming prime minister in 1868 Gladstone announced that his mission was 'to pacify Ireland' and he believed this could be done by moderate measures of reform designed to remove specific grievances of the Irish people. Although a zealous member of the Church of England, Gladstone did not hesitate to disestablish its sister church, the Protestant Church of Ireland, on the grounds that its official position and privileges were an affront to the Irish Catholic majority.

The Irish Church Act of 1869 ended the official connection of the Church of Ireland with the state and with the established Church of England. Of its substantial endowments about £5 million were given to Irish education, charities and for other public purposes, leaving some £13½ million with which the disestablished Church of Ireland could continue an independent existence.

The Land Act 1870

In 1870 Gladstone turned to the land problem, enacting without much opposition a Land Act which established the principle that tenants were not to be evicted except for non-payment of rent, and a tenant was to be compensated for improvements such as drainage or buildings he had made to his holding, even if he was evicted for non-payment of rent. There was also very limited provision for the purchase by the peasants of their holdings from the landlords. The Act was not a success; landlords raised rents and thereby kept their excuse for evicting defaulting tenants; little use was made of the land purchase clause. Gladstone also gave further proof of his wish to conciliate Ireland by introducing an Irish University Bill which would have given Irish Catholics a university of their own, but this was defeated by a narrow margin.

The Irish Home Rule League

Disraeli's ministry of 1874–80 avoided the Irish problem as much as possible, but during its term of office two important Irish movements emerged. The first was a political one, the Irish Home Rule League founded in 1873 and led by Isaac Butt, an Irish barrister; it demanded repeal of the Union of 1800 and the restoration of an Irish Parliament and government at Dublin. In the general election of 1874 fifty-nine Irish Home Rulers were returned to Westminster where Butt urged their cause in a conciliatory manner without evoking any response from the Conservative ministry. In the more forceful hands of Parnell, who supplanted Butt as leader in 1878, the Home Rule League became a powerful political force, especially during Gladstone's second ministry from 1880–5.

The Irish National Land League

The other movement lay even nearer the heart of the Irish problem, being concerned with the use and ownership of the land. In August 1879 a

An eviction in the west of Ireland 1881

number of Fenians led by Michael Davitt founded the National Land League for County Mayo. Its aims were to fight those landlords who raised rents and evicted tenants by a boycott of them and their agents. Besides working for a reduction of rents the League aimed at the eventual owner-ship of all Irish land by Irish peasant farmers. The League was backed by the money subscribed by American Fenian sympathizers and was there-fore able to give effective support to the victims of eviction. The politically astute Parnell realized the importance of this Land League as a parallel force to that of the Home Rule League. He therefore hastened to associate himself with it and to expand it into the Irish National Land League covering the whole country.

Charles Stewart Parnell

Charles Stewart Parnell first entered politics when he was returned in 1875 for Parliament as member for County Meath. He was both a Pro-testant and a landlord but strangely enough this proved a help rather than a hindrance, as it enabled him to stand outside and above the many jealousies and differences that divided the Catholic Irish agrarian and political leaders. Parnell showed great skill in uniting the various elements opposed to British rule in Ireland, and at Westminster by 1878 his biting and forceful speeches swept him into the leadership of the Irish Home Rule party in place of the more moderate Butt. Under Parnell organized obstruction to the work, debates and programme of the House of Com-mons became the rule in order to draw attention to the Irish cause. So much obstruction was caused by the disorderly behaviour of Irish Home Rule M.P.s, who carried debates to unheard of lengths or indulged in com-plete irrelevance when addressing the House, that the rules of procedure had eventually to be modified in 1881 by the introduction of the 'Closure' which gave power to end the debate.

The aims of Parnell have been variously interpreted. An older view regarded him as a deadly enemy of Great Britain, ready to sever the con-nection at all costs. Another view suggests that he was afraid of the violent elements in Irish politics and spent most of his time trying to restrain them, and that had Ireland been given a measure of Home Rule, he would have been satisfied. Others have seen him as a statesman who realized only too well the backward economic condition of Ireland and who knew that an improvement was only possible if Ireland remained associated with Great Britain, once Home Rule had been granted.

The policy of 'boycott'

When Gladstone became prime minister in 1880 for the second time the problem of Ireland had distinctly worsened because of the growing agri-cultural depression which had hit Ireland very hard indeed. As a result

185

the number of evictions had increased since 1880 and also the agrarian outrages known as 'moonlighting', in which landlords, their agents and sympathizers were murdered or assaulted. Those who took the lands of tenants evicted were dealt with by the method of 'boycott', so-called because it was first applied with effect to Captain Boycott, who was the agent of a large landowner in County Mayo. Parnell himself in a speech to a Land League Meeting in September 1880 had indicated the effectiveness of such a method:

'When a man takes a farm from which another has been evicted you must shun him on the roadside when you meet him – you must shun him in the streets of the town . . . in the shop . . . in the fair green and in the market place, and even in the place of worship, by leaving him alone, by putting him into a moral Coventry, by isolating him from the rest of his country as if he were a leper of old – you must show him your detestation of the crime he has committed.'

The Land Act of 1881

The government in desperation prosecuted Parnell and other members of the Land League for conspiracy, but the jury disagreed and the accused were discharged. In the disturbed situation the Liberal government resorted to a Coercion Act, which gave them emergency powers, including a suspension of habeas corpus and also wide powers of arbitrary arrest. Against this unfortunate background of coercion Gladstone introduced

186

his second Land Act in 1881; it was a more ambitious measure than the first, and conceded the principles of the 'three F's': fair rents, fixity of tenure and freedom of sale. The last concession was important: it meant that a tenant could sell to another person his legal interest in his tenancy, including the value of the improvements he had made. The Act also made provision for the Land Commission to advance up to three-quarters of the purchase price of a holding to a tenant whose landlord had agreed to sell it to him. Parnell's opposition and critical behaviour during the passage of the Bill led to his imprisonment in October 1881 in Kilmainham Gaol, Dublin.

The 'Kilmainham Treaty'; the Phoenix Park Murders 1882

The Land League's answer to the arrest of Parnell and its other leaders was to proclaim a 'no rent campaign' in which the tenants stopped payment of rents. The government was getting nowhere and the deadlock

'Gladstone committing treason at Kilmainham' April 1882

187

was broken by the so-called 'Kilmainham Treaty' by which Gladstone negotiated secretly with Parnell who promised to use his influence to end the disorders in Ireland, and call off the 'no rent campaign'. In return, an Arrears Bill was to be introduced to deal with the considerable arrears of rent that had resulted from the campaign of the Land League. Parnell and his companions were released from prison early in May 1882. Prospects for better relationships were suddenly dashed a few days later when the new Chief Secretary, Lord Frederick Cavendish, and the Under-Secretary, Mr Burke were murdered in Phoenix Park by an Irish revolutionary group known as the 'Invincibles'. Other murders and outrages followed and the government fell back on a new Coercion Act which gave even greater powers than previous ones. This state of affairs continued and when Gladstone resigned office in June 1885 he knew that his well intentioned efforts had not solved the Irish problem.

The Conservatives and Ireland 1885

Lord Salisbury now formed a stop-gap ministry. The Conservatives made a bid for Irish Nationalist support at the next election by opening discussions with Parnell in which they hinted that they might, if returned to power, bring in a Home Rule bill. As a token of their goodwill they reversed the Liberal policy of ruling Ireland through Crimes and Coercion Acts and carried the Ashbourne Lane Purchase Act; this made up to £5 millions available for loans to Irish tenants for the purchase of the land they farmed. Although Gladstone had by now made his momentous decision to adopt a Home Rule policy for Ireland, he did not give Parnell satisfactory guarantees and therefore Parnell ordered the Irish residents in Great Britain to vote for the Conservatives at the elections which were held in November 1885. In spite of this the Liberals succeeded in gaining a majority of 86 over the Conservatives. Parnell was returned with 86 Irish Home Rulers and thus held the balance between the two great English political parties, but because of the Liberal majority and of the conversion of Gladstone to Home Rule, he dropped his negotiations with the Conservatives and made ready to support their opponents.

The first Home Rule Bill and its rejection 1886

Gladstone formed his third ministry in February 1886. The news of his conversion to Home Rule had leaked out and had created considerable unrest among his party. Opposition to Home Rule came from two distinct groups within the Liberal Party; the aristocratic Whigs led by the Marquess of Hartington and the Imperialist-Radicals headed by Joseph Chamberlain. The first group was against Home Rule chiefly because Anglo-Irish landlords' interests in Ireland would be adversely affected by Home Rule, and because they thought the measure was going too far;

Chamberlain and his followers objected on the grounds that the proposed measure of self government for Ireland would make it all but independent and in a short time it would be no longer part of the British Empire. But the situation in Ireland was such that half-hearted measures would have been useless and Parnell had made it amply clear what the Irish expected: 'Whatever chance the English rulers may have of drawing to themselves the affection of the Irish people lies in destroying the abominable system of legislative union between the two countries by conceding fully and freely to Ireland the right to manage her own affairs.'

In introducing the first Home Rule Bill in the House of Commons on

189

8 April 1886, Gladstone made it clear that alternative and milder measures would be useless. He pointed out that in fifty-three years since 1832 there had been only two years in which no Coercion Acts had been enforced in Ireland. The result of the frequent application of such acts was completely to discredit the law in the eyes of the Irish: 'Our ineffectual and spurious coercion is morally worn out.' Gladstone's Bill proposed to set up a single chamber Irish Legislature in Dublin which would have powers of legislation over all Irish matters except 'reserved' subjects which affected the prerogative of the Crown, e.g. the declaration of war, the making of peace, control of defence, foreign and imperial relations, customs and excise, trade and navigation, communications and coinage. Executive power was to be exercised by a lord-lieutenant assisted by a Privy Council and advised by ministers responsible to the Legislature. Ireland was to make a financial contribution equal to one-fifteenth of the total United Kingdom budget. This would have left her with about 60% of the Irish revenue for the purposes of the Dublin Parliament and government. There was to be no representation of Ireland in the Parliament at Westminster. The Bill was strenuously opposed by the Conservatives and also by the hostile groups led by Hartington and Chamberlain. On the second reading the Bill was defeated by 343 to 313, with 93 Liberals voting against it. Because of this defeat, Gladstone decided to appeal to the country and a general election was held in July 1886, in which the voters decidedly rejected Home Rule, as the return of 316 Conservatives and 78 Liberal Unionists showed. Since the Conservatives had no more than a majority of 40 over the Gladstonian Liberals and Parnell's Home Rulers combined, these Liberal Unionists held the balance between the parties.

Conservative policy towards Ireland after 1886

A Conservative ministry under Lord Salisbury now took office with a policy towards Ireland diametrically opposed to that of Gladstone, and summed up in the phrase 'twenty years of resolute government will kill Home Rule'. It fell to A. J. Balfour, the new Chief Secretary for Ireland and nephew of Lord Salisbury to enforce this policy. To the surprise of many this seemingly languid aristocratic intellectual did this in so tough and persistent a way as to earn from the Irish the title of 'Bloody Balfour'. The Conservative policy was first to enforce the law and then to follow it with constructive reforms such as land acts which would relieve Irish economic distress. The Irish reply to the Conservative programme was the 'Plan of Campaign' which involved organizing the tenants to withhold their rents if their offers were not accepted by the landlords. Evictions followed and some bloodshed but Balfour was not deterred by these events.

Parnell and the Pigott letters

Parnell's reputation had been attacked in April 1887 by the publication in *The Times* of certain letters said to have been written by him shortly after the Phoenix Park murders. In these letters Parnell was alleged to have said that although he was sorry for Lord Frederick Cavendish, he considered that the Under Secretary, Mr Burke, got no more than his deserts. Parnell, who had originally denounced these letters as an impudent forgery, asked in 1888 for an official enquiry by a Select Committee of the House of Commons. The government did not grant this but in 1889 set up a special commission of three judges to investigate the whole matter. It was found that the letters had been forged by an impoverished journalist named Richard Pigott. Under cross-examination Pigott broke down, posted a confession of his forgery to *The Times* and fled the country to Madrid, where he shot himself.

The fall of Parnell 1890

This vindication of Parnell elated his followers and discomfited his enemies. Yet within a year his career as a politician was finished due to his being cited as a co-respondent in a divorce suit. For some years he had been living with Mrs Kitty O'Shea, the wife of an Irish M.P., Captain William Henry O'Shea, who condoned the affair in return for considerable sums of money from his wife and her wealthy aunt. Parnell made no defence in the suit. The whole thing caused a sensation and, as Victorian morality was offended, Parnell's position as leader of his party was now in question. In particular, Mr Gladstone, who greatly depended on the Nonconformist vote, demanded that the Irish Home Rule party must choose between Parnell and himself. The Irish Catholic bishops also threw their weight against Parnell, being equally shocked by this breach of morality. In spite of everything Parnell determined to fight it out and in December 1890 his position was debated for fifteen days by his party in the celebrated meetings in Committee Room 15 at the House of Commons. In the end only twenty-six Irish Home Rulers supported Parnell against forty-four who opposed him. Deprived of the leadership of his party, Parnell fought more fiercely than ever, but did not live long after this unhappy event, dying in October 1891. His death left the Irish Home Rulers much divided since it had been Parnell's masterful hand which had restrained many of the feuds that always ran close to the surface in this party.

Gladstone's second Home Rule Bill 1893

The general election in July 1892, gave Mr Gladstone, now aged eighty-three, a small majority of Liberals and Irish Home Rulers combined over the Conservatives and Liberal Unionists. Accordingly he took office in

August 1892 with Home Rule for Ireland in the forefront of his programme. The second Home Rule Bill that was introduced in 1893 differed
in structure from that of 1886, e.g. a two chamber 'Parliament' consisting
of a Legislative Council of 48 members and a Legislative Assembly of
103 members was proposed, and 80 Irish M.P.s were to sit and vote in the
Westminster Parliament. The Bill passed the Commons on its third
reading by 301 to 267 but was rejected by the Lords by 419 to 41. This
was a poor reward for the idealism and long sustained efforts of Gladstone
on behalf of Ireland; after 1885 he had never wavered in his belief that
Home Rule was the only just and practical solution of the Irish problem
and events in the twentieth century confirmed this. He now wished to
dissolve Parliament and ascertain further the views of the electors in the
matter, but his party, for whom Home Rule had been a difficult and
unlucky policy, were against this step.

Conservative measures to help Ireland

The rejection of Home Rule made Salisbury's third ministry, which took
office in 1895, press on with their alternative policy of 'resolute government' in which land purchase schemes were prominent. The Conservatives had already passed the Ashbourne Land Purchase Act in 1885: it was
followed by one in 1891 sponsored by Balfour. The 1891 Act enabled
money to be advanced by the state where landlord and tenant had agreed
on a sale but it achieved little because too much isolated bargaining was
involved. Another remedy attempted by Balfour was to set up the Congested Districts Board with the aim of helping emigration from crowded
and over-populated parts of Ireland. Light railways were built in the
remoter parts of Ireland in the hope that improved communications would
help the development of economic resources. Other measures were to
give Ireland in 1898 a system of local government similar to that of the
county councils and districts in England. Agriculture was also helped by
the establishment of the Irish Agricultural Organization Society which
spread knowledge about better farming methods. The Conservative
attempt to solve the land problem culminated in the Irish Land Purchase
Act of 1903 which was the work of Wyndham, the Irish Secretary. It was
cast along much bolder lines than previous Land Purchase Acts and
sought to deal with estates as a whole and to provide government funds to
encourage the landlord to sell. When the tenants had agreed with their
landlord a price for the estate, the Land Commission would advance the
money for purchase and also add an extra 12% as a bonus for the landlord. The tenants who bought their holdings paid for them over $68\frac{1}{2}$ years,
paying $2\frac{3}{4}\%$ on the money lent and a $\frac{1}{2}\%$ annual capital repayment over
the term of years. The Act led to large sales of land and made Ireland
predominantly a country of peasant proprietors.

The Third Home Rule Bill 1912

In spite of the failure of the Bills of 1886 and 1895 the Liberal Party remained committed to the policy of Home Rule for Ireland and in 1912 several factors prompted a further attempt by the Asquith ministry. Among these were the precedent of the grant of self government to the Transvaal and Orange Free State in 1906–7; the need of the Liberals, because of their reduced majority after the general election of December 1910, to secure the support of the Irish Nationalists in the Commons; finally the Parliament Act of 1911 made possible, after some delay, the enactment of Home Rule in spite of any veto by the House of Lords. In April 1912 the third Home Rule Bill was introduced into the Commons by the Prime Minister, Mr Asquith. By this Ireland would receive full internal self government with a Parliament and government of her own but she would remain within the British Empire: it was proposed to keep forty-two Irish M.P.s to represent her in the imperial Parliament at Westminster. The Irish Parliament was to consist of two Houses: an Upper House or Senate of forty members nominated in the first instance and subsequently elected by the four provinces of Ireland, and a Lower House of Commons of 164 members. On 16 January 1913 the Bill received its third reading in the Commons by 367 to 257, but a fortnight later the Lords rejected it by 326 to 69.

Resistance of Ulster to Home Rule

The Bill produced a fierce reaction from the predominantly Protestant six counties of Ulster. Already the Ulster Unionists who wished to preserve intact the connection with Great Britain and rule by the British Crown had anticipated the passing of this Home Rule Bill by establishing their own 'provisional government' and had organised an Ulster Volunteer force to defend this if necessary. The declaration of Lord Randolph

Ulster Volunteers at Portadown September 1912

Churchill in 1886 that 'Ulster will fight and Ulster will be right' now assumed an ominous significance. In September 1912 the Ulster Unionists under the leadership of Sir Edward Carson proclaimed a solemn covenant which was signed by hundreds of thousands of Ulstermen who pledged themselves never to recognize the authority of any Home Rule Parliament that might be set up at Dublin. The Liberal government made some concession to this opposition by offering to let Ulster contract out of Home Rule for a period of six years but this was unacceptable and in 1914 the Ulster Unionists began to arm their volunteer defence force by smuggling in arms from Germany. The Conservative opposition under Mr Bonar Law somewhat unscrupulously encouraged the Ulster Unionists in their resistance to the Liberal government. The Home Rule Bill would, by operation of the Parliament Act, become law in 1914, and in this year the tension mounted. In the spring the so-called 'Mutiny at the Curragh', showed that disaffection existed in the officer corps of the British army stationed in Ireland. They were faced with the probability of having to enforce the Home Rule Act in the disaffected province of Ulster. Many of these officers were of Protestant Anglo-Irish descent and the prospect was so distasteful to them that they were ready to resign their commissions rather than fight against the Ulster volunteers. The government had to compromise in this awkward situation by allowing those officers whose homes were actually in Ulster to 'disappear' temporarily from Ireland without prejudice to their subsequent service careers.

A conference of the leaders of all political parties summoned by King George V to discuss the deadlock that had arisen did not achieve anything, but the declaration of war in August 1914 led to an all-party agreement that the operation of the Home Rule Act for Ireland would be postponed until after the war.

19. The Conservative ascendancy and decline 1886–1906

Reasons for Conservative strength

Between 1886 and 1906 Conservative government prevailed, interrupted only by the Gladstone–Rosebery ministries of 1892–5. The decline in the fortunes of Liberalism was mainly due to the attempt of Gladstone to give Ireland Home Rule. The Liberal Party was seriously weakened by the breakaway of the Liberal Unionists led by Chamberlain; for the time being these Unionists remained an independent political group but after 1895 they were aligned with the Conservative Party. Home Rule was also unacceptable to the country at large for in the general elections of July 1886 a substantial majority opposed to it was returned, consisting of 316 Conservatives and 78 Liberal Unionists; on the other side there were 191 Gladstonian Liberals and 85 Irish Nationalists under Parnell.

Lord Salisbury's second ministry 1886–92

Lord Salisbury, who led the Conservative Party until shortly before his death in 1902, was a descendant of William Cecil, the trusted minister of Queen Elizabeth I. Salisbury had shown his ability in foreign affairs and

The Lobby of the House of Commons 1886. The five men in the centre are (from left to right): Joseph Chamberlain, C. S. Parnell, W. E. Gladstone, Lord Randolph Churchill and Lord Hartington

such success as had been won by Disraeli at the Congress of Berlin in 1878 was largely due to him. Foreign affairs indeed were his real interest and the office of prime minister he regarded as a duty to be undertaken rather than something eagerly to be sought after. Personally he was a rather detached, austere, Christian aristocrat whose view of society was a static one; he thought that the working classes, while entitled to fair treatment from those above them, should know their station in life and keep it, and not be unsettled by talk of democracy and equality. In another direction he had little in common with the brash and wealthy industrialists and manufacturers who were crowding into the Conservative Party at this time. Although Salisbury distrusted change the example of Disraeli's social reforms encouraged the enactment of similar measures in the period between 1886 and 1902.

Salisbury had a majority of forty over the Gladstonian Liberals and Irish Nationalists combined, but his position in the last resort depended on the votes of seventy-eight Liberal Unionists who followed Lord Hartington and Chamberlain. Salisbury had hoped that Hartington would form a ministry and offered to serve under him with the Conservatives: on his refusal Salisbury took office with an exclusively Conservative Cabinet. His ministry had a radical wing, the so-called 'Fourth Party', led by Lord Randolph Churchill, which was in favour of social reform in the tradition of Disraeli. As chancellor of the Exchequer and leader of the House of Commons Randolph Churchill seemed on the threshold of a brilliant political career but this was cut short by his ill-considered resignation in December 1886, made because he could not get the Prime Minister to enforce his demands for economy by reduction of the estimates for the Admiralty and War Office. To his surprise this resignation was accepted and he passed from the political scene before his ability could be fully tested. Salisbury now took the opportunity to improve his relationship with the Liberal Unionists by making one of them, Goschen, the new Chancellor of the Exchequer.

Reform of English local government structure 1888 and 1894

After the extension of the vote to all male householders in the countryside in 1884 it was logical that local government there should be made more representative. For centuries the justices of the peace sitting in Quarter Sessions had supervized local government activities in the country areas of England and Wales. An extensive reorganization was made by the County Councils Act of 1888 which set up sixty-two administrative counties and sixty county boroughs with areas taken out of the county territory. In the county or county borough there were to be councils consisting of councillors elected for three years by the ratepayers, and aldermen who were not to exceed in number one-third of the elected councillors. To these new authorities were transferred the old administrative functions of the justices in Quarter Sessions, such as maintenance of roads, bridges and asylums; the control of the police forces was entrusted in the counties to a joint committee of justices and county councillors and in the county boroughs to a Watch Committee. London was dealt with by a separate Act which made the area hitherto under the Metropolitan Board of Works into an administrative county in which there were two levels of authority exercised respectively by the London County Council and the Metropolitan Boroughs; the City of London because of its ancient rights was excluded from this reorganization. The reform of local government structure was completed by the Liberal government in 1894 by the District and Parish Councils Act which set up Urban and Rural District Councils within the county areas; below this second level Parish Councils were established in every parish where there were more than three hundred people. The chief duties given to the new Urban and Rural District Councils were those concerned with public health, sanitation and highways. The 1894 Act also provided that women, whether married or single, and if qualified to vote as ratepayers, could be elected as members of these District and Parish Councils.

Imperialism and its influence

Imperialism has varied interpretations but the British example from its beginnings in the seventeenth century involved the extension of the sovereignty and rule of the Crown over colonies acquired by settlement, conquest and cession and over protectorates created by treaty agreements with their native rulers. Between 1880 and 1914 British imperialism, sustained by political, economic and emotional factors which affected all levels of British society, moved towards its highest point of development.

The extent and outward greatness of the British Empire found varied expression: at the highest official level in the royal title: 'Victoria by the grace of God ... Queen of Great Britain and Ireland, ... Empress of India and of all the dominions beyond the sea', while the general public, after reassuring contemplation of the large areas of the earth's surface painted red in the atlas, knew it as 'the empire on which the sun never sets'. General optimism prevailed over its future; it was thought that the extension of self government since the Durham Report of 1839, together with the ties of a common descent, language and culture, would bring about a lasting association of the white-settled colonies such as Canada, Australia, New Zealand with Great Britain under the common sovereignty of the Crown. In the case of the Asian and African peoples of the Crown colonies, from British India downwards, their future was seen as one of long dependence on British rule; few people in 1897, the year of the Diamond Jubilee, foresaw the move to self government and independence which

197

'On the Road to Mandalay.' Somerset Light Infantry crossing the Twsa River in the Burma campaign of 1885–6

these Crown colonies made in the second half of the twentieth century.

Economically the empire was important to Great Britain which as an industrial country following a free trade policy was constantly looking for new markets overseas. The Lancashire cotton industry found outlets for its products in British India, Africa and the East; the self-governing colonies bought from Britain capital equipment for railways and port installations, besides a wide range of consumer goods. The empire was also a vast area of investment for British capital for the development of local resources, whether mining for diamonds, gold and copper, or the growing of tropical produce such as sugar, tea, coffee and rubber. Unemployment in Britain was relieved by emigration to the new lands of Australia, New Zealand, Canada and South Africa.

Emotionally imperialism affected the whole range of British society. Its upper class provided the governors, judges, and district commissioners for this empire; they assumed this role quite naturally as something appropriate to their birth and education, and usually exercised their power with a sense of duty towards those they ruled under the 'Pax Britannica'. The middle classes were the executives of the mining, planting, trading and banking activities of this empire; they also contributed to the missionary factor, important in the spread of British ideas through education given in the mission schools. For the working classes, newly literate through the provision of primary education, imperialism was frankly emotional; the pageant of empire was brought before them by the cheap newspapers and illustrated journals and by the ballads of the music hall. (For the more sophisticated readers of the middle classes there were the tales of Rudyard Kipling, the great journalist of empire.) From imperialism the British middle and lower classes received an agreeable sense of power somewhat resembling that which Palmerston had given them forty years before when he laid down the law to troublesome foreigners. Upon their uncritical senses was impressed a picture of Britain ruling, as it seemed, half the world, highlighted by colourful, picturesque scenes: India and its bejewelled Rajahs; the 'Soldiers of the Queen' on the 'Road to Mandalay' or watching the wild hillsmen of the North-West Frontier; the 'Fuzzy-wuzzies' of the Mahdi; the weary slog across the veldt in pursuit of the elusive Boers ('Good old de Wet – he's got away again').

Queen Victoria's Jubilees of 1887 and 1897

In June 1887, after fifty years of rule, Queen Victoria celebrated her Golden Jubilee. The Queen attended a thanksgiving service in Westminster Abbey together with rulers from many countries and the representatives of the self-governing colonies of the British Empire. Impressive reviews of the armed forces were held but more significant was the emphasis given by the celebrations to the importance of the empire. The

Queen Victoria at the time of her Golden Jubilee 1887

199

presence of the prime ministers of the self-governing colonies led to the first Colonial Conference which early in the twentieth century became the Imperial Conference. The discussions in 1887 were mainly concerned with imperial defence which at this time was chiefly based on sea power; the Australian colonies and New Zealand agreed to pay part of the cost of keeping a strong squadron in the Pacific.

Ten years later the Diamond Jubilee was celebrated with acclamation, if less elaborately, on account of the Queen's age and declining strength. Again the emphasis was imperial with the prime ministers of the self-governing colonies and contingents of troops from all over the empire taking part in the long procession from Buckingham Palace to St Paul's

Cathedral. Another Colonial Conference was held, presided over by Joseph Chamberlain, the Colonial Secretary. His plan for a political federation of Great Britain and the self-governing colonies received little support, but some progress was made towards preferential customs duties for British exports entering colonial markets, although Britain's free trade policy prevented any corresponding gesture in return.

Social reform

In the field of social reform the Conservative ministries made a cautious advance. The system of 'payment by results' which decided the amount of grant earned by primary schools after examination by school inspectors was abolished in 1890; this method had long been criticized because it produced unintelligent memorization of disconnected facts followed by a parrot-like repetition before the inspector. In 1891 the fees paid by parents for primary education in board schools were abolished. Technical education was helped by an Act of 1889 which authorized county councils and borough councils to provide such instruction. In 1890 the Housing of the Working Classes Act extended the powers of local authorities to clear insanitary areas and to carry out rehousing schemes. They were also given powers to acquire land compulsorily, to build houses for letting to working class people, and to close, repair, or demolish insanitary houses. In the same year a Factory Act for the first time enforced sanitary conditions inside factories and also regulated dangerous and unhealthy trades. A Shop Hours Act of 1892 prohibited the employment of young persons under 18 years, for more than seventy-four hours a week including meal times. In 1887 and 1889 Acts were passed for the provision of allotments

201

and smallholdings; it was hoped that this would slow down the movement of population from the countryside to the towns, but the local authorities concerned were slow to use their powers and the scheme had little success.

All these reforms, while commendable, were remote from the urgent problems of poverty and unemployment which increasingly beset British society at the end of the nineteenth century and which are described in chapter 20.

Gladstone's fourth ministry 1892–4

At the general election in July 1892 the Liberals and Irish Nationalists were returned with a combined majority of 40 over the Conservatives and Liberal Unionists. This enabled Mr Gladstone, now aged 83, to take office for the fourth and last time in the hope of settling the Irish question by the passage of a Home Rule Bill. He had some able men in his Cabinet, notably Harcourt, Chancellor of the Exchequer, Lord Rosebery, Foreign Secretary and as Home Secretary, H. H. Asquith. Besides Home Rule the Liberals were committed to the radical reforms of the 'Newcastle programme'; this included the disestablishment of the Church in Wales, payment of members of Parliament, reform of the House of Lords, the establishment of elected councils in parishes and the granting of a local veto on the sale of alcoholic liquor. The programme aroused intense opposition from the House of Lords and this, coupled with the fact that the government was dependent on the Irish votes in the Commons, made progress difficult. The passage of the second Home Rule Bill through the Commons and its rejection by the House of Lords has been described in chapter 18. Following this defeat Gladstone wished to dissolve Parliament but the majority of his party were against him; failure over Home Rule and his strong objection to the expenditure of money on the navy led to his final resignation and retirement from politics in March 1894. In May 1898 he died; there was widespread national mourning for one who had been the greatest parliamentarian, orator, and moral force in the politics of the Victorian era.

Lord Rosebery succeeds Gladstone 1894

Lord Rosebery, at the Queen's request, formed a government after Gladstone's retirement. As a Whig aristocrat and an owner of racehorses he was hardly acceptable to the 'Nonconformist conscience' of the Liberal Party which would have preferred Sir William Harcourt but he, because of his difficult and overbearing personality was impossible as a prime minister. A convinced imperialist, Rosebery was not at all happy with the commitment of the Liberals to Home Rule for Ireland, and altogether his ministry had a somewhat chequered existence. The most important measure of Rosebery's ministry was in the budget of 1894. Harcourt, as chancellor of the Exchequer, introduced a novelty in the shape of death duties in order to pay for increased expenditure on the navy. Basically this was that the property of a deceased person, whether in land or personal property, should be taxed according to the total value passing at his or her death; a graduated scale of duty was levied according to the value of the estate. This financial weapon introduced by Harcourt has remained ever since; Harcourt estimated that he would raise £14 millions by it, but under successive chancellors of the Exchequer the revenue from it has been multiplied many times over; in 1968–9 it produced £382 millions.

Other measures proposed by the Liberals were less successful. An Employers' Liability Bill which would have made employers liable for accidents due to negligence of themselves or their employees, was altered by the House of Lords who inserted a 'contracting out' clause which would have enabled a workman to agree with his employer that liability should not apply in his case; rather than accept this amendment the government abandoned the Bill. A Bill to disestablish the Church in Wales made such slow progress that it had not reached the committee stage by the time the Liberal ministry fell in 1895. Another measure, a Local Veto Bill, introduced by Harcourt, aroused even more opposition. This proposed to allow local areas to decide whether they would permit or prohibit the sale of alcoholic liquors in their particular localities. In June 1895 after its defeat on a sudden 'snap' vote, the government resigned. Lord Salisbury then formed his third ministry and won the general election in July; together the Conservatives and Liberal Unionists had a majority of 152 over their Liberal and Irish Nationalist opponents.

Salisbury's third ministry 1895–1902

Salisbury's Cabinet was a talented one; Salisbury himself, A. J. Balfour, Lansdowne, Hicks Beach and Joseph Chamberlain were all men of ability. It was Chamberlain whose personality stood out more than any other in this ministry, almost to the extent of becoming a 'shadow' prime minister, especially in negotiations with Germany over the possibility of an Anglo-German alliance. At the Colonial Office Chamberlain's strong leadership gratified British popular imperialism, now reaching its peak: for the Crown colonies he started a programme of financial aid, development of resources and better administration, while with the self-governing colonies he urged joint measures to promote imperial federation, imperial trade preferences and imperial defence. In fact Salisbury's third ministry was continuously dominated by imperial affairs from the Jameson Raid at the end of 1895, followed by Anglo-French tension in tropical Africa (Niger Valley, 1896–7 and the Fashoda crisis in 1898 after the Anglo-Egyptian reconquest of the Sudan), with the last three years to 1902 occupied by the South African war. Consequently social reform was

203

crowded out, although the first reasonably effective Workmen's Compensation Act was passed in 1897; this made it less difficult than hitherto for workmen (in a rather limited range of trades) to get compensation for injuries accidentally inflicted on them while at work. Under pressure from Chamberlain a parliamentary committee investigated the possibility of old age pensions and in 1899 reported in favour of them, but the cost of the South African war postponed their introduction.

The Jameson Raid 1895

The discovery of a rich goldfield in the Transvaal in the 1880s and its development by foreign companies led to serious tension between Britain and the Transvaal Boers. A large mining community of foreigners known to the Boers as 'Uitlanders', was attracted to the Rand area around Johannesburg; President Kruger and his Transvaal government not only taxed the mining companies heavily, levied high customs duties on imported mining materials and charged them dear for their dynamite, but also denied the Uitlanders the right to vote. With good reason Kruger feared for the independence of his country which because of its gold was threatened by the imperialist ambitions of Cecil Rhodes and his associates; they had already established the British South Africa Company in control of Rhodesia in the north and they regarded the Boer republics as tiresome obstructions to the further consolidation of British power in Southern Africa. Hence the Jameson Raid of 1895, which was an illegal invasion of the Transvaal by a force of British South Africa Company police under Dr Jameson, an official of the company and a friend of Rhodes; their plan was to link up with the Uitlanders of Johannesburg who were to rise in armed revolt. Disagreement among the Uitlanders at Johannesburg postponed the rising there, but notwithstanding, Jameson on 29 December 1895 invaded the Transvaal from the west; five days later his force surrendered to the Boer commandos at Doornkop, forty miles from Johannesburg. The raid discredited Rhodes who was obliged to resign his premiership of the Cape Province; it also greatly embarrassed the British government, which repudiated the whole business and put Jameson and his officers on trial for levying war against a friendly state. But foreign opinion assumed that the raid had official support; Kaiser William II implied this in his telegram to President Kruger congratulating him on maintaining 'the independence of your country against attacks from without'. A parliamentary inquiry of 1897 into the raid severely criticized Rhodes for his part but showed a certain reluctance to probe to the full the extent of Chamberlain's involvement in the matter.

Outbreak of the South African War 1899

The raid left the Transvaal Boers more suspicious than ever of British policy and this distrust spread to the Boers of the adjoining Orange Free State. The problem of the Uitlanders remained and the British government tried to negotiate better conditions for them through its High Commissioner in South Africa, Sir Alfred Milner. These attempts failed because of the relentless demands of Milner and the obstinacy of Kruger although the latter in mid-1899 was willing to concede votes for the Uitlanders providing that Great Britain would give up her 'suzerainty' over the Transvaal which she still claimed by the Conventions of Pretoria of 1881 and 1884. Britain rejected this demand and by the end of September 1899 both sides were preparing for war. Strengthened by the pledge of military support from the neighbouring republic of the Orange Free State Kruger on 9 October 1899 sent an ultimatum demanding that the British government stop sending reinforcements to South Africa. A counter-ultimatum from Britain followed immediately and war started on 12 October 1899.

Boer successes and British recovery 1899–1900

The Boers entered the war with high hopes of repeating the success they had won in 1881 at Majuba Hill; ever since then they had despised the military abilities of the British and the events of the first three months of this second war confirmed them in this attitude. Their mobility, skill in use of ground and cover and accurate markmanship enabled them to inflict a number of defeats on the British. The main Boer effort was the invasion of Natal with the aim of capturing the port of Durban and by the end of October they had reached the line of the River Tugela and besieged a large British force in Ladysmith. Kimberley and Mafeking on the western frontier of the Transvaal were also besieged by the Boers; these sieges immobilized large numbers of Boer troops and this mistaken strategy may have lost the Boers the war. Meanwhile they were helped by the blunders of their opponents; a field force of 30,000 men had reached South Africa under Sir Redvers Buller who instead of keeping it intact broke it up into three smaller forces and dispersed them over widely separated fronts. This gave the Boers their chance and in the 'Black Week' of 9–15 December 1899 the three British forces were defeated at Stormberg, Magersfontein and Colenso respectively with considerable losses of men and guns.

To retrieve this humiliating situation Lord Roberts was sent out as commander-in-chief with large reinforcements. The plan of Roberts was to carry the war directly with all his forces into the enemy 'heartlands' of the Orange Free State and Transvaal. His drive from the Cape Province on Bloemfontein and Pretoria put the Boers on the defensive; they withdrew from Natal and the Northern Cape to meet the thrust and although still winning local successes could not prevent the capture of Bloemfontein 205

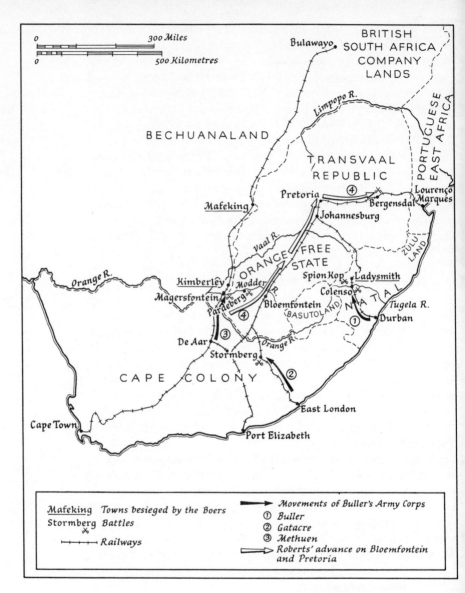

Map 10 The South African War 1899–1902

in March and Pretoria in June (1900). The remnants of the Transvaal Boer field army carried out a fighting retreat eastwards towards Delagoa Bay but in August fought their last field battle at Bergendal. President Kruger went into exile; the two Boer republics were annexed to the British Crown.

Guerilla warfare 1901–2

In spite of this the war dragged on; Boer resistance continued throughout 1901–2 with a skilful guerilla warfare carried out by determined 'bitter enders'– those Boers who were ready to fight to the last for their independence. Under leaders such as de Wet, de la Rey, Botha, and Smuts the Boer commandos struck at the British lines of communication in the Transvaal and Orange Free State and even raided far into Cape Province. Counter action by the British took the form of restricting commando movements by hundreds of miles of barbed wire strung along the railways and covered at strategic points by defended blockhouses. Complementary to this was a 'scorched earth' policy to deny the commandos food and shelter by burning the Boer farms and removing their inhabitants to internment camps. Conditions of sanitation and hygiene in these camps were bad leading to a death roll of 20,000 from typhoid and pneumonia; the exposure of the facts led to an outcry from the Liberals many of whom were opposed to the war and whose leader Campbell-Bannerman denounced the government's 'methods of barbarism'. In face of this the government was obliged to transfer the camps from military to civilian control and to improve conditions. By early 1902 the Boer commandos were finding it difficult to continue against the systematic drives of the British and peace negotiations were opened leading to the Peace of Vereeniging (May 1902). The Boers surrendered their arms and ammunition, accepted the sovereignty of the British Crown over them, but with the promise of self government in the future; £3 millions was given by the British government to repair and restock the Boer farms.

The war in perspective

So ended a war in which it had been necessary to use over 400,000 British troops (including colonial contingents) against about 80,000 Boers and at a cost of £250 millions. Once again disease had proved more deadly than the enemy's bullets; just under 6,000 British were killed but some 16,000 died from disease, chiefly typhoid fever. Like the Crimean War this war also revealed deficiencies in leadership, in the planning of operations, in the training and equipment of the troops, and their supporting services: the image of the exuberant imperialism of the late nineteenth century was tarnished by this expensive and rather inglorious war.

The death of Queen Victoria

Before peace was finally assured Queen Victoria died on 22 January 1901 after a reign of over sixty-three years. The war had clouded her last years

Four generations of the Royal Family. A photo taken in 1894 showing Queen Victoria holding her great-grandson (later Duke of Windsor); standing are her son (later Edward VII) and her grandson (later George V)

but in spite of failing health she had given the nation courageous leadership especially during the dark days of the early part of the war. Her long reign had raised the monarchy in public esteem; the Queen's sense of duty and her standards of morality and propriety coincided closely with those of the Victorian middle classes; her obstinacy and prejudice in dealing with ministers she did not like, such as Gladstone, remained unknown in detail until after her death when the relevant private papers and correspondence were published. Her death marked the end of an age which, although much criticized in our own time, was one of stability and outstanding achievement.

King Edward VII 1901–10

Queen Victoria was succeeded by her eldest son Albert Edward who at the time of his accession was in his sixtieth year. Because of his mother's jealousy and disapproval of his mode of life he had been excluded from matters of state at the highest level until nearly the end of her reign; nor had he been allowed to undertake royal political duties of major importance. Fortunately to counterbalance these disadvantages he had a wide knowledge of the world derived from foreign travel; his ability to speak French and German fluently gave him close personal knowledge of the rulers and statesmen of Europe and their policies. His modest intellectual abilities were compensated by his ease of manner with people and by that prerequisite of successful monarchy, a retentive memory. His sense of pageantry and occasion enabled him to revive very effectively the ceremonial of monarchy which had been neglected by his mother during the long years of her widowhood. His revival of court life which gave it gaiety and brilliance, his patronage of horseracing and field sports and his liking for good food were all acceptable to the luxurious and sophisticated Edwardian 'high society' with its retinues of servants and extravagant expenditure made possible by great wealth as yet untouched by the high taxation that came after 1914.

Balfour becomes prime minister 1902

The coronation of the new king was set for 26 June 1902 but his illness led to its postponement to 9 August. Lord Salisbury remained prime minister until the King's recovery was assured and then resigned; the new prime minister was his nephew, Arthur James Balfour. The ministry he formed with its preponderance of peers and squires was representative of Tory political society but it had few men of ability except Balfour himself, Lord Lansdowne and Joseph Chamberlain. Balfour, although a somewhat casual performer as leader of the House of Commons, was a man of high intelligence; in particular he had seen more clearly than other politicians the absolute need for this country to advance its educational

Arthur James Balfour, Prime Minister 1902–5

209

system and to strengthen its defences. Only if both these were improved could Great Britain face the future and live in a world threatened by the ambitions of Germany's world policy.

The Education Act 1902

The problem of state-supported education in England was complicated because religion entered very much into its background and politicians were reluctant to grasp this particular nettle. The Act of 1870 and subsequent Acts had set up a system of primary education which on the whole had worked efficiently but underlying it all there was the problem of the voluntary schools of the religious denominations partly maintained with the aid of government grants. Secondary education was in a less satisfactory state. Some provision of this had been made by the County Boroughs and County Councils under the Technical Instruction Act of 1889 and by a few School Boards, including the London School Board. In 1900 the activities of the School Boards in the realm of secondary education were shown to be illegal by the Cockerton Judgement: Mr Cockerton, an auditor of the Local Government Board had surcharged the London School Board for some of its expenditure on secondary education on the grounds that such expenditure was beyond their lawful powers; legal action followed and the auditor's action was upheld by the Court of Appeal. It was against this background that Balfour's Education Bill was introduced to clear up the whole situation; the Bill itself was largely the work of a senior official at the Board of Education, R. L. Morant. The Act resulting abolished the School Boards and placed primary, technical, and secondary education under the control of the local authorities, e.g. County Councils, County Borough Councils, or Urban District Councils where the population was over 20,000.

The most controversial part of the Act related to the voluntary schools of the various religious denominations; the managers of these were to provide the buildings and were to retain control of the appointment and dismissal of their teachers but otherwise their expenses were to be provided out of money from local rates. Strong opposition arose from the Nonconformists who objected to such maintenance of the schools of the Church of England which provided the great majority of the voluntary schools. To the Nonconformists the Act unfairly perpetuated the monopoly in education that had been held for so long by the Church of England; a number of Nonconformist 'passive resisters' served prison sentences for non-payment of their rates. Nevertheless Balfour's Education Act was a landmark in English education; it tidied up the whole structure and made a considerable advance possible, especially as far as secondary and technical education were concerned. An 'education ladder' resulted which made it possible for the abler children to win scholarships from their primary schools to the secondary grammar schools that the Local Authorities began to provide after the Act, or to the older endowed grammar schools which had been revived in the last quarter of the nineteenth century.

The reorganization of Britain's armed forces

The mounting tension due to the crises in Europe between the great powers made it essential for Great Britain to coordinate her system of defences: an indispensable instrument for this was the Committee of Imperial Defence. This had existed on paper before Balfour became prime minister but it was his especial contribution to shape it and make it an effective body. The Committee included the prime minister as chairman and the ministers responsible for Defence; it also had representatives of the Services and of the overseas Dominions. Attempts were also made during this ministry to carry out army reform which had been shown to be very necessary by some of the mishaps of the South African War of 1899–1902. Not much was achieved in this respect except the abolition of the office of commander-in-chief, and its replacement by the Army Council, a joint body of service and political chiefs at the highest level, which was to direct and control army organization and activities. More progress was made with naval defence chiefly due to the appointment in 1904 of Sir John Fisher as first sea lord at the Admiralty. In cooperation with Lord Cawdor, Fisher promoted the building of a new type of heavily-armed warship, the Dreadnought; to meet the threat from the new German high seas fleet he concentrated the Royal Navy in home waters rather than let it be dispersed all over the world. The first Dreadnought was launched in 1906; it upset German naval preparations because if they built warships of a comparable size they would have to widen the Kiel Canal (which was used by the German fleet in passing from the Baltic to the North Sea). The Cawdor–Fisher programme aimed at giving Britain a dozen Dreadnoughts before Germany could have replied with one; this lead was not realized because of the change of Government in 1906 when the Liberal ministry stopped this building programme until 1908 when the international situation made its continuation essential.

Joseph Chamberlain and tariff reform

In 1903 Joseph Chamberlain, then colonial secretary, raised an issue of fundamental importance and which split Balfour's government and the Conservative Party. This was tariff reform which meant placing protective duties on foreign imports and so challenging the free trade policy which Great Britain had followed for over fifty years. As the leading imperialist of the day it was natural for Chamberlain to make the spearhead of his attack imperial preference which would give both Great

211

Britain and her self-governing colonies mutual advantages in their trade relationships. During the South African War as an emergency measure there had been imposed a registration duty of 1s. a quarter on imported wheat. Chamberlain hoped that it would be possible to remit this duty on empire-grown wheat while retaining it for foreign wheat; he was offended when the Chancellor of the Exchequer in the budget in April 1903 abolished the duty altogether. In a speech in May at Birmingham which fell on the very receptive ears of the local manufacturers, Chamberlain proclaimed his abandonment of free trade and declared for imperial preference and for the imposition, if necessary, of duties on imports from foreign countries in retaliation for their protective duties on British exports. Within the rank and file of the Conservative Party there was considerable support for Chamberlain's views but they met strong opposition within the Cabinet where there were a number of influential free traders. Balfour himself, recognizing the serious issue that had arisen, tended to take a middle point of view. In September 1903 he declared that it would be expedient for the government to have power to impose retaliatory duties but that he himself was against taxation of food. Following the dismissal by Balfour in September 1903 of Ritchie, the free trade Chancellor of the Exchequer, a number of free trade ministers resigned: Chamberlain also resigned because he wanted freedom to preach his gospel of tariff reform. Balfour reconstructed his Cabinet as best he could but the issue that Chamberlain had raised was a present for the Liberal Party who were now provided with the excellent election battle cry of 'Protection will mean dear food.' In addition the Liberal Party had the further advantage that they were fighting a deeply divided Conservative Party; the boot of 1886 was now on the other foot.

Chamberlain founded the Tariff Reform League which organized meetings and published facts and figures in support of his cause. To the tariff reformers the basic facts were simple: formerly free trade had suited Great Britain's economy but now changed conditions made it positively harmful; industrial development in Europe and the United States of America had produced rival competitors in the world's markets who also by high protective tariffs virtually closed their own markets to imports from Great Britain. The confident predictions of ardent free traders such as Cobden, who thought that the British example of free trade would be imitated all over the world had not been fulfilled. Besides manufactures, agriculture suffered as well; the cheap grain of the North American prairies and meat from the Argentine had depressed British agriculture. There was also the alarming fact that these foreign industries with the secure home market given them by protective tariffs could dump their surplus produce in Great Britain almost regardless of the price they received for it. Chamberlain, with his ambition to make the British Empire a great world force on a unified basis, saw clearly that the first step was to bring about commercial unity within that empire and only the abandonment of free trade and the adoption of imperial preference would do this. To the arguments of his free trade opponents that his proposals would bring dear food and would mean the difference between 'the big loaf and the little loaf', Chamberlain replied that increases in food prices would be relatively small and that 'tariff reform means work for all'.

The Conservative decline and Balfour's resignation, December 1905

In January 1905 Balfour produced a formula which he hoped would heal the split in his party; this accepted the principle of imposing protective duties for the purposes of retaliation and negotiation, but it did not satisfy Chamberlain and the tariff reformers. The superficial unity which resulted was not enough to save Balfour's ministry whose measures for some time had incurred unpopularity among different sections of the public. The passive resisters against the Education Act of 1902 were biding their time, while the Licensing Act of 1904 had angered the temperance movement because it allowed compensation to the owners of public houses when they were closed on the grounds of redundancy, and although the money for this was provided from a fund raised by the liquor trade itself such compensation offended the temperance reformers who were numerous in the Liberal Party. An unwise measure of Balfour's government which allowed the importation of Chinese coolies into South Africa to work in the gold mines of the Rand, raised a storm of indignation. The degrading conditions of work and life for these Chinese labourers gave rise to the term 'Chinese slavery' and turned much moderate British opinion against the government. While the importation of coolie labour from India and China had been done in other parts of the British Empire, especially the West Indies, the policy itself was discredited and it was foolish to have revived it at this juncture. British working-class opinion which was solid against the government on the subject of 'Chinese slavery' was also influenced by the decision over the Taff Vale case. As the final court of appeal the House of Lords decided in 1901 that the Amalgamated Society of Railway Servants which had intervened in the dispute between the Taff Vale railway and its employees was liable for damages to the railway company for the loss caused by the strike it had organized. To their consternation British trade unions found that they were not protected by the legislation of the 1870s and their funds were therefore liable for damages in the case of any strikes they organized in furtherance of an industrial dispute.

The end of Balfour's ministry came through the forcing tactics of Chamberlain who now controlled the Conservative Party organization.

213

H

In November 1905 he demanded that the party should fight the next election on the issue of tariff reform. Under this pressure from Chamberlain and mistakenly believing that his Liberal opponents were too divided to form a ministry with any prospect of success, Balfour resigned on 4 December. The Liberal leader Campbell-Bannerman accepted the challenge and took office the next day; in the general election which followed in January 1906 the Conservative-Unionist party were routed.

20. Social problems and labour movements 1880–1900

Social justice lacking in Victorian society

The Golden Jubilee celebrations of 1887 and 1897 gave an outwardly impressive picture of Great Britain's national greatness and imperial power, but behind this lay a welter of social problems affecting a substantial number of the population living in conditions of squalor, poverty and frequent unemployment. This widespread poverty was in glaring contrast with the overall increase in the nation's wealth, most of which was possessed by a small minority of the population. The contrast between poverty and riches led social reformers and political thinkers to question the organization of a society which allowed this state of affairs. The twenty years from 1880 to 1900 are an essential part of the early history of the welfare state of the twentieth century because during these years the detailed and systematic work of social investigators and reformers

A London slum street: Dudley Street, Seven Dials, in the 1870s (by Gustave Doré)

215

made clear the very wide extent of poverty; only a programme of social justice backed by the full power of the state could grapple with so great a problem. Such a programme involved a complete break with *laissez-faire* which thought that the state should limit its activities to the maintenance of law and order, the protection of property and defence against external enemies; it should interfere as little as possible with the social and economic life of society which were matters best decided by the individuals who made up this society. Strongly as the Victorians had believed in *laissez-faire* by 1880 it had already been breached, e.g. the Factory Acts had restricted the right of the employer to work women and children for as long as he pleased; the Disraeli reforms of 1874–80 had used the powers of the state to promote social welfare collectively, e.g. Health and Housing Acts. By the early years of the twentieth century the pressing need for measures to relieve poverty, sickness and unemployment among the under-privileged had been accepted by public opinion and this brought the progressive abandonment of *laissez-faire*.

Homeless people applying for admission to a night refuge shelter (by Gustave Doré, from Blanchard Jerrold's London *1872)*

Economic factors influencing poverty

By the last quarter of the nineteenth century Great Britain had a large population for the most part living in urban industrialized areas, and dependent for their livelihood on an industrial system which manufactured for the home or overseas market. The workers, both skilled and unskilled, were at the mercy of the alternating slump and boom that affected the Victorian economy. In the last quarter of the nineteenth century increasing competition in the world market from rising industrial powers such as Germany and the U.S.A. brought economic depression far sharper than it had ever been in the period of economic expansion between 1850 and 1870. The position was worsened by the policy of free trade which left the British market wide open to competition from foreign manufactures and products. Some unemployment figures taken from the 1880s illustrate the extent of this depression; figures supplied by the trade unions showed that in 1883 about 3% of their members were unemployed; by 1884 it had risen to 8% and by 1886 to 10%. The position in the heavy industries was even worse with from 13% to 22% of the craftsmen unemployed during the worst years of the slump. For the unskilled labourer the position was correspondingly worse. A Scottish economist, John Rae, writing in 1884, and basing his comments on official figures, said:

'In the wealthiest nation in the world, almost every twentieth inhabitant is a pauper; according to poor law reports, one fifth of the community is insufficiently clad; according to medical reports to the Privy Council the agricultural labourers and large classes of working people in towns are too poorly fed to save them from what are known as starvation diseases; the great proportion of our population lead a life of monotonous and incessant toil, with no prospects in old age but penury and parochial support; one third, if not indeed one half, of the families of the country are huddled, six in a room, in a way quite incompatible with the elementary claims of decency, health or morality.'

Recognition of the problem of poverty

Subsequent investigations by Royal Commissions and by private persons amply confirmed the depressing picture given by Rae. When these facts relating to unemployment, poverty, ill health, sweated labour, and poor housing became known during the last twenty years of the nineteenth century public conscience was stirred. In the past people had thought not so much of the problem of poverty as of 'the poor', who were regarded as inevitable in any society, and who could be adequately dealt with by the Poor Law organization and by the efforts of private charity. Worse than that, there was the belief that 'the poor' were poor because of their own faults, their laziness, their thriftlessness and drunkenness. A change of

217

view came when people realized that poverty was not always due to the personal failings of an individual but more often was the result of the stresses, strains and failings of society. Contrary to the belief of *laissez-faire* these matters were not self-regulating and therefore the state must intervene to redress the balance. The readiness of politicians to do this was somewhat increased because by the Reform Act of 1884 the poor, unless in receipt of poor relief, had votes which could help the parties to obtain power. There was also the threat of Socialism which had recently shown itself in Europe: its plan to remodel society alarmed the ruling classes everywhere and in Britain this was a further reason for effective measures to alleviate poverty.

Charles Booth and his survey of poverty in London

In support of this change of opinion, detailed evidence began to pile up on a greater scale than ever before. There were several important Royal Commissions, which took evidence from hundreds of witnesses and issued voluminous reports: that of 1885 dealt with the housing of working classes: in 1886 the depression in trade and industry was considered and in 1892–4 the problems of labour and unemployment. Private investigations were even more important because they provided a more intimate and direct picture of the situation. A leading figure here was Charles Booth, who between 1886 and 1903 carried out a monumental survey of conditions relating to poverty in London. His *Life and Labour of the People of London* gave a mass of facts relating to employment, the causes of poverty, and other factors influencing the lives of the poor. The East End of London and Central London where conditions were worse, were examined on a house by house basis; the rest of London, street by street. In his survey, Booth divided the population into eight classes:

(*a*) the lowest class of occasional labourers, loafers and semi-criminals

(*b*) those with casual earnings – 'very poor'

(*c*) those with intermittent earnings

(*d*) those with small regular earnings, who with class (*c*) constituted the 'poor'

(*e*) those with regular standard earnings and who were above the line of poverty

(*f*) higher class labour

(*g*) lower middle class

(*h*) upper middle class

Booth fixed his poverty line at about £1 a week and on this basis found that there were a third of the population of London, amounting to nearly $1\frac{1}{4}$ millions, who fell below this line. His reports also showed the dismal background of life for the poor, living on an average of two to three persons in a room in conditions of squalor, leading inevitably to ill health, neglect

of children and a high death rate. He showed also the connection of under employment or casual employment with poverty and also the extent to which the elderly section of the poor suffered. Booth's final conclusion was that this great mass of poverty could not be solved by any combination of Poor Law and private charity: something beyond this was needed. The state must intervene and provide a minimum existence for the depressed 30%, and in the case of the elderly, old-age pensions. A few years later Seebohm Rowntree confirmed Booth's findings by his own investigations in the city of York. Rowntree showed that in York, 28% of the population were below the poverty line and he also demonstrated how poverty affected the physical standards of schoolchildren within this group. At a more popular level the facts and figures of Booth and Rowntree were effectively supplemented by pamphlets such as those written by the Salvation Army leader, William Booth: *Darkest England and The Way Out*, and *The Bitter Cry of Outcast London* of the Congregational minister Mearns.

The London dockers' strike 1889
A dramatic illustration of the grinding poverty suffered by the unskilled and casual workers was given by the London dockers' strike of 1889. This followed a successful strike in 1888 of girls employed in the sweated trade of matchbox-making involving very long hours of work for a pathetically small wage. The dockers were also encouraged by the success in 1889 of the newly formed Gasworkers Union which without striking had secured a reduction from twelve to eight hours in their working day.

219

Dockers waiting for work 1886

The dockers were casual workers who attended daily at the dock gates and who might perhaps get an hour's work one day and then no more work for several days. Their demands were that hiring of their labour should be for not less than four hours at a time and that there should be a minimum rate of pay of sixpence an hour. They also demanded the abolition of the very low piecework rates forced on them by the sub-contractors to whom the dock companies often let out the loading or unloading of ships. The strike which started in the London Docks in August 1889 was organized by Ben Tillett, John Burns and Tom Mann; 10,000 dockers came out. Much to the surprise of everybody, it was an orderly and well-organized affair. The dockers marched peacefully into the City and the West End to give publicity to their case. The dock owners made frantic

The dock strike 1889. Conciliation conference at the Mansion House. Ben Tillett and John Burns are in the foreground; Cardinal Manning is on the Lord Mayor's left

attempts to break the strike by importing 'blackleg' labour, but these failed. Public opinion was much impressed by the disciplined behaviour of the dockers and by realization of their plight and the strength of their case. Donations began to flow in to help the dockers and their families and after long negotiations their demands were conceded in mid-September.

The dockers had not only got their 'tanner' but also a trade union of their own; they had also set an example to unorganized labour which was quickly followed. The result of their strike was that within a year or so many trade unions were formed for unskilled or semi-skilled workers. A considerable stimulus was also given to recruitment to trade unions that already existed. An outbreak of strikes followed which demanded a living wage, the limitation of hours of work, the abolition of overtime and the regulation of piecework rates. The differences between these new unions and the old craft unions were considerable. The latter were small and rather exclusive organizations preoccupied with the special position and rates of pay of their own particular skilled trade; they emphasized friendly society benefits in connection with sickness, unemployment and old age and were reluctant to imperil their funds by strikes. In sharp contrast the new unions were far more 'activist' and far readier to use such funds as their low rate of membership subscriptions allowed for strike action to get better conditions; they were also a force in the foundation of a workers political party to reorganize society.

British Socialist and Labour movements

The compelling evidence of official and unofficial reports, the industrial unrest shown by strikes and the knowledge that both the Liberal and Conservative parties were unlikely to make sufficiently radical changes, led in the 1880s and 1890s to new political parties and groups aiming at substantial changes in the political and economic structure of British society. Some of these new groups derived their inspiration from Socialism in Europe which had been given a powerful stimulus by Karl Marx's *Das Kapital*, published in 1867. Marx taught that society would be changed by violent revolution but this idea appealed to relatively few British Socialists.

The Social Democratic Federation. One of the first Englishmen to read *Das Kapital* was H. M. Hyndman, no downtrodden worker, but a prosperous stockbroker. Converted by its doctrines he founded in 1881 the Democratic Federation which in 1884 was renamed the Social Democratic Federation. The S.D.F. rejected piecemeal reform and instead demanded social revolution; its programme included the provision by the state of relief works for the unemployed. Its militancy was shown in

*'Bloody Sunday',
13 November
1887. The rioting
in Trafalgar
Square*

February 1886 when it organized a demonstration of unemployed which turned into a large scale riot through the West End of London. In November 1887, in defiance of a prohibition by the Commissioner of Police, the S.D.F. sponsored another Sunday demonstration in Trafalgar Square. A pitched battle (long remembered as 'Bloody Sunday') followed between the police and troops and the demonstrators; over a hundred people were injured and two subsequently died of their injuries. The S.D.F. made little appeal to the moderate trade unions and its proposals for revolutionary action were rejected by other Socialist groups, notably the Fabians, but it contributed to the growth of a militant trade unionism among unskilled workers and also had a hand in the foundation of the Independent Labour Party in 1893.

The Fabians. An interesting and more lasting influence in the movement for political and social reform was the Fabian movement. It was founded in January 1884, and was composed almost entirely of middle-class intellectuals. Some of these were highly individual characters: Bernard Shaw, Sydney Webb, Beatrice Webb, Graham Wallas and Annie

Besant. The significance of the name, which derived from Fabius Maximus, the Roman general who had done much to save his country in the wars against Carthage, was that it indicated a policy of patient waiting and then striking hard. The Fabians derived their political ideas from two main sources, the tradition of Radical Liberalism of J. S. Mill, and from European socialism. They rejected the revolution and class struggle preached by Marx and confidently believed that a socialist society, which they thought was common sense, could be attained by gradual and non-revolutionary methods.

Fabian Socialism preached the establishment by democratic means of collective control of the means of production in the interests of the community in contrast to the economic individualism of capitalism with its profit-making motives. They were nothing if not methodical in their approach: instead of vague sweeping plans they specialized in detailed studies of individual social and political problems in order to establish the facts for action. Their early programme contained the following:

1. Extension of democracy with votes for all, including women. Payment of M.P.s and more democracy in local government.

2. A wide extension of government powers and activity in housing, health, education, and poor relief.

3. The placing under national ownership and control of such public utilities as railways, canals, water, gas, docks, tramways; also the nationalization of coalmines.

4. Social equality was to be promoted by greater educational opportunities and by high taxation of unearned incomes.

The Fabians never became numerically large but remained a small influential pressure-group. Their methods of influencing public opinion were those of educators based on their vast output of political pamphlets, full of precise and verified information, and supplemented by lectures. Their social contacts included some of the senior civil servants in Whitehall who were often glad to avail themselves of the superior knowledge of the Fabians about social problems, to which the governments of the day were now obliged to give increased attention. In political life the Fabians most substantial achievement was in the local government of London where for many years their ideas were put into practice by the progressive majorities of the London County Council and of some of the Metropolitan boroughs. They also made a contribution to the advance of the Labour Party in the twentieth century; much of the programme of the Labour ministries of 1945–51 was derived from Fabian ideas.

The Independent Labour Party. The hesitant attitude of the Conservative and Liberal parties to the urgent social needs that had been revealed led to the formation of a Labour Party which should represent

223

*'Not a wise Saw.'
Keir Hardie
wants a real
workers' party
1903.*

the working classes directly with a programme of its own. In the 1870s
and 1880s there had been a few 'Labour' candidates returned as M.P.s,
but they were not organized in any party and generally voted with the
Liberals; politically they were more akin to Liberal Radicals than
Socialists. It was the election in 1892 of Keir Hardie, a Scottish miner,
as M.P. for West Ham that brought the first modern Socialist to the
House of Commons. In 1893, a conference attended by representatives
of various Labour and Socialist organizations met at Bradford under the
chairmanship of Hardie and this led to the foundation of the Independent
Labour Party. The new party was to be completely independent of existing parties, with its own programme of Socialism aiming at the collective
ownership of the means of production, distribution and exchange, and
with its own parliamentary candidates. During the next few years the
I.L.P. had little success with its parliamentary candidates, but it played
an important part in persuading the Trades Union Congress to enter
politics; it was trade union support and money which made possible the
Labour Party of today.

The Labour Representation Committee 1900–6. In February 1900
a conference attended by representatives of most of the Trade Unions,
the Fabians, the S.D.F., and the I.L.P., met in London. The conference
appointed a Labour Representation Committee to build up a distinct
Labour Group in Parliament with its own whips and its own policy: it
was to cooperate with any political party ready to promote legislation in
the direct interest of Labour, and to oppose any party whose measures
had the opposite tendency. J. Ramsay Macdonald, afterwards prime

224

minister of the first Labour government in 1924, was appointed secretary to the Committee. In the elections of 1900, the new party had fifteen candidates, but only two, one of them Keir Hardie, were returned. It did much better in 1906 when Labour opinion, alarmed by the threat of the Taff Vale judgement of 1901 to the future existence of trade unions, rallied strongly to the new party; twenty-nine candidates of the Labour Representation Committee were elected M.P.s.

It is interesting to speculate about the influence of the infant Labour Party on the Conservatives and Liberals. Probably it was not taken very seriously until after the general election of 1906 but before then the Conservatives had made a conciliatory gesture with their Unemployment of Workmen Act (1905); this foreshadowed the abandonment of poor relief as administered under the harsh principles of the Act of 1834. One of the last things Balfour did as prime minister was to appoint the Commission on the Poor Law and Unemployed in December 1905. The Liberals may well have been more alarmed than the Conservatives at the new party for it had been general for working men with votes to give them to the Liberals rather than to their rivals; it is significant that the Liberals ministries between 1906 and 1914 actively appeased working-class opinion by favourable trade union legislation and numerous measures of social reform.

21. The Liberal reforms 1906–14

The Liberal victory 1906

After the resignation of Gladstone in 1894 the Liberal Party had been divided by personal rivalries and political dissension and matters did not improve until 1898 when Sir Henry Campbell-Bannerman became their leader. His parliamentary skill and devotion to party interests did much to revive a sense of unity and purpose within the Liberal Party. When Balfour resigned on 5 December 1905, Campbell-Bannerman accepted the King's invitation to form a ministry. His ministry was a strong one and included H. H. Asquith, as chancellor of the Exchequer, Sir Edward Grey as foreign secretary, and several newcomers, who were subsequently to make their mark. Among them was David Lloyd George who went to the Board of Trade, and R. B. Haldane, who became secretary for War; the inclusion of John Burns, a Labour M.P. as president of the Local Government Board was a significant bid for the support of the new Labour Party.

The general election in January 1906 brought a landslide for the Liberals at the expense of the divided and unpopular Conservative Party. Working against the Conservatives was the split in the party over tariff reform which Liberal propaganda skilfully exploited with the slogan that 'your food will cost you more', while the Nonconformists had not forgotten Balfour's Education Act of 1902. The discreditable aspects of the South African War such as the internment camps, followed by the scandal of Chinese coolie labour in the Rand gold mines, also told against the Conservatives. The Liberals won 377 seats, which gave them a majority of 84 over all the other parties combined. Only 157 Conservatives and Unionists were returned; there were 83 Irish Nationalists, 29 Labour and 24 'Lib–Labs'.

The Trade Disputes Act 1906

The flood of Liberal social reforms did not come until after Campbell-Bannerman's retirement in April 1908, but while he was prime minister some important measures were carried. In 1906 the Trade Disputes Act remedied the grievances of trade unionists over the judicial decision in 1901 of the House of Lords in the Taff Vale case, which had decided that trade unions were legally liable for the actions of their members during a strike, if such actions resulted in loss or damage to their employers. The Act of 1906 reversed this decision and placed the trade unions in a privileged position by exempting them from legal actions for damages resulting from strike action. The Lords did not oppose this Trade Disputes Bill, but in 1906 and 1908 they rejected two Education Bills which had passed the Commons and which sought to modify the provisions of Balfour's Education Act of 1902.

Haldane's army reforms

The worsening European situation together with the defects in organization revealed by the South African War made army reform urgent. This was carried out between 1907–8 by Haldane, the secretary for War. He was a distinguished lawyer, personally well acquainted with Germany, and who realized the extent of her aggressive ambitions. In his reorganization of the land forces of Great Britain, Haldane had two aims: to provide an expeditionary force of six infantry divisions and one cavalry division, together with supporting services such as supply and medical. At long last a General Staff was created to deal with planning of operations, intelligence and organization. Home defence was to be based to a great extent on a territorial army which was formed out of the old militia, the volunteers and yeomanry cavalry, totalling about 300,000. To provide a reserve of officer material, senior and junior divisions of Officers' Training Corps were formed in the universities and public schools. Haldane encountered certain difficulties in these reforms; some of his party objected to increased army estimates and he could not use conscription to raise the size of the army since this was utterly unacceptable to British opinion.

Asquith becomes prime minister 1908

H. H. Asquith, who succeeded Campbell-Bannerman as prime minister, was a barrister by profession and had been home secretary in the Gladstone and Rosebery ministries of 1892–5. Although personally rather reserved, Asquith was a man of great intellectual capacity and this enabled him to dominate parliamentary debates with his precise and compelling arguments. Lloyd George became chancellor of the Exchequer, and Winston Churchill, who had left the Conservative Party over the tariff reform issue, took Lloyd George's place at the Board of Trade. The partnership of these two men, temperamentally and socially so different, was to play a decisive part in the establishment of health and unemployment insurance. Over the next six years the influence of the left wing of the party carried the Liberals into a programme of social reform which aimed at using the power and resources of the state to minimize poverty in old age, ill health and unemployment. This programme did not involve any wholesale reorganization of society in a socialist sense; indeed, in the spirit of the individualistic 'self-help' doctrines of the nineteenth century, it insisted that the benefits (apart from old-age pensions) should be partly financed by contributions from those who benefited.

H. H. Asquith, Prime Minister 1908–16. From a photo taken in 1923

227

Old-age pensions

The most urgent need was for some form of old-age pension to be given as a right to old people with insufficient means of livelihood. Joseph Chamberlain and Charles Booth had urged such pensions in the 1890s; a Royal Commission on the Aged Poor had discussed the matter, but had mistakenly concluded that the Poor Law Guardians could and would do something for these old people. The Commission somewhat complacently comforted itself with the idea that pauperism as such was slowly disappearing, but at the same time disregarded the fact that much grinding poverty remained. A more realistic view was that of Charles Booth who said: 'A pension would lift from very many old hearts the fear of the workhouse at the last.' Financial considerations caused hesitation because the investigations of Booth and others had shown that the numbers of aged poor to whom a pension must be given were very considerable. There was also the opposition of the private voluntary charity societies, the Friendly Societies, and the industrial insurance companies, who thought their interests would be adversely affected in some way or other if old-age pensions were given on such a scale. As chancellor of the Exchequer, Asquith had promised to introduce old-age pensions as soon as there was a budget surplus. This happened in 1908, and in planning his budget for this year Asquith made provision for the payment of old age pensions from national funds. In the budget carried by Asquith's successor as chancellor, Lloyd George, a maximum pension of 5s. a week was granted to those over seventy, who had an income of less than 8s. a week. Those with incomes between 8s. and 12s. a week were also eligible, but for a reduced amount of pension. There were no contributions payable, nor was there any loss of the parliamentary vote as was the case for those at this time who were in receipt of Poor Law relief. The number of people who applied for pensions in the first full year, 1909–10, was over 650,000, a figure greater than anticipated and clear proof of the extent of poverty. The cost in the first year was nearly £8 millions; by 1914 nearly a million people were in receipt of old age pensions. Though the pensions paid were small, their social effect was enormous since they removed from the elderly poor the fear of the workhouse and a pauper's grave.

The Royal Commission on the Poor Law and Unemployed

While by 1909 some provision had been made by old-age pensions for the elderly poor, the problem of other destitute poor remained. A Royal Commission on the Poor Law and Unemployed had been appointed in 1905 and in February 1909 it issued two reports, a majority report and a minority report. The members of the Commission included officials directing Poor Law administration at the Local Government Board, and social investigators like Charles Booth and Mrs Sidney Webb. The Com-

mission carried out a full investigation into the working of the Poor Law and also of what means there were outside the Poor Law for dealing with distress that arose from unemployment, particularly during periods of severe industrial depression. The majority report, while it proposed to retain the Poor Law as such, wished to humanize it and also to make its administration more expert and efficient. It recommended that the elected Boards of Guardians, which controlled the Union workhouses, should be abolished, and their functions taken over by County Councils and County Borough Councils, who would administer the Poor Law through Public Assistance Committees, helped by voluntary aid committees connected with voluntary charitable organizations. The Poor Law was to be renamed 'Public Assistance' and outdoor relief would be called 'Home Assistance'. Other recommendations were for insurance against unemployment and ill-health and the establishment of Labour Exchanges.

The minority report, largely due to Mrs Webb and her husband, Sidney Webb, agreed with the majority that the guardians should be abolished, and that their duties should be taken over by local authorities. But the minority report disagreed with the majority over keeping the Poor Law as framed in 1834; it demanded its abolition and the allocation of its functions in relation to children, the elderly and unemployed to local authorities, who were to set up special committees to care for these classes of poor, and to provide medical services for them. The minority report also called for a Ministry of Labour, which would be responsible for the preventing or minimizing unemployment by means of Labour Exchanges, providing industrial training, and by an organized programme of public works during times of economic depression.

The reports aroused great public interest, but the recommendations of

229

both were resisted by the President of the Local Government Board, John Burns, a one-time Socialist and leader of the dockers strike in 1889. The fact was that he was dominated by his permanent officials; nevertheless some small changes were made to humanize the administration of the Poor Law. Fortunately other ministers such as Lloyd George and Churchill were working on projects that had been recommended by the reports, notably unemployment and health insurance. When the upheaval caused by the budget of 1909 and the political struggle over the powers of the House of Lords was ended, the way was clear for the great measure of the National Insurance Act of 1911.

The budget of 1909

As chancellor of the Exchequer, Lloyd George was obliged to raise £15 millions extra revenue in his budget for 1909. Naval expenditure had increased with the building of the new Dreadnoughts which public opinion demanded to meet the threat of the German navy. Old-age pensions had proved more expensive than anticipated and Lloyd George and Winston Churchill were preparing costly new schemes for health and unemployment insurance. Without hesitation, Lloyd George determined to get this extra money from the wealthy, and in particular from landowners, whom he singled out as the representatives of wealth and privilege who could well afford to spare some of their money to help the poor and under privileged. His budget raised income tax to what seems to us today the very modest maximum of 1s. 2d. in the pound, with graduations below this for smaller incomes; allowances for children were also made to those with incomes of under £500 a year; on incomes over £3,000 a year, a modest surtax at 6d. in the £ was levied. Higher duties were placed on tobacco and spirits and there was an increase in the liquor licence duties. But the most controversial measure of the budget was the land value duties, which were directed at Lloyd George's particular enemies, the great landowners. Their basic principle was that landlords whose land had appreciated in value had been enriched without any effort on their part and therefore it was right that this 'unearned increment' should be taxed for the benefit of the community. The budget proposed that a duty of 20% should be paid on increases in the site value whenever property changed hands, and other duties and taxes on appreciation in land or rental values were also to be levied.

Conflict with the House of Lords

To assess these land duties, a complete valuation of all land would be necessary, and it was this enquiry into the source of their capital gains that irritated the landed interest most. The House of Lords now committed itself to the defence of privilege and property. Lloyd George gladly took up the challenge; he had already referred to his budget as a 'war budget' for the purpose of 'raising money to wage implacable warfare against poverty and squalidness'. In his Limehouse speeches of 1909, he attacked the House of Lords for its attitude, referring to the dukes as costing 'as much to keep up as two Dreadnoughts and they are just as great a terror and they last longer'.

Lloyd George had made the Lords appear as the obstinate champions of privilege, but a more important matter was whether the Lords would use their veto to reject the budget. If they did, they would break the well established constitutional principle that 'control of the purse' and money matters in general belonged to the House of Commons alone. King Edward, fearing a head-on clash between Lords and Commons, tried to use his personal influence to persuade the Lords not to force the issue in this way, but they unwisely refused to recognize that constitutional practice was against them in the matter and in November 1909 they rejected the budget by 350 to 75. This produced a sharp reaction by the Commons who denounced this rejection as unconstitutional and as an invasion of their rights. Asquith now asked the King for a dissolution of Parliament, which was granted in December 1909.

The regulation of the powers of the House of Lords

The general election of January 1910 returned 275 Liberals, 273 Conservatives, 82 Irish Nationalists and 40 Labour M.P.s. With the Labour and Irish Nationalist votes the government had a majority of 124; as in the 1880s and 1890s, the balancing power of the Irish Nationalists was decisive, and to secure their votes the Liberals promised to pass a Home Rule Bill for Ireland. In April 1910, to regulate the powers of the Lords over money Bills and other Bills which had passed all three readings in the Commons the Parliament Bill was introduced and received a first reading in the Commons. Asquith stated in no uncertain terms that if the Lords rejected this Bill the government would ask for a dissolution of Parliament after previously obtaining from the King a promise to create sufficient peers to carry the Bill through the House of Lords. The budget of 1909 was now reintroduced into the Commons and passed by a majority of 93; on presentation to the Lords it was accepted by them without a division. A week later, and amidst the intense party strife, King Edward VII died on 6 May 1910.

The new King George V inherited a difficult situation, but the shock caused by his father's sudden death gave him the opportunity to call a conference between the parties to see if the deadlock could be peaceably resolved. Between June and November 1910 their representatives, four on each side, met in conference. While considerable agreement was reached about the restriction of the Lords' powers over money Bills, the

231

conference otherwise failed: the Conservatives wished to retain the powers of the Lords over certain types of Bills which they described as 'organic': in particular, they wanted at all costs to stop the promised Home Rule Act for Ireland. As Asquith wished to find out what support he had from the electors for the proposed Parliament Bill, he secured a dissolution of Parliament in November 1910. The general election which followed produced a result almost identical with the election of the previous January; the overall majority of the government with its Labour and Irish Nationalist supporters was now 126.

Between February and May 1911, the Bill passed through the three readings in the Commons; in the Lords the third reading had been reached by 20 July; a strong and vehement opposition had arisen among some of the Lords who received the name of 'diehards' or 'last-ditchers'. At this stage Lord Lansdowne, the leader of the Conservatives in the Lords, was told by the government that they had asked the King to create sufficient Liberal peers to pass the Bill, if Conservative opposition persisted. The 'diehards' said this was bluff, but the more serious-minded peers realized that if the Parliament Bill was rejected there would be large and prompt creation of Liberal peers, perhaps amounting to 500, which would profoundly change the composition of their House. On 10 August 1911, the Bill passed the Lords by 131 to 114 votes.

The Parliament Act 1911

The provisions of the Parliament Act of 1911 were:

1. The House of Lords lost its powers of amending or rejecting any money Bill which was certified as such by the Speaker. If the Lords withheld their assent to a money Bill for more than a month it might be presented for the Royal Assent and so become law without the Lords' concurrence. A money Bill was one which was concerned with all aspects of the raising, spending and administration of public money.

2. Bills other than money Bills, passed by the Commons in three successive sessions and rejected each time by the Lords, could then be presented for the Royal Assent and so become law; this gave the Lords a two years suspensory veto in the case of non-money Bills.

3. The maximum life of Parliament was reduced from seven years to five.

The National Insurance Act 1911

While the Parliament Bill was being so fiercely debated another Bill of far-reaching importance had been introduced. This was the National Insurance Bill; its Part I covered health insurance, and Part II unemployment insurance.

232   The aim of Part I was to make available to the working man medical

services which he could not normally afford. Voluntary organizations to achieve this, such as Friendly Societies and sick clubs, already existed in Britain; these paid sickness benefits and by contracts with local doctors provided a basic medical service for their members, but even so probably not more than a third of the working population were covered by such arrangements. Lloyd George had been impressed by German social insurance schemes and was determined to introduce similar ones in Britain. He decided to work through the existing voluntary organizations, thus side-stepping a powerful opposition; he had also to conciliate the doctors, many of whom were strongly opposed to the scheme. He accepted the principle of insurance contributions which were to be made in varying proportions by the employer, the employed, and the state. The Act fixed the weekly contribution at $9d.$: $4d.$ from employees, $3d.$ from employers, and $2d.$ from the state: this was to be represented by a stamp affixed to an insurance card. Hence arose the outcry of the opposition that the government were turning the people into a nation of 'stamp-lickers'. The benefits were $10s.$ a week sick pay, $30s.$ maternity benefit and the provision of medical attention and medicines; the scheme only applied to workers whose wages did not exceed £160 a year. It was to be administered by the existing Friendly Societies, industrial insurance companies and the trade unions, which, for the purpose of the Act, were known henceforth as 'Approved Societies'. The scheme was a limited one since it provided no consultant or hospital services except for persons suffering from tuberculosis, nor did it include the members of the family of the worker insured, but it was the beginning of the National Health Service of today.

Part II of the Act was concerned with unemployment which over the

233

last thirty years had intensified because of the rising total of the working population and the dependence of the British economy on the fluctuation of demand in the world market. In 1900, to relieve the unemployed worker and his family there existed the Poor Law, Friendly Societies, and private charitable organizations. The Poor Law was ill-suited to deal with the situation as it gave relief not as a right but as a matter of grace and behind it was the assumption of moral failure: that is, there was work available if the working man really wanted it and really looked for it. A break in this attitude came with the Unemployed Workmen Act of 1905, which not only tried to deal with the problem of unemployment by setting up local committees to help men to find work, but also stated the principle that a man had the right to expect work in society, and if he was unemployed to be treated in some other way than through the ministrations of the Poor Law.

In 1908, Winston Churchill, President of the Board of Trade, called to his assistance William Beveridge, a social investigator and journalist who had worked at the Toynbee Hall settlement in the East End of London and was therefore well acquainted with the problems of poverty due to unemployment or under-employment. Beveridge strongly urged that there must be some means of communication between employers and workmen, and for this he recommended labour exchanges, or 'clearing houses' where the unemployed worker could sign on and so indicate his need and employers could notify vacancies which these unemployed might fill; authorized by an Act of Parliament in 1909, the first eighty-three Labour Exchanges opened in February 1910. As a novelty they took time to gain acceptance from both employers and workers, but by 1914 they were filling some 3,000 vacancies a day.

Due to Churchill's efforts, Labour Exchanges were followed by a scheme of unemployment insurance which became Part II of the National Insurance Act of 1911. In its original form the scheme covered only a few trades notoriously subject to fluctuations of employment, such as building, iron-founding, shipbuilding, engineering. As in the case of Health Insurance, there was a triple contribution from workers, employers and the state. Benefit was small, totalling 7s. a week, limited to fifteen weeks in any one year and depending on the number of contributions paid during employment. About $2\frac{1}{4}$ million workers came under Part II of the 1911 Act, but it was extended to all manual workers except farm labourers and domestic servants in 1920.

Child welfare

The early years of the twentieth century witnessed a considerable attempt to help children from infancy to adolescence and also to do something for the welfare of mothers. Statistics showed that while the general death rate had fallen sharply to about 17 per thousand of the population, the infant mortality rate remained very high: in 1899 it was 163 per thousand. The growth of primary education had shown that very many children who attended school were poorly clad or badly undernourished. The bad results of this were shown by the medical examination of recruits who offered themselves for the armed services during the South African War; nearly 40% were rejected for physical disabilities.

Due to the efforts of enlightened medical officers of health and a number of private individuals, a maternity and child welfare movement emerged in the first years of the century. Emphasis was on the provision of clean milk for babies that could not be breast fed, and also the provision of health visitors to help and assist the mother in the bringing up of the newly-born child. Many local authorities now began to appoint health visitors and their existence was officially recognized by the Maternity and Child Welfare Act of 1918. A higher standard of midwifery and the establishment of infant welfare centres made their contribution to the reduction of infant mortality rates which dropped from 128 per thousand in 1905 to 95 per thousand in 1912. (In 1960 the rate was 25 per thousand.)

The chronic poverty of parents below the line of subsistence led to undernourishment of their children. To remedy this, school meals were started, first on a voluntary basis and later under the powers given by the Education (Provision of Meals) Act of 1906. This Act enabled local authorities to spend the proceeds of up to $\frac{1}{2}d$. rate on providing school meals; by 1914 over 150,000 needy children were being provided with these meals. Children's Care Committees were also set up by this Act: their aim was to follow up cases of children who were having school meals and to give help and advice to their parents. A school medical service was set up by an Act passed in 1907 to carry out a medical inspection of all primary school children. It was followed in 1912 by grants from the Board of Education to make possible medical attention, particularly in cases relating to the eyes, ears and teeth of children.

The Children Act of 1908 consolidated and added to previous legislation relating to the protection of children. It dealt with cruelty to children by parents and others, forbade their employment for begging, and made unlawful the sale of tobacco to them. Other legislation tackled the problem of adolescent and child delinquents. Child offenders were no longer to be sent to prison to be contaminated by older prisoners while awaiting trial but were to be sent instead to remand homes; their offences were to be considered by juvenile courts with special procedures whose aim was treatment under the supervision of the court and its probation officers rather than punishment. For older offenders between 16 and 20 reformatories known as Borstals were started in 1907; they derived their name from the Kentish village where the first one had been established.

Industrial legislation

In 1906 a Workmen's Compensation Act amended the previous Act of 1897 by forbidding any contracting out of the Act: workmen and employers could no longer make private bargains to exempt themselves from the provisions of the Act. The Act applied to all workers earning less than £250 a year, except the armed forces and police. Besides compensation for accidents, arising out of, and in the course of employment, compensation was also provided by the Act for certain industrial diseases such as lead poisoning. The Coal Mines Regulation Act of 1908 was the first Act to regulate the hours of male workers; because of the hard and dangerous nature of coal mining, the Act said that miners should not work more than eight hours underground in any one day. The Shops Act of 1911 helped overworked shop assistants by enforcing hours of closing, and by giving a half-holiday every week and adequate time for meals. A more glaring evil, that of the sweated industries, was regulated by the Trade Boards Act of 1909. A sweated industry was one in which the workers worked in their own homes or in 'sweat-shops' at piece work rates, making clothing, dresses, matchboxes, lace and chains. These industries had no trade union organization to bargain with their employers; wage rates were exceedingly low but the sweated workers had to accept them or starve. The Act of 1909 set up Trade Boards with representatives of employers and workers in four sweated trades, giving them power to fix legal minimum piece and time rates of wages for each trade.

In 1908 Osborne, a Liberal trade unionist, had objected to payments made by his union to the Labour party; the House of Lords decided such payments were illegal. The Trade Union Act of 1913 legalized political activities for trade unions, but members could 'contract out' of payment to the political funds of their union.

Housing and town planning

A Housing and Town Planning Act of 1909 extended the existing powers of local authorities to clear slum areas and prohibited the building of back-to-back houses. It also, for the first time, gave local authorities planning powers in respect of future development of land, but these powers were so hedged in by limitations about compensation for property injuriously affected by the proposed planning that little was done under the Act. The results were unfortunate, because lack of town planning showed itself in the rash of 'ribbon development' after the war of 1914–18.

The suffragettes: 'Votes for Women'

The atmosphere in which the Liberal ministries had enacted their reforms was hardly a peaceful one, being marked by fierce political criticism and agitation, together with frequent and protracted strikes. To this

236

*Mrs Pankhurst
and her daughter
in prison garb*

disturbed background was added the 'Suffragette Movement' demanding votes for women. This was an offshoot of the movement for the emancipation of women which had developed in the last half of the nineteenth century. Emancipation of women involved the removal of legal disabilities in respect of their own property; admission to higher education and the learned professions; the right to vote and to become a member of Parliament. By 1900, some progress had been made. The Married Women's Property Act of 1882 gave a woman control over her own separate property, instead of putting it under the control of her husband when she married. In education, most British Universities opened their lectures to women and some admitted them to degrees, but Oxford and Cambridge withheld full membership and degrees. In local government by the District and Parish Councils Act of 1894, women could be elected as members of these bodies; they could also be members of Boards of Guardians and Education Committees.

In 1903, the Women's Social and Political Union was founded by Mrs Emmeline Pankhurst, the widow of a Manchester lawyer of advanced political views. The movement had two wings, a moderate group, which wished to work by peaceful persuasion, and a militant-activist group prepared to take any step which would attain the desired end of votes for women. This militant group split off from the original movement in 1908, calling itself the Women's Freedom League. Down to 1909, the methods of the suffragettes were relatively mild, e.g. large-scale demonstrations, heckling Cabinet ministers at political meetings, and the distribution of pamphlets urging their cause. A more violent phase opened in 1909, possibly due to anger and disappointment with a Liberal government which had failed to act progressively by giving women the vote. Suffragettes now openly damaged property, breaking plate-glass windows in clubs and shops in the West End, setting houses, railway stations, and churches on fire, and slashing pictures in the National Gallery; for these offences they gladly accepted imprisonment. In 1913, the suffragette Emily Davison, jumped from the rails at Tattenham Corner to try and bring down the King's horse that was running in the Derby of that year, losing her life in the attempt. Many of the suffragette prisoners went on hunger strike; to prevent them dying as martyrs for the cause they were forcibly fed by the prison authorities. The number of these prisoners became embarrassingly large and to clear the prisons of them the government resorted to the powers given by the so-called 'Cat and Mouse' Act

The funeral procession of the suffragette Emily Davison 1913

238

of 1913, whereby the Home Secretary could release prisoners on licence which was revoked should they repeat the offence for which they had originally been imprisoned. The violence shown by the suffragettes did their cause little good and moderate public opinion was against them, although two attempts to give them the vote before 1914 nearly succeeded. In 1911, a private member's Bill, which would have enfranchised all women householders, received a second reading and in 1912, the government in their Franchise and Registration Bill were ready to accept an amendment to this which would have given women the vote, but this was ruled out of order by the Speaker and the Bill was abandoned. The situation was transformed by World War I, when nearly two million women replaced in factories and offices those men called up for military service; women's war work brought public opinion behind the idea that they were worthy of the parliamentary vote. The Representation of the People Act, 1918, gave the vote to all men still unfranchised and also to women over thirty, either single women householders, or the wives of householders. In 1918 another Act enabled women to be elected to Parliament and in 1919 Viscountess Astor became the first woman M.P. to sit in the Commons. Finally in 1919, the Sex Disqualification (Removal) Act made it generally possible for women, married or single, to hold any civil or judicial office and to practice any civil profession or vocation.

Reform interrupted by the war of 1914–18

The last years of the Asquith ministry, between the passing of the Parliament Act in 1911, and the outbreak of war in August 1914, were overshadowed by political strife at home arising from the passage of the Third Home Rule Bill for Ireland, with the likelihood of civil war if it was enforced, and also by the international tension leading to World War I (see chapters 18 and 22). Social reform was now halted by the concentration of national resources and energy on the war, but the Liberal ministries by their measures had done much to shape the pattern of British history in the twentieth century. The next phase of social reform, comparable in extent and vigour, did not come till the third Labour ministry of 1945–50.

22. British foreign policy 1865–1914

The eclipse of Palmerstonian diplomacy

The failure of Palmerston to save Denmark from the aggression of Austria and Prussia in 1864 was a severe reverse for British policy, or as *The Times* expressed it: 'The humiliation and the consciousness of failure which afflict the public mind are the measure of the exultation of those whose policy has prevailed so completely over our own'. The adroit and forceful diplomacy of Palmerston which had kept the affairs of Europe 'in trim' for so long on behalf of the 'eternal interests' of Britain was rendered obsolete by events in Europe between 1864 and 1871 when by successful wars against Denmark, Austria and France, Prussia under the leadership of Bismarck had united Germany. A new power had been created in Central Europe, with a large and efficient army, an industrious and obedient people, and directed by a man who had slight respect for international law. British policy since 1815 had regarded the strengthening of central Europe as providing a bulwark against the ambitions of France and Russia but before the nineteenth century was out it had become clear that the new Germany, far from assisting a balance of power, was a nation whose ambitions were working against its maintenance.

The Victorian interpretation of Germany

In the 1870s British politicians and diplomats rather uncomfortably adjusted themselves to this new situation which made their previous policies towards Europe look both obsolete and misinformed. Since 1815 and especially since the creation of the Second Empire in 1852 Britain had regarded France as her most dangerous enemy, but this view exaggerated the aims of France as much as it did the power and efficiency of her army. At the same time the aims of Prussia and Bismarck were misunderstood and with this went a sentimental interpretation of German character. Victorian Britain saw Germany as a land of peace, beer gardens, flaxen-haired maidens, and very far removed from 'blood and iron'. German culture and philosophy were also much admired but with little realization of their more unpleasant implications of aggression and war. The achievements of 'blood and iron' between 1864 and 1871 leading to the 'power-state' of the German Empire were a shock to the Victorians.

The weakness of Britain in 1870–1

In 1870 British opinion was quite unprepared for the defeat of France. At the outbreak of war *The Times* said: 'France brings an army into the field, Prussia only an armed people . . . there will be hard fighting on the Rhine, in the Baltic, or it may be in the heart of Germany.' A career diplomat, Sir Robert Morier, made the confident forecast: 'There is little doubt that the Prussians are not yet ready and that a great portion of Germany will be occupied before the decisive battle is fought, which will be somewhere in the interior of Germany.' Caught off balance, all Great Britain could do was to secure a promise from France and Prussia that they would respect the neutrality of Belgium in accordance with the treaty of 1839. As the war progressed an attempt was made to form a league of neutral powers which should mediate between France and Prussia, with the hint of more drastic collective action if this failed, but Britain, because of her suspicion of Russia gave lukewarm support and nothing was achieved. Finally when Bismarck imposed harsh peace terms and demanded Alsace and Lorraine from France, Gladstone protested but was ignored by Bismarck who contemptuously referred to him as 'Professor' Gladstone. Further proof of the weakened position of Britain was given at the end of October 1870 when Russia made a unilateral denunciation of the Black Sea neutrality clauses of the Treaty of Paris of 1856. All that Gladstone's Foreign Secretary, Granville could do, was to hold a face-saving conference at which the sanctity of treaties in general was affirmed, quite disregarding the fact that part of one had been torn up because the power that did so knew that no other powers were prepared to fight for a matter of principle. The Disraeli ministry of 1874–80 showed more spirit in its conduct of foreign policy; in 1875 Bismarck was probably prevented from making a second war on France by the vigorous representations of Britain and Russia. Disraeli's action in the Eastern Question in 1876–8, though perhaps open to criticism, was done with energy and resolution and as the representative of a state whose history and resources made her a great power.

The policy of 'splendid isolation'

During the last twenty-five years of the nineteenth century British foreign policy had first of all to adjust itself to the Europe that had been changed by the rise of German power and to the alliances and counter-alliances that developed out of this new situation. Secondly there was the maintenance of British imperial interests, including the strategic bases and routes of empire in face of the competitive imperialism of the European powers who in these years were staking out their claims to colonies, protectorates, concessions and spheres of influence in Africa and Asia.

To the first problem the general answer was the policy of 'splendid isolation' of Lord Salisbury. The essence of this policy was that Great Britain, while always ready to cooperate with other powers in the maintenance of peace, would 'go it alone' and remain uncommitted to foreign alliances; the policy was possible because of Great Britain's naval power, her empire, and her economic strength in the world. In dealing with the second problem Great Britain had the advantage that she was already the leading imperial power and this position she would and could maintain, while willing to make concessions to other powers where her vital interests were not affected.

Lord Salisbury's non-committal attitude

In all three of his ministries Lord Salisbury was foreign secretary as well as prime minister. It was in his second ministry from 1886 to 1892 that the features of 'splendid isolation' were most clearly seen; his last period in office from 1896 to 1902 marked the beginnings of a movement away from this policy. Our relations with France and Russia were cool, due in the case of the first power to our occupation of Egypt in 1882 and in the case of the latter, to British support of Turkey at the Congress of Berlin in 1878. With the Triple Alliance powers of Germany, Austria–Hungary and Italy, Britain's relations were at this time rather more cordial since Salisbury regarded this alliance as being a stabilizing force in Europe and fundamentally peaceful in its aims, but even so he acted cautiously in view of the complicated diplomacy of Bismarck during these years. The German statesman's greatest fear was a two-front war launched simultaneously by France and Russia; if Great Britain could be drawn into the Triple Alliance the pressure on Germany would be reduced should this war break out. The approaches made by Bismarck to Salisbury to achieve this resembled his constant efforts to maintain an understanding with Russia by the 'reinsurance' policy. But in conformity with the policy of isolation Salisbury kept clear of the committments that would follow if Great Britain entered the Triple Alliance. The most that Salisbury would do was to make an understanding with Italy over the Mediterranean which was extended in 1887 into an agreement between Great Britain, Austria–Hungary and Italy by which they undertook to maintain the *status quo* in the Near East and to uphold the integrity of Turkey.

In 1889 Bismarck made a proposal to Salisbury for an Anglo-German Treaty which would have pledged both countries to common action in the event of a French attack upon either of them. Bismarck asked for an open public treaty but Salisbury hesitated in his reply to this proposition which would have made Great Britain a fourth member of the Triple Alliance; some months later he gave a noncommittal answer, saying that in a parliamentary state such as Great Britain there were certain difficulties about making such an alliance. In other respects, Salisbury was ready to keep on friendly terms with Germany as the Anglo-German Treaty in 1890 showed. This recognized a British protectorate over Zanzibar and also that Uganda lay within the British sphere of influence in East Africa; in return Britain ceded Heligoland in the North Sea to Germany. The

Germans considered this a great gain because of their naval ambitions in connection with the opening of the Kiel Canal.

Reappraisal of British foreign policy after 1890

After 1890 Great Britain was forced to reconsider her foreign policy and for this a number of factors were responsible. An important one was the change in German policy brought by the dismissal of Bismarck in 1890; no longer could the Triple Alliance be considered as a force for peace in Europe. Instead there were the ambitious designs of Kaiser William II and his advisers leading to an expansionist world power policy; Germany must have 'a place in the sun'. The colonial ambitions of France, Germany and Russia also caused Great Britain anxiety, especially by the seizure of strategic bases. Commercial rivalry from Germany meant that British exporters found themselves undercut in their customary markets by cheaper German goods; 'made in Germany' became the bane of British industrialists. The hitherto unchallenged position of the British navy, on which her world power rested, was threatened by the creation of a German navy. The Navy Bills of 1898 and 1900 outlined German aims in this respect although it was not till 1906 that the full extent of the German naval challenge was revealed.

The isolation of Great Britain was particularly emphasized by the system of alliances that had come into being in Europe; in opposition to the Triple Alliance there was now the Franco-Russian alliance of 1893 and in pursuit of their aims these alliances might take action against Great Britain's interests. The feverish colonial expansion of the times gave ample opportunity for this and even for the members of the opposed alliances to act together against Great Britain. Thus in 1894 there was a Franco-German agreement to oppose the activities of the British Royal Niger Company in the Niger Valley. German designs to take over part of the Portuguese Empire in Africa were now taking shape; if successful they would have given her the strategic area of Delagoa Bay on the Indian Ocean, thus threatening the British position in Southern Africa. Because of the strength of imperial sentiment which reached a peak in Britain in the 1890s no British government could ignore such threats; a stiffening of the British attitude followed and also a movement away from isolation whose disadvantages were becoming painfully apparent. In 1895 Britain declared that it would regard the penetration of the Upper Nile Valley by another power as an unfriendly act, a declaration that was later put into effect by Kitchener in 1898 when he gave the French expedition under Major Marchand an ultimatum to quit Fashoda.

Great Britain and the Far East

The movement of Great Britain away from isolation was tentative and

243

gradual but it received an impetus from events in the Far East, whither Anglo-Russian hostility had shifted. In this area, now that the authority of the Chinese Empire had crumbled, Japan was the only power capable of checking Russian expansion. Great Britain made friendly approaches; in 1894 she agreed to give up her privileged consular courts in Japan and followed this by refusing to join Russia, France and Germany in their pressure on Japan which compelled her to restore the Liao-Tung peninsula and Port Arthur to a defeated China. The wisdom of finding a friend for Great Britain in the Far East was justified by subsequent events. On the pretext of ill treatment of German missionaries, Germany in 1897 seized the port of Kiao-Chow from China; Russia followed this by occupying the more valuable base of Port Arthur in 1898, and Great Britain, not wishing to be left behind in the power struggle in the Far East, obtained a lease from China of Wei-hai-wei, opposite Port Arthur.

British diplomatic approaches 1898–1901
In 1898 Salisbury, who remained convinced of the soundness of the policy of isolation, tried to improve relations with Russia and France by negotiation. His attempt to do this with Russia failed and the Russian seizure of Port Arthur made the situation worse, but with France there was more success. A friendly agreement was made to settle Anglo-French claims in the Niger Valley, and this survived the tension that arose between the two nations over the Fashoda incident later in the same year. Between 1898 and 1901, Joseph Chamberlain, who as colonial secretary was becoming increasingly concerned for the safety of the British Empire in a hostile world, engaged in diplomatic conversations with the aim of bringing about an Anglo-German alliance; somewhat optimistically he thought it would be possible to bring in the U.S.A. as well. The project failed because of the tortuous diplomacy and excessive demands of the Kaiser and his ministers, the hostility shown by the German press and people to Great Britain during the South African war, and to German naval expansion which in the long run threatened Great Britain.

The Anglo-Japanese Alliance 1902
Basically Great Britain was faced by a closed system of European alliances, both of which cold-shouldered her. The formal break from isolation came in 1902, and after Salisbury had handed over the foreign secretaryship to Lord Lansdowne. An alliance was made in January 1902 with Japan, to protect Britain's interests in a region where she felt particularly vulnerable – the Far East. The treaty provided for mutual aid if either Britain or Japan was attacked by more than one power; the special interests of Japan in Korea were recognized; in 1905 the scope of the treaty was extended to cover India and South East Asia. The treaty was largely the work of

Lord Lansdowne and it is clear that Lord Salisbury and his Cabinet were not enthusiastic about it. Nevertheless it marked a decisive step away from 'splendid isolation' in British foreign policy and indicated to the diplomatic world that Britain might well make other agreements to maintain peace and to protect her interests.

The Anglo-French Entente 1904

This more flexible diplomatic course on which Britain had embarked enabled her to improve relations first with France and then with Russia. In 1900 relations between Britain and France were poor due to the friction arising from their colonial rivalries in Africa and Asia; the Fashoda incident in 1898 had brought them to the brink of war. A compelling motive for both countries to improve their relationship was their common fear of the aggressive German policy that increasingly revealed itself.

Discussions to settle their differences started early in 1902 and negotiations were carried further in March 1903 when King Edward VII made a courtesy visit to President Loubet in Paris; the King's affability did much to abate the anti-British feeling which had hitherto been strong. The critical stage came in July 1903 when President Loubet accompanied by his Foreign Secretary, Delcassé visited London for conversation with the Foreign Secretary, Lord Lansdowne. After protracted bargaining over the points at issue an Anglo-French Convention was signed in April 1904; this defined and regulated the colonial interests of Britain and France in various parts of the world. France recognized our position in Egypt without insisting on any time limit for our occupation; and Britain recognized the special French position in Morocco and that France should have a free hand there to administer this country. France abandoned her fishing rights on the 'treaty' shore in Newfoundland and in

King Edward VII's visit to Paris 1903

return received some compensation in West Africa where the frontiers in Northern Nigeria, Gambia and the Ivory Coast were modified in her favour. Although primarily a friendly agreement over colonial problems and not a binding alliance, the *Entente* was interpreted in Europe and especially by Germany as a prelude to the closer association of Great Britain with the Dual Alliance of France and Russia.

The first Moroccan crisis 1905–6

It was not long before the *Entente* was put to the test. The crushing defeat of the Russians by the Japanese in the war of 1904–1905 made Russia, for the time being, a very weak partner in the Dual Alliance. Russian relations with Britain were also strained by the Dogger Bank incident of October 1904, when the Russian Baltic fleet on its way to the Far East had fired on British fishing trawlers in mistake for Japanese torpedo-boats. The Kaiser and his advisers therefore thought the time was ripe for a counter-attack against the Anglo-French *Entente*. In March 1905 the Kaiser landed at Tangier and assured the Sultan of Morocco, who was under pressure from France, that he could have the assistance of Germany to protect him if he wanted it. Germany now demanded that the whole problem of Morocco should be brought before an international conference. With their ally Russia in difficulties in the Far East, the French had to give way and appease Germany; the Foreign Minister, Delcassé was dismissed and the conference demanded by Germany agreed to. Then followed a German attempt to weaken France further by enticing Russia away from her alliance with France into the German camp. In July 1905 the Kaiser by personal negotiation with Czar Nicholas II at Bjorko, a Baltic island, induced him to sign a treaty aligning Russia with Germany but the Foreign Ministries of both countries rejected the treaty as unworkable. Britain now pledged diplomatic support to France and more significantly for the first time entered into discussions with France about joint military and naval co-operation. It was also made clear to Germany that Great Britain would not remain indifferent to any wanton attack on France by Germany over Morocco. The conference demanded by Germany on Morocco met at Algeciras in January 1906. It was a signal failure for Germany because her viewpoint was supported only by Austria–Hungary and her plan for dividing Morocco into spheres of influence was rejected. It was also a demonstration of the effectiveness of the new friendship between Great Britain and France. The conference authorized the establishment of an international police force for Morocco but entrusted the supervision of this to France and Spain. Germany withdrew in some discomfiture but five years later she made Morocco the background for another international crisis. The setback at Algeciras strengthened the hand of the 'big navy' influences in Germany; the Kiel

Canal was widened and the German naval programme increased. Efforts by Britain by negotiation with Germany to stop this race in naval armaments failed, while the lack of any real wish on the part of the great powers to disarm made The Hague Conference on Disarmament of 1907 an almost complete failure.

The Anglo-Russian Convention 1907

In 1906, and with active French encouragement, Great Britain began to improve her relations with Russia. The immediate aim was to clear up differences in those parts of the world where friction had arisen, e.g. Persia, Afghanistan and Tibet. One difficulty in doing this was the dislike felt by British Liberals for the Czar and his autocratic rule, and in particular, the ruthless suppression of the popular demonstrations in St Petersburg in 1905. The Anglo-Russian Convention signed in August 1907 regulated the position of Russia and Britain in Persia by dividing this country into spheres of influence: Russia was assigned the northern part, a neutral area was left in the middle, while the southern area bordering on the Persian Gulf fell to Britain. Afghanistan was recognized by Russia as being a British sphere of interest while Britain undertook to respect the sovereignty of its ruler. In the case of Tibet both powers agreed not to interfere and to recognize the suzerainty of China over this country.

The Bosnian crisis 1908

In 1908 the Balkans cast their shadow over the peace of Europe. The Congress of Berlin in 1878 had granted the administration of Bosnia–Herzegovina to Austria; in October 1908 Austria–Hungary without consulting the signatory members of this Congress annexed Bosnia–Herzegovina, so marking another stage in the partition of the Turkish Empire. A strong reaction came from Russia; there had been an understanding with Austria that if Bosnia was taken, Russia should be compensated by the opening of the Straits from the Black Sea into the Mediterranean; the disasters Russia had recently suffered in the Far East at the hands of Japan made her the more anxious to secure compensation in Europe. War between Russia and Austria with the latter supported by Germany seemed imminent but Russia's ally, France, was unwilling to fight over this issue and British influences were working for a peaceful settlement. Realizing that if she made war on Austria, Germany would fight as well, Russia finally backed down in the spring of 1909.

The German Naval Law of 1908

For Britain the rising European tension of these years was complicated by the steady growth of the German naval building programme which by their Naval Law of 1908 sanctioned the building of four capital ships

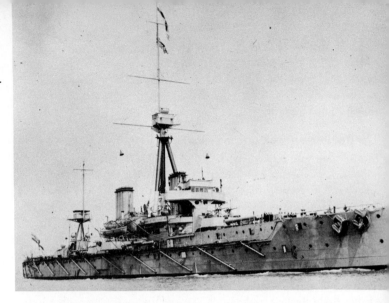

annually. The British request for a reduction of this was refused by Kaiser William who contemptuously disregarded the very real anxiety felt by Britain at this threat to her naval power on which depended her safety from invasion and the maintenance of her food supplies from overseas. This rebuff was followed later in 1908 (October) by an interview the Kaiser gave to the *Daily Telegraph* in which he made some extravagant statements about the 'distortions' of the British press in misrepresenting his 'offers of friendship' to England and that it was only his personal influence which had restrained France and Russia from attacking Britain during the South African War. In the face of all this the Liberal government, which on taking office had reduced naval expenditure, was obliged to increase its programme; its proposal to build four capital ships in 1909 was advanced by patriotic agitation to eight – 'We want eight and we won't wait.'

The Agadir crisis 1911

In 1911, Morocco was the scene of a second international crisis. The French government had sent an expedition to help the Sultan who had trouble with rebels at his capital of Fez, and it looked as if France was extending her control over the country. The German government began to demand compensation and sent a gunboat, the *Panther,* to the Moroccan port of Agadir ostensibly to protect German nationals (there were none there) but in reality to stake a claim for a German naval base on the Atlantic coast of Morocco. The strength of the Anglo-French *Entente* was once again tested. Grey, the British Foreign Secretary, gave his diplomatic support to France and the attitude of Britain in the event of war was

248

emphasized by the speech of Lloyd George at the Mansion House in the City of London in July 1911. He made it clear to Germany that she was running great risks if she made war on France on the assumption that Britain would remain neutral in the conflict. The Germans eventually took the hint but tension remained between the countries and the British fleet was alerted as war was thought to be a distinct possibility. The Committee of Imperial Defence was summoned to a special session by Prime Minister Asquith, to consider the military situation. Against Admiralty opposition it was decided to give priority, in the case of war, to the despatch of an expeditionary force to reinforce the French in Europe. The crisis ended by September and Germany was compensated by the cession to her of part of the French Congo.

The united front of France and Britain in the Agadir crisis strengthened the hands of the German 'big navy' groups. An increase in German naval expenditure followed, leading to a corresponding increase in that of Britain. In an attempt to come to a workable agreement with Germany over naval expenditure, the British government early in 1912 sent Lord Haldane to Germany to discuss the matter with the German ministers. The Germans made an offer to slow down their naval building programme, if in return Britain would guarantee to be neutral in a war between Germany and the Dual Alliance of France and Russia. This was unacceptable to British policy which feared that in such a war Germany might seize the Channel ports. At the end of 1912, by agreement with France, the British battle fleet assumed responsibility for the Channel and the North Sea, and the French navy did the same in the Mediterranean. In spite of these and other measures to concert their defences, there was still no formal military or political alliance between Great Britain and France.

The Balkan Wars 1912–13

The last phase of the slow drift to war was enacted in the Balkans between 1912 and 1914. The seizure of Bosnia in 1908 by Austria and the capture of Tripoli, Cyrenaica, and the Dodecanese Islands off the coast of Asia Minor by Italy in 1911 showed that Turkey would have great difficulty in defending the remains of her empire in Europe. Four Balkan states coveted Turkish territory in Europe, while in the background were the wider aims of the great powers. Thus Russia sought to control the Straits leading into the Mediterranean and to occupy Constantinople; Austria–Hungary had economic ambitions in the Balkans and the Aegean Sea, while Germany was building the Berlin–Baghdad railway to carry her influence through the Balkans into Asia Minor and towards the Persian Gulf. There was great danger for Europe that a general war would break out because of the rival ambitions of Russia and Austria in the Balkans.

At the end of 1912, Greece, Serbia, and Bulgaria, with Russian encouragement, allied together against Turkey and in a short and successful war completely defeated her. This success alarmed Austria because these states were the satellites of Russia, and Austria could not allow any extension of Russian influence in the Balkans without compensation for herself. She feared the Slav triumph there might prove to have an unsettling effect upon the Slav peoples of her ramshackle empire, and behind Austria–Hungary was Germany, who saw her expansionist aims in the Near and Middle East being cut in two by this expansion of Russian influence in the Balkans. The British Foreign Secretary, Grey, realizing the danger of this new situation called a conference of powers to prevent the war spreading. This was held in London early in 1913 and was mainly concerned in re-drawing the map of the Balkans in view of the changes made by the First Balkan War. While the Conference was in session, the victorious Balkan powers quarrelled amongst themselves and Bulgaria was attacked by her late allies Greece and Serbia, together with Rumania. The Turks took the opportunity to recover some of their lost territory near Constantinople. Of the Balkan powers, Serbia had done best out of these wars and this especially had alarmed Austria–Hungary; she now determined to attack the successful Slav nationalism typified by Serbia and in the gamble of war assert her mastery over the Slav people of her empire.

The last eighteen months before Europe was swept into war were marked by a general intensification of warlike preparations. Both the German and British navies were increased, while the period of service for French and Russian conscripts was increased from three to three-and-a-half years. By the end of 1913 Germany had assured Austria–Hungary of her full support in the event of war, even should this be a general European war. In both countries the military leaders' views increasingly prevailed over those of the politicians and diplomats.

Archduke Franz Ferdinand and his wife shortly before their assassination at Sarajevo, 28 June 1914

The Sarajevo murders and the outbreak of war, July 1914

On 28 June 1914 the Archduke Franz Ferdinand, heir to the thrones of the Austrian and Hungarian monarchies, and his wife, were murdered by Bosnian terrorists at Sarajevo, the capital of Bosnia. The assassins had been equipped and instructed by a terrorist organization in Belgrade. Here was the opportunity the military chiefs had been waiting for: everything was right, time, place and victim. With the assurance of the Kaiser's support, Austria on 23 July despatched an ultimatum to Serbia: its demands were almost impossible but Serbia accepted them. Austria's reply was to break off diplomatic relations and two days later, on 28 July 1914, to declare war on Serbia. Russian and then French mobilization followed: Germany had done this by 1 August and declared war on Russia on 2 August and on France the following day.

Great Britain's ultimatum to Germany, 4 August 1914

The British Cabinet was divided over the grave decision it must now make because of these catastrophic events in Europe. Three viewpoints emerged: firstly that full naval and military support should be given to France and her allies; secondly that Great Britain should give only naval assistance and make no military intervention in Europe; and lastly that complete neutrality in the conflict should be followed. Germany had already made a clumsy bid for the neutrality of Britain which was of vast importance to her schemes: had Britain remained neutral it would have been as the spectator of the defeat of France with the certain prospect of war sooner or later with Germany. The violation of Belgian neutrality by Germany on 4 August ended the divisions within the Cabinet save for a few ministers who remained firm against war. On the same day the British government sent an ultimatum to Germany asking for assurances that Belgian neutrality would be respected. No answer was received and by midnight on 4 August, Great Britain was at war with Germany.

23. Great Britain and World War I (1914–18)

The British reaction to war, August 1914

Once the decision had been taken the British people rallied strongly behind their government although they had little realization of the length of the war ahead or of its appalling toll of life and resources; their determination was strengthened by the ready aid that came from the self-governing Dominions of Canada, Australia, New Zealand, South Africa and the other lands of the British Empire.

In some respects Great Britain was not unprepared for this war; her navy was large and had an unbeaten record while her army, thanks to the reforms of Haldane, was of good quality although very small compared with the huge conscript armies of the European powers. Economically Great Britain was strong and as the wealthiest creditor nation in the world had large overseas investments which could be realized to finance her war effort and that of her allies.

Among the early measures of the government on the home front were the closing of the banks for three days, raising Bank Rate to 10%, and suspension of the gold standard. The Defence of the Realm Act ('DORA') of 8 August 1914 gave special powers to the government; civilians who threatened public safety and the defence of the realm could be tried by court-martial, while newspapers might face prosecution if they published war news not contained in the official 'hand-outs'.

On the war front, the navy which had been kept fully mobilized since the summer manoeuvres in July, was sent to its action stations in the North Sea. Four infantry divisions and one cavalry division (approximately 100,000 men) of the British Expeditionary Force were sent to France to fight on the left wing of the French armies opposing the German thrust through Belgium into France.

The German offensive in the West 1914

The German plan drawn up some years before 1914 by Field marshal Schlieffen was to crush France in six weeks by an overwhelming attack and then to switch their forces for a knock out blow against Russia. The right wing of their advance into north-eastern France took the form of a gigantic sweep through Belgium which aimed at the encirclement of Paris from the west and the final defeat of the French armies to the south-east of the city. By mid-August, and after pushing aside Belgian resistance, the two German armies of their right wing totalling about 600,000 men

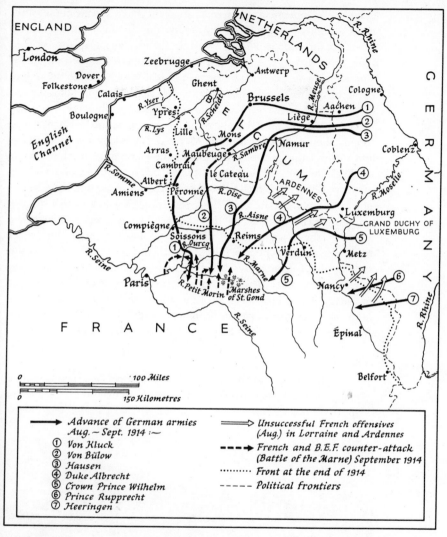

ENGLAND

London
Dover
Folkestone
Calais
Boulogne

English
Channel

R. Somme

Amiens
Albert

Arras
Cambrai
le Cateau
Péronne

Lille

R. Lys

R. Yser
Ypres

Zeebrugge
Ghent
Mons
Maubeuge
R. Sambre

Brussels
Liège
Namur

Antwerp

Aachen
Cologne

NETHERLANDS

R. Rhine

R. Meuse

R. Scheldt

GERMANY

Coblenz

R. Moselle

ARDENNES

Compiègne
Soissons
R. Ourcq

Paris

FRANCE

R. Seine

R. Oise
R. Aisne

Reims
R. Marne

R. Petit Morin
Marshes
of St. Gond

Verdun

Luxemburg
GRAND DUCHY OF
LUXEMBURG

Metz

Nancy

Épinal

Belfort

R. Seine

R. Rhine

① ② ③ ④ ⑤ ⑥ ⑦

0   100 Miles
0   150 Kilometres

Advance of German armies
Aug. – Sept. 1914 :—
① Von Kluck
② Von Bülow
③ Hausen
④ Duke Albrecht
⑤ Crown Prince Wilhelm
⑥ Prince Rupprecht
⑦ Heeringen

Unsuccessful French offensives
(Aug.) in Lorraine and Ardennes

French and B.E.F. counter-attack
(Battle of the Marne) September 1914

Front at the end of 1914

Political frontiers

Map 11   The war in the west 1914

were pouring into France. The British Expeditionary Force came up on
the left of the fifth French army opposing this German mass and contact
was first made near Mons. Both French and British were borne back by
the weight of the German attack but in a fighting retreat from Mons the
B.E.F. inflicted heavy casualties on the Germans. In a hard fought
action at Le Cateau on 26 August the British Second Corps drew Von
Kluck's army westward and away from its correct line of advance. By the

253

first week of September the German armies of the right wing of the movement were becoming over extended after their rapid advance and were losing the direction laid down by the Schlieffen plan; a gap also began to grow between Von Kluck and the neighbouring army under Von Bülow. Von Kluck who according to the plan should have passed to the west of Paris, turned eastwards thus exposing his flank to attack along the line of the River Marne. The French and British successfully counter-attacked this flank and advanced through the gap between the two German armies, forcing them to retreat from the Marne to the line of the River Aisne, and so thwarting at the eleventh hour the German plan for victory in the West in 1914. A new threat to the B.E.F. came from a German offensive down the North Sea coast of Belgium to capture the Channel ports of Dunkirk, Calais and Boulogne, through which British supplies and reinforcements came, but the flooding of the land between the sea and Ypres by the Belgians forced the Germans to concentrate their attack on Ypres and Armentières. The great salient covering these towns was successfully defended by British troops in the first battle of Ypres (October and November 1914) but at the price of using up what remained of the B.E.F. By December 1914 the war of movement had ceased and both sides dug themselves in to trenches which stretched continuously from the North Sea to the Swiss frontier. (See Map 11.)

The pattern of the war

By 1915 the pattern of the land war was fully revealed. The battlefield was dominated by the fire power of machine guns and artillery which stopped all movement; the armies were held down in the long lines of

Trench warfare – a scene from the French line 1916

A bombing raid early in World War I

trenches protected in front by their barbed-wire entanglements. Both sides tried to break this deadlock by large-scale offensives prefaced by very heavy artillery bombardment but until the allied breakthrough in the autumn of 1918 both sides failed in these attempts which brought heavy losses in men. The land war on the Western front thus became a war of attrition with each side trying to wear down its opponent and then to deliver a knock out blow.

At sea the war produced one large-scale battle between the British and German fleets at Jutland in 1916, together with a few smaller actions, e.g. Coronel (November 1914), the Falkland Islands (December 1914), and Dogger Bank (January 1915). Throughout the war the allied powers maintained naval supremacy which enabled them to dominate the sea routes of the world, to open and supply new fronts in the Eastern Mediterranean and to impose an economic blockade on Germany and her allies. The German reply was an audacious, and for a time very successful, submarine campaign directed against the merchant shipping of their enemies. Air power made its appearance but compared with the Second World War it was not very extensive or important. The primitive aeroplanes could help the artillery on to their targets and take air photos but

255

Damage from a Zeppelin raid on the East End of London

their use for bombing was restricted by their limited range and the small size of bombs available. Both sides used the air arm for anti-civilian purposes but the civilian casualties and damage inflicted were insignificant compared with those of 1939–45.

The Gallipoli campaign 1915

In 1915 an attempt was made by the allies to break the deadlock in the West by attacking Germany's allies in Eastern Europe; this involved striking at Turkey and also the rear of Austria–Hungary by way of the Balkans. It was thought that if the Straits leading into the Black Sea from the Mediterranean were captured a way would be opened through which Russia, whose war effort was now flagging, could be supplied with arms and ammunition. Russia's need for these was admittedly great, but the fact was that at this stage the Western allies were themselves short of shells and weapons. This plan for an eastern campaign was strenuously opposed by the senior commanders of both the French and British armies who were obsessed by the idea of breaking through in the West and finally enveloping the enemy's forces in a great decisive battle. Against this view civilian opinion (notably Lloyd George and Winston Churchill) maintained that by shifting the attack to weaker spots of the enemy's front much could be achieved; in an eastern campaign it would be possible to combine military and naval forces in a successful operation with considerable political consequences in Eastern Europe. Success would save Serbia, now at her last gasp; Greece would move to the allied side and Bulgaria would be prevented from entering the war on the side of

Map 12 The Gallipoli campaign 1915

Germany, while Turkey might well abandon her German alliance.

The Gallipoli campaign of 1915 was a joint Anglo-French operation although British and Dominion troops and the British navy played by far

257

the larger part. The operation was mounted with a good deal of hesitancy and there was a lack of planning and organization on the military staff side. In February 1915 an attempt was made by a naval expedition without supporting troops to force the Straits. This silenced the forts at the entrance but then ran into a Turkish minefield; after losing several ships from this hazard, the British Admiral commanding refused to risk any more in an attempt to force a way through. At this stage the Turks had not organized their defences on the Gallipoli peninsula and if troops had been available to follow up the naval bombardment, it is probable the peninsula could have been taken. When the allied land forces made their landings in April, tactical surprise had been lost; Turkish reinforcements were in position and defences had been constructed. 30,000 British, Australian and New Zealand troops were landed but their advance out of the beach heads was uncoordinated and they were unable to break through the Turkish defences on the higher ground. In August the British commander General Sir Ian Hamilton made a second attempt to capture the peninsula; a landing was made further north at Suvla Bay with the object of outflanking the Turkish defences. The landing succeeded but once again the momentum of the attack slowed down on moving out of the beach heads; the Turks remained in possession of the vital high ground from which they could not be dislodged. It was now clear that failure could not be reinforced any more and the decision was taken to evacuate the British forces; this was done without loss in December 1915 and January 1916. The results of failure in this inspired but thoroughly mismanaged campaign were serious for the allied cause: Greece became hostile and regretted allowing Britain and France to occupy the Salonika bridgehead; Bulgaria joined the central powers, and Russia was isolated from effective help from the West. (See Map 12.)

British failure in the West 1915

On the Western front in 1915 the allied cause did not prosper; in February their hold on the Ypres salient was weakened by German attacks in which gas was used for the first time. The superiority of defence against attack was again shown by the failure of the British offensives in this year at Neuve Chapelle, Aubers Ridge, Festubert, and finally at Loos where 50,000 British were killed, wounded and missing for the capture of a few hundred yards of enemy territory. These failures brought a government crisis in Great Britain where public opinion was disturbed by the failure to provide the vast quantities of high explosive shells needed in the preliminary bombardment before an attack was made. A reconstruction of Asquith's ministry took place in which a number of Conservatives were admitted as ministers. Lloyd George became minister of Munitions to deal with the shell shortage and in recognition of the vital importance to the war effort of organized labour, Arthur Henderson, Secretary of the Labour Party, was given ministerial office with Cabinet rank. By the Munitions of War Act (1915) the government, for the duration of the war was given wide powers covering the prohibition of strikes and lock-outs, the assumption of direct control of munition factories, and the direction of labour to wherever it was most needed.

The Battle of the Somme 1916

In 1916, the allies made attempts to coordinate their attacks in France, in Italy (which had joined the allied side in May 1915) and in Russia. Their schemes were frustrated by the German Commander Falkenhayn who launched an attack on the French fortress of Verdun with the object of bleeding the French army to death by operations designed to produce the maximum casualties. This battle which lasted from February to the end of June, led to very high casualties on both sides; Verdun was not captured, but the allied plan for a simultaneous offensive was disrupted. The losses of the French at Verdun led to the major part in the allied offensive being taken by the British armies in France which now numbered a million men. The Battle of the Somme opened on 1 July 1916; once again there was the optimistic belief that given sufficient men and heavy artillery preparation the German trench defences could be breached and the open country beyond reached where the horse-cavalry would then become the spearhead of the advance. In the event, cruel disappointment followed; the artillery preparation, heavy though it was, did not eliminate all the German machine-gun nests many of which survived and took heavy toll of the closely packed advancing British and French infantry; 60,000 casualties were suffered by the British armies on the first day of this fearsome battle. Little enemy ground was won but the attack was continued and the battle did not end till November; by that time, British casualties were over 400,000 and the French, who had taken a part in the later stages of the battle, lost nearly 200,000 men. To this allied failure in the West were added other setbacks in 1916. Russia, which had played a considerable part in relieving the pressure of the Germans in the West by her offensives in East Prussia in 1914 and against the Austrians in Galicia in June 1916, now began to show signs of collapse due to enormous casualties, lack of war equipment, and inefficient direction of the war by the Czar and his advisers. Rumania which had entered the war on the allied side in August 1916 had been eliminated by a strong German–Bulgarian invasion in the autumn of the same year.

The war at sea 1914–15

In the autumn of 1914 a German armoured cruiser squadron under Admiral Graf von Spee from the China station, after sinking two of

Admiral Cradock's ships at the Coronel off the coast of Chile (1 November), was surprised by a British squadron at the Falkland Islands; four of the five German cruisers were sunk (8 December). By the early months of 1915 the German commerce raiders, both cruisers and armed merchantmen, had been accounted for. Nearer home the German fleet made a number of nuisance raids, shelling Scarborough and Hartlepool on the north-east coast of Britain but on their third attempt they suffered serious losses. They now sought a way to reduce British naval supremacy by a naval weapon which had been developed shortly before 1914, the U-boat (*Unterseeboot*) or submarine. As early as the spring of 1915, Germany moved towards a policy of unrestricted sinking, i.e. all vessels, British or neutral, found in a war zone around the British Isles would be sunk at sight without inspection or warning. Among the sinkings was that of the liner *Lusitania* in May 1915, with a loss of over eleven hundred civilians, many of them American citizens. This had a noticeable effect upon American opinion and was the first major event to harden the opinion of the U.S.A. against Germany and which eventually led to her entry into the war. In April 1916, the American President Wilson addressed a stiff note to Germany about her unrestricted U-boat campaign; under pressure from this the Germans relaxed it for the time being.

The Battle of Jutland 1916

The major aim of British naval strategy was to keep its fleet supremacy intact and this largely explains why there was only one major battle at sea, that of Jutland on 31 May 1916. The British commander Admiral Jellicoe fought a cautious action, the exact details of which were disputed long after their happening, but in the words of Winston Churchill, 'Jellicoe was the only man on either side who could lose the war in an afternoon'; in particular Jellicoe feared the dangers to his fleet from German torpedoes and minefields. The battle opened with an action between Beatty's squadron of battlecruisers and the German vanguard. After suffering considerable losses, Beatty sought to lure the main German fleet commanded by Admiral von Scheer towards the British battle fleet under Jellicoe some fifty miles away. The approach of Jellicoe led to complicated avoiding manoeuvres by the German fleet, which made great use of torpedoes, smokescreens, and the bad light caused by mist. Jellicoe was also cautious and turned away his fleet to avoid this torpedo attack. In the gathering darkness, the German fleet was able to make a retreat eastwards to its ports, slipping behind the main fleet under Jellicoe. It was not seriously harassed in this homeward retreat because caution deterred Jellicoe from setting his destroyer flotillas on the retreating Germans; there is also some doubt about his possible disregard of a wireless message from Admiralty intelligence which had intercepted a message from Ger-

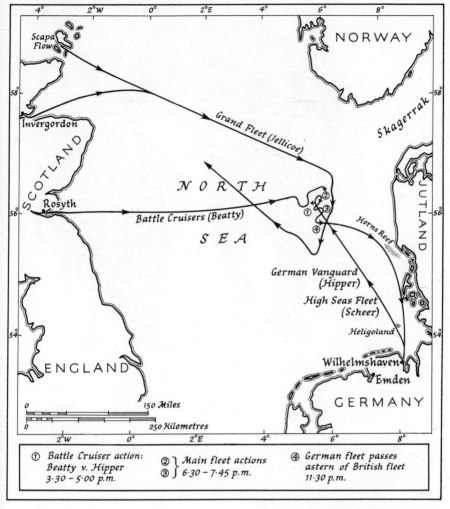

Map 13 The Battle of Jutland 1916

man sources giving the homeward course of the German fleet. While the British fleet had suffered greater losses of ships and men than its opponent, and technical defects of its ship design, guns and signalling equipment had been revealed, nevertheless British naval supremacy remained intact. The Germans did not risk another fleet action after Jutland and instead turned to intensive use of the submarine as a means of countering British naval supremacy. By the beginning of 1917 the German High Command had decided to resume unrestricted submarine warfare regardless of the effect this would have on the opinion and actions of the U.S.A.

261

Lloyd George and Winston Churchill 1916

Lloyd George becomes prime minister, December 1916

The events of 1916 led to a growing dissatisfaction on the part of the British public with the conduct of the war. The losses at Jutland and the failure and casualties of the Somme offensive together with the elimination of Serbia and Rumania were dispiriting. There was also the 'Easter rebellion' in Dublin which many people thought had been put down with unnecessary severity. On the home front, civilian morale was adversely affected by the growing shortage and cost of food and other goods; conscription had been imposed to meet the demand, so it seemed, for more men to be slaughtered in futile offensives. The Coalition, which had been formed in May 1915 by the entry of Conservatives into Asquith's Liberal government, was an uneasy one. Asquith himself came under strong criticism for his direction of British war policy; there was the widespread belief that he was opposed to the vast extension of government controls needed to mobilize the nation's resources for war purposes. There was also the realization of the need for a small inner War Cabinet to take charge of the direction of war policy. This distrust of Asquith's leadership led to high level intrigues behind the scenes and also a newspaper agitation in the *Daily Mail* and *Daily Express*, which backed the claims of the Conservative leader Bonar Law and also those of Lloyd George who had become war minister on the death of Lord Kitchener in May 1916. The crisis was reached in December 1916 when a proposal was made for the formation of a small War Cabinet of three or four ministers under the nominal direction of Asquith; the latter, after first accepting, then rejected a scheme which would have left him a mere figurehead. Lloyd George and the Conservative ministers of the Coalition then resigned, forcing Asquith to do the same on 5 December. The next day Bonar Law made an unsuccessful attempt to form a ministry, whereupon the King was advised to send for Lloyd George who formed a Coalition ministry: this was based on the support of a minority of Liberals who followed him rather than Asquith and of the Conservatives led by Bonar Law.

The new Prime Minister had already distinguished himself by his stormy, impetuous and successful methods. The hour had called forth the man; Lloyd George had the energy and capacity for getting things done which were essential for this crisis in Britain's fortunes. Equally important, he had an excellent sense of public relations and how to get over his ideas to the public at large and to know what they were thinking at this time of crisis; in this he was aided by his superb oratory which was so persuasive it was said that 'he could charm the birds from the trees'. To give more forceful direction to Britain's war effort, Lloyd George created a small inner War Cabinet of five ministers who were freed from any departmental responsibilities.

The year 1917 tested the new management to the full. One vital problem was the renewed U-boat offensive which struck at Britain's food supplies and nearly succeeded in starving us out of the war; the other was military deadlock in the West where once again failure attended the efforts of the generals to make a breakthrough and deliver the final knockout blow. Another adverse factor was the crumbling of Russia's war effort followed by revolution in 1917 and her withdrawal from the war early in 1918. Amidst all these difficulties allied morale was raised by the entry of the U.S.A. into the war in April 1917.

Germany's U-boat campaign 1917

The resumption by Germany early in 1917 of an unrestricted submarine warfare against allied and neutral shipping was a desperate effort to force a decision and to break the economic blockade of Germany; it was a gamble but nevertheless one which nearly succeeded for in the month of April 1917, the U-boat sinkings of allied shipping mounted to one million tons of which 600,000 were British. Not only did the U-boat campaign deter neutral ships from approaching British harbours, but its rate of sinking was such that even the extended capacity of British shipyards could not make up these colossal losses. By the middle of May, the situation was serious with probably not more than two or three weeks' food supply left in Britain. The estimates of the British Admiralty, curiously enough, agreed with those of the German High Command which had calculated that this unrestricted submarine offensive would force Britain into starvation and surrender by 1 August 1917. There was the possibility that an organized convoy system would save many ships from sinking by U-boats but the Admiralty was critical of this method, declaring that it would not work. Lloyd George, by direct intervention, now brought about a trial of the convoy system and its success was soon demonstrated. By the end of July 1917, owing to its adoption, the number of sinkings had greatly decreased and by September 1917 the losses of shipping had fallen to about 200,000 tons a month. The organized convoy together with the intensified use of anti-submarine devices such as depth charges, 'Q' ships and minefields finally contained the U-boat menace for good.

Failure of the French offensive, April 1917

On land, Lloyd George was seeking for a way out of the deadlock and he thought this could be achieved by attacking the central powers in the East rather than the West; he proposed a knock-out blow directed against Austria. But this project met the severest opposition, not only from the British commander Sir Douglas Haig and his Chief-of-Staff Robertson but also from the French who saw the expulsion of the German troops from the soil of France as the first and greatest object to be attained. Eventually Lloyd George was persuaded into accepting the plausible plans of the new French Commander-in-Chief, General Nivelle, who had recently succeeded Marshal Joffre. Nivelle's plan was to attack in Champagne where the German front was relatively lightly held; he promised a complete breakthrough, which in the light of past experiences was exceedingly optimistic. Meanwhile the German armies in the north had carried out a strategic retirement to what was known as the Hindenburg Line; this movement itself dislocated the proposed Nivelle operation. The German intelligence service also had ample knowledge of the impending French offensive and consequently their front in Champagne was strengthened so that when the French offensive opened in April 1917, it met with failure and instead of a complete breakthrough, only some six hundred yards of territory was captured at the cost of immense casualties. The renewal of the offensive for some three weeks brought about mutinies in the French armies who were no longer willing to be sent to death on the barbed-wire entanglements. Complete demoralization of the French armies was only prevented by the judicious measures taken by General Pétain, the defender of Verdun. By a combination of firmness and leniency and by remedying the grievances of the troops over leave and by improving conditions for units resting after duty in the front line, discipline was restored.

The Passchendaele offensive 1917

The utter failure of Nivelle's 'big push' was followed by another disaster, that of the Passchendaele offensive mounted in the late summer of 1917 under the direction of Sir Douglas Haig. The obvious strategy for both French and British was to await the reinforcements that the entry of the U.S.A. would bring but Haig was convinced that it would be possible by mounting a great offensive in Flanders for the British army to win the war. The War Cabinet brought Haig's plan under severe criticism but Haig brushed aside their objections and was supported by the Admiralty which hoped that a successful offensive would enable the German submarine bases on the Belgian coast to be put out of action.

The area for the attack, to the east and north east of Ypres, was ill-chosen. Not only was it flat country easily observed by the enemy, but most of it was reclaimed marshland whose drainage system was soon churned up by the artillery bombardment and this, coupled with the fact that heavy rains ensued during most of the offensive, made it into an impassable morass; though these facts were pointed out by his intelligence service, Haig disregarded them and persisted week after week in his attack. A very heavy artillery barrage preceded the attack but this did not silence the German machine-gun posts ensconced in concrete pill-boxes. For three months the British troops struggled in this ocean of slime, water

265

and horror, but their commander would not desist. In the event, only a few thousand yards of territory were gained and the casualties amounted to 400,000; a sad commentary on Haig's declaration earlier to the War Cabinet that he had 'no intention of entering into a tremendous offensive involving heavy losses'.

Italian defeat; overthrow of Czarist Russia 1917

To the French and British failures on the Western front in 1917 were added two other disasters: the first was on the Italian front where, at the end of October 1917, a German–Austrian offensive broke through the Italian line at Caporetto. After losing over half a million men, the Italians with the help of French and British troops stabilized their front on the line of the River Piave, not far from Venice. The other setback for the allied cause was the exit of Russia from the war at the end of 1917. The rule of the Czars was utterly discredited and in March 1917, Czar Nicholas II was forced to abdicate. A moderate democratic government under Kerensky now took charge and for a short time Russia continued in the war, but with a rapidly diminishing effort. In October the real revolution was achieved when Lenin and Trotsky, the Bolshevik leaders, overthrew Kerensky and established their rule, at the same time seeking an armistice with Germany. By March 1918, the new Russian revolutionary government had made peace with Germany, so releasing nearly fifty German divisions (over half a million men) for service on the Western front.

U.S.A. enters the war, April 1917

Under President Woodrow Wilson the U.S.A. had followed a policy of neutrality but at the same time the President had tried to mediate between the belligerents in the hope of bringing about peace. In November 1916 Wilson was re-elected to a second term of office as president largely on the basis of his declared intention to keep the U.S.A. out of the war. The situation was sharply altered by the unrestricted German submarine warfare of the early months of 1917 which sank a number of American merchant ships; at the same time Germany intrigued with Mexico, inciting the latter country to attack the U.S.A. in the hope of recovering some of the territory she had lost to the U.S.A. over eighty years previously. On 6 April 1917 the U.S.A. declared war on Germany. This was a tremendous stimulus to the allied cause, but its results took time to show themselves; the American army had to be built up practically from scratch. On the other hand, the U.S.A. could and did make timely advances of financial credit to the allies; this was particularly vital to Britain who, by this time, had nearly exhausted her dollar assets and credits in the U.S.A.

Peace negotiations 1916–17

After two years of indecisive war it was not surprising that there should be a movement in favour of a negotiated peace; this originated in civilian circles but was unacceptable to the generals on both sides who were inflexibly bent on total victory over their opponents. While the allied powers in 1916 would have been content with a peace which restored the prewar state of affairs, Germany insisted on territorial gains, e.g. the prewar state of affairs, Germany insisted on territorial gains, e.g. control of Belgium and retention of Alsace-Lorraine and part of Poland. define their respective war aims. Germany, because of her extensive ambitions, did not do so, but the allied powers declared that they were fighting for the restoration of Belgium and Serbia and also for the principle of self-determination which would give independence to Magyar and Slav peoples of the Austro-Hungarian Empire.

In 1917 Austria–Hungary opened negotiations with France and Great Britain for a separate peace; these failed because Austria–Hungary was closely dependent on Germany and the allies required that Austria should join them against Germany as the price of peace. 1917 also saw the triumph of the generals over the civilians in Germany where they secured the dismissal of Chancellor Bethman Hollweg who had been willing to consider a negotiated peace. In August 1917 Pope Benedict XV made comprehensive proposals, aiming at a peace in which neither side would be the victor. The allied powers were critical of this move on the grounds that Germany was not to be trusted in peace negotiations unless she would state clearly all her territorial aims, and also because of her declared refusal to restore Alsace–Lorraine to France.

President Woodrow Wilson's 'Fourteen Points'

On 8 January 1918 President Wilson in an address to Congress set forth a peace programme in his 'Fourteen Points'. His most important proposals were: open diplomacy and no more secret treaties; freedom of the seas in peace and war; removal of international trade barriers; reduction of armaments; full regard for interests of colonial populations; evacuation of Russian, Belgian and French territory, including restoration of Alsace–Lorraine to France; self government for the peoples of the Austro–Hungarian Empire and for the non-Turkish peoples of the Ottoman Empire; restoration of independence of occupied Balkan states; the formation of an independent Polish state; the creation of a League of Nations to guarantee the independence of all states. Because of their wide scope and the idealism behind them, the 'Fourteen Points' made a great impression on world opinion at this critical stage of the war, but in the peace negotiations of 1919 Wilson was to find the practical application of their principles a very difficult matter indeed.

A tank in action

The war situation at the beginning of 1918

Early in 1918 Germany made a final effort to win the war on land in the
West. There were compelling reasons for this: the U-boat campaign of
1917 to starve Britain had failed and the German home front was beginning to crack under the strain of war, the growing shortage of food and the
siege economy imposed by the allied blockade. The position was even
worse in the case of Germany's allies, particularly in the Austro-
Hungarian Empire where the rising disaffection of its non-German
peoples pointed to an impending collapse. It was essential for Germany
to strike a decisive blow in the West before the American armies reached
France to shift the balance in favour of the allies. The elimination of
Russia from the war made this possible; Germany had been able to
transfer half a million of her troops from the Eastern to the Western front
and at the beginning of 1918 had a numerical superiority over the French,
British and Belgians in this area.

On the allied side the setbacks of 1917 had slowly brought about
measures for a unified direction of the war effort. Towards the end of
1917 a Supreme War Council was set up at Versailles and agreement
was reached, somewhat grudgingly, between the French and British
commanders in France to set up an inter-allied pool of reserves which
could be used to help each other if the Germans should launch an offensive.
The prospect was further improved for the allies by the arrival of
American troops, although their organization and training proceeded
too slowly in the opinion of the battle-weary French and British.

The allies also had other advantages denied to the Germans. Their
war industries had more abundant supplies of raw materials whereas

268

those of Germany were starved of these and were forced to use inferior substitutes. More important, as far as the battlefield was concerned, the British had developed a weapon which was to break the static warfare of the trenches. This was the 'tank', a combination of armour, fire power and mobility. It was first used in the later stages of the Battle of the Somme in 1916 and in November 1917 showed its great possibilities in a surprise attack in the area of Cambrai where a deep penetration of the German lines was made, although unfortunately the ground won could not be consolidated. By contrast the Germans were slow to develop the idea of the tank or to find any effective counter-measures against it. In the air allied power slowly edged ahead of the Germans and in 1917–18 development were made which foreshadowed the far greater use of air power in the Second World War of 1939–45. Thus a beginning was made with tactical bombing of the enemy's supply lines, railways, ammunition dumps and preparation was made in 1918 for bombing of the German industrial areas such as the Ruhr.

The German offensives in 1918

The British sector of the Western front was chosen by the Germans for their spring offensive of 1918; their blow was designed to strike at the weakest part of the British line between Cambrai and St Quentin, and if success was attained here the German High Command planned a further offensive against the northern sector of the British front. Overall their aim was to break through, capture the Channel ports and so isolate the British forces from their French allies to the south. On 21 March 1918, the German offensive opened. Aided by a heavy artillery barrage and a thick fog which covered the countryside, the German armies drove through the fifth British army and threatened the key railway centre of Amiens. In some places they made a forty mile advance, in sharp contrast to the limited movement of the offensives in 1916 and 1917. Eventually the German advance was stopped by the resistance of the remnants of the fifth army and the arrival of French reserves, but the German success forced the allies to coordinate more effectively the command of their armies. On the 14th April 1918, Marshal Foch was appointed commander-in-chief of the allied armies in France, and although his power over the commanders of the British and American armies was persuasive rather than compulsory, the appointment was a change for the better.

Early in April the Germans mounted another offensive further north, aiming at the important railway junction of Hazebrouck. As in March they were helped by thick fog; the front they attacked was thinly held because the British expected that any further German attack would be made further south in the neighbourhood of Arras. The Germans made a great bulge ten miles deep in the British line, but by the end of

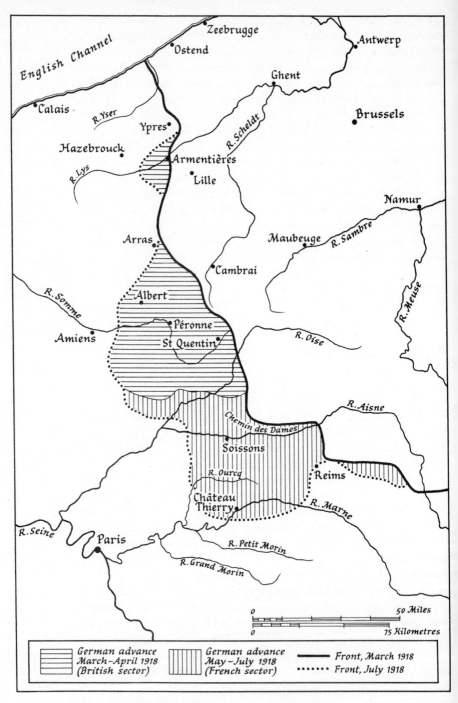

Map 14 The German offensive in 1918

April with French help the front was stabilized. At the end of May a third German offensive was mounted against the French on the Chemin-des-Dames by an advance across the River Aisne on to the line of the River Marne to the south. Eventually this offensive was contained by elastic defence tactics on the part of the French whereby the initial attack was met by lightly held outposts after which the wearied attackers were confronted by strong defences further back.

In spite of these successes German military strength was declining; they could no longer make good the losses they suffered. Their last major

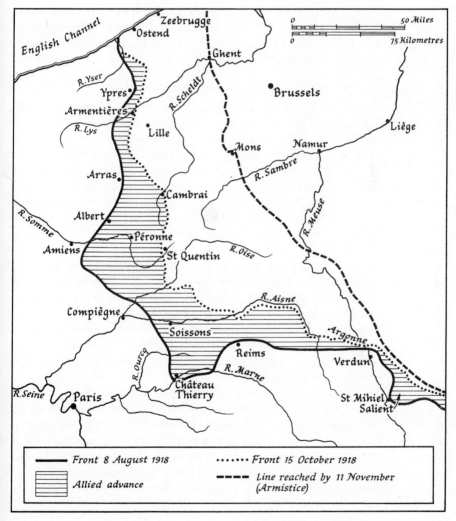

Map 15 Victory in the west 1918

effort was in July 1918 when they attacked in the area of Reims but their failure enabled the French to counter-attack with marked success, and this indicated the turn of the tide. A week later the attack by the fourth British army in front of Amiens confirmed this. The German defences were penetrated by a large spearhead of tanks and an advance of eight miles made on the first day. The extent of this British success led the German Commander Ludendorf to say that 'August 8th was the blackest day of the German Army in the history of the war; it put the decline of our fighting power beyond all doubt'. But even so the German army to a great extent maintained its cohesion and discipline right down to the Armistice of November 1918 in the fighting during the grand offensive mounted by Marshal Foch in September in which all the allied forces in France took part. It was only after hard fighting that the British forces stormed the 'Hindenburg line', while to the south the Americans were checked in the Argonne.

The end of the war, September–November 1918

Events in Eastern Europe now hastened the end of the war. By the beginning of October the Bulgarians had been driven out of the war by a joint French, British and Serbian attack from Salonika, while Turkish resistance, as was shown by the rapid advance of Allenby's armies through Palestine into Syria, was crumbling fast. These events together with the critical military situation in the West forced Ludendorf and the new German Chancellor, Prince Max of Baden, to ask President Wilson on 3 October for an armistice, but with the military and political situation moving so fast in their favour the allies could take their time over this. On 30 October Turkey capitulated, followed by Austria–Hungary on 5 November after their defeat by the Italians at Vitorio Veneto. Germany could continue no longer: worn down by hunger and enemy propaganda and disillusioned with their leaders the German people broke into revolt. On 9 November the Kaiser was forced to abdicate; two days earlier the German envoys were informed of the allied armistice terms by Marshal Foch at Rethondes in the Forest of Compiègne. The terms were stiff: evacuation of invaded French and Belgian territories: surrender of 5,000 guns and 25,000 machine-guns; allied occupation of Germany to the west of the Rhine together with the bridgeheads of Cologne, Coblenz, Mainz and Strasbourg, with a neutral zone forty kilometres wide on the east bank of the river; the surrender of the German navy and the continuance of the blockade until the armistice terms were fulfilled. A time limit of seventy-two hours to expire at 11 a.m. on 11 November was set for acceptance of these terms. At 5 a.m. on 11 November the German envoys signed and the signal went out: 'Hostilities will cease along the entire front on 11 November at 11 a.m. French time.'

*The W.R.A.F.
join in the
Armistice
celebrations*

British war attitudes

What had been the attitude of the British people to this colossal conflict?
In 1914 an intense feeling of patriotism swept the country which was
expressed at recruiting meetings and at mass demonstrations of support.
After much heart searching most intellectuals accepted the war as a
crusade against a tyrannical Prussian militarism and as being in defence
of civilization: it was 'the war that will end war' (H. G. Wells). The
appeal for a million volunteers by Lord Kitchener ('Your King and
Country needs you') met a swift response and within a few months there
were more volunteers than could be equipped and trained. An indis-
criminate anti-German feeling sprang up; Lord Haldane was driven from
the Cabinet because he had once expressed admiration for Germany and
its culture; unlucky people whose names were German-sounding were
in danger of being denounced as spies and the owners of dachshund dogs
hastily disposed of such embarrassing pets. Generally the civilian 'front'

273

showed a remarkable, if blind trust in its political leaders and military chiefs, in spite of the obvious blunders that were made by both, while civilian bloodthirstiness towards the 'Huns' was certainly not shared by the British 'Tommies' fighting them in France. These civilian attitudes continued even after the blood baths of the Somme and Passchendaele, although by that time a number of writers in prose and poetry gave a far different and more realistic picture of the war, moving sharply away from the idealistic exaltation of the poems of Rupert Brooke in the early days; instead they showed up the horror and pity of war. H. G. Wells, in his *Mr Britling Sees it Through*, reflected the disillusionment of the average person with the cruel facts of war as they became increasingly revealed. More effectively, two soldier poets, Siegfried Sassoon and Wilfred Owen, exposed the filth, the squalor, the futility, the waste and horror of war, particularly as it had been shown in trench warfare and the 'great offensives'.

In common with the other combatant nations the cost in lives of this war for Great Britain was a high one. Over 6 million men had been in her armed forces and of these $\frac{3}{4}$ million were killed with $1\frac{3}{4}$ millions wounded. Most of the war dead were physically and intellectually the best of their generation and their loss was irreparable. The contribution this 'missing generation' could have made to national life would almost certainly have prevented much of the political incompetence of the postwar years.

The introduction of conscription 1916

In 1914 Great Britain was a country which prided itself upon the freedom of its citizens whether in respect of their personal liberty or their right to control their property. War needs brought limitations of these freedoms on an increasing scale; under powers derived from Defence of the Realm Acts and other statutes the government took control of a wide range of privately owned industries, including railways, coal mines, munition factories and flour mills.

The idea of universal military conscription in time of peace or war was unacceptable to British opinion as an unwarrantable encroachment of the state on individual liberty, and the success of Lord Kitchener's appeal which had provided over a million volunteers in the first year of war encouraged the hope that conscription might be unnecessary. But by the autumn of 1915, the high casualty rates and the demands on man power made by military operations on the Western front, both defensive and offensive, brought conscription steadily nearer. The Derby scheme of recruitment launched in October 1915 tried to keep the principle of voluntary enlistment; of those who attested for service the bachelors would be called up before married men. The comparative failure of this scheme led to the first Military Service Act in January 1916, which

A recruiting poster early in World War I

provided for the conscription of bachelors; in May 1916 it was extended to all physically fit men, single or married between the ages of eighteen and forty-one; later men up to the age of fifty-one became liable for service. The measure was accepted as a distasteful necessity, but also as the fairest one that could be adopted in view of the increasingly grim war situation. Opposition to it came from about 16,000 men who had conscientous objections of various kinds to fighting or any participation in the

275

war effort. An indignant public labelled these objectors as 'conchies'; about 1500 of the more extreme objectors spent the rest of the war in prison, but the more moderate ones were allowed to serve in non-combatant corps, in ambulance duties, or working on farms.

Women and the war effort

The wave of patriotic feeling brought a remarkable change in the attitude of the suffragettes who had harassed the Liberal ministers in the years immediately before 1914. Mrs Pankhurst turned a somersault to become an ardent patriot and rallied most of her followers behind the war effort, although her youngest daughter Sylvia moved leftwards into the pacifist camp. The government was slow to make use of this female enthusiasm, partly because the dislocation of war led to considerable male unemployment in the first stages of the war. But the rising tide of voluntary recruitment to the armed forces, followed by conscription in 1916 brought large scale employment of women especially in the munitions factories where the number of women employed rose from 250,000 in 1915 to over 800,000 in 1918. The transport industry was also an important employer of women as bus and tram conductresses and ticket collectors; office work, both government and private, absorbed large

Women factory workers in World War I

numbers of women. In closer contact with the war were the large numbers of women who joined the nursing services at home and overseas and the various auxiliary services such as the Womens Auxiliary Army Corps Services (W.A.A.C.S.), the Womens Royal Emergency Naval Services (W.R.E.N.S.) and Womens Royal Air Force Services (W.R.A.F.S.).

The activities marked a decisive stage in the emancipation of British women. It was recognized by all but an obstinate minority that women's war services entitled them to the parliamentary vote which was given to most women over thirty by the Representation of the People Act (1918). More important were the social and economic effects. War work gave very many women for the first time the economic independence and freedom of movement necessary to live as free individuals and to escape from the old codes of behaviour which had restricted their social relationships, especially with the male sex. Outwardly the wartime expression of this was the disappearance of the chaperons for single women who now went unaccompanied in public where the more daring of them actually smoked: the adoption of more sensible clothing with the abandonment of tight corseting and a shortening of skirts to a few inches above the ankles.

Labour and the war

The enormous demand for war supplies of all kinds made the civilian labour front a vital part of the war effort and the government therefore had to pay constant attention to industrial relations. Its major problems on this front were the prevention of strikes, the maintenance of the

277

K

efficiency of the labour force and the filling of vacancies caused by the call up of men for the armed forces. A first step was to win the support of the trade union leaders, some of whom were Labour M.P.s, and who were brought into closer consultation by giving them minor ministerial appointments in the government; a further gesture was the Excess Profits Duty levied on wartime profits as organized labour not unnaturally resented the large profits that factory owners were making. Relying on this support the government in its Munitions of War Act (1915) prohibited strikes, introduced compulsory arbitration for disputes and took powers to direct labour to where it was most needed which in practice meant 'dilution', i.e. semi-skilled or unskilled labour would do the work of skilled craftsmen. The government had to act cautiously in the exercise of these sweeping powers but apart from a few awkward strikes on Clydeside and in South Wales managed to avoid serious trouble. In this matter it was helped by responsible trade union leaders and also by public opinion which regarded strikes as a betrayal of the men in the trenches; some of the popular newspapers launched campaigns against the strikers urging that 'Put 'em in uniform' would be the answer.

The need to maintain efficiency in the labour force led to important changes in the licensing laws in the shape of a drastic restriction of the over-generous opening hours for public houses which prevailed at the outbreak of war. With increased wages drunkenness, especially in the industrial areas, had become a serious problem, leading to inefficiency and bad time-keeping. Drinking time was heavily cut; taxation of beer and spirits was increased and in Carlisle and Enfield Lock where there was a concentration of munitions factories state control of public houses was

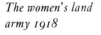

The women's land army 1918

introduced. The results were not only beneficial as far as war production was concerned but on the longer term it brought a sharp reduction in the amount of drunkenness.

Food rationing

Although Great Britain relied on imports for the greater part of her food supply, serious shortages did not show themselves until the middle of 1916. The poorer section of the community were hit by the rising prices of staple commodities such as bread but the more affluent suffered no discomforts. Conditions changed sharply in 1917; in London and the larger towns long queues appeared for bread, potatoes and coal. A Ministry of Food had been set up at the end of 1916 but its original policy of voluntary rationing in 1917 was not very effective. The success of the German U-boat campaign in 1917 which reduced Britain's food stocks to a few weeks' supply made government control of food distribution and compulsory rationing of civilian consumers inevitable. At the end of 1917 sugar was rationed, followed in the spring of 1918 by meat, tea and butter; local Food Control Committees were set up to issue ration cards and coupons to the civilian population. Other measures were subsidy payments to keep down the price of bread and potatoes, and the restriction of meals served by restaurants and other eating places. A crash programme of ploughing up grassland for arable crops was launched to increase home production of bread grains, and a force of 'Land Girls' was recruited to help out the shrinking labour supply of the farms.

24. Postwar Britain 1919–22

The background of postwar Britain

The Armistice was received with profound rejoicing as a release from a war that had lasted too long and at too great a cost both of lives and resources. At the time it seemed that it must herald a future in which things would be better; surely a society could be fashioned where there would be greater equality, better housing, more educational and health services, and work for all. The twenty years between 1919 and 1939 were an ironic commentary on these immediate postwar hopes; the progress towards a better society during these years was painfully slow and could be not unfairly described as stagnation punctuated by small advances. Some of the political and social reasons for this failure are suggested below, and economic factors are given in chapter 26.

Firstly there was a major political antagonism which breached the unity of the nation. The fight was on between the forces of the 'traditional' governing and possessing classes, (finding expression mainly in the Conservative Party) and the rising Labour movement organized for both political and industrial action. The former wanted to keep the workers firmly in their place, to dictate wage rates and terms of employment, to curb as much as possible trade union activity and not to go beyond very modest and frugal schemes of social reform lest higher taxation should result. Against this Labour stood embattled, not always very skilfully as the general strike in 1926 showed, in its fight to protect workers' living standards and to advance social security and welfare schemes. On the whole Labour was outmanoeuvred by its opponents between the wars, and after the disastrous break up of the second Labour government in 1931, it was very much on the defensive as a political force. But its two periods of office (1924 and 1929–31) showed its will to govern and apply its political beliefs in the face of major handicaps such as a lack of an absolute majority in Parliament and an economic crisis of unparalleled severity in 1930–1.

Lastly the attitudes of the British people seemed to lack buoyancy during this postwar period; a certain apathy and bewilderment was never far away and this resulted in a preference for safe compromises and uninspired leaders; in this vital field of leadership the loss of the 'missing generation' was increasingly felt. Other attitudes were those of estrangement or escape. Thus the war veterans were hostile to the older generation and to those of their own age groups who had not fought in the war. They found it difficult to adjust themselves to postwar society and became bitter about the muddled peace settlements and the economic troubles that persisted; more and more it seemed that their sacrifices had been in vain and they could only regard the slogans coined by the politicians, such as 'A war to end war', 'Homes fit for heroes' with cynical mockery. Among the older generation there was a deep wish for escape from the war years and a return to the secure and ordered world they had known before; they deplored the disastrous effect of the war on standards of behaviour and of living and wished themselves back in a world where the pound was worth twenty shillings, domestic servants were in abundance, the working classes knew their place and kept it and where there were no 'temporary gentlemen' masquerading as officers.

The general election, December 1918

The Armistice of 11 November 1918 was followed by a general election. This was urgent for various reasons; the Parliament elected in 1910 had exceeded the span of life allowed by the Parliament Act of 1911 by nearly three years; the electors must give their mandate for the period of reconstruction which lay ahead. There were also political party reasons which influenced the speed with which the election was held and the way in which the appeal was made to the electorate. Lloyd George, the successful war leader, wished to continue in power as a great peace minister; he had split the once mighty Liberal Party by his part in the dismissal of Asquith and if he was to continue as prime minister the support of the Conservatives was essential. The Conservative-Unionist Party under Bonar Law saw their chance to make a political recovery at the expense of the divided Liberal Party, realizing at the same time the immense appeal value of Lloyd George; these two influences brought about an electioneering coalition between the Lloyd George Liberals and the Conservative-Unionists.

Their appeal to the electorate was on the grounds that they had won the war and could now win the peace; in support of this they issued a rather cautiously worded plan for reconstruction which included housing, Home Rule for Ireland without Ulster and, what was nearer to their hearts, de-control of industry. But soon a more disreputable note crept into the coalition programme and its electioneering promises, in response to a popular demand for vegeance on Germany that had arisen and was being unscrupulously fanned by some newspapers. Germany would be made to pay the whole costs of the war; in the words of Lloyd George the 'uttermost farthing' would be exacted while one of his more exuberant supporters talked about squeezing 'the German lemon until the pips squeaked'. There was also a demand for punishment of war criminals which led to the cry 'Hang the Kaiser'. With such a torrent of emotional support behind him the coalition of Conservatives and Lloyd George

281

Liberals went swiftly ahead in what was known as the 'coupon' election; Asquith had scornfully called the endorsement of the candidature of the Lloyd George Liberals as giving them the 'coupon'. The general election took place in late December; the appeal was to an electorate increased by the provisions of the Representation of the People Act of 1918 which had given the vote to all men over 21 hitherto unfranchised and to women over 30 who were householders or the wives of householders; as an exceptional measure the vote was given to men between 18 and 21 who were serving in the armed forces. In spite of the hysteria and feeling aroused only 59% of the electorate voted in this general election, the results of which were declared on 28 December 1918.

With the return of 335 Conservative-Unionists and 133 Lloyd George Liberals the Coalition secured a large majority; in addition it could rely on support from 23 Conservatives and 25 Irish Unionists who had not stood under the coalition 'coupon'. The largest opposition party was that of Labour which increased its strength to 63 M.P.s.; only 28 pro-Asquith Liberals were elected. The elections in Ireland had returned 73 Sinn Fein M.P.s. who in support of their demand for independence for Ireland refused to take their seats at Westminster. Behind the shop window of the Coalition it was clear that the Conservatives had gained most from this political manoeuvre, while the split between the Asquith and Lloyd George Liberals and the competition of the Labour Party made Liberal recovery to anything like its former position impossible.

The prime minister of the coalition ministry was Lloyd George; by general acclaim the outstanding figure of leadership of the war years, it remained to be seen if his imagination, energy, eloquence and adroitness would produce similar results in peacetime. Bonar Law, leader of the Conservatives, was Lord Privy Seal and leader of the House of Commons: he was an able parliamentarian whose quiet and restrained manner contrasted sharply with the exuberance of the Prime Minister and whose wise advice on many occasions influenced Lloyd George to abandon some of his wilder schemes. Other ministers of ability were Lord Birkenhead, the Lord Chancellor; Austen Chamberlain, Chancellor of the Exchequer; the Foreign Secretary A. J. Balfour, a former prime minister, and Winston Churchill, at this time still a Liberal, who became secretary of state for war.

Demobilization of the armed forces

At the beginning of 1919 the immediate domestic problem for the government was to bring about the change-over of the British economy from a wartime organization to a peacetime basis. A first step in this was the demobilization of the armed forces, which at the end of the war amounted to over six millions, and the return of all this manpower to civilian life and

*Demobilization –
handing in
weapons and
equipment*

employment. The official plans for orderly demobilization were based on
the idea of giving priority of release to skilled craftsmen who were essential
to get the wheels of industry moving and so provide jobs for the main
body of the demobilized. This scheme caused discontent because it
favoured those who had been the last to be called up; large scale demonstrations and riots took place in the transit camps where troops were
awaiting demobilization. A change in policy followed and the principle of
'first in, first out' was applied; by the end of 1919 over four million men
had been released from the forces. A strong but short-lived economic
boom coincided with demobilization; this upsurge in demand was due to
abundant purchasing power brought by war profits, war savings and the
gratuities paid to ex-service men. Until the spring of 1920 unemployment
remained low, the October 1919 total being under half a million which was
below the official expectations for the immediate postwar period.

De-control of industry 1919–22

During the war the government had set up an elaborate apparatus of
control over the key sections of the nation's economy e.g. railways,
munitions, coal mining and shipping; to direct the activities of these
industries new ministries had been created or special commissions
appointed. There was also control of food by rationing and in addition a
system of price controls which regulated prices in various commodities.
The whole situation raised the problem of how far post-war de-control
was to go; the industrial and business community pressed urgently for

283

complete de-control because it deeply distrusted the idea of any government interference with the working of the economy. On the other hand there was an influential minority opinion which realized that public utilities such as electricity and transport, could in the national interest be put under state control, but in the event private interests prevailed; attempts to set up public boards for the generation and distribution of electricity were defeated in Parliament and such powers as the government took under a Ways and Communications Act in 1919 to control transport and the supply of electricity were very slight indeed.

One by one the various controls were abolished; shipping in 1919; food rationing in 1919–20 and price control in 1920. The government munition factories were sold as soon as possible and also the large stock of 'government surplus' war stores; much of this was sold at 'give-away' prices which depressed the market for some time ahead. The wartime ministries of Munitions, Shipping, and Food were ended by the beginning of 1921. Government control of the railways ended in August 1921 and in the same year a Railway Act was passed which brought about an amalgamation of the many companies of prewar days and formed them into four distinct railway systems which lasted down to 1947 when the railways were nationalized by the Labour government. The four great groups of private ownership which were now constituted were: the Great Western railway; the London Midland and Scottish; the London and North Eastern railway; and the Southern railway.

Great Britain and the peace treaties

At the same time as it wrestled with the postwar problems of the home front, the Coalition government faced the equally important task of making peace. In January 1919 the delegations of the victorious allies assembled in Paris to discuss the terms of peace that were to be given to the defeated powers Germany, Austria, Bulgaria, Turkey, and Hungary. While there were as many as seventy delegations whose members claimed they had participated in the war against Germany and her allies, the actual terms of peace were decided by a much smaller group rather in the same way as at the Vienna Congress of 1815. There were five powers who really counted: Great Britain, France, the U.S.A., Italy, and Japan; gradually the 'Big Five' became the 'Big Four' and finally the 'Big Three'; (Great Britain, France and the U.S.A.). The outstanding personal figures in the 'Big Three' were Lloyd George for Great Britain, Clemenceau for France and President Woodrow Wilson for the U.S.A.

The treaties were shaped in two ways, by discussions among the innermost circle of Lloyd George, Wilson and Clemenceau, and by commissions and committees which worked out the details. Lloyd George played a considerable part in this peace making; his subtle and adroit

Peacemaking at Versailles 1919. From left to right: Lloyd George (G.B.), Orlando (Italy), Clemenceau (France) and Woodrow Wilson (U.S.A.)

mind delighted in the political problems and tensions that had to be resolved, but he was under pressure from the home front for a severe peace, particularly as regards payment for the cost of the war by Germany. There was also the problem of the severe and uncompromising attitude of Clemenceau who demanded a peace which would give France security regardless of the effects on Germany, and which meant permanent occupation of a demilitarized Rhineland and the creation of the left bank Rhineland territories into a separate state under French control. At the other extreme there was President Wilson who was a political idealist and who wished to make his scheme for a League of Nations prominent in the peace settlement together with some of his 'Fourteen Points' especially those relating to 'self-determination' and the disposal of the German colonies. By the middle of March the drift of events caused Lloyd George great concern because he considered the French demands for reparations grossly excessive in amount and their plans for the Rhineland and a Polish state unreasonable. Communism was showing itself in Central Europe and Lloyd George feared it might get a hold in Germany if the peace terms were too severe. He therefore wrote a memorandum entitled 'Some considerations for the Peace Conference before they finally draft their terms', in which he urged general moderation towards Germany in the framing of the peace terms.

The Treaty of Versailles, 1919

The treaty terms were presented to the German delegation early in May; after protesting at their severity they finally signed in the Hall of Mirrors at Versailles on 28 June 1919.

285

The main terms of the treaty were:

1. France recovered Alsace–Lorraine; Belgium received Eupen and Malmédy.

2. The Rhineland was to be demilitarized and the left bank to be occupied by allied forces for fifteen years; the Saar coalfield was to be worked for fifteen years by France in compensation for the destruction of her own coalfields in Northern France during the war.

3. Plebiscites were to be held to decide the future of Schleswig, East Prussia, and Upper Silesia.

4. The state of Poland was reconstituted but Danzig became a Free City under the League of Nations.

5. The German conquests from Russia made by the Treaty of Brest–Litovsk became independent states e.g. Lithuania, Latvia and Estonia; Finland also became independent.

6. The German colonies were placed under the mandate of the League of Nations who entrusted their administration to various powers, e.g. Great Britain, France, Belgium, Japan, South Africa, Australia and New Zealand; some provinces of the former Turkish Empire e.g. Syria, Palestine and Iraq were also placed under mandate.

7. Germany was to pay reparations to cover the cost of the war and war pensions; the amount was unspecified but was to be determined in detail by a Reparations Commission.

8. The German armed forces were to be limited to an army of 100,000 men with no tanks or aeroplanes, and to a small navy.

9. Germany acknowledged her responsibility for starting the war – the so-called 'war guilt' clause.

10. The treaty incorporated the idea of the League of Nations and its Covenant but Germany was not admitted to this League whose aim was to secure peace and disarmament.

The Versailles treaty was followed by separate treaties with Austria, Bulgaria, Hungary and Turkey. The merits and demerits of the Versailles settlement have been widely discussed; probably the most objectionable features were the reparations and 'war guilt' clauses: regarding the latter it must be said that Germany's opponents were not entirely blameless in this respect. The territorial clauses were more moderate than would have been imposed had Germany won the war; German nationalist propaganda which labelled the treaty as a *Diktat* provided an excuse for the aggressions of Hitler after 1933. More important was the lamentable disunity that arose among the victorious powers and which on the longer term gave little chance of the successful working of the treaties. A major misfortune was that the United States had not ratified the treaties because President Wilson could not get the two-thirds majority in the Senate necessary for this, while the increasing obsession of France with security and reparations made British cooperation with her difficult; Italy was a dissatisfied power because her territorial and colonial aims were ignored in 1919.

Reparations, security and disarmament 1921–2

Difficulties soon arose in the working of the peace treaties and while Lloyd George worked hard to ease matters, not a great deal of success attended his efforts. Basically the situation was that Germany, although defeated, was wriggling on the hook of reparations and trying to evade her undertakings to pay these; France was dissatisfied with this and sought not only the exact fulfilment of the treaty by the Germans but also security for herself in Europe; Lloyd George had to face this difficult French attitude virtually unaided since the other allied great power, the U.S.A., had by 1920 withdrawn from Europe and its affairs. In 1921 Lloyd George sided with the French over reparations which were fixed for Germany at £6,600 million. When in December 1921 a default in payment of reparations was threatened by Germany this brought Lloyd George and Briand, the French Premier, together in conference, and for a time it looked as if not only would agreement be reached by the two powers over reparations but also there might be an Anglo-French *entente* which would satisfy France's anxious desire for security in Europe. It was also hoped to bring back Russia into the European community and a conference was called at Genoa in April 1922 to discuss the economic problems of Europe. Unfortunately, Briand fell from power in France and was displaced by Poincaré, whose attitude towards Germany was severe and unyielding. At Genoa where twenty-nine European states were represented, including Germany and Russia, it seemed for a moment that something would be achieved to bring about economic reconstruction and political peace in Europe. Unfortunately the French sabotaged this conference and announced that they would take individual action if Germany defaulted on her reparation payments. The Russian proposal for the settlement of the prewar Czarist debts, considerable amounts of which were held by French investors, were unacceptable and prevented a resumption of normal relations by the Western European states with Soviet Russia.

The Genoa conference was a failure; had it succeeded it would have greatly enhanced Lloyd George's reputation. The failure was only partly offset by the agreement reached at the Washington conference on disarmament (November 1921 to February 1922). One particular topic discussed was the Pacific and Far East, an area in which the U.S.A. was greatly interested and which explains her participation in this conference. It was not possible to reach any agreement on the reduction of land forces but in the matter of naval armament considerable progress was achieved. 287

A ten-year ban on construction of warships was agreed to and a ratio for the fleets of the U.S.A., Great Britain, Japan, France and Italy was laid down. A four-power treaty between the U.S.A., Great Britain, Japan and France guaranteed the *status quo* in the Pacific and this brought to an end the alliance between Great Britain and Japan which had lasted since 1902.

The 'Easter rebellion' and after

A major domestic problem which called for solution when the Coalition government took office in 1919 was that of Ireland where the situation had been radically affected by the war of 1914–18. Britain's preoccupation with the war provided an obvious opportunity for Irish nationalism to assert itself. The postponement of the operation of the Home Rule Act of 1914 on the outbreak of war had not helped the moderate Irish Home Rule Nationalists under Redmond and had given an impetus to the views of more revolutionary organizations whose aim was an independent republic. These included Sinn Fein ('Ourselves alone') – the party of Arthur Griffith, which aimed at the political, economic and cultural separation of Ireland from Britain, the Irish Volunteers which had been organized in 1913 as a reply to the Ulster Volunteers, and the Citizen Army of the Socialist Republican Party led by Larkin and Conolly.

Easter Sunday 1916 was chosen by the revolutionary groups as the day for attack on British rule in Ireland but last minute developments made success look unlikely and therefore discussions took place with a view to postponement of action. Nevertheless the rising was prematurely started on Easter Monday by the Citizen Army and left-wing Dublin Volunteer elements who seized the key points in Dublin, proclaimed a republic and attacked the British garrison which was taken by surprise. Aid from Germany in the shape of arms had been negotiated by Sir Roger Casement, but the ship carrying them was intercepted and Casement who landed from a German submarine on the coast of Kerry with the aim of postponing the rising, was captured and later tried, convicted of treason and executed. British reinforcements converged on Dublin and after nearly a week of street fighting the Irish were forced to surrender. The execution of fourteen of their leaders was a mistake; it made reconciliation between Britain and Ireland almost impossible and the memory of the martyrs of 1916 greatly increased support for insurgent Irish nationalism. For the rest of the war Ireland simmered under British rule; Lloyd George made an unsuccessful attempt to find a solution in 1917 by summoning a representative gathering of Irish politicians, while the extension of conscription to Ireland in 1918 was generally resisted.

Guerrilla war 1919–21

At the general election of December 1918, 73 Sinn Fein candidates were elected, with 25 Unionists and 7 Nationalist Home Rulers representing pro-British and more moderate opinion. The Sinn Feiners refused to take their seats at Westminster and instead met in Dublin in an assembly they called the *Dail Eireann* and on 21 January 1919 proclaimed an Irish Republic with Eamon de Valera as president; other leading figures were Arthur Griffith, Michael Collins and Cathal Brugha. The infant republic appealed for recognition to the powers then making peace at Paris but they failed to get this although some American financial help was later obtained. Within Ireland the republic had to build up its own structure of government in competition with the existing British one; gradually their own courts, taxation system and control of local government emerged, but since British rule could only be finally overthrown by fighting it, war started early in 1919 and continued until July 1921.

The first major target of the Republicans was the Royal Irish Constabulary; individual policemen were shot, attacks were made on their barracks and a general boycott enforced against them and their families. The British government's reply to these terrorist methods was through the notorious 'Black and Tans', who were ex-soldiers recruited to fill the thinning ranks of the Royal Irish Constabulary, and also the 'Auxiliaries' who were drawn from ex-officers; in addition to these there was a large force of British regular troops in Ireland. By 1920 the pattern of the war was fully revealed; it was basically a fairly large scale guerrilla war of 'hit and run' attacks on convoys and barracks, the destruction of government records, kidnapping of individuals, shooting of hostages, searching of houses and interrogating their inmates, curfew in the towns, the burning of property, and atrocities and counter-atrocities by both sides. The south and south-western parts of Ireland were most affected but the war had its counterpart in Northern Ireland where the Ulster Protestant Volunteers attacked the Catholic Irish minority.

In the midst of this war the British government enacted the Government of Ireland Act (December 1920); this divided Ireland into Northern Ireland (Ulster) and Southern Ireland, giving both parts Home Rule, but reserving the power of taxation for the Parliament at Westminster. Ulster somewhat reluctantly accepted this new status but events in Southern Ireland had gone too far to make acceptance possible there. Almost at the same time as the British government committed itself to the policy of partition it introduced martial law in the counties of south and south-west Ireland where opposition was greatest; this enabled military courts to carry out summary trials of those caught with arms or participating in acts of hostility to British rule. The guerrilla warfare intensified as a result of this step and casualties rose on both sides. Meanwhile political opinion in Britain had swung against the policy of the government and its use of 'Black and Tans' and their vicious methods; there was growing

*Black and Tans
searching a Sinn
Feiner 1920*

realization of the futility in the long run of the policy of reprisals. Influential voices were heard in favour of a negotiated peace and the grant of Dominion status to Ireland. The Coalition government now had to decide whether to push on relentlessly with its policy of force to the bitter end or reverse it and move towards conciliation. It decided on the latter course and a truce was arranged for Monday 11 July 1921.

The Anglo-Irish Treaty, December 1921; the Irish Free State 1922–3

Lengthy negotiations followed and finally a conference for a treaty met in London on 11 October 1921. The Irish delegation was led by Arthur Griffith and Michael Collins; the representatives of Ulster were notable absentees. Basically Lloyd George's policy was to settle with the offer of Dominion status for Ireland, although this status clashed with the idea of an independent and sovereign Irish Republic which was held by many of the Irish leaders; in particular there was great difficulty over the oath of allegiance to the Crown which Dominion status involved. Eventually Lloyd George, by rather misleading promises over Ulster and its boundaries, persuaded the Irish delegation to abandon their original idea of a republic in external association with the British Commonwealth for Dominion status within the Commonwealth. Difficulties still arose over the form of the oath of allegiance to the Crown and at this stage (5 December) Lloyd George delivered an ultimatum to the Irish delegates; either they must sign a treaty at once or war to the limit would follow. Rather surprisingly they signed on his terms recognizing that, although the treaty fell short of their ambitions, it conceded much and could be used as a base for a further advance later on. Thus the Irish Free State came into existence with Dominion status similar to that of Canada. Great Britain was granted the use of some Irish ports for her navy and the Irish Free State assumed liability for certain financial payments, notably those in connection with the annuities due under the Land Purchase Acts. Northern Ireland could, and did, contract out of the treaty and so kept the status given her by the Act of 1920; a basic British condition was that Northern Ireland should not be coerced into a united Ireland.

On 2 January 1922 the Dail ratified the treaty but by a very narrow majority (64 to 57); on January 22 the British authorities handed over their powers to a provisional government, pending the drafting of a constitution for the new state which was finally promulgated in December 1922. The signing of the Treaty led to a serious split between Arthur Griffith and de Valera; the latter strongly objected to the oath of allegiance to the Crown which conflicted with his idea of a republic in external association only with the British Commonwealth. De Valera now formed a new party, the Republican Party, and in this he was backed by many of the left-wing members of the Irish Republican army. Civil war followed and the provisional Government had to take stringent measures to suppress the opposition of the Republican irregulars. It took nearly a year to do this and there was considerable loss of life and much damage to property, particularly of the country's railway system. One of the casualties was Michael Collins, Commander-in-Chief of the Dail's forces; Arthur Griffith had died a few weeks earlier. Only after this bitter civil war was it possible for the Irish Free State to start its separate existence under the presidency of W. G. Cosgrave in 1923.

25. Tory and Labour 1922–4

The decline of the Coalition

After 1920 political strain increasingly showed itself in the Coalition government whose successful working depended on the union of the talents and reputation of Lloyd George with the political support of the Conservative Party; Lloyd George was an outstanding leader but a leader without a substantial party. In politics, as in many other matters, there was a natural wish to get back to the old order of things, and this meant ending the Coalition and returning to strict party government. At first the Conservative Party was by no means unanimous about ending the Coalition, for there were a number of influential Conservatives who regarded Lloyd George as an indispensable leader; there were also some who urged the fusion of the Conservative and Liberal parties into a combined anti-Socialist front. Among these supporters of the Coalition were Austen Chamberlain, Lord Birkenhead, Lord Balfour, and to some extent Mr Bonar Law. The section of the Conservative Party that was most hostile to the Coalition was the right wing element of diehard imperialists and unionists who were much offended by the policy Lloyd George had followed of giving Ireland an independent Dominion status which they thought was an evil omen for the future of the British Empire. By the beginning of 1922 Lloyd George himself realized that his position was becoming precarious. He had come under increasing criticism for his apparent carelessness over the sale of honours which had been handed out on a great scale and which could be almost openly bought by a suitably lavish contribution to the party funds of either the Lloyd George Liberals or the Conservative Party. Yet there was a reluctance among his senior Conservative supporters to throw everything into the melting pot and to risk the chances of a general election and this kept the Coalition alive until the autumn of 1922.

The Chanak crisis 1922

It was the policy of Lloyd George in the Eastern Mediterranean that cast doubt upon his skill as a political leader and which eventually resolved the hesitations of the Conservatives about the continuation of the Coalition. Since the overthrow of the Turkish Empire Lloyd George had encouraged the expansionist aims of the Greeks to the extent of supporting their occupation of the south-western part of Asia Minor. This policy antagonized France who was suspicious of British ambitions in the Near East; it also alarmed Russia who feared that it might herald another intervention against her regime through Turkey. The situation was changed by the dramatic success of the Turkish republican leader Mustafa Kemal who rallied his countrymen against the invading Greeks. By September 1922 Kemal had driven the Greeks into the sea at Smyrna and the Chanak crisis then followed. This was caused by the victorious Turks moving towards the Straits Zone, an area on both sides of the Dardanelles leading up to the Black Sea and which was occupied by French and British troops. If the Turks did not respect this neutral zone then clearly war with Turkey would follow. The British Cabinet asked the self-governing Dominions to send contingents to help Great Britain in this impending war. Generally their response was unfavourable since the Dominions considered British action in this crisis was inconsistent with their independent Dominion status. An ultimatum was sent to the Turks ordering them to withdraw from the neutral zone, but the British General Harington, commanding at Chanak, saved the situation by delaying action on this until tempers had time to cool and negotiations could be carried out with the Turks. The crisis was ended by the Convention of Mudania by which the Turks agreed to respect the neutral zone.

The end of the Coalition government, October 1922

The Chanak crisis and the part Lloyd George played in it decided the Conservative leaders to reach a decision about the future of the Coalition. Either they must continue it and fight another general election under the leadership of Lloyd George or else it must be ended. Many Conservatives thought that in such a general election the Conservative Party might be routed and that Lloyd George would drag down their party in the same way as he had his own. The Conservative Party leaders called a meeting of the party at the Carlton Club on October 19. Much would depend on the attitude of Bonar Law who now emerged as an alternative prime minister to Lloyd George. At this meeting Balfour and Austen Chamberlain spoke in favour of continuing the Coalition but a vehement speech against it was made by Stanley Baldwin, a junior minister, and then Bonar Law declared that the Coalition should be ended by the Conservative Party leaving it. The vote in favour of this was 187 to 87. Following this Lloyd George tendered his resignation and that of the Coalition government to the King who then asked Bonar Law to form a government.

The ministry of Bonar Law 1922-3

The Cabinet formed by Bonar Law was not particularly distinguished. His choice of ministers was limited by the reluctance of some of the senior Conservative ministers of the Coalition, including Austen Chamberlain, to accept office because they considered that it had been a mistake to end the Coalition. Stanley Baldwin was promoted to the office of chancellor of the Exchequer and Lord Curzon became foreign secretary; most of the remaining ministers were drawn from the right-wing backbenchers of the party. For the general election held in November 1922 Bonar Law gave the watchwords 'Tranquillity and stability'. The Conservatives gained an overall majority of about 80 with 345 M.P.s, although their Liberal and Labour opponents polled jointly far more votes. The Liberal showing was still respectable with 54 M.P.s supporting Asquith and 62 for Lloyd George's National Liberal Party, but the most significant result was the advance of Labour; from 63 M.P.s in 1918 their strength increased to 142 and the total vote polled by the party was very nearly doubled.

The premiership of Bonar Law ended in May 1923 when, stricken by a mortal illness, he resigned office. During his ministry the major pre-occupation was foreign affairs in which Lord Curzon had both success and failure. The success concerned the negotiation of a treaty with Turkey to restore peace in the Eastern Mediterranean. At the Lausanne Conference Curzon shaped the details of a peace which included arrangements for a demilitarized zone on either side of the Straits; rules for the navigation through the Straits, and decisions regarding disputed areas such as Eastern Thrace and Mosul in Northern Iraq. A more difficult problem was the French and Belgian occupation of the Ruhr early in 1923 which was due to their annoyance over the default of Germany over the delivery of reparation goods such as coal and timber. Great Britain did not agree with French policy over this and the wartime *entente* between France and Britain was now brought to the verge of extinction. Curzon tried to mediate between the French and German governments emphasizing that the capacity of Germany to pay reparations should be more accurately investigated and that the whole matter was related to the question of inter-allied war debts. This constructive attitude was undermined by the action of the new Prime Minister, Baldwin who after a personal discussion with Poincaré went over to the French point of view.

Early in 1923 Great Britain made a settlement with the U.S.A. of her war debts which amounted to £978 millions. The negotiations were carried out by the Chancellor of the Exchequer, Baldwin, and the British government reluctantly accepted the best terms he could obtain viz. repayments were to be spread over a period of 62 years, together with a moderate rate of interest on the capital outstanding.

Baldwin's first ministry 1923–4

When Bonar Law resigned in May 1923, he made no direct recommendation about his successor to the King, although it is possible he may have favoured the claims of Stanley Baldwin. The alternative candidate was Lord Curzon, who personally was very sure that his long career, which included the appointments of viceroy of India and foreign secretary, must give him the coveted post of prime minister. But the King summoned

Baldwin, largely on the grounds that it would not be possible to have Lord Curzon as premier because he was a peer; Lord Balfour, whom the King consulted, pointed out the difficulties that his uncle, Lord Salisbury, had experienced when prime minister through being in the House of Lords. Curzon was stunned by the news that the King had sent for Baldwin, and considered that this was a slur on his career and his status as a peer; nevertheless he continued as foreign secretary under the new Prime Minister.

There was some surprise at the promotion of Baldwin to the premiership but there were few acceptable alternatives available. His political career had been somewhat uneventful since he first became an M.P. in 1908. He had shown himself a good House of Commons man and was respected for his patience and humour; his careers as president of the Board of Trade and as Chancellor of the Exchequer had been successful and had obviously marked him out for promotion. His reputation in his party had been enhanced by his speech at the celebrated Carlton House meeting which decided the fate of the Coalition. There is no doubt he successfully projected an image of himself as an honest, plain-dealing, pipe-smoking Englishman, which reassured the man in the street, but in many respects he was limited and conventional in his outlook.

Only a few changes were made by Baldwin to Bonar Law's Cabinet, the most notable being that Neville Chamberlain became chancellor of the Exchequer. The new ministry pursued a somewhat uneventful career through the second half of 1923, but in October the political scene was galvanized by the sudden declaration of Baldwin that only the adoption of a protectionist policy could solve the country's economic difficulties. This point of view is understandable when considered in relation to the unemployment figures which had been steadily mounting; in October 1923 they stood at over 1,350,000. While Baldwin genuinely believed that a protective tariff could do much to solve unemployment, he had other motives for urging this change of national policy. He realized that the adoption of protection as Conservative policy would reunite the party which had been splintered when the Coalition broke up in 1922, and that if successful it would weaken the strongest remaining supporters of a free trade policy, the Liberal Party. To secure a mandate for this new policy a general election was necessary and with some reluctance the King granted a dissolution on 16 November 1923. While Baldwin's purely party aims were successful in so far as the Conservative Party fought as a united party, it was nevertheless substantially defeated in the general election, losing 87 seats and thus its overall majority in the House. The Liberal and Labour parties increased their numbers; Labour gained 49 seats to give it a total of 191 M.P.s, and the Liberals, who had been reunited by the challenge to free trade, raised their total from 116 to 159.

The political possibilities of this situation were that there could either

295

be a coalition of Conservative and Liberals (which was unlikely) or a minority government based on the Labour Party which would probably rely for general support on the votes of the Liberal Party. The feeling grew that Labour must be given its chance: Asquith, who held a dominating position at this particular moment, considered that there was no reason why a Labour government should not be tried, and added: 'that it could hardly be tried under safer conditions'; some Conservatives also saw possibilities in the situation, that Labour in any case was a minority and it might well discredit itself in its management of the nation's business. The Baldwin ministry met the new Parliament in January 1924 and very soon had an amendment of 'no confidence' carried against it by the joint votes of the Labour and Liberal parties. Baldwin resigned and on 22 January the King asked Ramsay MacDonald, the leader of the Labour opposition, to form the first Labour government.

The first Labour government, January to November 1924

The party that took office in 1924 was a mixed one; it was not exclusively a workers' party since it had many middle-class members. Certain elements can be distinguished: trade union leaders headed by J. H. Thomas and J. R. Clynes; members of the Independent Labour Party, such as Philip Snowden, F. W. Jowett, and Clement Attlee, and a Socialist 'ginger group' from Clydeside including such colourful characters as James Maxton, David Kirkwood, and John Wheatley. There were also some Fabian representatives, including Sydney Webb, the high priest of the movement, and also some Liberals who joined Labour because they despaired of the future of their original party.

Ramsay MacDonald, the first Labour Prime Minister, had been elected leader of his party in 1922. He had been an early member of the I.L.P.; in 1900 he had become secretary of the newly-founded parliamentary Labour Party and in 1912 he had become its treasurer. To some extent he had suffered political eclipse during the war owing to his pacifist convictions. His climb to the leadership of the party in 1922 had been much assisted by his skilful work with the advanced Socialist wing of the party; they mistakenly believed that he was their man and in 1922 they gave their support to him for leadership of the party, which enabled him to gain a small majority over his rival, J. R. Clynes. Outwardly MacDonald had an engaging and distinguished appearance, and a poetical eloquence that raised great expectations even if it disregarded hard facts. In truth he was not a revolutionary Socialist but rather one who believed in the gradual conversion of British society to a Socialist basis; his greatest fear was lest the revolutionary 'wild men' should upset the Socialist 'apple cart' and thus discredit his discreet leadership; he also thought it essential to keep the Labour Party well clear of the Communist International.

The Cabinet that MacDonald assembled was a judicious cross-section of the various elements in his party together with a few distinguished non-party personalities, such as Lord Haldane, who became lord chancellor. MacDonald himself, besides being prime minister, took the office of foreign secretary. Five ministers were appointed from the trade unionist ranks, notably Arthur Henderson at the Home Office, and J. H. Thomas as secretary of state for the colonies; this was rather less than might have been expected since the bulk of the Labour members represented trade union interests. The left of the party had representation in the Cabinet in the persons of J. W. Wheatley as minister of Health, and F. W. Jowett as first commissioner of Works. It is clear that MacDonald wished to give to the public at large an impression of moderation and respectability in his Cabinet.

Home affairs

The first Labour government has been criticized for the slightness of its achievements on the domestic front but it must be remembered that they were inexperienced in the conduct of government and that they were dependent on the Liberals for support in the House of Commons. On the whole they showed a certain amount of enlightenment in their approach, and a greater awareness of the pressing social needs of the time even if the results were not very impressive. In unemployment insurance the gap between benefit periods which had previously existed was abolished and the position was improved for those who hitherto had been unable to draw unemployment pay because they were not covered for it by their contributions. In education the number of scholarships for secondary education was increased and the scheme for state scholarships to the Universities was extended. A Housing Act, sponsored by the minister of Health, J. W. Wheatley, gave more generous subsidies for longer periods to Local Authorities to encourage them to build houses for letting to working-class tenants at controlled rents; this was a considerable advance over the previous Acts of 1919 and 1923. In spite of its promises the Labour government was ineffective in dealing with the bugbear of unemployment; the most it achieved was a few public works schemes to build roads and to extend the electricity system. The Labour Chancellor of the Exchequer, Snowden, was reluctant to grant money for such purposes; his economic thinking was fashioned along conventional *laissez-faire* free trade lines and he earned the applause of the Liberal Party when his budget reduced taxation and also abolished the McKenna protective duties which had been levied on certain imports since 1915.

Labour and foreign policy

In foreign affairs the Labour government had more success due to their 297 more international approach and outlook; the Prime Minister, who was also foreign secretary, scored a personal success in his negotiations in this field. Better relations were established with France by the agreement over the Dawes Plan for the fixing of adjusted reparation figures and the stabilizing of the German mark after the devastating inflation of 1923. When the inflexible Poincaré was succeeded in May 1924 by the more liberal-minded Herriot, Anglo-French relations became distinctly harmonious, and at the London Conference in July agreement was reached over the implementation of the Dawes Plan and the evacuation of the Ruhr by the French: by his work at this conference MacDonald made a contribution to the peace of Europe by bringing about German–French reconciliation. The Labour government sent a strong delegation to the Assembly of the League of Nations in September 1924. MacDonald, with the close support of Herriot, proposed ways and means whereby through the use of arbitration in disputes between nations, security and ultimately disarmament could be achieved. As a result the League Assembly accepted the 'Protocol for the Pacific Settlement of International Disputes' by which disputes between nations would either be dealt with by the Court of International Justice or otherwise by arbitration. The Labour Party fell from power before it had time to ratify Great Britain's adherence to this instrument and the Conservative government which followed rejected it.

Amidst much bitter opposition from Conservatives and Liberals, the Labour government entered into negotiations with Russia. These took the form of official recognition of the Soviet Union as the lawful successor of the Czarist rulers, and negotiations for a commercial treaty combined with a settlement of British claims in respect of the loans that had been raised by the Czarist government on the London market. A commercial treaty was signed and also a general treaty which provided for later negotiation in respect of the prewar debts and other British claims for property confiscated at the time of the Russian revolution. When negotiations under this second treaty had been successfully completed, the treaty promised that Great Britain would make a loan to Soviet Russia; it was this last proposal for a loan to a Communist state that aroused the wrath of the political opponents of Labour.

The fall of the Labour government was brought about by its handling of the 'J. R. Campbell' case: Campbell was the editor of a Communist paper in which he had written an article urging soldiers not to fire on their fellow-workers in case of an industrial dispute or during wartime. The government started a prosecution for sedition, but a week later cancelled proceedings; their action led to the tabling of a Conservative vote of censure and also a Liberal amendment calling for a Select Committee of Inquiry into the government's conduct. The government announced that

298

they would make this a matter of confidence and if defeated would ask for a dissolution of Parliament. On 8 October the hostile amendment was carried against the government by 364 votes to 198. The next day parliament was dissolved and a general election fixed for 29 October.

The 'Zinoviev letter' and the defeat of Labour

The election campaign was marked by an all-out attack by the Conservatives and Liberals on the general policy of the Labour government. Its pro-Russian policy came particularly under attack and it was not difficult to smear Labour as being pro-Communist and pro-Russian and as preferring the interests of Russia to those of Great Britain and her empire. The counter-attractions of the 'sane, common sense' government promised by Baldwin undoubtedly prevailed in the electors' minds, especially those of the floating voters. Four days before polling day came the sensation of the 'Zinoviev letter' and while its importance in deciding the election result has been exaggerated it made victory certain for the Conservatives. The letter appeared as a communication to the British Communist Party signed by Zinoviev, the head of the Communist International. It gave instructions for action to ensure the ratification of the Anglo-Russian treaty which the letter saw as a prelude to the achievement of an armed revolution to establish the dictatorship of the proletariat in Great Britain. The original of the letter had never been seen; it was only copies that had come into the possession of the Foreign Office and the *Daily Mail*. While the Prime Minister knew of the existence of the letter, his preoccupation with his electoral campaign seems to have prevented him from dealing with it firmly and decisively. The Foreign Office, knowing that the *Daily Mail* would certainly publish their copy of the letter, and considering it to be authentic, sent a letter of protest to the Russian *chargé d'affaires* in London and also to *The Times* for publication. The weight of evidence indicates that the Zinoviev letter was a forgery, although the Conservative government which followed Labour declared that according to secret-service information it was authentic; whatever the truth it was a last-minute bombshell which clinched the Conservative victory at the polls four days later.

The election was a substantial triumph for the Conservatives who increased their vote by over two and a half millions to eight millions, winning a total of 419 seats. Labour although it lost 40 seats nevertheless increased its vote by over one million; its membership in the new Parliament was 152. For the Liberal Party the election of 1924 appears as the point of no return in the twentieth century; it lost 116 seats, mostly to the Conservatives, and now had only 40 members. This crushing defeat signalled the return to the traditional two-party system of British politics.

26. The British economy 1919–39

The general problem of the economy

The Coalition government as part of its appeal to the electorate after the four years of war had made general promises of a better society in which there would be a higher standard of living and security of employment. While something was done between 1919 and 1939 to improve conditions the fact remains that the results fell far short of the expectations of social reformers or of the British working classes. One major reason for this was the state of the British economy between the wars. During this period its rate of productivity increased too slowly; it relied too much on the 'old' industries such as cotton, coal mining and shipbuilding which found it increasingly difficult to compete in world markets, and its direction was too much influenced by bankers and businessmen who thought in terms of the successful nineteenth-century economy which had lasted down to 1914.

No government during this interwar period was able to find a solution which would bring Britain well and truly out of the economic doldrums. The proof of this was shown by the very high level of unemployment; between 1921 and 1939 it did not fall below one million and in the years between 1931 and 1935 it was over two millions. This unemployment was particularly severe in the 'depressed areas' such as Lancashire, the north-east coast and South Wales where the cotton, shipbuilding and coal mining industries were located. The government did very little to create employment by planned government expenditure in spite of the demonstration by the economist J. M. Keynes that only such action could mobilize the unused resources of the economy; the Bank of England and the Treasury thought this idea dangerous and inflationary. The advice of the orthodox economists was to let the slump work itself out as had been done in the nineteenth century; only when deflation had worked through the economy would there be an upswing in investment, production and employment: in social terms this meant unemployment for millions of people.

The burden of debt

In 1914 Great Britain's National Debt was about £650 millions; by March 1919 it had increased some twelve times to around £7,500 millions; £6,000 millions was internal debt and £1,000 millions external debt borrowed for war purposes from the U.S.A. The effects of this mountain of debt were generally adverse for the British economy between the wars.

The heavy annual charge for interest on this debt brought much higher direct taxation than had prevailed before 1914, while awareness of the debt and its cost confirmed successive British governments in their opposition to the controlled inflation urged by Keynes for economic expansion, which would have increased the total of government debt. As repayment of the vast sum of debt was impossible, the government attempted to lessen the burden by conversion operations by which debt holders agreed to convert their holdings to lower rates of interest. In 1921 £630 millions of war debt was converted to a lower rate of interest ($3\frac{1}{2}\%$) and a larger conversion in 1932 brought £2,000 millions of War Loan down from a 5% rate to $3\frac{1}{2}\%$, thus saving £23 millions in annual interest charges.

Great Britain's external debt involved a payment in dollars of interest and capital to the U.S.A. and this was a drain on our gold and currency reserves. The question of British debts to the U.S.A. was complicated by the fact that Great Britain was owed money by her wartime allies, notably France and Italy, but she could get no repayment from them. Nevertheless, in 1923, Great Britain negotiated a debt settlement with the U.S.A. by which she agreed to pay 3% interest for ten years and thereafter $3\frac{1}{2}\%$ for fifty-two years, together with repayment of capital by annually increasing instalments. Payments under this agreement were made by Great Britain to the U.S.A. down to the period of the world economic crisis of 1930–1.

The return to the gold standard 1925

In 1914 the British unit of currency, the pound sterling, was on a gold standard basis, i.e. its value was equal to a fixed amount of gold (123 grains Troy weight). Under the system, gold to any amount could be freely imported into, or exported from, Great Britain. The amount of gold held determined the amount of currency available either in gold coins or Bank of England notes, the amount of the latter being strictly controlled under the Bank Charter Act of 1844. Down to 1914 gold sovereigns and half-sovereigns circulated freely and banknotes were convertible on demand into the equivalent amount of gold. Nearly all world currencies were linked to gold, thus giving stable exchange rates between them.

On the outbreak of war in 1914 Great Britain suspended the gold standard and prohibited the export of gold; the greatly increased wartime currency needs were met by inconvertible Treasury £1 and 10s. notes. This managed paper currency was continued until 1925 when the decision was taken to return to the gold standard modified to the extent that gold coins and convertibility of notes were not restored. Unfortunately this return was made at the old pre-war parity of £1 equals 4.86 U.S. dollars, and while this satisfied conservatively minded financiers and bankers who had been insisting that 'the pound must look the dollar in the face', its deflationary results were serious. The pound was now over-valued in relation to the U.S. dollar and also in respect of the currencies of those countries which had returned to the gold standard but at a parity lower than prewar. As a result British exports became over-priced so increasing the already marked decline in Britain's share of the world export market. The return to a gold standard was one of the factors contributing to industrial depression and unemployment within Britain which could not pay its debts in the world by exports of goods and so was increasingly forced to settle the claims of its creditors by export of gold. In the world economic crisis of 1930–1 the strain of maintaining the gold standard became too much and it was abandoned in November 1931 by the National government.

Population and its distribution

Between 1919 and 1939 the population of Great Britain and Northern Ireland increased by approximately four millions of which about three and a half millions was due to the natural increase by excess of live births over deaths; the balance of about half a million was accounted for by the return to Great Britain, owing to economic depression, of those who had previously emigrated to the U.S.A., Canada and Australia. The trend of a falling birth-rate which first showed itself in the 1870s was continued during this period and the curve moved down sharply in the 1930s; in 1940 the crude birth-rate figure for Britain was 14.6 per 1,000 (1964 18.4 per 1,000). The spread of birth control methods, the realization that fewer children meant better chances for their upbringing and a higher standard of living for the family, and the pessimism induced by the economic depression and likelihood of general war, all contributed to a falling birth-rate. Nevertheless population growth was maintained by a steady decline in the death rate which in 1930 was 11.7 per 1,000 compared with 18.4 per 1,000 in 1900. This fall in death rates was substantially helped by the improvement in infant mortality, i.e. of those who died before they were a year old. In 1920 infant mortality was 80 per 1,000; by 1940 it had fallen to 57 per 1,000 (1960=25 per 1,000). The decline in deaths in all age groups was brought about by the interaction of the following factors: an improved environment due to proper drainage, pure water supplies and better housing, the advance in medical knowledge and its greater availability through national health insurance, the development of infant welfare and child care, and a more varied and better balanced diet.

The distribution of this increased population within Britain continued to follow the pattern that had shown itself so strongly in the second half of the nineteenth century, viz. a movement from the countryside to the towns. The great urban areas expanded outwards in the interwar period

302

by the building of straggling suburbs; increased mobility was given by electrified railways, bus services and motor transport, so enabling workers to travel daily from these suburbs to their work, in contrast with the nineteenth-century practice of living within walking distance of the factory or office. There was also the beginning of the dispersal of industry in new areas away from the coalfields which had determined the location of industry in the nineteenth century; the availability of industrial power from electricity and oil made this change possible. At the same time a population drift began to show itself from depressed regional areas such as South Wales, Tyneside and Clydeside due to the depression in their heavy industries of coal mining, iron and steel and shipbuilding. It was London, the South-East and the Midlands, where the prospects of work were better owing to new industries and greater regional prosperity, which attracted most of this shift in population.

The 'old' industries

The postwar era brought increasing difficulties for Britain's 'old' staple industries such as cotton, coal, iron and steel, and shipbuilding. Down to 1914 these had been the mainstay of Britain's free trade economy providing the bulk of the consumer and capital goods which were exported to pay for our large imports of food and raw materials. Due to adverse factors such as rival and more efficient foreign producers, tariff barriers, and economic crises these industries saw their share of export markets steadily shrink after 1919.

Cotton. In 1913 the British cotton industry, largely concentrated in Lancashire, was at the peak of its prosperity, having in that year a labour force of 620,000, and exporting seven million yards of cotton cloth, chiefly to markets in India and the Far East. Wartime shortages stimulated cotton textile industries in Japan and India, working with modern machinery and with the advantage of very low wage rates; against these Lancashire found it impossible to compete. By 1938 its exports were only a fifth of the 1913 figure and its labour force had declined to 378,000.

Coal. Like cotton, coal in the years immediately before 1914 had been steadily expanding its output and the peak output of the British coal industry of 287 million tons was reached in 1913, of which 73 million tons were exported. Apart from a lucky break in 1923 when the French occupation of the German Ruhr and its mines brought boom conditions for British coal exports, British coal entered a period of slow decline. The industry was dogged by strikes and the lengthy one in 1926 lost export markets to German and Polish competitors; British mines had too many high cost producers where the seams were narrow and difficult to work; 303

more ominous was the long-term trend against coal with an increasing use of fuel oil for ships and power stations. Compared with the output and exports for the years 1900–14 the figures for 1919–39 show a decline of 8% in output and 20% in exports of British coal.

Iron and steel. While Britain in 1919 had a large capacity for iron and steel production much of her plant was old fashioned compared with that in Europe and the U.S.A. Her steel output was generally geared to the needs of shipbuilding and railways and demand from both these industries, especially shipbuilding, fluctuated widely in the 1920s. Some recovery came in the 1930s due to the imposition of a 33% duty on foreign imports in 1932 and to agreement with European steel producers to limit their exports to Britain. With the home market assured and with a rising demand for rearmament, shipbuilding and motor vehicle production, the British iron and steel industry, compared with the 1920s, increased its output between 1930 and 1938 by 16%.

Shipbuilding. In 1914 Great Britain was the biggest builder of merchant ships with 60% of the total world output. After a boom in 1919–20 to replace the tonnage sunk during the war, and when two million tons were launched from British yards, the industry went into recession apart from a prosperous period between 1927 and 1929. The sharp contraction of world trade and low freight rates made it impossible to shipowners to give orders for new ships, besides which British yards met increasing competition from foreign builders. A moderate recovery came in the 1930s; a government loan enabled the Cunard *Queen Mary* to be built and naval rearmament stimulated activity, but some shipbuilding areas such as Jarrow on Wear remained permanently depressed with unemployment rates of 50% or more.

Aids to the economy in the 1930s

Judged by the fortunes of Britain's 'old' industries the picture of the economy between the wars was a cheerless one but in the 1930s a number of factors brought a measure of improvement which enabled Great Britain to weather the world economic crisis perhaps better than some other industrialized countries. The abandonment of the gold standard in 1931 and the decision to let the £ find its own value against the U.S. dollar made British export prices more competitive in world markets. The adoption of a protective tariff and import quotas in 1932 gave British manufacturers and farmers an assured share of the home market (see chapter 30). Due to the heavy fall in world prices of commodities imported by Britain, especially foodstuffs, the cost of living fell. The economy was stimulated in the 1930s by a building boom made possible

304

by the low cost of labour and materials, and also low interest rates for house mortgages; after 1935 the annual output of the industry was over 350,000 houses, mostly built in the more prosperous areas such as London, the South-East and Midlands.

The 'new' industries

If Britain's 'old' industries were flagging, her 'new' ones were showing an encouraging growth in the 1930s; of these the most important were motor vehicles, electricity and chemicals. The scientific knowledge on which these industries were based had been established in the second half of the nineteenth century but its practical application for everyday use was the work of technicians and engineers in the first half of the twentieth century.

Motor vehicles. In 1914 nearly 200 separate British firms were making cars and lorries bearing their names, although at 34,000 vehicles the total output was small. The interwar years saw the introduction of American techniques such as the assembly line and the use of standardized components; these raised annual output to nearly 500,000 by 1939 and also reduced the cost of cars so bringing them within the reach of those with moderate incomes. Mass production also reduced the number of firms making cars to 20 by 1939 since many of the earlier manufacturers had been very small-scale producers of cars 'hand tailored' to their customers' requirements. The expansion of this industry is shown by the increase in its labour force from about 120,000 in 1923 to 250,000 in 1938.

Electricity. Between 1880 and 1914 the British electricity industry which included the generation and distribution of electricity and the manufacture of electrical plant had solved many of its technical problems but had not yet achieved a massive break-through in its effects on industrial and domestic life; before World War I steam power was strongly entrenched in industry and gas lighting predominated in public buildings and private houses. The interwar years were decisive in the development and use of electricity. The Central Electricity Board, created in 1926, concentrated generation in large-scale power stations in contrast to its previous production by a host of small local stations operating at different voltages and frequencies; it also built a national grid for the distribution of electricity. Industry in the 1920s began to turn increasingly to electricity as a source of power and its possibilities for the railway system were shown by the successful electrification carried out on the Southern railway system. Equally impressive was its advance on the domestic front where electricity supplanted gas as an illuminant and began its increasing contribution to higher living standards by making possible electric cookers, stoves, vacuum cleaners, radio and telephones. The industry also became an important exporter of generators, motors, transformers and cables; the increase in its labour force from 145,000 in 1923 to 341,000 in 1938 was significant.

Chemicals. By 1914 the British chemical industry had a large output of 'heavy' chemicals such as sodas and acids, of which the soap, textile, paper and glass industries were bulk users. After 1919 the technical progress of the industry was concentrated on many new products which were to have a far wider effect on everyday life. The most important of these were dyestuffs (the German monopoly of production of these before 1914 had created difficulties for Britain in World War I), artificial fibres, plastics, fertilizers, paint solvents, drugs and synthetic rubber; most of these were synthesized from coal-tar and petroleum derivatives.

One of the most successful of these developments in the interwar period was rayon. This 'man-made' fibre derived from the pioneer work in the 1890s of Chardonnet, Cross and Bevan and was commercially produced after 1900 by the firm of Courtaulds as an alternative to the costly natural silk derived from the silkworm. By the 1930s rayon had become widely used in women's outer and under wear and stockings; it became competitive in price with natural fibres such as cotton and was also used industrially, notably in tyre manufacture. Another socially important development was the widening range of drugs produced by the chemical industry. In the late 1930s the first antibiotics such as penicillin and the sulphonamides were developed, making possible the control of 'killer' illnesses such as pneumonia and meningitis. This period also saw the development of the early insecticides such as DDT which later became of international importance in the destruction of the malaria-carrying mosquito.

Agriculture

British agriculture entered the postwar era in an optimistic mood; the Corn Production Act of 1917 had guaranteed grain prices for six years, while prices for other farm products remained high until the boom broke in 1920–1. Tenant farmers had prospered during the war and although farm workers' wages had risen, rents had not: all this led many tenants with the aid of borrowed money to buy the farms they occupied from their landlords; several million acres changed hands between 1919–20. The sharp fall in world grain prices in 1920 saddled the government with a subsidy payment of £35 millions under the terms of the Agriculture Act of 1920 which had extended the guaranteed prices of the Act of 1917 for another four years. The call for economy and the pressures still exercised by the need for 'cheap food' for a predominantly industrial population led the government to repudiate its promises and to repeal the act of 1920, thus removing guaranteed prices for grain. Minimum wage rates for farm workers also disappeared until they were reinstated by the Wages Board Act of 1924.

Over the next ten years conditions were very difficult for most British farmers. Their reactions resembled those of the great depression of the 1880s, e.g. a turning away from grain-growing and concentration on more profitable activities such as milk, meat, fruit and vegetable production: the acreage for grain-growing fell from 7.4 million acres in 1921 to 5.3 million in 1931. But a heavier blow came with the world economic slump of 1931; British farmers by 1933 were getting a quarter less for their products compared with 1929. For many farmers this was the end of the road although the mixed farm relying largely on family labour could often survive. The government was forced to intervene to save farming from complete ruin and a series of support measures from 1932 onwards achieved this. Marketing Boards, notably for milk, brought price stability and control over producers' outputs; duties and import quotas restricted the import of foreign food, with preferences for empire producers such as Australia and New Zealand; producers of sugar beet, fat cattle and wheat were given guaranteed prices by government subsidy payments; agricultural land was freed from the payment of local rates. Overall it was a revolution in government policy towards agriculture; the threat of war in the 1930s and the consequent need for greater self sufficiency in food was an influential factor, while the adoption of protection for British industry against foreign competition gave agriculture a logical claim for equivalent measures to underpin it. In the late 1930s confidence began to return to British farming in time for it to make a large contribution to the feeding of the nation during World War II.

27. Labour and industrial relations 1919–27

Postwar aims of Labour

The British Labour movement entered the postwar era organized for action on two fronts: political activity through the parliamentary Labour Party and the allied Socialist groups, and industrial action through the trade unions. Its declared aims reflected a basic division within the movement; on the one hand there were moderate and reasonable demands for improved social services, social security, guarantees of employment, higher wages, and better working conditions which contrasted with the other more revolutionary demand for the overthrow of capitalist ownership of industry and for the establishment of workers' control. The first and more moderate demands Labour thought were justified by the sacrifices, work, and privations it had suffered during the war; the demand for the overthrow of capitalist control of the means of production stemmed from the triumph of the Russian revolution of 1917, which had caught the enthusiasm of the more revolutionary Labour leaders in Western Europe, who believed that the same revolution could be carried out in their own countries. However, only a small but militant minority of British Socialists followed the revolutionary trend; the great majority were more moderate and opposed to the idea of any revolutionary upheaval. The Labour Movement, both in the trade unions and Parliament, was dominated in the 1920s by cautious and moderate men, such as Arthur Henderson and J. R. Clynes who had held minor office in the Coalition government under Lloyd George.

The political prospects of Labour had been improved by extensions in its organization and membership; it had set up local party organizations in the constituencies and had widened its membership by enrolling members who were non-manual workers. Its political programme was set out in a manifesto entitled *Labour and the New Social Order*. This advocated increased social security measures including a national minimum wage, the nationalization of basic industries such as railways, coal, and electricity, the levying of higher taxation (including a capital levy on the wealthier classes) for social welfare and to reduce the burden of the National Debt.

Although the Labour Party had extended its appeal to 'brain workers', it still largely relied upon the trade unions for its momentum and financial support; there had been a significant increase in trade union membership which had risen from four million in 1913 to eight million in 1919, and amalgamations which had taken place had created large and powerful unions such as the General and Municipal Workers and the Transport and General Workers. The Trades Union Congress which had met annually since 1868 now increased its effectiveness by setting up a standing general council with executive powers to act during the interval between the meeting of one congress and its successor, and with close working links with the parliamentary Labour Party. On the whole this working alliance between the Labour Party and the trade unions reflected the moderate tendencies of the leading figures in both movements, although there was an active minority on the extreme left which derived its inspiration from the Russian revolution. There was also a Communist Party of Great Britain, formed in 1920, but this was cold-shouldered by the Labour Party which rejected its requests for affiliation.

Attitude of the Coalition government

The militant mood of British Labour was seen very soon after the armistice when in January 1919 the Clydeside workers in the engineering and shipbuilding yards called for a general strike if a forty-hour week was not granted. The three years from 1919 to 1921 were marked by widespread and costly strikes, followed by more settled conditions between 1922 and 1925 and then by the general strike of 1926. The reaction of the Coalition government alternated between force, which was used to break the Clydeside strike in 1919, and a readiness to discuss grievances: such discussion was designed to be a safety valve sufficient to prevent any real structural changes in the relationship of employers and workers. There were also a number of legislative measures which the government could exhibit as proof of its benevolent intentions towards the workers, e.g. a temporary Wages Act which forbade reductions in wages, the continuation of the wartime Rent Restriction Acts, a Housing and Town Planning Act (1919) to promote the building of houses to be let at low rents to workers. But these measures did not add up to very much and the government was stalling on the demand of the workers by a judicious mixture of bluff and evasion. A very good example of this was the summoning of the National Industrial Conference in February 1919. It was attended by 300 representatives of employers in major industries and 500 representatives of the principal trade unions who met to discuss ways and means of improving industrial relations. The conference accepted the recommendations of a Joint Committee of employers and trade unionists for a maximum working week of forty-eight hours and for government-sponsored measures to lessen unemployment. The government announced its general acceptance of these recommendations but did nothing to give them legal force; it was content to keep the talking going as a way of taking the steam out of the demands of Labour. The conference dragged on ignominiously until the middle of 1921 when the trade union members, realizing they had been hoodwinked, resigned. The evasive attitude of the government in this matter was similar to its behaviour in connection with the major recommendations of the Sankey Commission on the coal mines.

The Sankey Commission on the coal industry 1919

In 1919 coal mining had a labour force of 1,200,000 and was one of Britain's most important industries. De-control proved slow and difficult; the miners were in no mood for compromise and in January 1919 they demanded nationalization of the industry, a six-hour day and a 30% wage increase, and threatened a strike if these demands were not met. Lloyd George, faced with this serious threat to the economy, skilfully bought time by getting all concerned to agree to the appointment of a Coal Industry Commission which should investigate the industry and its problems. This commission, known as the Sankey Commission from the name of the high court judge who presided over it, was made up of representatives from the mine owners, miners, and industrialists, together with three economists. It carried out an extensive probe into the industry, examining its profits, royalty payments, conditions of work and housing for the miners; the miners' representatives were successful in building up a strong case for nationalization largely because of the damaging admissions they elicited from the mine owners and royalty owners during the hearing of evidence. In March three interim reports were submitted by the Commission; the most important was that of the Chairman Sir John Sankey and the three industrialists, which took a middle position between the recommendations of the miners' representatives and that of the owners. The Chairman's report recommended a seven-hour day, to be reduced eventually to six hours; a wage increase of 2s. a day, and a levy of 1d. per ton to improve housing in the mining districts. More important, it declared for nationalization because the existing system of ownership was condemned by the evidence that had been placed before the Commission.

The Government and miners accepted the Sankey interim report but difficulties arose when the Commission reported again in June 1919. This time there were four distinct reports and while all had common ground in recommending the creation of a Ministry of Mines and the nationalization of coal royalties, the Commission was divided over state ownership of the mines. Not unnaturally the mine owners opposed this and were supported by two of the industrialist members. Although the Government had earlier accepted the principle of nationalization it now began to temporize over the issue on the ground that the Commission had not finally presented a unanimous report. A strike of Yorkshire pitmen for the shorter hours and higher pay recommended in the interim report turned public opinion against the miners, and it was also represented as an act of indiscipline because the mines were still under government control. The Prime Minister, in August 1919, adroitly took advantage of this to reject the Commission's recommendations for nationalization. A Coal Mines Act (1919) gave the seven-hour day and two later Acts in 1920 extended the duration of government control of the mines to 1921 and made provision for pithead baths and other amenities for the miners. All this did not bring peace or efficiency to the industry; the miners felt that they had been bluffed by the Commission and the owners were scared by their narrow escape from nationalization.

Industrial unrest 1920–2

By the middle of 1920 the postwar boom had faded out and a period of sharp depression in British industry followed which lasted through 1921 and 1922; this was particularly marked in the iron and steel industry, in shipbuilding and engineering, and unemployment by the middle of 1921 had reached over two millions. Besides unemployment the depression brought sharp reductions in wages, and organized labour reacted strongly against this by strikes and demands that the government must provide work, or maintenance. The coal miners were the most active in protesting against reduction in wages; in their industry the situation had become critical because early in 1921 the government decided, on the grounds of growing unprofitability, to de-control the mines and hand them back to their private owners on 31 March 1921. This meant that the industry's wage structure would have to be reconsidered and the miners' cherished object of getting a national settlement for the whole industry under a national wages board, rather than negotiating local agreements for each coal mining district, was threatened. The coal owners announced new scales of wages to come into force when they regained control of the mines and almost all the new scales involved reductions in wages ranging from 10% to 40%; the miners refused the terms and went on strike on 1 April. They now called for the support of the two powerful unions, the Transport Workers' Federation and the National Union of Railwaymen, who were associated with the miners in the so-called 'Triple Alliance', a grouping which had shown its power before 1914; this could only mean a strike by these two unions in sympathy with the miners. When strike orders were issued to the railwaymen and transport workers a large scale stoppage appeared imminent and the government reacted by declaring a state of emergency under the Emergency Powers Act of 1920; the armed forces were ordered to stand by and volunteers were recruited to assist in the maintenance of order and distribution of essential supplies. The day before the strike was due to start, the Prime Minister invited the miners' leaders to an urgent meeting to discuss a temporary solution for the wage problem. The rejection of this invitation by the miners caused a split in

311

the Triple Alliance, and the other two unions withdrew their strike notices. The miners were left alone to carry on the struggle which they did until the beginning of July 1921 when their defeat brought a settlement of wages on a district, and not a national, basis; reductions varied according to the district, but in some areas, notably South Wales, they were sharp and amounted to nearly half the previous levels paid. Strike action in two other major industries, engineering and shipbuilding, in 1922 led to the same result; the strikers lost and were forced to take wage reductions which were also enforced in the building and printing trades, and on the railways.

Large-scale, organized demonstrations by unemployed in the winter of 1920–1 took place in London and other large cities, followed in 1922 by the first of the hunger marches of unemployed men. These demonstrations led the government to extend the period for which unemployment benefit could be drawn; originally this had been for only fifteen weeks in the year. By an Unemployment Insurance Act of March 1921 two periods of benefit of sixteen weeks each were granted, but between these there was a gap during which no benefit was payable. This extra benefit, which soon became known as the 'dole', was subject to certain tests and could only be paid to those 'genuinely seeking' work, and official investigations to prove this were much resented by the unemployed. In November 1921 the Unemployment Fund was authorized to make small payments to the wives and children of unemployed workers, since these dependents were not covered for any benefits by workers' contributions to the insurance scheme. When the dole ran out during the 'gap' period, the unemployed and their families were forced on to the Poor Law which gave outdoor relief at widely differing rates. This placed a very heavy burden on the rates especially in working-class or industrial areas which were the least wealthy in rateable values.

The Samuel Commission 1925–6

In the coal mining industry an uneasy peace followed the wages settlement in 1921; matters were helped by the temporary prosperity of the industry due to increased exports of British coal during the period of the French occupation of the German mines of the Ruhr area in 1923. A new wages agreement between the mine owners and the miners was negotiated in May 1924 which made small additions to the miners' wages; this lasted only a year when the owners gave notice in June 1925 to end the agreement on the grounds that the profitability of the industry had sharply decreased and it could no longer afford to pay these wages. The owners stated that they could only pay the standard wage with no additions and that increased wages depended on the miners working longer hours, viz. an eight-hour day. The Miners' Federation rejected these terms with the

312

support of the General Council of the Trades Union Congress; an embargo on the movement of coal after the miners had come out on strike was agreed. The miners' stoppage was due to begin at midnight on 31 July; at the very last minute the government gave way and the Prime Minister, Baldwin, met representatives of the miners. Pending an inquiry into the organization of the industry the Government promised a subsidy of not less than £10 million to cover the losses that were being made by the industry if the miners would call off the strike and the embargo on the movement of coal. A Commission under the chairmanship of Sir Herbert Samuel was appointed to investigate the problems and organization of the coal mining industry. Meanwhile the government, alarmed by the temper and attitude of the trade unions, made outline plans to meet the possibility of a general strike. These were based on the Emergency Powers Act of 1920 and included a scheme for controlling road transport to distribute food and essential supplies. This emergency distribution was to be carried out on a regional basis; England and Wales were divided into ten areas with civil commissioners directing affairs with the aid of local committees.

In March 1926 the Samuel Commission made its report. It rejected the demands of the miners for nationalization and also the owners' proposals for increasing the hours of work. Its chief recommendations were that the industry must reorganize itself under private ownership by eliminating small and unproductive mines and by seeking new outlets for coal sales especially to electricity producers; there must be greater cooperation between miners and mineowners which would be helped by the provision of amenities such as better housing and pithead baths, holidays with pay, and the raising of the wages of surface workers. It also recommended that coal royalties should be nationalized; the Sankey Commission had also done this but its proposals had been ignored. The Commission accepted the need for a temporary reduction of wages in order to reduce the working costs of the industry and place it on a competitive basis. The government gave a lukewarm acceptance to the Commission's recommendations and said it would give legislative effect to them in due course subject to agreement by both miners and owners, which it was already abundantly clear would not be forthcoming.

The general strike May 1926

In April 1926 it became clear that a head-on collision was impending; the miners and owners were in no mood for compromise. The miners' leader, A. J. Cook, summed up their attitude in his slogan 'not a penny off the pay, not a minute on the day'. The mine owners, thinking in terms of lower wages and longer hours, were confident that they had the Conservative government behind them and looked forward to a conflict which

313

should settle the issue in their favour by beating the miners into surrender. The owners issued lock-out notices to take effect on 30 April, but on this day under pressure from the Prime Minister, they made a final offer for a wages agreement on a national basis; basically these took wages back to those set in 1921 with the addition of longer hours, viz. an eight-hour day for at least three and a half years. The miners rejected this offer; further negotiations took place on Government initiative to see if the miners would accept the proposed reductions, providing schemes for reorganization were set on foot. In advance of the rejection of this proposal the government had declared a state of emergency and local authorities had been alerted to put into effect plans prepared in case of a general strike. The trade union delegate executives who had assembled in London had not yet declared a general strike although they had received the plans of the General Council of the T.U.C. for support of the miners. On 1 May the trade union representatives by an overwhelming majority gave their assent to the proposals for support of the miners. These were referred to not as a general strike but as 'proposals for coordinated action', and were to be made effective by the individual unions calling out their members on a prearranged basis. The deadline for action was midnight on Monday, 3 May 1926.

Even at this late hour negotiations took place to avert a general strike. These were carried out between the government and the Industrial Committee of the trade unions which had intensive discussions with the Prime Minister over the week-end. By Sunday both sides had apparently agreed on a formula which if accepted by the miners could put off the general strike and also end the disputes in the coal industry. Late in the evening of Sunday, 2 May, when final agreement seemed near the Prime Minister called for the representatives of the Industrial Committee and handed them a letter in which he declared that negotiations were at an end. His excuse for this was that a lightning strike by printers at the *Daily Mail* office was 'a gross interference with the freedom of the press' and also 'a challenge to the constitutional rights and freedom of the nation'. More important, the government indicated that it would not continue negotiations under the threat of a general strike and it demanded the unconditional withdrawal of the instructions issued for this. It seems probable that a small group of the Cabinet including the Prime Minister himself were overruled by the strong-arm majority who wanted a showdown with the trade union movement.

The unconditional surrender demanded by the government placed the trade union leaders in an impossible position and within twenty-four hours the general strike passed from being a threat to a reality for the British public as they found on the following day, Tuesday 4 May. The General Council's plan for action was to call out on strike all the workers in the major service industries followed by those in other key industries. If necessary the remaining unions were to call out their members on strike at a later date. Those on strike on the first day included the workers in the transport industries, both rail and road, the dockers, the printing trades, the iron and steel workers, the building trades, and those workers in the electricity and gas industry producing industrial power. There was a very full response in the industries concerned and solidarity often approached 100 per cent. The extent of the strike is shown by the fact that out of a total of just over four and a quarter million members of the trade unions over three million of these were actually called out on strike.

The course of the general strike

Although in some respects the general strike was carried out in a 'sporting spirit' there were serious implications behind it. Within a day or two the transport of persons and goods by public transport had virtually ceased and the maintenance of food supplies was threatened. There was also the possibility that revolutionary violence might show itself. In its efforts to preserve order and maintain supplies the government was helped by the fact that majority public opinion was against the general strike; it also had the assistance provided by a miscellaneous force of volunteer organizations. From those of the country's citizens who opposed the strike were recruited large numbers of volunteers who were given jobs driving trains, buses, trams, acting as special constables, loading and unloading food lorries. While the activities of the train and bus drivers were sometimes amateurish and led to some damage and accidents, they

Student volunteers unloading bacon at the London docks during the general strike

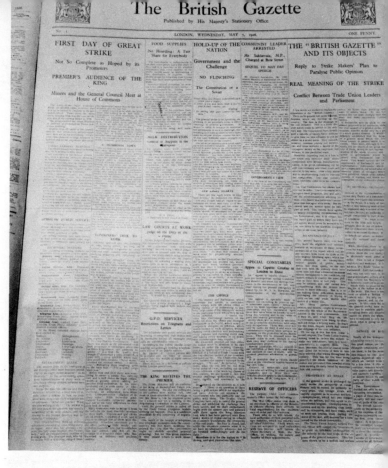

The British Gazette of 5 May 1926

nevertheless enabled a skeleton transport service to operate during the last days of the strike. The government also had very wide powers under the Emergency Powers Act; these enabled it to take over land and buildings and to prohibit meetings if disorder was anticipated and to take strong action against those who promoted sedition or disaffection among the armed forces or the civilian population. Baldwin and his ministers defended the use of these powers by referring to the menace of the strike: 'Constitutional government is being attacked; the general strike is a challenge to Parliament and is the road to anarchy and ruin.' The importance of the control of media of communications was shown during the strike. No daily papers were printed but a number were improvized; the *British Gazette* published by the Government and its control of the B.B.C. gave it considerable advantages in the presentation of its case, while the T.U.C. replied with its publication the *British Worker*.

On the strikers' side organization at the centre was probably less effective. At the T.U.C. headquarters there were some who were not very

316

enthusiastic for the strike because of their underlying anxiety that it might wreck the trade union movement. The strike savoured too much of revolution and the constant reiteration by the government of its illegal aspects, i.e. attacking the constitution, undoubtedly carried weight with some of the more moderate T.U.C. leaders. An exception was the energy

THE
BRITISH WORKER
OFFICIAL STRIKE NEWS BULLETIN
Published by The General Council of the Trades Union Congress

| No. 2. | THURSDAY EVENING, MAY 6, 1926. | PRICE ONE PENNY |

The British Worker of 6 May 1926, issued by the Trades Union Congress

WORKERS CALM AND STEADY

Firmer and Firmer Every Day of Strike

BLACKLEGS FAIL

The third day of the General sees the situation unchanged. The working class is holding firmly and tenaciously to the position it has taken up.

The easy assurance of anti-strike people, that it would be "over in a couple of days," that it would soon be sick of it," that "anyway the Government will make heaps of volunteers to run the trains and things" has vanished quickly. It has given place to a growing anxiety.

"It" is not over. The strikers are growing more determined as the days pass. They are not drifting back to work. On the contrary.

The trouble everywhere is to keep the men at work who have not been ordered to strike.

It is as to getting the "trains and things" running with "volunteers" the first day's boasts have failed to materialise. The bus service remains a skeleton—an even bonier skeleton than yesterday.

Few London buses are being run by a policeman. Here and in the provinces the same. But what does it all amount to? It all Manchester, for example, three tram drivers!

A few buses, a few passenger vans. But the mines are still, goods traffic has ceased, the docks are closed, the factories are closing.

Of all the O.M.S. in the world get them going again. Only disorganised workers can do that. The organised workers, solid, determined, calm, are refusing to do until justice is done to their cause.

The third day. And still everything—complete calm, complete order.

Anti-strike propagandists are set on, are going of a riot here and a riot there and a... *(continued on Page Six, Column Three)*

WEATHER

Wind northerly, moderate or fresh; strong at times locally; variable sky, some showers of rain or hail; perhaps local thunder; rather cold.

LABOUR'S REPLY TO THE PREMIER

General Council's Conditions for Reopening Discussions

"UNFETTERED ATMOSPHERE"

The following is the reply of the General Council of the Trades Union Congress to the Prime Minister's statement as to possible terms of peace:—

Mr. Baldwin, in the House of Commons on Wednesday, said :—

"No Government in any circumstances could ever yield to a general strike. The moment it was called off unconditionally the Government were prepared to resume negotiations."

The General Council is ready, at any moment, to resume negotiations for an honourable settlement. It enforces no conditions for resuming preliminary discussion with the Government on any aspects of the case.

It is obvious, however, that at this stage, with no knowledge of the subsequent line of policy that the Government intends to pursue, the General Council cannot comply with

the Prime Minister's request for an unconditional withdrawal of the strike notices.

The General Council, it must be remembered, was not responsible for the breakdown of negotiations. The strike was due to the Government's refusal to secure a withdrawal of the lock-out notices in the mining industry, and to its action in provocatively taking the side of the coalowners and in breaking off negotiations at a time when the General Council was sincerely seeking a peaceful settlement.

The conditions that govern the reopening of discussions should be different from the conditions governing the withdrawal of the notices for the general strike; and inasmuch as the Government was responsible for the breaking-off of negotiations, any preliminary parleys with a view

Contd. at foot of Col. Two, Page Eight

OUR REPLY TO "JIX"

The General Council urges the men and women of Great Britain not to be stampeded into panic by the provocative utterances of the Home Secretary.

The inference contained in his broadcast appeal for special constables on Wednesday evening, to the effect that the Trade Union Movement was violating law and order, is quite unjustifiable.

Only on that same afternoon, in fact, the General Council of the Trades Union Congress had officially urged every member taking part in the dispute to be exemplary in his conduct and not to give any opportunity for police disturbances.

The General Council had also asked pickets to avoid obstruction and to confine themselves strictly to their legitimate duties.

There is no need for the panic which the Home Secretary seems intent on provoking. The strikers are standing firm, and they mean to conduct themselves in the disciplined, quiet and orderly manner.

The unnecessary and unwise action of the Home Secretary is more likely to imperil good order than to preserve it.

HOW THE "B.W." CAME OUT

A Sudden Police Raid— and After

AMAZING SCENES

Eight o'clock last night. A hundred difficulties had to be overcome. But they had been overcome. And the BRITISH WORKER was all ready for printing.

The last line of copy had been sub-edited and set. The last stereo plate had been made and fastened in place on the presses. All was ready.

Swarm of Police

The big crowd of members of the Distributive Section of the Paper Workers' Union, who had been waiting with their cars and cycles outside, very patiently, for three hours and more, raised a cheer. Then—from the half-finished new Daily Mail building across the street emerged a policeman—two policemen—five—ten—twenty—fifty or more. Round the corner came a dozen mounted men.

They pushed the waiting workers away from the front of the office, and held them by a cordon 50 yards away. Then a number of plain-clothes men, headed by a detective inspector, entered the building and ordered that the machines should not be started.

Warrant from "Jix"

Mr. Robert Williams saw the Inspector, who explained that they had a warrant from the Home Secretary to search for and seize all copies of the DAILY HERALD of May 4, all material used in producing it, or which might be used in producing any document calculated to impede measures taken for the maintenance of essential services.

It was quickly made clear that what really interested them was less the DAILY HERALD of May 4 than the BRITISH WORKER of May 5.

The inspector requested that a dozen copies of the paper should be run off for submission to the City Commissioner. If the Commissioner approved, we could go ahead. If not—he was sorry, but——.

He went off with his copies, leaving some of his men in charge.

Continued on Page Eight, Col. Four

Published for the General Council of the Trades Union Congress by Victoria House Printing Company, 2, Carmelite Street, London, E.C.4. Telephone (8 lines): 837 City.

317

*Improvised
transport for City
workers during the
general strike*

and activity shown by Ernest Bevin, who headed the strike organization committee. Greater enthusiasm and action was shown by the local strike committees that came into being all over the country, and which did much to keep the strike alive. These committees were powerful locally because it was through them that permits were issued for the transport of essential goods and for work under certain strictly-defined conditions. Other of their activities were the organization of picketing and the publication of local strike bulletins which were designed to counter the news broadcast by the B.B.C. or published in the *British Gazette*.

The collapse of the strike

By the end of the week it was clear that the General Council of the T.U.C. was very much on the defensive, although the morale of its supporters in the country at large remained unimpaired. The General Council feared the fight to the finish which the government was clearly going to give them, and they began to cast around for some way out of the impasse. On Saturday, 8 May, the Prime Minister made a conciliatory broadcast asserting that the door was not closed to negotiations providing that the strike was called off; he also emphasized that the strike was an attack upon the community. Sir Herbert Samuel, who had been chairman of the recent Commission on the coal industry, now came forward as an unofficial mediator. His aim was to focus attention on the coal miners' strike which was the primary cause of the trouble; if this could be settled on agreed terms then the general strike could be called off by the T.U.C. He proposed that negotiations between the miners and coal owners should be reopened and that for the time being the government should continue its subsidy to the coal mining industry and that no revisions of wages should take place until reorganization of the mines had been

318

brought about. The weakness of this was that Sir Herbert Samuel was acting quite unofficially and there was no guarantee that the government would accept the terms of his memorandum, and his proposals, because they envisaged some eventual reduction of wages, conflicted with the miners' slogan of 'not a penny off the pay'. The General Council accepted the Samuel memorandum and called upon the miners to do the same. This was refused to the extreme disappointment of the General Council, who could reasonably argue that the miners must make concessions and that they could not expect the rest of the trade union movement to remain on strike indefinitely on their behalf. Two days of argument could not shake the miners from their refusal to accept these terms and on Wednesday, 12 May, a deputation from the T.U.C. waited on the Prime Minister at 10 Downing Street. Their purpose was to tell him of their decision to call off the strike, coupled with a request that victimization of the strikers should be avoided. Baldwin gave general assurances but no more. The General Council of the T.U.C. tried to cover up its enormous defeat by pretending that the terms of the Samuel memorandum were official and that negotiations for ending the mining dispute would be resumed. All this accorded very ill with the declaration made by Baldwin on the B.B.C. the same evening that the strike had ended virtually on terms of unconditional surrender. The decision to end the strike was received with dismay by very many of the rank and file who saw this as a betrayal not only of their own cause but particularly that of the miners who were now abandoned. For some days further the general strike continued unofficially in the provinces and this was encouraged by the action of some employers who indulged in semi-victimization of those strikers who now returned to work. The Prime Minister had to make it clear that the government would not tolerate any abuse by employers of the present position to exact reductions in pay. So ended the general strike; fortunately it was of short duration for had it been prolonged violence probably would have taken place. Whatever the rank and file might think, the leaders of the trade union movement had learnt their lesson; they would be very reluctant to give hostages to fortune by embarking on another general strike.

Mr Baldwin at 10 Downing Street after the T.U.C. had informed him that they had called off the general strike, 12 May 1926

The coal strike remained and Baldwin was far less successful in his attempts to settle this. He made proposals along the lines of the recommendations of the Samuel Commission but these were rejected both by the miners and the mineowners. At this he lost patience and apart from an Act to suspend the seven-hour day in the mines and a Mining Industry Act to give effect to some of the recommendations of the Samuel Commission, he left the miners and coal owners to fight it out between themselves. The obstinacy of the owners gradually wore down the resistance of the miners and all hopes of a national agreement on wages for the

319

industry had disappeared by September. Following this there was a slow drift back to work, usually on the basis of district agreements with the owners; these were unfavourable to the miners, generally giving them longer hours and less wages. This prolonged strike inflicted great hardship on the miners and their families, while the shortage of British coal led to unemployment in many industries which were dependent on it for their source of power; large quantities of coal had to be imported from Poland and Germany to keep the works moving. The industrial slump after 1929 brought unemployment and short-time working for the coal mining industry, and by 1936 its labour force had declined by over 200,000 men.

The Trades Disputes and Trade Unions Act 1927

While Baldwin had shown statesmanship and moderation at the time of the general strike, he was less successful in restraining his right-wing supporters who wished to keep trade unionism on the run as was shown in the Trades Disputes and Trade Unions Act of 1927. The chief provisions of this Act were:

1. general and sympathetic strikes were made illegal;

2. trade union members had to 'contract in' if they wished to pay contributions to their union's political fund in support of the Labour Party, thus reversing the former rule of 'contracting out';

3. Civil Service trade unions and associations could not be affiliated to the Trades Union Congress;

4. restrictions were imposed on picketing.

The British trade union movement now entered a period of temporary decline; its membership slumped because of the damage to morale brought by the defeat of the general strike and the high unemployment of the 1930s, while the Act of 1927 made strike action difficult. The Labour Party whose income from the political levy was considerably reduced by the 'contracting in' principle, made repeal of the Act an urgent objective of its political programme, but it was unable to achieve this until 1946.

28. Baldwin's second ministry, November 1924–June 1929

Baldwin's political programme

Apart from the timely advantage of the Zinoviev letter to scare the voters, Baldwin led the Conservatives to victory in the election of 1924 on a programme that lacked definition and precise details. Its appeal lay in its generalities which were comforting to a large part of the electorate which hankered after the stability of the prewar years before 1914. Baldwin successfully conveyed the impression to many that he was an honest man with no politician's tricks, but in the long run this was no substitute for a clear-cut policy. Personally rather indolent, Baldwin believed in the value of judicious inaction in politics rather like Walpole and his maxim of 'letting sleeping dogs lie', although in the critical matters of the general strike of 1926 and the abdication of King Edward VIII in 1936 he acted with vigour and determination.

His family background among the iron masters of the West Midlands made him aware of the social tensions in industrial Britain arising from the relations of capital and labour. His fear was that these tensions might lead to social revolution unless harmony between the classes could be established; he expressed this in his 'Peace in our time and land' speech (March 1925): 'We stand for peace, we stand for the removal of suspicion in the country. We want to create an atmosphere, a new atmosphere in a new Parliament in which the people can come together.' His wish was that Conservative policy should work towards this end but the general strike, worsening economic conditions, and opposition from 'hard liners' of his party made progress slow.

Widows, orphans and old-age pensions 1925

This wish to appease working-class opinion brought a modest programme of social reform. The Minister of Health, Neville Chamberlain was responsible for this; he was a capable administrator but lacked both personal appeal and imagination. Nevertheless his achievements in social reform during the 1920s were considerable, although they have been obscured by his unfortunate record as prime minister in the years 1937–40. In 1925 he sponsored a Widows, Orphans and Old Age Contributory Pensions Act which extended the scope of the existing Health Insurance Scheme set up by the Act of 1911. All who contributed to this scheme were now, in return for small extra payments, covered for a pension of 10s. a week, starting at age 65, without means test. Pensions of 10s. a week and 7s. 6d. a week respectively were to be paid to widows and orphans. While this scheme was intended as far as possible to be financed by contributions, there was a gap to be bridged which was done by a contribution from the Treasury which by 1937 amounted to about £40 millions a year when over twenty million people were insured under the scheme. One criticism of the Act was that there were many people of limited means who were not insured under the Act of 1911 and this was not remedied till 1937 when an Act brought them into the scheme as voluntary contributors.

Unemployment insurance

Unemployment, as for all governments in the postwar years, proved a far more intractable problem. The major difficulty was that the high level of unemployment during these years had exhausted the resources of the Insurance Fund which had been built up by contributions from insured workers. To meet this difficulty the principle had been adopted of regarding state-sponsored unemployment benefit as being of two kinds: one was the standard benefit covered by contributions, and the other was known as extended benefit which was not so covered. By an Unemployment Act of 1927 the Conservative government abolished the distinction between standard and extended benefits and gave what was called transitional benefit to those unemployed who had exhausted the payments they were entitled to under their contributions. To qualify for transitional benefit the unemployed worker must show a minimum number of past contributions and also must satisfy the requirements that he was genuinely seeking work. Those unemployed who could not satisfy these tests, and in the late 1920s they averaged over a million people were thrown back on relief from the Poor Law authorities. This created many difficulties because of the large number of Poor Law authorities with their different standards and attitudes to the giving of relief. Some were generous, some were niggardly, and some tried to impose the old hated tests associated with the days of Victorian Poor Law relief and the workhouse. The position was worst in the depressed industrial areas where the rateable value of property was low. There were complaints of lax administration by certain Boards of Poor Law Guardians who were giving generous scales of relief paid from borrowed money. To counter this the government in 1927 carried an Act which gave them power to supersede the elected guardians where this was happening, and this power was exercised in three cases – at West Ham, Chester-le-Street and Bedwellty. Nevertheless, the unsatisfactory nature of the powers of the Poor Law guardians to relieve distress from unemployment pointed urgently to the need for a coherent national policy to deal with the relief of

unemployment.

The Local Government Act, 1929

Chamberlain's most ambitious measure was the Local Government Act of 1929. This recognized the need to reduce the number of local government authorities and to reorganize the areas they covered, and also the need to extend the services they provided. The major provisions of the Act were:

1. In the interests of efficiency the numbers of Urban and Rural District Councils were reduced and 33 'all purpose' Municipal Boroughs were created.

2. The powers of the County Councils over roads, public health and town and country planning were increased.

3. The Poor Law guardians created by the Act of 1834 were abolished and their powers and duties were transferred to the County Councils and County Borough Councils. These authorities were to administer poor relief through Public Assistance Committees which would deal with the problems arising from poverty in a more specialized way than the old Poor Law.

4. To encourage economic efficiency by reducing costs in industry and agriculture, the Act gave an extensive amount of de-rating. All agricultural land was entirely exempted from local rates while industrial buildings and railways systems were de-rated to a 25% basis. Treasury grants totalling some £40 millions were to be paid to the local authorities in compensation for the loss of these rates.

5. Treasury grants to local government finances were to be calculated on a 'block' grant basis, instead of the previous 'percentage' grant. The 'percentage' grant hitherto used had favoured the wealthier authorities, since the Treasury paid an agreed percentage of the schemes initiated by these authorities: the 'block' grant was calculated more precisely on local needs and aimed at helping the poorer local government areas.

The Equal Franchise Act 1928

The Equal Franchise Act of 1928 gave the parliamentary vote to all women over twenty-one, on the same basis as for men over twenty-one. It was realized that the Act of 1918 which gave the vote to women over thirty under certain conditions, had been unnecessarily cautious, and that no disastrous results had followed from their enfranchisement.

Foreign policy

The foreign secretary in Baldwin's Ministry was Austen Chamberlain. He quickly reversed the internationalist trend of the Labour government, especially in connection with the friendly approaches to Russia; the Anglo-Russian trade treaties which had been drafted were now aban-

323

doned. All this was acceptable to most Conservatives who were firmly convinced that the sinister hand of the Communist International was everywhere in the world and was in particular working insidiously for the disintegration of the British Empire and its commercial interests. This hostility was carried too far when in May 1927 the police raided the office of Acros, an Anglo-Russian trading organization. The raid was made in search of a War Office document alleged to be concealed in this building, and also in the hope of finding further incriminating documents and evidence of anti-British Communist activity. In the event very little was found but it provided an excuse to break off British diplomatic and trading relations with Soviet Russia.

In much the same way as they distrusted the pro-Russian policy of Ramsay MacDonald, so the Conservatives also disliked his interest in the Geneva Protocol which would have given effective enforcement to the decisions of the League of Nations in the maintenance of peace. This Protocol was dropped by the Conservatives, but to their credit they made an important attempt to strengthen the forces for the maintenance of European peace by their association with the signing of the Locarno Pact in October, 1925. This was done at a meeting of the principal European powers at Locarno on Lake Maggiore.

One major aim of Locarno was to satisfy the deep wish of France for security in Europe. Locarno provided for a pact of non-aggression between Germany and France and the reference of all disputes to arbitration; it gave a guarantee of the German western frontiers and for the demilitarization of the Rhineland. Great Britain and Italy were guarantors of this and promised to aid any victim of its breach. The principle of arbitration was also to apply to Germany's relations with her eastern neighbours, Poland and Czechoslovakia. In the interest of better relations with the rest of Europe, Germany was admitted to the League of Nations.

While the Locarno Pact was a considerable achievement, and especially for Austen Chamberlain, nevertheless the government did not really live up to the spirit of it and do anything very much to foster collective international security. Disarmament also was distrusted by the Conservatives and during this ministry little was done to promote it; the naval disarmament conferences between Britain and the U.S.A. failed largely because of Britain's obstinacy about making concessions. In protest against the stagnant and indifferent attitude of the government to matters of collective security and disarmament, Lord Cecil, who was head of the British delegation to the League of Nations, resigned from the Cabinet in 1927.

Defects of Conservative policy

In retrospect the achievements of Baldwin's second ministry were largely two: the weathering of the general strike (see chapter 27) and the social

324

legislation carried through by Neville Chamberlain. In other respects Baldwin attached considerable importance to a policy of inaction which he thought would prolong the life of his ministry and enable him to continue 'the endless adventure of governing men'. In face of Britain's economic difficulties this was inadequate and probably Baldwin's greatest failure was his lack of a constructive policy to deal with unemployment. The return to the gold standard in 1925 was a mistake and led to the overpricing of British exports in overseas markets with consequent unemployment at home; the government was reluctant to use its borrowing powers to provide funds for public works or development projects which would have absorbed much of this unemployment. Increasingly its policy was one of drift, hoping that the economy would right itself, and behind all this was a fundamental wish to preserve intact the capitalist structure and control of industry.

Liberal and Labour programmes

Of the two rivals of the Conservative Party, the Liberals had long been torn by the feud between the supporters of Asquith and those following Lloyd George. With a general election in the offing, a serious attempt was made in 1928–9 by the Liberals to heal the divisions within their party and to make an effective attempt to revive their political influence. The spearhead of this Liberal revival was Lloyd George, not only full of political ideas but also in control of the party political funds: Asquith had resigned the party leadership in October, 1926 leaving Lloyd George as the dominating force in the Liberal revival. From 1924 onwards, the Liberals published a number of realistic reports on matters affecting the country's welfare. These included reports on coal and power and also one in 1928 called *Britain's Industrial Future*. This recommended the placing of basic industries, such as gas and electricity, under public boards, and also a widely based attack on unemployment by the launching of a national development programme which should build houses, roads and extend the use of electricity; such a programme was to be financed by the provision of cheap money by expanding credit facilities. In the spring of 1929 the Liberals carried their development plan to cure unemployment a stage further in a pamphlet *We can conquer unemployment*; it promised a cure for unemployment within a year, without any increase of taxation. The Liberal programme set a hot pace for the Labour Party which in 1928 published its policy in *Labour and the Nation*. This was largely a copy of the Liberal plan for reducing unemployment by public works and although the document proclaimed that the Labour Party was a Socialist Party, it played down some aspects of Socialism, such as nationalization of industry, apart from advocating that this should be done in the case of coal mining.

325

The general election, May 1929

The general election was fixed for 30 May 1929. The Conservative programme was largely one of claiming that things were getting better and that 'safety first' was the best policy for the country to follow. While this had some appeal, the majority of the electors decided it was not good enough; the Labour Party won 288 seats, thus making them for the first time the largest party in the Commons. The Conservatives were not far behind with 260 M.P.s, but the greatest disappointment was suffered by the Liberals who only had 59 members in the House in spite of putting forward 513 candidates at this election. Baldwin rejected the idea of a coalition with the Liberals and when he resigned on 4 June he advised the King to summon Ramsay MacDonald to form a government. MacDonald was very ready to do this, although Labour had no majority over the other two parties combined: the political situation of a minority government probably appealed to him because it meant a cautious policy and the avoidance of radical Socialist measures, of which he had become increasingly distrustful.

29. The second Labour ministry, June 1929–August 1931

The Labour Cabinet and its problems

The new Labour Cabinet was essentially a moderate one and reflected the right and centre of the party, whose outlook plus their unhappy experiences of the General Strike predisposed them against any extreme measures. It was these moderates who received office; two-thirds of the new Cabinet had been ministers in the first administration of 1924. This time there were no left-wing Socialist ministers except Lansbury, who was given a seat in the Cabinet with the unimportant department of First Commissioner of Works. Arthur Henderson, because of his seniority in the party, claimed and received the appointment of foreign secretary, rather against the wishes of the Prime Minister. A novelty was the first woman Cabinet minister, Miss Margaret Bondfield, who became minister of Labour. In the country at large there was the hope that this new ministry would sweep away the cobwebs and provide some refreshing change after the stagnation of the Conservative government. This was not to be, and in any case the new ministry lacked majority control in the House of Commons; it depended in general on a sufficiency of support from the Liberals and also on a reasonably cooperative House of Lords. Even if things went well its task was not going to be an easy one; it had the misfortune to begin its career just as a great world economic crisis revealed itself. Faced with this economic crisis the counter-measures of the Labour government were uninspired, but it is doubtful if their Conservative opponents would have done any better. In the event this second Labour government was overwhelmed by the intensity of the depression which descended upon Great Britain and other countries.

Labour and unemployment

One major difficulty which Labour had to tackle was that of unemployment. At the end of 1929 the unemployment figure was about $1\frac{1}{2}$ millions; during 1930 it rose steadily and alarmingly to over 2 million by the middle of the year: in October it was over $2\frac{1}{4}$ millions. Another indication of the scale of the crisis, especially for an industrial nation like Britain, was the sharp decline in exports: in 1929 these were worth £839 millions; in 1930, £660 millions, and in 1931 only £461 millions. The minister in charge of unemployment, J. H. Thomas, found it heavy going. He started schemes for public works involving construction of roads and improvement to railways, but this did no more than scratch the surface of the

327

problem. He found great difficulty in getting any money from the economically minded Chancellor of the Exchequer, Philip Snowden, and also received very little sympathy from the Treasury and departmental officials. This limited treatment of the problem of unemployment caused a lively discontent within the Labour Party. There were two main groups of critics – one was the extreme Independent Labour Party members, who demanded that real Socialist measures should be tried, and the other a radical section headed by Sir Oswald Mosley. Mosley drew up a streamlined programme for an unorthodox attack on the problem of unemployment. It called for 'pump-priming' by the extensive creation of bank credit, the adoption of tariffs and the granting of subsidies to British agriculture. The scheme was submitted to the Cabinet, but rejected by it; the failure to get to grips with the bogey of unemployment increased the tension within the Labour Party. Mosley subsequently resigned in disgust and formed his own party called the 'New Party', which in the later 1930s became the British Union of Fascists.

A related problem was that of unemployment insurance payments. The Labour government did its best to ease conditions for payment of unemployment insurance, especially for those unemployed who had only a minimum number of contributions. They modified the requirement of the Conservative government that those seeking benefit should be 'genuinely seeking work', but overall their measures let in a considerable number of people whose claims to unemployment benefit proper were somewhat doubtful. The government's policy was criticized not only by the Conservatives, who accused it of being wasteful, but more particularly by the Independent Labour Party members; they were committed to the principle of 'work or maintenance' and were disgusted to think that a Labour government had not provided this. Meanwhile the unemployment insurance fund was becoming hopelessly insolvent: the numbers of unemployed drawing transitional benefit increased from 120,000 in 1929 to 500,000 in 1931; the cost rose from £51 millions to £125 millions, and against this there was no more than £30 millions paid in contributions by employers and employed.

Domestic legislation 1929–31

A Coal Mines Act was enacted in 1930 which gave the miners a seven and-a-half-hour day instead of the eight-hour day they had been working. Quotas of production were fixed for mining districts, together with minimum prices in order to discourage mine owners from making wage cuts; attempts were made to reorganize the industry by amalgamation schemes. Other legislation of this government was a Housing Act in 1930 which made slum clearance possible, and which also tried to bring about an orderly rehousing of the slum dwellers. An Agricultural

Marketing Act in 1931 set up marketing boards of producers in various branches of the agricultural industry, the aim being to promote orderly marketing and to support the market price of farm produce.

Some attempted legislation failed, e.g. an Education Bill which sought to raise the school leaving age to fifteen was rejected by the House of Lords. There was also a Bill to amend the hated Trades Disputes Act of 1927. Rather ingeniously it tried to make sympathetic strikes, but not general strikes, legal; the Bill was dropped because of the heavy amendments made to it in committee, chiefly by the Liberals. The Liberals were also displeased that the Labour government had not produced any measures to bring in proportional representation. A Bill for electoral reform was introduced, but as it went no further than making possible the use of the alternative vote, it did not meet the Liberal wish for full-scale proportional representation.

Foreign and imperial affairs

As in their first ministry in 1924, Labour showed more decision and grip in its dealings with foreign affairs than with those at home. The Foreign Secretary, Henderson, achieved a great reputation at Geneva, where the League was now working for comprehensive disarmament, following the signing of the Kellogg–Briand Pact outlawing war. The British government gave its general assent to the reference of disputes in which it might be involved, to the permanent court of international justice sitting at The Hague; the British Dominions followed suit. Diplomatic relations were resumed with Russia in October 1929 and in the following year an Anglo-Russian commercial treaty was negotiated. The problem of Germany's reparation payments was now being finally settled by the Young Plan, but Snowden, the Chancellor of the Exchequer, upset international harmony by rather brusquely demanding and getting better terms for Britain at this settlement. A conference on naval disarmament was held in London in 1930; MacDonald presided, and it was attended by U.S.A., Great Britain, France, Italy and Japan. Agreement was reached between the U.S.A., Great Britain and Japan over the maximum tonnage of various types of warships for their navies, and that a five years 'holiday' for building warships should be observed.

In imperial affairs the major problem was that of India where there was an increasing demand for more self government than had been given by the Montague–Chelmsford reforms in 1919. The Simon Commission which had been appointed by the Conservative government in 1927, made its report in June 1930; it recommended an advance to responsible government for the Indian provinces and further discussion about the type of central government that should be established. The Labour government was embarrassed by the mass civil disobedience that had

329

spread through India owing to the policy of the Congress Party led by Gandhi and the Nehrus. The repressive measures necessary to check this civil disobedience were distasteful to the Labour government and it tried conciliation through the Round Table Conferences. The first of these met in London in November 1930, but unfortunately it was boycotted by the Congress Party: only the representatives of the Indian princes attended, but agreement was reached that eventually an all-India Federation should be set up.

Labour's financial policy

The year 1931 proved fatal to the second Labour government, when a combination of internal and external financial problems brought about its fall. As far as the management of the country's finances were concerned, the Labour Party was handicapped by its uninspired, conventional approach, and by the fact that its Chancellor, Snowden, was a convinced free trader. Financial difficulties began in 1930, due to declining revenue and increased expenditure on the social services; the budget was unbalanced and this had to be remedied by slight extra taxation. Snowden obstinately refused to extend the life of the safeguarding duties on gas mantles, cutlery, lace and fabric gloves, because this offended his free trade principles. In retrospect it seems strange that the Labour Party should have been so hidebound in their attachment to free trade, since the climate of opinion about this was undergoing a rapid change and it would have been possible for them to have taken advantage of this.

Labour's action over the safeguarding duties enraged the Conservative protectionists. Baldwin had accepted safeguarding and imperial preference as an official part of Conservative policy, but this did not satisfy the 'United Empire Party', sponsored by the press barons, Lord Beaverbrook and Lord Rothermere. They demanded duties on foreign food and complete preference in the British market for empire foodstuffs; their programme envisaged an economic bloc consisting of Great Britain and the empire, and which was sealed off economically from the rest of the world. The 'Empire Free Trade' group attacked Baldwin because his tariff policy was, in their opinion, far too half-hearted. A personal feud developed between Baldwin and Beaverbrook and Rothermere, which led in 1930–1 to Empire Free Trade candidates standing against official Conservative candidates at by-elections. But in this as in other crises, Baldwin at bay showed surprising powers of retaliation: he flayed the press barons for the unscrupulous use they made of their newspapers in their bid for political power and successfully confirmed his position as party leader. which had been threatened by the Empire Free Trade attack.

Rising unemployment, which at the beginning of 1931 was over two and a half millions, played havoc with the government's financial plans; heavy borrowing became necessary to support the insolvent Unemployment Insurance fund. The Conservative opposition stepped up its demands for economy measures and this led Snowden to appoint a Committee on National Expenditure, presided over by Sir George May to review government expenditure and make recommendations.

The crisis deepens; Labour's economy proposals

In May and June, 1931 Austria and Germany were involved in financial crises which led to a rapid withdrawal of foreign short term credits. The German gold and foreign exchange reserves were rapidly drained away and in June, President Hoover of the U.S.A. proposed a year's moratorium, or standstill, on payments of war debts and reparations. In spite of help from foreign central banks, the German financial crisis was not contained and spread to other central European countries.

At the beginning of July, Great Britain appeared unshaken by this economic crisis, but during the second half of the month foreign credits began to be withdrawn and this was reflected in a steady drain on the Bank of England's gold reserves. On 31 July, the day after Parliament had adjourned for the summer recess, the May Committee report was published. It drew a gloomy picture of Britain's financial state, forecasting a budget deficit of not less than £120 millions for 1932. To correct this its recommendations were a small increase in taxation and large scale reduction in unemployment expenditure by a 20% cut in unemployment benefit, together with 15% reduction in the pay of civil servants, teachers, police and the armed forces. The effect of this report was to shatter foreign confidence in Great Britain, which appeared to be nearly bankrupt. Withdrawals of foreign credit balances continued apace and the Bank of England was obliged to seek supporting credits from central banks in France and the U.S.A. but these gave only temporary relief.

The Labour government now faced two unpleasant facts: the first was that it commanded little, if any, confidence, either at home or abroad in its ability in financial matters, and secondly that its only chance of recovery would be by drastic economies at the expense of the unemployed. If the necessary steps to balance the budget were not taken, the government was advised that the pressure on the pound would continue and eventually Britain would be forced off gold and the pound devalued. The moment of crisis for the Labour government had arrived: its Cabinet must decide, and decide quickly, whether or not it was prepared to enforce a policy of strict economy to ward off a financial crash.

The Cabinet crisis over economy measures

The decision was thrashed out at Cabinet meetings spread over five hectic days (19-23 August). Before this MacDonald had meetings with the leaders of the two opposition parties, at which he indicated to them in general terms that his government would follow a course of economy. The Cabinet economy committee, working under the revised figure of a budget deficit of £170 millions by April 1932, rather than the figure of £110 millions estimated by the May Committee, increased its list of economies to £78½ millions. The matter now came back to the Cabinet on 19 August, when economies of £56 millions were agreed. The General Council of the T.U.C. and the Labour Party Executive hastened to inform the Cabinet of their emphatic opposition to economies of this nature and extent. A Cabinet meeting on 21 August left the economies at £56 millions, but this figure did not satisfy the opposition which had been led to believe that they would be on a much larger scale. Unmistakable signs of a split within the Cabinet now appeared, particularly over the question of achieving economies by reductions in the rate of unemployment benefits. It was clear to MacDonald and Snowden that if they were to gain sufficient support in Parliament from the opposition to carry them through the crisis, they must pitch their figure of economies higher. They attempted this at a Cabinet meeting on Saturday, 22 August when against the opposition of a minority of ministers led by Henderson, the total of economies was raised to £88 millions, including a 10% cut in unemployment allowance.

The next day MacDonald told the King that because some ministers would also certainly resign in opposition to the proposed economies, the continuance of the government was uncertain. Then followed consultations by the King with the Liberal and Conservative leaders, Samuel and Baldwin. From these talks was born the idea of a 'National' government of all three parties, under the leadership of MacDonald, as being the best way out of the crisis. The same evening a decisive Cabinet meeting was held, at which MacDonald made it clear that the granting of American credits in support of the £ depended on the full economies being enforced, and that if the Cabinet were divided on this matter, resignations must follow. A bare majority of the Cabinet were in favour of the proposed economies: the large minority included influential Labour leaders, such as Henderson, Clynes and Lansbury.

Resignation of MacDonald and formation of a National government

Because of this fundamental disagreement, MacDonald announced his resignation, received those of his Cabinet, and announced that he would now advise the King to call a conference of all three party leaders. The following day, Monday 24 August, MacDonald met the King, together with Baldwin and Samuel; the King invited MacDonald to form a broadly based 'National' government, to include all three parties. With the support of Baldwin and Samuel, MacDonald agreed to do this. The news of this came as a bombshell to the Labour ministers, who assumed that a Conservative–Liberal coalition government would succeed them; they were also unaware of the role for which MacDonald had groomed himself during the past fortnight. To the majority of his colleagues it was a 'sell-out', and they quickly disassociated themselves from his action; only three of them, P. Snowden, J. H. Thomas and Lord Sankey, were willing to participate in the new government. The various Labour organizations, such as the Parliamentary Labour Party and the T.U.C. endorsed this opposition to the National government, and Henderson was elected leader of the Labour Party in Parliament.

There has been much speculation over the causes of the fall of the second Labour government, and the part played therein by Ramsay MacDonald. Smarting under defeat, the Labour Party saw its fall originating in the plans of international financiers who had brought on an artificial crisis in which they subsequently dictated their terms and demanded their pound of flesh at the expense of the unemployed. From such unsavoury origins it was carried forward, so Labour critics alleged, by deliberate planning by MacDonald himself. His reasons for doing this are variously given; his personal vanity, which made him wish to continue in the dramatic role of prime minister of a National government with Conservative and Liberals serving under him: his dislike for his own party and its 'cloth cap' attitudes and addiction to controversial Socialist measures; in other words, that his political beliefs had been corrupted and eroded by the sweets of office and the allurements of high society.

A more balanced view of the matter is that, although MacDonald was greatly attracted by the idea of a National government, this was brought about not by his own scheming but by the interaction of other forces which favoured its creation. Thus, Baldwin was far too experienced a politician to underestimate the difficulties facing him if he formed a Conservative–Liberal coalition and together they had to solve the problem of unemployment and a financial crisis; it would be far better to attempt all this under the more comfortable umbrella of a National government, so that responsibility for any failure could be spread as widely as possible. Finally King George V appears to have played a decisive part by his persuasive pressures on MacDonald to undertake the formation of a National government and by encouraging Conservatives and Liberals to participate in this.

30. The National government to 1937

Economy measures, September 1931

The all-party character of the government formed by Ramsay Mac-Donald in August 1931 and the crisis it had to solve were reflected in a small Cabinet of ten ministers; four of these were Labour, four Conservatives and two Liberals, although outside the Cabinet Conservative ministers predominated with a sprinkling of Liberals.

The immediate task was to solve the financial crisis, and this meant a budget which should put into force the economy measures necessary to restore confidence in Britain's position with the foreign banks which were supplying credits. Snowden, the Chancellor of the Exchequer had to make good a deficit of about £70 millions in the current year and a prospective deficit of £170 millions in the next full year. To bridge this gap the budget imposed extra direct taxation of about £50 millions and extra indirect taxation of £24 millions; the balance of the economies came from cuts in the pay of ministers, judges, M.P.s, teachers, police, armed forces and the allowances of the unemployed. The reductions originally proposed were 15%, except in the case of the unemployment allowances which were set at 10%. These reductions were greatly resented by teachers, police, and armed forces, and were subsequently reduced to 10%.

Britain goes off gold, September 1931

While the formation of the National government had led to the provision of credits totalling £80 millions from the U.S.A. and France, foreign confidence in the pound still remained weak and the drain of gold continued. On 14 September the naval ratings of the squadron at Invergordon, in protest against the reductions in pay and dependants' allowances, refused to man their ships. The news of what appeared to be a mutiny in the British navy undermined the remnants of foreign confidence and the drain on gold accelerated, reducing the Bank of England's gold reserves to a low level. In view of this the government had no option but to abandon the gold standard to which Britain had returned in 1925, and this was done on 21 September 1931; it was an ironic commentary on the previously declared aim of the National government to save the pound. The pound was now allowed to 'float' and so find its own value in terms of the dollar; the rate settled at around 3.40 dollars to the pound. This measure gave some help to British exports since the pound was no longer over-valued in terms of foreign currencies.

The general election, October 1931

Although Prime Minister, MacDonald was in a weak position. Very few of his own party supported him, and he came increasingly under pressure from the Conservatives who were demanding a general election at the earliest possible moment. They saw great possibilities in this: firstly, it would increase their representation in Parliament, and secondly, they could fight the election on the issue of a protective tariff. This tariff policy was unacceptable to the Liberals in the National government, and also to the Labour Chancellor of the Exchequer, Snowden. Nevertheless, for appearances sake, if nothing else, the idea of the National government had to be preserved. This could best be done by saying that the emergency still continued and that it could be dealt with only by a National government after the electors had given it a further mandate for this purpose. The issues presented to the voters at the election at the end of October 1931 were thoroughly confused: there was a general manifesto from the National government, but each party issued its own as well, and the Conservatives strongly emphasized their favourite point that only a protective tariff could save British industry and reduce unemployment.

The election was marked not only by the confusion of issues presented to the electors, but also by a good deal of political abuse. The Conservatives could easily make capital out of the mistakes and follies of the Labour government, and insinuate that only Conservative policies could save the country. The Liberals denounced the tariff proposals and there was much bitterness in the Labour camp where those who supported MacDonald in his National government denounced their former colleagues who followed the leadership of Henderson. In the election campaign it was

335

the uncommitted lower-middle-class voters who came under the strongest pressures; they were stampeded into voting for the National government by threats of inflation, similar to that which had hit Germany in the 1920s and of the loss of their savings, whether in the Post Office Bank or in a Friendly Society. The National government romped home with an enormous majority of 497. Of the parties the Conservatives did best, gaining 210 seats; the Liberals, although they increased from 59 to 72 M.P.s suffered a sharp decrease in their percentage of total votes polled. Labour representation, including five I.L.P. members, was only 52 M.P.s, but the proportion of total votes polled in their favour did not greatly decrease, showing that the hard-core of working-class supporters had remained faithful. This election highlighted the defects of the British electoral system, since Labour, although polling 31% of the votes cast, only received 9% of the membership of the Commons. After the election the Cabinet reverted to its normal size of twenty ministers of which eleven were Conservatives, five Liberals and four Labour. In a reshuffle of offices Neville Chamberlain became chancellor of the Exchequer in place of Snowden who received a peerage and the office of Lord Privy Seal; at the Foreign Office Lord Reading was displaced by Sir John Simon.

The abandonment of free trade 1931–2

The Conservatives in the National government forced the pace over tariffs to the obvious distrust of the Labour and Liberal ministers who could do nothing to prevent it. In November 1931 the Abnormal Importations Bill was rushed through Parliament, giving power to impose up to 100% *ad valorem* duties on a large range of manufactured products. The reason for this emergency legislation was to prevent flooding of the British market by foreign manufacturers who now realized that a full scale of tariffs was not far away. In December, the Horticultural Products (Emergency Provisions) Act gave powers to control imports of fresh fruit, vegetables and flowers. The abandonment of free trade was completed in February, 1932, by the Import Duties Act. This imposed a duty of 10% *ad valorem* on all goods coming into the United Kingdom, except those which already carried duties at various rates under earlier measures such as the Safeguarding of Industries Act, or those commodities, such as cotton, wool, iron ore, maize, which were on the 'free list' and so paid no duty. Empire products were to be exempt from these duties for the time being until the matter of imperial preference had been further discussed and agreed upon by Great Britain and the self-governing Dominions. A special body, the Import Duties Advisory Committee, was set up with the duty of making recommendations for duties in the first instance, or recommending higher or lower duties as seemed desirable to them. The work of this committee soon raised duties on most manufactured foreign goods; in general it gave Britain a moderate tariff ranging from 10% to 20%.

The Statute of Westminster 1931

In November 1931 the important Statute of Westminster was enacted. The application of the principle of self government embodied in the Durham Report of 1839 had, by the early years of the twentieth century, brought the white-settled colonies of Canada, Australia, New Zealand and South Africa to a condition of virtual independence. Even so there still remained certain legal inferiorities for these self-governing Dominions, e.g. legislation of their Parliaments might be declared void or inoperative because it was repugnant to the law of England; they were still subject to British legislation such as the Merchant Shipping Acts; their laws could have no extra-territorial effect over their subjects.

The Statute of Westminster, by removing these legal inferiorities, established the independence of the Dominions from any control by the United Kingdom Parliament. It also declared that because of the importance of the Crown as a symbol of the free association of the members of the British Commonwealth and because of the common allegiance of its members to the Crown, that any changes in the law of succession or the Royal Style and Titles would require the assent of the Dominion Parliaments as well as that of the Parliament of the United Kingdom.

The Ottawa Conference 1932

In July 1932 the Imperial Economic Conference met in Ottawa. Its proceedings were not as harmonious as had been expected; the Dominions were reluctant to make concessions over British manufactured goods which competed with their own established industries; they demanded free entry for their agricultural produce into the British market, and also a tariff on foreign imports of such commodities. On balance the result was favourable to the Dominions rather than to Great Britain: nearly 80% of all Commonwealth exports to Britain were given duty-free entry and their position in the British market was further improved by the raising of the British tariff against the products of foreign foodstuff producers; duties on these were raised from 10% to 20% and in particular the two important commodities of wheat and linseed were taken off the 'free list'. The adoption of a tariff policy had already disquieted the free trade Liberal and Labour ministers; the imperial preference measures of the Ottawa agreements proved the last straw. In September 1932 two Liberal ministers, Sir Herbert Samuel and Sir Archibald Sinclair, and the Labour Lord Privy Seal Viscount Snowden, resigned. The harassed Prime Minister who was striving desperately to keep his National government together could hardly deny that it was now Conservative in everything but name.

Unemployment policies of the government

During the years 1931–5 unemployment did not fall below the two million mark and in these circumstances the maintenance of a genuine insurance scheme based on payment of contributions to cover benefits for those unemployed, became impossible. The National government was obliged to attempt a reorganization of unemployment insurance in order to deal with the problem of the large number of unemployed who were not strictly entitled to unemployment benefit payments. In 1931 contributions were increased, benefits reduced and the period of payment of benefits shortened. Transitional payments for those who were outside contributory insurance cover were to be assessed under a 'means test' and paid by the Public Assistance Committees, which had been set up when the old Poor Law Guardians had been abolished in 1929. The result was a reduction in the cost of unemployment benefits, partly because under the 'means test' many people lost the benefits they had been paid under the relaxed rules introduced by the second Labour government. There was considerable resentment over the application of the 'means test', which was associated with the old Poor Law procedures. Overall there was disappointment that the government, which had virtually promised that it would deal effectively with the problem of unemployment, had no positive remedies for reducing the large number of unemployed. In fact it almost openly admitted that large scale unemployment could not be reduced to any great extent in the foreseeable future. This complacent attitude was not forgotten and told heavily against the Conservative Party in the general election immediately after the end of World War II in 1945.

The distinction between insurance payments as of right and relief payments outside insurance was carried further by the government in their

Jarrow unemployed marching to London 1936

Unemployment Act of 1934. This set up two distinct bodies, the Unemployment Assistance Board, and the Unemployment Insurance Statutory Committee. The Unemployment Assistance Board took charge of those unemployed who had exhausted their entitlement to benefit and it acted on the principle that this large-scale problem was a national responsibility, and for which a common standard of relief must be fixed. It would no longer do to shuffle off the problem to the local Public Assistance Committees; there was the aim, if possible, of removing this problem from the field of politics, whether central or local. Some delay was experienced in bringing the Unemployment Assistance Board into full operation, because it turned out that its national scales of relief were lower in some cases than those given by local Public Assistance Committees. After hasty readjustment the scheme took effect in 1937 and lasted till 1948, when new social security provisions took its place. The Board whose funds were provided by the Treasury made its payments subject to a means test as had been done in the case of the transitional benefits from 1931 onwards; the household and family were treated as a unit in respect of the total income earned in each week, and relief was assessed on this basis. The system was intensely disliked because those members of the household who were employed had to bear part of the cost of maintaining other members of the household who were unemployed.

Besides providing financial aid, the Unemployment Assistance Board made an attempt to provide welfare services, e.g. Government Training Centres where unemployed could be retrained for new jobs. Their success was moderate and the same was true of the government's attempt to help what became known as distressed or special areas such as South Wales and Tyneside where unemployment was very high; industry was encouraged by tax concessions and by the development of special trading estates to establish itself in these areas.

The Unemployment Insurance Statutory Committee under the chairmanship of Sir William Beveridge was given charge of national unemployment insurance based on contributions from employed workers. The slow fall in unemployment after 1935 enabled the fund to be kept in credit and a reserve built up for emergencies. Unemployment insurance was extended to agricultural workers in 1936, but domestic servants, nurses, civil servants and railwaymen remained outside this unemployment scheme.

The growing threat to world peace after 1931

To the difficulties of the domestic situation was now added an alarming deterioration in foreign affairs. In September 1931 the Japanese committed an act of aggression against China, a fellow member of the League of Nations, by invading Manchuria. This was a severe test for the League

339

of Nations; its difficulties soon became apparent, e.g. there was little enthusiasm for the idea of collective action against Japan in an area remote from Europe; there was even sympathy with the aggressor, and a major drawback was that the U.S.A., the greatest power in the Pacific, was not a member of the League. In 1932 the possibility of joint British–American action in the matter was spoilt by the attitude of the British Foreign Secretary, Sir John Simon, who seemed only too anxious to appease Japan, and who was distrustful of the motives of the U.S.A. There was also a background of growing pacifist feeling in Great Britain, and the calculating prudence of the National government told it not to go against this swing of public opinion, however harmful it might be in the long run for Britain. Once again it illustrated the capacity of the National government for taking short-term views. The result was that Japan continued her defiance of the League, set up a puppet state in Manchuria, resigned from the League of Nations and after 1937 waged open war on China.

Concurrently with these developments in the Far East, the European situation took an ominous turn for the worse. Superficially in 1931 the situation looked more hopeful; the allied occupation of the Rhineland had been ended and the economic crisis had forced the general abandonment of reparation payments. A disarmament conference had been summoned in the hope that it would be possible to bring European armaments down to the level that had been imposed on Germany by the peace terms. The conference which met at Geneva in February 1932 soon ran into difficulties: Germany's demand for equality of status in armaments with the other great European powers was opposed by France who sought security against any future German aggression, although Great Britain was ready in principle to concede the German demand. By 1932 the situation was dramatically altered by the change that came over German politics: the moderate Centre Party Chancellor Brüning resigned and was succeeded by the right wing Nationalist government of Von Papen. Germany now withdrew temporarily from the disarmament conference but the takeover of power in March 1933 by Hitler and his National Socialist Party soon made agreement impossible. Hitler at first pleaded his pacific intentions and then evaded a realistic disarmament plan that the conference had prepared by withdrawing from the conference and resigning from the League of Nations in October 1933. His career of bluff and blackmail leading to a revolution of destruction had begun and for the floundering British politicians of the 1930s he presented a far more formidable and sinister problem than had Bismarck for their Victorian predecessors.

The rapid rearming of Germany by Hitler in defiance of the Treaty of Versailles after his seizure of power in 1933, and its accompanying threat to the peace of Europe, was something even the National government could not ignore. In 1934 it made small increases in the R.A.F., pretending at the same time that Germany's lead in the air was not as great as supposed. In March 1935, in an official White Paper, the government announced that in view of the failure of disarmament policies and the rearming of Germany, British armed forces must be increased as soon as possible.

Baldwin becomes prime minister June 1935

In May 1935 the Silver Jubilee marking twenty-five years of rule by King George V was celebrated throughout Great Britain, the Dominions and empire. The occasion evoked a sincere expression of public feeling because the King commanded in full measure the respect and affection of his subjects for his long devotion to the exacting duties of his office. In June changes were made in the government: Baldwin became prime minister in place of MacDonald. Apart from the inclusion in the Cabinet of Anthony Eden, other ministerial changes were not particularly inspiring, while Winston Churchill who for the past two years had been giving prophetic warnings about the extent of German rearmament, still remained outside the government. Although very largely made up of Conservatives the reconstructed government still clung to the title of 'National' which in the difficult situation at home and abroad still had some political value.

A general election was held in November 1935. Baldwin chose the time for this skilfully; his own political image as the pilot who could weather the storm was as yet unimpaired and he adroitly met public anxieties over the critical foreign situation by playing up the government's support of the League of Nations, while also promising a moderate amount of rearmament. The electors responded by giving the National government a majority of between 240 and 250 over its opponents; the decline in Liberal strength continued, but Labour made a strong recovery from 52 M.P.s to 154.

Weakness of British policy

It was not easy for the government to deal with the problem of the dying peace. Both Baldwin and Neville Chamberlain, especially the latter, had limited horizons in international affairs, and were survivals of the balance of power era. British foreign policy in this crisis fluctuated between rearmament and old style diplomatic bargaining and support for the League of Nations, although it probably distrusted the basic principles of this organization. The government were well aware of the widespread pacifist sentiments which arose from disillusionment with the 1914–18 war and which had been fortified by the war literature of the late 1920s: this made them hesitate in being too militant for fear that this would be a loser in a general election. The success of the Peace Pledge Union and the

341

M

National Peace Ballot in which 40% of the parliamentary voters cast an overwhelming vote in favour of disarmament and the League of Nations, encouraged Baldwin in his policy of soothing talk, 'sealed lips' and half-measures, and also doubtful deals, such as the Hoare–Laval proposals, to sweep awkward international problems under the carpet. The British government was ready to overlook the repudiation by Hitler in March 1935 of the arms restriction clause of the Versailles treaty, since he followed this by a declaration of his peaceful intentions and made an offer to negotiate over armaments. This led Great Britain to conclude the Anglo-German Naval agreement of 1935, by which Germany could build her fleet up to 35% of the size of the British navy.

The Abyssinia crisis 1935–6

The tension building up in Europe was complicated by Italian aggression against Abyssinia (Ethiopia). In 1935 Abyssinia appealed to the League of Nations for mediation to solve the dispute which had arisen with Italy over frontier incidents. The League, preoccupied with German unilateral denunciation of the Versailles treaty, delayed action. British public opinion rallied strongly to the side of the League; the Foreign Secretary, Sir Samuel Hoare, in a speech in September at the Assembly of the League in Geneva, made it clear that Great Britain stood by the principle of the Covenant and collective action against unprovoked aggression. In October 1935 the Italian attack on Abyssinia started. The League took action, but only to the extent of imposing partial financial and economic sanctions on Italy. It was not long before the fervour of the British government for collective action through the League against the aggressor Italy began to decline. Sanctions, if they were to be really effective, might well bring about a general war over Abyssinia; this possibility had been recognized by France and Great Britain, who were the two major powers most concerned with the matter. In spite of their earlier support for the principles of the League, Great Britain and France now favoured a negotiated settlement rather than the imposition of effective sanctions against Italy, such as military action, a naval blockade and closure of the Suez Canal. The imposition of oil sanctions, which might well have halted Italian aggression, was held up in the League through the influence of Laval, the French Foreign Minister.

The Hoare–Laval proposals, December 1935

Early in December, Hoare, while passing through Paris en route for Switzerland, concerted proposals with Laval for a settlement which should be submitted to the League; their terms involved the cession to Italy of over half of Abyssinia. These terms which were prematurely disclosed by Laval to the French press on 9 December, brought a sharp public reaction, both in Great Britain and France. The proposals made complete nonsense of all talk of collective security through the League of Nations, and worse than that, showed only too clearly that aggression paid handsome dividends. Baldwin was shaken by the storm of criticism from the British press and people: after appealing for blind trust in his government and its policies, he was obliged to admit that the deep feelings shown by the British people was grounded in 'conscience and honour' and that in face of this his government was abandoning the Hoare–Laval proposals.

Baldwin did not disclose the reason for the British government countenancing these shameful proposals but it was basically the military unpreparedness of Britain which made him anxious to avoid a war with Italy fearing that if this happened Hitler would be given further opportunities for influencing European affairs. Both France and Great Britain wanted Italy as an ally against Hitler and were therefore prepared to go to great lengths of appeasement to achieve this. If these were the inner motivations for British policy, outwardly a gross deception had been practised on the British public in view of the continued emphasis that its government had laid on a policy of collective security through the League of Nations. The downward trend continued: by May 1936 Abyssinia had been conquered and annexed by Italy and in June sanctions against Italy were abandoned by Britain.

German reoccupation of the demilitarized Rhineland, March 1936

A more serious crisis in British policy was brought about by the reoccupation, in March 1936, by Germany of the demilitarized zone of the Rhineland. This was a clear breach of the Versailles and Locarno treaties: France, who was most directly affected, wanted military action to restore the situation, but could get no promise of assistance from Britain. Instead, British politicians and influential opinion, especially *The Times*, swallowed the ground bait laid by Hitler at the time of the reoccupation of the Rhineland: this took the form of wide proposals for securing the peace of Europe over the next twenty-five years. At this stage British policy moved clearly towards appeasement of the dictators and this was shown by official attempts to minimize the importance of the German reoccupation of the Rhineland by reference to the 'injustice' of the Treaty of Versailles. Hitler's proposals for European peace were also treated very seriously, although it soon became obvious that these were no more than propaganda in aid of his Rhineland coup of March.

The Spanish Civil War 1936

A few months after the German reoccupation of the Rhineland there occurred another event which brought profit to both Hitler and Mussolini and corresponding discomfort to the Western democracies. This was the Spanish Civil War in which the Spanish Republic was attacked by right-wing forces headed by the army under General Franco. The war quickly assumed international importance: Mussolini and Hitler welcomed the opportunity to try out their tanks and aircraft in support of Franco, pretending that they were doing this in order to check Communism and disorder. An International Brigade of anti-Fascist volunteers from all over the world, together with some Russian planes and tanks, strengthened the Republican resistance. The British government came out strongly for a policy of non-intervention and with some difficulty carried the French government with it in this matter. Germany and Italy adhered officially to this agreement, but flagrantly broke it by sending a stream of 'volunteers' amounting to 30,000 and 80,000 troops respectively to help Franco; the British government got little credit for its non-intervention policy because of the obviously unfair way in which it was working.

British opinion was strongly affected by this war; a clear-cut division into 'left' and 'right' emerged. Although atrocities had been committed by both sides, the Nationalists had been particularly brutal; most British opinion inclined to the side of the Republicans and there were insistent demands that help should be given them. To many of the British public the government gave the impression that it favoured the side of the dictators and Franco, and this increasingly brought the Government's foreign policy under suspicious criticism. Attempts were made by British Communists and left-wing Socialists to form a 'Popular Front' and to promote working-class unity against Fascism. This had little success because it was rejected by the Labour Party, which distrusted any collaboration with the Communists. Opinion in favour of the 'left' was mobilized by the Left Book Club whose vigorous if partisan books about contemporary political issues were widely read.

The Abdication crisis 1936

On 20 January 1936, King George V died. His death and funeral ceremonies brought an impressive demonstration of the respect and affection in which he was held by his subjects who recognized his human qualities and the endeavours he had made as king. The new King took the title of Edward VIII; few of his subjects at the time of his accession could have foreseen that his reign would last but eleven months. It was thought by many that the friendliness and charm he had shown as prince of Wales would now be carried further as king, and that he would bring the monarchy into closer touch with the people. He was fitted to do this because he disliked court ceremonial and soon made changes in this, much to the dismay of the conventional court personnel.

344

In the summer of 1936 the American and European press gave publicity to the King's friendship for and attachment to Mrs Ernest Simpson, an American lady married to a London stockbroker. The British press, under a self-imposed censorship made no mention whatever of this, although the facts were known to the Cabinet and court circles. Baldwin, although his grip on the general run of political business was now at a low ebb, braced himself for the delicate constitutional problem that had now arisen. His intervention was prompted by the fact that in October Mrs Simpson was divorced from her second husband; the King told Baldwin on 16 November that he intended to marry Mrs Simpson. The King clearly regarded his marriage as a private matter, but the Cabinet did not. To them it was a matter of the highest constitutional importance and one in which the King must accept the advice given him by his ministers. The government opposed the marriage on the grounds that generally it would be unacceptable to the majority of the King's subjects and that it was incompatible with the public

345

duties of the office of the sovereign. Although a considerable minority of his subjects supported the King's right to make a marriage of his own choice and to remain king, majority opinion both in Britain and the Dominions was against him.

On 3 December the British press broke its silence and the bewildered subjects of the King learned of the situation for the first time. It was necessary to find a solution quickly to prevent this delicate matter becoming the subject of political debate. The King had already made clear to Baldwin his intention to abdicate if his marriage to Mrs Simpson was opposed. His final decision to do this was given to the government of 5 December and announced by Baldwin to the Commons on 10 December. A Declaration of Abdication Bill was rapidly enacted by 11 December and on the same day the King, now a private citizen, after a broadcast speech of farewell to his former subjects, left for exile and marriage in

INSTRUMENT OF ABDICATION

I, Edward the Eighth, of Great Britain, Ireland, and the British Dominions beyond the Seas, King, Emperor of India, do hereby declare My irrevocable determination to renounce the Throne for Myself and for My descendants, and My desire that effect should be given to this Instrument of Abdication immediately.

In token whereof I have hereunto set My hand this tenth day of December, nineteen hundred and thirty six, in the presence of the witnesses whose signatures are subscribed.

SIGNED AT
FORT BELVEDERE
IN THE PRESENCE
OF

1937 to Mrs Simpson. He was succeeded by his brother, who took the title of George VI. The solution of this crisis, whereby the traditional position of the Crown in the constitution had been preserved, was undeniably a triumph for Baldwin. It was also his last political action of importance; on 28 May 1937 he resigned as prime minister, to be succeeded by Neville Chamberlain.

31. Great Britain and the dying peace 1937–9

Peace by appeasement

Whatever criticisms may be made of Chamberlain's conduct of British foreign policy, it will be agreed that he inherited a very difficult situation. World peace was falling into ruins; the aggression of the Berlin–Rome–Tokio axis steadily increased; the League of Nations had failed in its aim of preventing war and protecting the weak against the aggressor. In this situation the policy of Chamberlain was that of appeasement of Germany and Italy by direct negotiation and discussion. Until March 1939 he pursued this policy with relentless zeal and the conviction that he was right, as was shown by his touchy resentment of any criticism. In these negotiations Chamberlain aligned France with Britain, but France, torn by internal dissension, was by now hardly a great power, in spite of her outwardly imposing system of alliances with the 'Little *Entente*' and Soviet Russia. Great Britain, although she had started to rearm, was still weak; public opinion opposed the thought of war, although by 1937 many of the left-wing opponents of rearmament realized it was necessary if aggression was to be halted.

Why did Chamberlain believe that he could secure peace by appeasement by discussion with the dictators? Probably it sprang from his businessman's view of human nature, e.g. that it was always possible to do a deal with an opponent on agreed terms, with the underlying implication that he would honour his bargain and fulfil the terms of the contract. Unfortunately the standards of his opponents were those of the gangster, based on bluff, threats and blackmail. While the policy of appeasement gained time for British rearmament, especially in the air, this was not Chamberlain's first aim. Until March 1939 he consistently gave priority to the negotiation of a settlement with Hitler which he was confident would prevent war. A subordinate but important part of Chamberlain's policy was that in these negotiations Italy could be played off against Germany.

The conduct of appeasement

In his policy of appeasement Chamberlain at first commanded considerable support: many people, and also the leading newspapers, recognized that our position was so weak that there were few practical alternatives. A small right-wing section of British society enthusiastically supported appeasement because it cultivated the friendship of Hitler and Mussolini,

348

whom it fondly believed to be the saviours of society against Communism; perhaps Hitler could be turned against Bolshevik Russia and thereby make the future of the British Empire secure. Appeasement was essentially a personal policy and throughout was controlled by Chamberlain, who kept negotiations closely in his own hands with the aid of a small inner circle of his Cabinet, including Lord Halifax, Sir John Simon and Sir Samuel Hoare. Significantly Chamberlain distrusted and often disregarded the advice of the permanent officials of the Foreign Office; he was also critical of the career diplomats, many of whom were convinced of the unwisdom of appeasement. Instead Chamberlain gave his entire confidence to Sir Horace Wilson, a senior civil servant lacking experience in foreign affairs, but a man who showed a good deal of skill in adapting things to the way Chamberlain wanted them to go. In May 1937 the key appointment of British ambassador in Berlin was given to Sir Nevile Henderson, who believed in appeasement and who did all he could to further Chamberlain's aims by concealing the worst features of the Nazi regime and whose despatches home were sometimes misleading. It was also noteworthy that the two great powers of the U.S.A. and Soviet Russia were cold-shouldered until too late by Chamberlain. He disliked President Franklin Roosevelt of the U.S.A., possibly because his 'New Deal' savoured of Socialism, while Russia was suspect because of its Communist principles.

The dismissal of Anthony Eden

One obstacle to the progress of Chamberlain's policy was his Foreign Secretary, Anthony Eden, who spoke out against appeasement and insisted on the need for supporting one's friends rather than making concessions to obvious enemies. In particular Eden was opposed to Chamberlain's ardent wish to open negotiations for reconciliation with Mussolini, because the latter had shamefully broken the Non-Intervention Agreement to withdraw the so-called 'volunteers' who were helping Franco in Spain to defeat the Republicans. To Chamberlain, negotiations with Mussolini took precedence over the sounder principles Eden advocated and consequently he was ready to get rid of his Foreign Secretary: By the threat of his own resignation, Chamberlain, at a Cabinet meeting on 19 February 1937, forced the resignation of Eden. There was general dismay at the sacrifice of Eden and the whole business was seen as the most naked appeasement of Hitler and Mussolini, both of whom disliked Eden because of his criticism of their regimes. The new Foreign Secretary was Lord Halifax, who was more in sympathy with Chamberlain's policy, although by no means entirely so. In April 1937 Chamberlain's cherished project for an Anglo-Italian agreement was achieved: it provided for the stabilization of the positions of both powers

349

in the Mediterranean and also made arrangements for the withdrawal of 'volunteers' from Spain, but only when the war had ended.

The German seizure of Austria, March 1938

Meanwhile a sinister demonstration of Nazi aggression in Europe had taken place. In February 1938 the Austrian Chancellor Schuschnigg was forced, under threat of German invasion, to recognize the Nazi Party in Austria and to take some of its members into his government. His attempt to hold a referendum about the future of Austrian independence led to his forced resignation and a German occupation on 11 March 1938. This brutal extinction of the Austrian Republic shocked even Chamberlain but it did not deter him from his policy of 'discussion' with the perpetrator of the outrage.

Hitler and Czechoslovakia

More important than Austria in Hitler's schemes of conquest and the establishment of his 'Third Reich' was Czechoslovakia. Created in 1919 as one of the succession states of the old Austro-Hungarian Empire, it occupied an important strategic position in Central Europe; it was well developed industrially and was allied to France and had links with Soviet Russia. It also had within its frontiers three million Germans, the Sudeten Germans, and these provided a convenient excuse for Hitler

Neville Chamberlain meets the French Prime Minister, M. Daladier, for talks over the Czech crisis, 18 September 1938

to start a campaign of promoting internal disorder as a prelude to invasion and conquest.

While Chamberlain hoped to restrain German action over Czechoslovakia, his immediate difficulty was that to France Czechoslovakia was a vital interest as the most important of her 'Little *Entente*' allies. There was the possibility that France would fight in defence of Czechoslovakia; this Chamberlain was determined to prevent, while at the same time compelling Czechoslovakia to make concessions to Germany. By mid-September 1938 the German pressures on Czechoslovakia had intensified, but no mobilization in defence of the Czechs was ordered by the French government. Chamberlain now made a dramatic intervention in the shape of a personal meeting with Hitler.

The negotiations at Berchtesgaden and Godesberg

On 15 September Chamberlain made his first flight in an aeroplane in a desperate attempt to preserve peace. He met Hitler at his mountain retreat at Berchtesgaden where, with the aid of an interpreter, a three-hour conversation took place. Hitler, to Chamberlain's disappointment, showed little readiness to bargain in detailed terms, but he made it fully clear that nothing would stop him from making war to achieve his aims; the meeting revealed that an essential requirement of Hitler's for further negotiations was the immediate cession of the Sudeten German lands. This meant the virtual dismemberment of Czechoslovakia and the loss of

Mr Chamberlain at the Godesberg meeting with Hitler, 22 September 1938

her strategic frontiers, but Chamberlain, to preserve peace, was ready to agree to this. France followed Britain's lead; heavy pressure was put on Czechoslovakia to accept this dismemberment of their country and the abandonment of their alliance with Soviet Russia. It was made clear to the Czechs that if they refused they would be left alone to meet any German invasion; under these intolerable pressures the Czechoslovak President Benes submitted.

On 22 September Chamberlain had his second meeting with Hitler at Godesberg. He found that Hitler, baulked of his war, had stepped up his demands; these included an immediate occupation by German troops of the German-speaking areas of Czechoslovakia. Chamberlain made an angry protest to Hitler that this was an ultimatum and would imperil the plans for orderly negotiations, but he got few concessions except an extension of the time limit for occupation and the assurance from Hitler that 'he had no more territorial demands to make'.

The Munich meeting and its results

The memorandum Chamberlain brought back from Godesberg was rejected by the British Cabinet on 25 September; the French and Czechoslovak governments did the same. Meanwhile Hitler hurled his abusive threats at the Czechoslovaks, France partially mobilized her forces and Great Britain thought she would be at war within a few days. Hurried preparations were made by the civilian authorities to put into effect civil defence measures, such as evacuating women and children, digging slit trenches and distributing gas masks. Time was quickly running out when, on the evening of 27 September, Chamberlain received a reply to a meassage he had sent to Hitler by Sir Horace Wilson. It was an invitation from Hitler to continue negotiations and invited Chamberlain to help bring the Czechs to reason. The meeting was to take place at Munich; France and Italy would also attend. The news of the invitation to Munich was announced by Chamberlain to a tense House of Commons, which received the information with undisguised relief, regardless of the fact that it must almost certainly involve the sacrifice of Czechoslovakia.

At Munich Chamberlain and the French Prime Minister, Daladier, conceded to Hitler what they had shortly before refused when they rejected the Godesberg memorandum. Within a week Czechoslovakia was to hand over those parts of her territory inhabited by Germans; these areas included her powerful frontier fortifications which the Germans thus gained without firing a shot; what remained of Czechoslovakia was to be guaranteed by Britain and France. Before leaving Munich Chamberlain had a private meeting with Hitler at which he secured his signature to a document he had drafted himself, in which

Mr Chamberlain speaking on his return from the Munich meeting with Hitler, 30 September 1938

they both agreed to consult in a similar way on any future problems. On his return to London Chamberlain exultantly proclaimed that this signed promise by Hitler meant 'peace for our time'.

In spite of the triumph of Hitler, it was not difficult for Chamberlain and his government to defend the Munich agreement on the grounds that the alternative was war; probably a majority of the British people, showing a strange indifference to the fate of Czechoslovakia, accepted this argument, although not without feelings of shame. In the debate in the Commons on the agreement the Labour Party leader, Attlee, condemned it as a bitter humiliation; Winston Churchill gave an eloquent and sombre warning that it was only the beginning of further humiliations

A Spitfire squadron of the R.A.F., May 1939

unless we made a stand for right and freedom. By the beginning of 1939 opinion on the balance sheet of Munich began to change; there was a fuller realization of what had been lost by the sacrifice of Czechoslovakia and that, in spite of Chamberlain's belief about 'peace for our time', war had only been postponed for a little while longer. The time gained by Munich enabled Great Britain to hasten her rearmament. This involved the expansion and equipment of all three services, navy, army and air force. The greatest progress in this respect was made with the R.A.F. which was expanded in men and planes and provided with the celebrated 'Hurricanes' and 'Spitfires'. More ships had to be built for the navy, especially in connection with its anti-submarine role. As in 1914, it was decided that the army should send an expeditionary force to fight in France if she was attacked. This necessitated the expansion of the army and the provision of up-to-date equipment, especially of motorized vehicles, although ironically we were deficient in that weapon which we had pioneered in the World War I, the tank. The Germans had profited from our experience, as they were to show when their Panzer divisions overran France in 1940. Civil defence of the home front was another important consideration and in 1938-9 extensive A.R.P. preparations were made. These included the provision of fire services, air raid shelters and plans for the evacuation of people from big towns.

The extinction of Czechoslovakia, March 1939

In spite of criticism from a small section of his own party and of the attempts to form a 'Popular Front' of all who opposed Fascism to replace the National government, Chamberlain remained firmly in control, confident that his policy had succeeded. His hopes in this respect were shattered when on 15 March 1939, by a brutal invasion coup, Hitler extinguished the last remnants of Czechoslovak independence. A German protectorate was proclaimed over Bohemia–Moravia, while Slovakia and Ruthenia became puppet states under German control. Chamberlain's denunciation of this glaring breach of faith by Hitler marked the turning away from appeasement and a drastic change in British policy.

Great Britain and Poland

Within a week of devouring Czechoslovakia Hitler switched his aggression towards Poland. He demanded that the Free City of Danzig should be ceded to Germany and that alterations be made to the Polish corridor between Germany and East Prussia. Chamberlain now reversed his former policy of refusing any commitments to help threatened European countries by announcing at the end of March that the British government would give all possible help to enable Poland to keep its independence. Astonished critics pointed out the rashness of this undertaking without

354

Map 16 The growth of Hitler's 'Third Reich' 1935–9

the assistance of Russia, a power with whom Chamberlain had resolutely refused to have any dealings. This new move was a gamble by Chamberlain to frighten Hitler but it failed in its intended effect as Hitler's war programme had gone too far to be stopped. He had already given orders for the attack on Poland to be made at the first suitable moment; he rejected proposals from President Roosevelt for non-aggression treaties; he denounced the Anglo-German Naval Agreement of 1935 and in May 1939 he tightened his military alliance with Italy.

Anglo–French negotiations for Russian support

In an attempt to support their commitments in Eastern Europe, Britain and France, in the summer of 1939 tried to get the assistance and co-operation of Russia. Although France had a pact of alliance with the Soviet Union, this did not now mean very much; the new negotiations were a reversal of Chamberlain's former policy of no dealings with Soviet

355

Russia. Both sides were guarded in their attitudes; Russia distrusted the Western powers because of their action over Czechoslovakia, while the Western powers were enthusiastic about a military alliance with Russia only in so far as it would deter Hitler from his designs on Poland. While these negotiations were proceeding, Hitler, in spite of his denunciations of Communism, had opened up talks with Russia. Stalin was ready to do a deal with Hitler to ensure his own position which in the existing situation was not very secure, while Hitler, with the prospect of a campaign in Poland, wished to be free from Russian intervention. On 23 August a Russo–German Treaty was signed, giving a ten years non-aggression pact and the promise of neutrality in wars against third parties. There was also a secret agreement over the division of territorial interests in Eastern Europe, the main point being that if Poland was partitioned, both Russia and Germany would divide the spoils. Hitler could now attack the isolated Poland and defy Britain and France to do their worst.

The final negotiations

In the last week of August Hitler, now sure of an understanding with Russia, had issued secret orders for the attack on Poland to be made early on 26 August. Nevertheless the firm attitude of Poland herself and France and Britain led to last minute negotiations. Chamberlain and Daladier made it absolutely clear to Hitler that they would support their commitments to Poland and this made him hesitate. He tried to buy off British opposition and to divide her from France and Poland by offering to guarantee the future of the British Empire, but would make no concessions regarding Poland. Although further negotiations continued between August 28 and 31, in the hope of continuing negotiations between Germany and Poland, these proved in vain since Hitler was determined to have his war and to treat Poland in the same way as Czechoslovakia. Early on the morning of 1 September 1939 German forces invaded Poland.

Britain declares war on Germany, 3 September 1939

The British and French declarations of war on Germany were not made until 3 September, due to an attempt by Mussolini, who so far had not joined Germany in war, to bring about a last minute conference with Hitler. Britain and France agreed in principle, providing German forces were withdrawn from Poland, but in the situation this was impossible to expect. On the morning of Sunday 3 September Chamberlain announced to the people of Britain that they were at war with Germany. His broadcast reflected his bitter disappointment at the failure of his steadily pursued policy of appeasement by negotiation, but there was no admission that this policy and its author had been in any way wrong.

Postscript

In 1939 the British people faced the grim realities of war and all its hazards in a far less confident mood than in 1914. Between the wars their morale had been depressed by uninspired leadership, lost opportunities, social discord and economic hardship; there was also the bitter reflection that in spite of 'the war to end war' with its great loss of life, another conflict of unknown extent now confronted them. The situation was accepted stoically if fatalistically, and this may partly explain the continued acceptance of Chamberlain as prime minister. He strengthened his government by bringing in two of his severest critics, Winston Churchill and Anthony Eden, but the Labour and Liberal leaders refused to serve under him.

After the destruction of Poland in September, a 'phoney' war ensued in the West with the French and British armies in defensive positions along the eastern frontier of France. In April 1940 the storm broke with the German invasion of Norway, against which the British counter-measures failed. The leadership of Chamberlain could not survive this set back, although he obstinately and tenaciously clung to his position against the tide of criticism from many members of his own party and from the Labour opposition. At this critical stage a truly national government was urgent, and with a leader other than Chamberlain. On 10 May 1940, the day the Germans began their blitzkrieg invasion of the Netherlands and Belgium, Chamberlain resigned. Winston Churchill became the nation's leader; three days later he announced his policy of relentless war for total victory, warning the British people that the price of this would be 'blood, toil, tears and sweat'.

357

A bed-time story for evacuated children, December 1939

Meanwhile the situation worsened as the German Panzer divisions tore into France, forcing her surrender in early June. Providentially the Dunkirk evacuation saved most of the British Expeditionary Force as a garrison for the island fortress Britain had now become. More important were the precious R.A.F. fighter squadrons and their pilots who by their sacrifice ensured victory in the battle of Britain in September 1940 and so made possible the survival of Britain in the greatest crisis of her history.

Glossary

'Ad valorem'. 'To the value of'. Customs duties are levied as a percentage of the value of imported goods at the port of entry.

'Agent provocateur'. A government agent who by pretending sympathy for the aims of a revolutionary movement is accepted as a member of the group. He then encourages them to overt action, having previously betrayed their plans to his employers.

Apostolic succession. Authority is given to the bishops and priests of the Christian Church to exercise their sacred office by the laying on of hands at the sacrament of ordination. The Catholic Church claimed an unbroken chain of succession going back to the Apostles of the early Christian Church of the New Testament. The Oxford movement maintained that, in spite of the Reformation, this Apostolic succession was preserved in the Church of England.

Artisan. A mechanic or craftsman; a skilled workman who has learnt his trade by serving an apprenticeship.

Ballot. Secret voting, as opposed to the older method of open voting in which a voter declared his choice by word of mouth.

Census. The official numbering of the population. First done in Great Britain in 1801; repeated (except 1941) at ten-year intervals.

Cholera. An infectious and often fatal disease resulting from contamination of food and drink by human and animal excreta. Prevalent in Asia but spread to Europe in waves of infection in the nineteenth century, especially between 1830 and 1870.

Conurbation. A large grouping of towns in continuous contact brought about by the building of factories and houses for an increasing population, e.g. London, the Midlands, Lancashire.

Doldrums. A region of calm near the Equator where the North East and South East Trade winds meet and neutralize each other: hence to be 'in the doldrums' is to make little or no progress.

359

Embezzlement. Theft committed by someone who has had money or other property entrusted to him in his capacity as a clerk or servant.

Franchise. (i) The right to vote; (ii) the right to send a Member to Parliament.

Freeholder. One who owns land free from any burdensome obligations to a superior landlord.

Habeas Corpus. The legal process by which a British citizen is protected against arbitrary imprisonment. The writ of habeas corpus, obtained from a high court judge, orders the gaoler to 'produce the body' of a prisoner in a certain court at a certain time.

Jubilee. A special occasion for rejoicing, e.g. the fiftieth and sixtieth anniversaries of the accession of Queen Victoria.

'Laissez-faire'. The doctrine of minimum interference by government in the political, economic and social affairs of the citizens.

Leaseholder. One who holds his land or house for a fixed term of years subject to payment of rent to the ground landlord.

Metaphysics. A branch of philosophy which is concerned with the first principles of things, e.g. being, substance, space, time etc.

Molestation. Harassing or interfering with an individual, e.g. a non-striker, in a hostile manner.

Nuisance. An act or omission by an individual or corporate body whereby the health, amenities and enjoyment of life by the public are adversely affected, e.g. allowing the accumulation of decaying refuse, releasing noxious fumes etc.

Picketing. A method used by a trade union to persuade employees not to work during a strike, usually by placing a small detachment or picket of strikers at the factory gates.

Protectorate. A territory that was brought under British control, but not annexed, either by Royal Proclamation or by treaty with the native ruler.

360 **'Q' ships.** Used in World War I to combat the U-boat menace. Usually

small 'innocent' looking tramp ships or fishing vessels with cleverly concealed guns.

Rack rent. The highest possible rent that can be demanded by the landlord having regard to the supply of, and demand for, land or houses.

Radical. A political attitude which demands drastic and fundamental reforms and which rejects limited or piecemeal reforms as unsatisfactory or useless. (From Latin *radix*, 'root'.)

Rent roll. A landlord's register of his tenants with the amounts of rent due from them.

Reparations. Compensation paid by a defeated country for the damage it has done during the war to its opponents.

Suzerainty. Sovereignty or paramount authority over another state.

Voluntary School. An elementary (primary) school established by a religious denomination, e.g. Church of England, and maintained by voluntary subscriptions from its members.

Yeoman. A small farmer owning the freehold of the land he cultivates.

Book List

Reference

G. M. Young and W. D. Hancock (Eds.), *English Historical Documents*, vol. X II (1), *1833–1874* (Eyre and Spottiswoode)

G. D. H. Cole and A. W. Filson, *The British Working Class: Select Documents 1789–1875* (Macmillan)

D. J. Butler and J. Freeman, *British Political Facts 1900–1967* (Macmillan)

E. N. Williams, *A Documentary History of England*, vol. 2, *1559–1931* (Pelican)

B. R. Mitchell (with P. Deane), *Abstract of British Historical Statistics* (Cambridge University Press)

General works

E. L. Woodward, *The Age of Reform* (Oxford University Press)

A. Briggs, *The Age of Improvement* (Longmans)

R. C. K. Ensor, *England 1870–1914* (Oxford University Press)

J. A. R. Marriot, *Modern England 1885–1932* (Methuen)

C. L. Mowat, *England Between the Wars 1918–1940* (Methuen)

A. F. Havighurst, *Twentieth Century Britain* (Harper and Row)

Biography

N. Gash, *Mr Secretary Peel* (Longmans)

G. D. H. Cole, *Robert Owen* (Cass)

S. E. Finer, *The Life and Times of Sir Edwin Chadwick* (Methuen)

P. Guedalla, *Palmerston* (Benn)

A. Briggs, *Victorian People* (Odhams)

R. Blake, *Disraeli* (Oxford University Press)

P. Magnus, *Gladstone* (Murray)

C. Woodham Smith, *Florence Nightingale* (Constable)

Lady Longford, *Victoria R.I.* (Weidenfeld and Nicholson)

C. C. O'Brien, *Parnell and his Party* (Oxford University Press)

P. Magnus, *Edward VII* (Penguin)

K. Young, *Balfour* (Bell)

R. Jenkins, *Asquith* (Collins)

T. Jones, *Lloyd George* (Oxford University Press)

Political topics

J. R. M. Butler, *The Passing of the Great Reform Bill* (Cass)

A. Briggs (Ed.), *Chartist Studies* (Macmillan)
N. Gash, *Politics in the Age of Peel* (Longmans)
D. Southgate, *The Passing of the Whigs 1832–1886* (Macmillan)
J. Vincent, *The Formation of the Liberal Party 1857–1868* (Constable)
M. Cowling, *1867, Disraeli, Gladstone and Revolution: the passing of the Second Reform Bill* (Cambridge University Press)
A. M. MacBriar, *Fabian Socialism and English Politics 1884–1918* (Cambridge University Press)
Lord Beaverbrook, *Decline and Fall of Lloyd George* (Collins)

Economic history

J. H. Clapham, *An Economic History of Modern Britain*, 3 vols. (Cambridge University Press)
D. S. Landes, *The Unbound Prometheus* (Cambridge University Press)
G. P. Jones and A. G. Pool, *A Hundred Years of Economic Development in Great Britain 1840–1940* (Duckworth)
S. Pollard and D. W. Crossley, *The Wealth of Britain 1085–1960* (Batsford)
P. Mathias, *The First Industrial Nation* (Methuen)
W. Ashworth, *An Economic History of England 1870–1939*
E. L. Jones, *The Development of English Agriculture 1815–1873* (Macmillan)
C. S. Orwin and E. H. Whetham, *A History of British Agriculture* (Longmans)
R. S. Sayers, *A History of Economic Change in England 1880–1939* (Oxford University Press)
S. Pollard, *The Development of the British Economy 1914–1950* (Arnold)
J. M. Keynes, *The Economic Consequences of the Peace* (Macmillan)

Social history

R. J. White, *Waterloo to Peterloo* (Heinemann)
G. M. Young, *Victorian England: Portrait of an Age* (Oxford University Press)
G. D. H. Cole, *A Short History of the British Working Class Movement 1789–1947* (Allen and Unwin)
R. Robson (Ed.), *Ideas and Institutions of Victorian Britain* (Bell)
G. Faber, *The Oxford Apostles* (Pelican)
W. E. Houghton, *The Victorian Frame of Mind* (Yale University Press)
J. Simmons, *The Railways of Britain* (Routledge Kegan Paul)
M. Robbins, *The Railway Age* (Penguin)
T. Coleman, *The Navvies* (Penguin)
B. Disraeli, *Sybil* (Penguin)
C. Woodham Smith, *The Great Hunger* (H. Hamilton)

C. Hobhouse, *1851 and the Crystal Palace* (Murray)

F. M. L. Thompson, *English Landed Society in the Nineteenth Century* (Routledge Kegan Paul)

M. K. Ashby (Ed.), *Joseph Ashby of Tysoe 1859–1919* (Cambridge University Press)

J. Arch, *Autobiography* (McGibbon and Kee)

F. Thompson, *Lark Rise to Candleford* (Oxford University Press)

B. Webb, *My Apprenticeship* (Penguin)

S. Nowell Smith (Ed.), *Edwardian England* (Oxford University Press)

C. Petrie, *Scenes from Edwardian Life* (Eyre and Spottiswoode)

C. F. G. Masterman, *The Condition of England* (Methuen)

M. Bruce, *The Coming of the Welfare State* (Batsford)

R. Fulford, *Votes for Women* (Faber)

G. Dangerfield, *The Strange Death of Liberal England* (McGibbon and Keen)

A. Marwick, *The Deluge* (Penguin)

Wilfrid Owen, *Poems* (Chatto and Windus)

Siegfried Sassoon, *Collected Poems* (Faber)

Siegfried Sassoon, *Memoirs of an Infantry Officer* (Faber)

E. Blunden, *Undertones of War* (Collins)

C. E. Montague, *Disenchantment* (McGibbon and Kee)

R. Graves, *Goodbye to All That* (Penguin)

J. Symons, *The General Strike* (Secker and Warburg)

G. Orwell, *The Road to Wigan Pier* (Secker)

Colonial and imperial history

C. E. Carrington, *The British Overseas* (Cambridge University Press)

W. D. Hussey, *The British Empire and Commonwealth 1500–1961* (Cambridge University Press)

J. A. Williamson, *A Short History of British Expansion*, vol. 2 (Macmillan)

Naval and military history

E. Holt, *The Boer War* (Putnam)

Winston Churchill, *The World Crisis 1911–18*, 3 vols. (Butterworth)

B. H. Liddell Hart, *The Real War 1914–18* (Faber)

C. Falls, *The First World War* (Longmans)

C. Barnett, *The Sword Bearers* (Eyre and Spottiswoode)

Winston Churchill, *The Second World War*, vol. 1, *The Gathering Storm* (Cassell)

Index

365

367